Modularity in Knowledge Representation
and Natural-Language Understanding

Modularity in Knowledge Representation and Natural-Language Understanding

edited by Jay L. Garfield

A Bradford Book
The MIT Press
Cambridge, Massachusetts
London, England

Second printing, 1989
© 1987 Massachusetts Institute of Technology

This book was set in Palatino by Asco Trade Typesetting Ltd., Hong Kong, and printed and bound by Halliday Lithograph in the United States of America.

Library of Congress Cataloging-in-Publication Data

Modularity in knowledge representation and natural-language understanding.

"A Bradford book."
Bibliography: p.
Includes index.
1. Psycholinguistics.   2. Cognition.   3. Languages—Philosophy.   4. Vision.
5. Neurolinguistics.
I. Garfield, Jay L., 1955–
P40.M6   1987   401'.9   86-34415
ISBN 0-262-07105-3

for Jonas, Joshua, and Abraham

Contents

Preface

Many of the essays in this volume were contributions to a workshop of the same name held in June 1985 at Hampshire College in Amherst, Massachusetts. I gratefully acknowledge financial support for the workshop from the Alfred P. Sloan Foundation; the Systems Development Foundation; Five Colleges, Inc.; the UMass/Five College Cognitive Science Institute; the Departments of Linguistics, Philosophy, Psychology, and Computer and Information Science of the University of Massachusetts; Hampshire College; and the School of Communications and Cognitive Science of Hampshire College. Thanks for advice, assistance, and logistical support for the workshop are due especially to Kathy Adamczyk, Mary Ann Palmieri, James Rucker, and the Hampshire College Office of Special Programs for handling many of the details, but also to Barbara Partee, Lyn Frazier, Charles Clifton, and Michael Arbib for many helpful suggestions and for much encouragement along the way.

For help in producing this volume, I thank James Rucker, Ruth Hammen, Leni Bowen, Randolph Scott, Kira Shepard, and Peter Winters for logistical support, Blaine Garson for giving me the time to complete the work, and Neil Stillings and Sally for their assistance with the introduction. Finally, I thank Jerry Fodor for writing *The Modularity of Mind*, which is the obvious efficient cause of all this.

Introduction: Carving the Mind at Its Joints
Jay L. Garfield

With the publication of *The Modularity of Mind* (Fodor 1983), a number of
ideas that had been current or at least implicit in cognitive theorizing over
the previous two decades crystallized into a single recognizable hypothesis: The mind is not a seamless, unitary whole whose functions merge
continuously into one another; rather, it comprises—perhaps in addition to
some relatively seamless, general-purpose structures—a number of distinct, specialized, structurally idiosyncratic modules that communicate with
other cognitive structures in only very limited ways. According to this
hypothesis, these modules include, roughly, the input systems (including
certain components of the perceptual systems and of the language-
understanding system) and certain components of the output systems
(including processes involved in motor control and language production).
The hypothesis contrasts these modules with the presumably nonmodular
structure of, for example, long-term memory, or the cognitive structures
underlying general knowledge.

As a preliminary characterization of what it is for a system to be a
cognitive module, Fodor proposes five diagnostic questions and a rough
sketch:

> 1. Is it domain specific, or do its operations cross content domains?
> . . .
> 2. Is the computational system innately specified, or is its structure
> formed by some sort of learning process?
> 3. Is the computational system "assembled" (in the sense of being
> put together from some stock of more elementary subprocesses) or
> does its virtual architecture map relatively directly onto its neural
> implementation?
> 4. Is it hardwired (in the sense of being associated with specific,
> localized, and elaborately structured neural systems) or is it imple-
> mented by relatively equipotential neural mechanisms?
> 5. Is it computationally autonomous . . . , or does it share horizontal
> resources (of memory, attention, or whatever) with other cognitive
> systems?

> ... Roughly, modular cognitive systems are domain specific, innately specified, hardwired, autonomous, and not assembled. (pp. 36–37)

This preliminary characterization gives way to eight properties which, Fodor argues, are jointly characteristic and diagnostic of the modularity of particular cognitive systems. Though Fodor does not distinguish these properties with respect to weight or priority, subsequent theoretical and experimental practice and some philosophical reflection lead me to distinguish four as "major criteria" and four as relatively minor (not in the sense that they are of less theoretical importance, but rather in the sense that they play less active roles in actual research in cognitive science). The major criteria are domain specificity, mandatoriness, informational encapsulation, and speed. Modular systems are hypothesized to have these four properties, central systems to lack them.

The four minor criteria are lack of access by other systems to intermediate representations, shallow output, neural localization, and susceptibility to characteristic breakdowns. The first two of these criteria play lesser roles than the major criteria because of the difficulty of designing experiments to test for their presence (but see chapters 2 and 3 of this volume for studies bearing on both criteria), the second two because of the relatively undeveloped state of cognitive neuroscience (a situation that is, happily, on the mend—see Churchland 1986 and chapters 17 and 19 of this volume for examples of neuroscientifically informed theorizing about modularity). It is perhaps easiest to see how these criteria play out by examining how Fodor wields them in arguing that input systems, including the language input system, are modules in this sense. I turn first to the major criteria.

Fodor discusses the domain specificity of the phonetic-analysis module as follows:

> Evidence for the domain specificity of an input analyzer can be of a variety of different sorts.... For example, there are the results owing to investigators at the Haskins Laboratories which strongly suggest the domain specificity of the perceptual systems that effect the phonetic analysis of speech. The claim is that these mechanisms are different from those which effect the perceptual analysis of auditory nonspeech, and the experiments show that how a signal sounds to the hearer does depend, in rather startling ways, on whether the acoustic context indicates that the stimulus is an utterance.... The rather strong implication is that the computational systems that come into play in the perceptual analysis of speech are distinctive in that they operate *only* upon acoustic signals that are taken to be utterances. (pp. 48–49)

Turning to the more general language-perception module, Fodor argues in a similar vein:

> ... the perceptual system involved [in sentence perception] is presumed to have access to information about how the universals are realized in the language it applies to. The upshot of this line of thought is that the perceptual system for a language comes to be viewed as containing quite an elaborate theory of the objects in its domain; perhaps a theory couched in the form of a grammar for the language. Correspondingly, the process of perceptual recognition is viewed as the application of that theory to the analysis of current inputs....
>
> To come to the moral: Since the satisfaction of the universals is supposed to be a property that distinguishes sentences from other stimulus domains, the more elaborate and complex the theory of universals comes to be the more eccentric the stimulus domain for sentence recognition. And ... the more eccentric the stimulus domain, the more plausible the speculation that it is computed by a special-purpose mechanism. (p. 51)

Clearly this form of argument can be generalized to all sorts of modules covering all sorts of domains, and also to the micro-domains that are hypothesized to be the provinces of submodules. The point is just that where input domains are eccentric enough (and important enough) to place peculiar demands on the input systems, special-purpose processes are advantageous.

The second of the major criteria is mandatoriness. The idea is that modules, prominently including the input systems, perform their functions automatically when given the stimuli that normally trigger them. We lack the ability to prevent them from computing. In the case of language (as Fodor notes on pp. 52–55), we just can't help hearing an utterance of a sentence in our home language as a sentence rather than an uninterpreted sound stream. Similarly, we can't help perceiving an object in our visual field as an object rather than a two-dimensional array of varying hues and intensities. On the other hand, we appear to have some voluntary control over which grocery store we go to or which research problems we tackle. Hence, modular processes appear to be mandatory whereas central processes appear to be optional. Such mandatoriness—if indeed mandatoriness does serve to demarcate some modular faculties—is easily explained from an evolutionary point of view if one attends to the claim that the domains over which cognitive modules operate are important to the organism. In a hostile world, one would not want one's object-recognition module "switched off" at the wrong moment.

The third of the four central properties of modules is informational

encapsulation. Encapsulation is one of the most intriguing properties ascribed to modules by the modularity hypothesis, and it is the property that
figures most prominently in much of the debate about the modularity of
particular systems (witness the fact that it is a central issue in nearly every
chapter in this volume). Nevertheless, it is one of the most difficult of the
central properties to detect experimentally (see chapters 2–4). As Fodor
concedes, and as the debate in this volume documents, encapsulation is a
vexing issue in psycholinguistics. It is easier to get a handle on this property by considering an example Fodor draws from visual perception:

> ... When you move your head, or your eyes, the flow of images
> across the retina may be identical to what it would be were the head
> and eyes to remain stationary while the scene moves. So: why don't
> we experience apparent motion when we move our eyes? Most psy-
> chologists now accept one or another version of the "corollary dis-
> charge" answer to this problem. According to this story, the neural
> centers which initiate head and eye motions communicate with the
> input analyzer in charge of interpreting visual stimulations. Because
> the latter system knows what the former is up to, it is able to discount
> alterations in the retinal flow that are due to the motions of the
> receptive organs.
>
> Well, the point of interest for us is that this visual-motor system is
> informationally encapsulated. Witness the fact that, if you (gently)
> push your eyeball with your finger (as opposed to moving it in the
> usual way: by an exercise of the will), you *do* get apparent motion.
> Consider the moral: when you voluntarily move your eyeball with
> your finger, you certainly are possessed of the information that it's
> your eye (and not the visual scene) that is moving.... But this explicit
> information, available to you for (e.g.) report, is *not* available to the
> analyzer in charge of the perceptual integration of your retinal stimu-
> lations. That system has access to corollary discharges from the motor
> center *and to no other information that you possess.* Modularity with a
> vengeance. (p. 67; emphasis in original)

A cognitive process is informationally encapsulated if it has access to only
the information represented within the local structures that subserve it. It is
the *lack* of access to the knowledge about what the finger is doing that
demonstrates the encapsulation of the visual-analyzer-cum-head-and-eye-
movement system. It is important to note both the connection and the
distinction between informational encapsulation and domain specificity. If
a module subserves processing with respect to some domain (e.g. visual
object representation in scene recognition), then to say that it is also
encapsulated is to say, over and above the fact that it subserves only object
representation, that it has access only to information about the mapping

from the optic array to the objects and the illumination that typically are causally responsible for such arrays. Domain specificity has to do with the circumstances in which a module comes into use; encapsulation has to do with the information that can be mobilized in the course of that use.

The final member of this quartet is speed. Modules are very fast. This speed is, on the Fodorian view, accounted for by the mandatoriness, the domain specificity, and the encapsulation of modules. Because they are mandatory, no deliberation is required to set their operations in motion; because they are domain specific, they can trade on fortuitous features of their domains in the evolution of efficient dedicated computational architectures; because they are encapsulated, there is only so much information that they can take into account in their processing.

Central processes are, on this view, slower than the modular peripheral processes. Because the process of belief fixation and revision is (mostly) rational and sensitive to evidence, and because—given suitable circumstances—anything can become relevant to anything else, the processes responsible for maintaining our store of standing general knowledge cannot be unencapsulated; because we can believe things about anything, they cannot be domain specific; because of the difficulty of operating with such large, unconstrained domains, these processes are slow. This is why, according to Fodor and his followers, parsing a complex sentence by hand or solving a problem in chess or arithmetic takes time, whereas on-line sentence understanding or scene recognition happens in an instant despite the fact that the problems solved by the visual or the linguistic input system are arguably much more complex than those solved so laboriously by central systems. (Though, as Fodor notes in chapter 1 of this volume, the fact that the frame problem is not nearly so daunting for humans as it is for machines indicates that something awfully fast is going on in our central systems of knowledge representation, although we don't really understand what it could be.)

The first two of what I call the minor criteria for cognitive modules concern the access of central systems to the representations over which the modules' computations are defined. Modules yield relatively shallow outputs to central systems, and central systems have no access to intermediate representations generated by modules. Shallowness of output would be guaranteed by encapsulation and required by speed, though how much information can fit in a cognitive capsule and how rich a representation can be generated how quickly from a capsuleful are, to be sure, empirical matters. Thus Fodor argues (conceding the highly speculative nature of the arguments) that the output of the linguistic input system are "representations which specify, for example, morphemic constituency, syntactic structure, and logical form," and that sentence processing does not "grade off insensibly into inference and the appreciation of context" (p. 93). (See chapters 2 and 8 of this volume for the opposing picture.) Fodor also suggests that the output of the visual object-recognition system might be something like Rosch's (1976) basic categories, e.g. *dog* rather than *poodle* or *animal*.

Central processes have limited or no access to the intermediate representations computed by modules. Thus, although a great deal of data must be represented by my visual system regarding the intensity of illumination on various surfaces surrounding me, none of the very-low-level data utilized early in visual processing are available to introspection—only the inventory of objects, and their gross "perceptible" features, appear. And I have only the most speculative and theory-governed idea about the intermediate stages of my own linguistic processing. This opacity of modular systems, on the Fodorian view, is also a consequence of their speed and automaticity. If they were to be constantly open to query by central processes, or to maintain a large inventory of stored intermediate representations, speed would suffer and central control could come to interfere with automaticity. An alternate explanation of the unavailability of such intermediate levels of representation to introspection is offered by Marslen-Wilson and Tyler in chapter 2.

Finally, modular systems are neurally localized and subject to characteristic breakdown. These characteristics flow naturally from the evolutionary considerations that explain the existence of rapid dedicated processes and explain both their relatively fixed architecture and their speed. The modularity hypothesis, when thus linked to neuroscience, gains additional support from the fact that (as Fodor notes on pp. 98–99) the only cognitive systems that have been identified with specific areas of the brain, and with specific, idiosyncratic structures, are those that are most naturally thought of according to the other criteria as modular: perceptual analysis systems, language, and motor control. (See chapter 17 of this volume for a discussion of the connection between modular cognitive systems and brain structure.) The differential susceptibility of modular (as opposed to central) systems to characteristic breakdowns is then easily explicable in terms of brain pathology, and it is not surprising that the most localized cognitive functions are most susceptible to specific traumatic or pathological degradation.

Of course, there is no principled reason for thinking that no nonmodular systems are localized, in which case one might expect to find characteristic breakdowns in those systems. Thus, if it turned out that some types of memory or some range of general-purpose inferential abilities (say induction) were neurally localized, these might then suffer characteristic breakdowns as a result of local trauma or pathology, though this would not, by itself, constitute evidence for their modularity. Hence these two properties may be more weakly tied to the remainder of the characteristics of modular systems than the remaining six.

With this brief sketch of the properties the modularity hypothesis ascribes to cognitive modules, the modularity hypothesis can be restated more fully: The mind comprises not only central systems that can take advantage of any and all information at their disposal and each of whose representations are globally sensitive to all the other representational states and processes of the organism, but also a number of modular systems dedicated to sensory and linguistic input analysis and to linguistic and motor output. The operation of these systems is mandatory, domain specific, and fast; they are informationally encapsulated; they yield only a specific, relatively shallow level of representation to central processes; and they are realized in specific, dedicated neural architectures. Central systems, in contrast, are slower and more subject to voluntary control in their operation, are unencapsulated, are typically neurally scattered, and operate with a semantically much richer set of representations. Modular processes are blind; central processes deliberate.

It is clear that the modularity hypothesis is an empirical claim. There is no obvious *a priori* reason why the mind has to be that way. Indeed, there is much cognitive theory (some of it represented in this volume) committed to the view that the mind is considerably more unitary and seamless than this hypothesis would have it. It is also clear that the modularity hypothesis is really a set of hypotheses, for it claims not only that there are modules but also that a very specific cluster of properties hang together to characterize those modules. Like any plausible empirical claim in a live science, the modularity hypothesis raises important questions and sets an agenda for research. I now turn to some of these implications of the modularity hypothesis for empirical research in cognitive science.

When I say that the modularity hypothesis defines a research agenda, I mean that it suggests particular questions or kinds of questions to ask and certain experimental paradigms as likely to yield valuable data, and that it demarcates certain areas of cognitive performance as likely to be worth intense investigation, and perhaps others as less rewarding. The fact that this agenda is established is merely a consequence of the viability or plausibility of the hypothesis, at least in some form; it does not require that the hypothesis be true. Rather, the necessity of testing the hypothesis against the facts sets the research agenda.

The modularity hypothesis, simply taken as a working assumption, immediately poses two large questions that cry out for empirical work: Which cognitive functions are mediated by modular structures and which are not? What is the precise location of the boundary between modular input/output processes and isotropic central processes? Though these two questions are closely related, and though their answers (assuming for the moment the truth of the hypothesis) are undoubtedly mutually dependent, they are conceptually distinct.

The second question is really a question about the degree of semantic poverty (in Fodor's terminology, the "shallowness") of the representations delivered by input modules or received by output modules. This problem is addressed in rather direct fashion in chapter 2 by Marslen-Wilson and Tyler, who argue that the dedicated cognitive structures responsible for language understanding deliver a very rich structure—a discourse representation—as their output. One would expect, if this account turns out to be true, that the corresponding output structures would take equally "deep" structures as their inputs. This view contrasts dramatically with Fodor's view (also adopted by Forster, Hornstein, Weinberg, Carroll and Slowiaczek, Clifton and Ferreira, and Frazier) that the representations delivered by this module contain only syntactic information. Similar questions concerning the visual module are addressed in part IV of this volume. These questions also bear directly on the issue of informational encapsulation, since (as Marslen-Wilson and Tyler note in chapter 2), if the structures delivered by these fast, mandatory processes are as semantically informed as discourse representations, these processes must have access to a good deal of information over and above that which is traditionally thought of as syntactic.

The first question is also concerned with the details of the architecture of a modular mind, but it is directly concerned with what input and output processes turn out to be modular. Is, for example, object recognition accomplished in humans by a single module? How about scene analysis? Is all of the sense of taste subserved by a single module, or are there several? Are the visual and auditory linguistic input modules distinct? Are both these processes modular? The list of specific empirical questions for future research limned by this question is long indeed, and if the hypothesis remains viable each particular question appears fascinating in its own right.

A further question arises concerning the cluster of properties enumerated by Fodor. Do the properties in fact hang together in a theoretically fruitful way? Even if the mind turns out to be modular, might it turn out that various modules have some but not all of the Fodorian properties? One could imagine, for instance, that some cognitive function has all but neural localization, or that another lacks mandatoriness, though when in operation it has all the other relevant characteristics. Fodor concedes that many of his arguments for the integrity of the cluster are merely suggestive. Discovering that they are as tightly bound as modularity theorists argue they are would raise the level of plausibility of the considerations he adduces. Discovering their separability might well lead to intriguing reconceptualizations of the architecture of the mind.

Over and above setting this rather large research agenda, the modularity hypothesis embodies two specific claims about the methodology of cognitive science, both of which are addressed directly in this volume. The first is that theories concerning the structure of peripheral processes and the representations over which their operations are defined should be far easier to achieve than theories of the operation of central processes. This consequence of modularity theory issues from the characterization of central processes as Quinean and isotropic—that is, from the fact that the degree of confirmation or plausibility of beliefs, or the meanings of representations, depend on the global properties of the representational system and may be sensitive to variations in the plausibility or meaning of representations that might at first sight be conceptually rather remote. To the degree that central systems have these properties, they are subject, as Fodor notes in chapter 1 below, to outbreaks of the "frame problem"—a difficulty neatly skirted by modules in virtue of their informational encapsulation.

Fodor's recommendation, and that of other orthodox modularists, is to study the modular peripheral processes first, and only when they are relatively well understood to essay the more amorphous central systems. Anti-modularists argue that such a bifurcation of theory and effort is in principle impossible, in virtue of the seamless character of cognition, and point out that much progress appears to have been made in the study of such centrally located abilities as attention, memory, inductive reasoning, and problem solving. (However, if the modularity hypothesis is correct, one should be wary of generalizing models that are successful in these domains to the domains subserved by the modular systems.) Strategies that work in Quinean, isotropic domains will typically be ill suited to fast, mandatory processing. Strategies useful to modules trade on the encapsulated nature of the knowledge required for the processing tasks they are set.

The second methodological moral of modularism concerns the role of neuroscience in cognitive science. Inasmuch as the innate, "hardwired," neurally localized character of cognitive modules is part and parcel of the hypothesis, research on the localization of proposed modular functions is essential to its confirmation. What is more, the discovery of neurally localized cognitive functions that might not hitherto have been suspected of modularity might shed new light on cognitive architecture. Finally, if it turns out that there are localized dedicated processors responsible for a wide range of cognitive abilities, the prospects for convergence in neuroscience and the cognitive psychology of modular systems will be bright indeed. All these considerations suggest that research guided by the modularity hypothesis will involve collaboration between neuroscientists and cognitive scientists from other domains who have hitherto moved in quite different theoretical circles.

An interesting feature of most discussions of modularity—particularly Fodor's, but also those found in parts I–III of this book, is that the only alleged module ever discussed in depth is the language input module. (The only other module that has received serious attention in the modularity literature is the visual object recognition module, but the literature there is considerably more sparse than that in modularity-inspired psycholinguistics.) This is particularly surprising in view of the fact that both modularists and anti-modularists stake their theoretical positions on observations concerning natural-language understanding—the anti-modularists point to the apparent involvement of much general knowledge in such seemingly rapid and mandatory processes as discourse understanding, and the modularists to the apparent encapsulation and data-driven character of syntactic parsing. Arguments concerning the degree of modularity enjoyed by language processing (and, by implication, concerning the truth of the modularity thesis) are to be found throughout this volume, but a few comments are in order concerning the reason that the linguistic module occupies such a central position in this debate.

In the first place, the study of language processing promises to highlight the nature of the interface between modular input systems and nonmodular central processes. It is clear that, whether or not some or all portions of the language input system are modular in Fodor's sense, the cognitive structures responsible for language understanding deliver, in a remarkably short time, mental representations corresponding to the content of the discourse being processed. It is also clear that the initial stages of this process involve the on-line interpretation of phonological, orthographic, or visual information by a primarily data-driven system which perhaps uses, or at least is characterizable by, a set of powerful interpretive algorithms, and that the final stages involve significant interaction between information coming into the system on-line and the listener/reader's general knowledge.

Moreover, and perhaps most important, recent research in linguistics, psycholinguistics, and semantics has offered a fairly detailed, though still radically incomplete, picture of the processing stages involved in this language-understanding process and of some of the computational principles operative at some of these stages. The degree of articulation of linguistic and psycholinguistic theory is unparalleled in the domain of theories of specific cognitive processes (particularly the theory of input systems). Again, the closest rival, by a good margin, is vision, and this is indeed the other hotbed of modularity theory. The upshot of all this is that in the language system we have an input system for which we can frame detailed hypotheses concerning the degree of modularity of specific components (or constellations of components) of the system—hypotheses that suggest practicable experimental procedures. We can ask, for instance, whether the processes responsible for discourse representation share information with syntactic analyzers, or whether syntactic analysis affects phonetic analysis. We can probe the relative speed of syntactic and semantic processing. We can even test for the interaction or independence of the generation of such intermediate representations as S-structure and logical form.

This is not to say that these hypotheses are uncontroversial, or that the results of these studies are unambiguous. Much of this book attests to the degree of controversy surrounding these claims and studies. But it is to say that here there is something to talk about, and that the level of discussion is high in virtue of the antecedent body of theory concerning language understanding and knowledge representation.

There are two other, related considerations that help explain the prominence of linguistic modules in discussion of modularity; both of these also suggest the relevance of considerations of innateness and of neural localization to modularity theory generally, but specifically to theory of the language system. These are the body of language-acquisition theory and the phenomena of aphasia. Among the plausible candidates for cognitive modules among humans, the language-understanding and language-production systems demonstrate the most easily studied pattern of postnatal development. The principles that govern postnatal development provide striking evidence for the biological basis of these systems and for their relative autonomy from other cognitive systems. This is powerful evidence for their modularity. There is the additional methodological benefit of the availability of data and theory concerning language learning and learnability, which benefit provides important clues to the structure of the modules and submodules together comprised by the language system. Grimshaw's contribution to this volume is a nice example of theory trading on this methodological asset.

The frequency and the varieties of aphasias, coupled with recent developments in imaging technology, also count in favor of studying language as a vehicle to understanding the modularity of mind. Aphasias give us clues to the modular cognitive structure of linguistic processing systems (by demonstrating the patterns of breakdown to which they are susceptible) and clues to the neural infrastructure of linguistic processing and the way it maps onto the relevant processes. The language systems exhibit the greatest variety of such pathologies, and so are unique in the degree to which such pathologies contribute to our understanding of them. Again, the only other system that comes close is vision. Elegant exploitation of the relevant neurological and cognitive data is in evidence in Arbib's and Stillings's contributions to this volume.

Despite this preeminence of language in the study of modularity, there is good reason, beyond the general desire to expand our knowledge in cognitive science, to desire evidence concerning modularity from other cognitive domains.

Most obvious, the generality of modularity theory is a bit suspect if—even if its predictions should be borne out in the domain of language understanding, and even if its explanations of phenomena in that domain should be compelling—it is silent about all other input and all output processes. One might fear, and with good reason, that the success of the theory trades on artifacts of the linguistic domain.

There are other, more specific reasons for pursuing research in this paradigm on other modules. For one thing, as noted above, one of the great virtues of the modularity hypothesis (irrespective of its truth or falsity) is the degree to which it facilitates the collaboration of neuroscientists with other cognitive scientists. Other candidate modules, including input systems corresponding to aspects of sensory processing (particularly in the visual module, as noted by Arbib and Stillings), as well as motor output systems, appear to be rather localized in the central nervous system. It would appear that modularity theory could benefit from research pursuing the degree to which, and the manner in which, this localization issues in the other properties associated with cognitive modules.

Finally, the need to examine other cognitive modules is indicated by the desirability of psychological theory encompassing infrahuman as well as human organisms. In light of the obvious phylogenetic continuity between humans and other animals in many dimensions of cognitive and neural function, an important test of any psychological theory—particularly any theory that is broader in scope than the "higher" reasoning or linguistic processes, such as modularity theory—is its ability to mesh with data from other species and with evolutionary neurobiology. This desideratum is particularly salient in the case of the modularity hypothesis in virtue of the evolutionary arguments offered in its defense, in virtue of its applicability to all input and output systems, and in virtue of its neurobiological component. Now, inasmuch as it is impossible to learn much about language processing across species, it would appear that in order to make use of interspecific comparisons we ought to study other cognitive systems which we presumably share with infrahuman organisms (e.g., the systems involved in object recognition, in visuo-motor coordination, or in auditory and tactile perception) within the framework of the modularity hypothesis. Arbib's investigation of visuo-motor coordination in toads is a heartening development.

The chapters in this book are grouped in four parts. Those in part I (Modularity and Psychological Method) contribute to the discussion of the methodological consequences of the modularity hypothesis, either by directly addressing methodological issues, as do Fodor and Tanenhaus et al., by essaying new methods in psychological research inspired by the hypothesis, as does Forster, or by questioning directly the methodological utility of the cluster of properties Fodor has identified in carving the mind at its joints, as do Marslen-Wilson and Tyler.

The chapters in parts II and III are all concerned specifically with language processing. Those in part II (Semantics, Syntax, and Learnability) address questions concerning the interaction between semantic or general knowledge and syntactic processing, the internal structure of the processes responsible for syntactic processing, whether or not distinct submodules can be detected within the linguistic input module, and the implications of language-acquisition theory for the structure of linguistic modules. Part III (On-Line Processing) comprises discussions of real-time language perception and understanding. These chapters take up the question of whether or not such processes are modular in character, and also questions concerning the internal structure of the modules that might accomplish this task.

The chapters in part IV (The Visual Module) ask the same kinds of questions about vision (though with more emphasis on neurological underpinnings) that the earlier chapters ask about language. This, of course is the only part of the book in which biological and cross-species evidence is brought the bear on these issues, and the only part in which the relationship between the modularity debate and the debates about methodological naturalism versus methodological solipsism in cognitive science is addressed.

Despite this grouping of chapters, it is important to note that many are closely related to others that appear in other parts. There are, indeed, many plausible ways to group these studies. For instance, Marslen-Wilson and Tyler address many of the same issues discussed by Clifton and Ferreira and by Frazier. Flynn and Altmann raise somewhat similar questions about the modularity thesis. Many of the chapters in parts I and II make use of on-line-processing data, and many of those in part III are concerned with the relationship between syntax and semantics.

There is diversity here on a number of dimensions. A wide range of views regarding the truth of the modularity thesis are represented, from staunch defense to deep skepticism. Among the contributors are neuroscientists, psychologists, linguists, and philosophers. Some are concerned with broad methodological questions, some with limning the marcostructure of the mind, and others with the micromodular details of hypothesized modules. Knowledge representations, language processing, and vision are discussed. This diversity, the multiplicity of dimensions on which it occurs, and the excellence of the science underlying all these positions seem to me to be the best indications of the value of the modularity hypothesis as a stimulus to good cognitive science.

I

Modularity and Psychological Method

Introduction

Jay L. Garfield

The modularity hypothesis distinguishes sharply between input systems (tentatively including the language-processing system and the perceptual systems) and central cognitive system (including those responsible for much of long-term memory and general-purpose reasoning). The distinction is drawn in terms of a cluster of properties argued—principally by Fodor (1983)—to be both coincident and characteristic of modular input systems: domain specificity, mandatoriness, speed, and informational encapsulation. Input systems are argued to be fast, mandatory, informationally encapsulated, and domain specific; central processes are hypothesized to be typically slow, optional, informationally porous, and general purpose, communicating freely among themselves and receiving input from and sending output to all the modular input and output systems.

This challenging hypothesis has a number of theoretical and methodological implications for research in cognitive science, many of which are addressed in the following four chapters. In fact, one can say with justice that the modularity hypothesis functions as a scientific paradigm (in Kuhn's [1962] sense) within contemporary cognitive science. That is, it functions as a model for other, often more specific, hypotheses; it defines and generates research problems, and it determines (or at least suggests) specific research strategies and methodologies. Each of these chapters demonstrates the paradigmatic influence of the modularity hypothesis.

Once the hypothesis is on the table, an important goal of psychological research becomes the determination of the boundaries between input modules (or output modules, which I will ignore in this discussion) and central processes. To put this goal in the form of a slightly less metaphorical question: What are the essential features of the final representations passed by each input module to central processes? Where does fast, mandatory, encapsulated processing end and deliberation begin?

Two closely allied questions concern the hypothesis itself: How useful is this quartet of criteria for carving the mind at the joints? More specific, do these four criteria actually hang together to the degree that Fodor has argued? The first question could be answered in the negative if it turned out either that the mind is substantially more seamless than the modularity hypothesis asserts it to be or that, while it is modular in structure, the distinction between modular and nonmodular processes does not coincide with the Fodorian property cluster. The second of the above questions, which concerns the integrity of the quartet, is more fine grained. Fodor's arguments for integrity are indeed persuasive, but they are (as he concedes) not demonstrative. What would count as demonstrative would be lots of empirical data. It could turn out, e.g., that while input systems are characteristically fast, mandatory, and domain specific, they are not informationally encapsulated (see chapter 2 below).

A further goal of psychological research inspired by the modularity hypothesis is the investigation of the internal modular structure, if there is any, of the principal cognitive modules. To what extent are their subcomponents informationally encapsulated and domain specific? (Presumably the properties of speed and mandatoriness are inherited by submodules from their supermodules.) The more global modularity hypothesis and research on the boundaries of the macromodules of mind hence serve as paradigms for more local hypotheses and for research concerning more local boundaries.

An intriguing question concerning the structure of psychological theory is raised not so much by the modularity hypothesis in isolation as by its sharing the theoretical scene with the theoretical movement that has come to be known as connectionism. As Tanenhaus, Dell, and Carlson note in chapter 4, the modularity hypothesis and connectionist hypothesis are often seen as orthogonal or, if relevant to one another, incompatible. What is more, in view of the emphasis in research on boundaries in the human information-processing system suggested by the modularity hypothesis and the emphasis on the investigation of parallel, massively integrated processing strategies suggested by the connectionist hypothesis, there is reason to wonder how these two independently plausible models can be integrated.

The modularity hypothesis suggests that theories of the central processes and theories of the modules will looks substantially different from one another, and that the methodologies for investigating the two sorts of processes will be radically distinct. For instance, theories of the modules will typically be accounts of processing mechanisms that are data-driven, architecturally rigid, and autonomous in their functioning. Theories of central processes will reflect the seamlessness of commonsense knowledge and inferential mechanisms, and might well take note of considerable individual differences in skill, inferential ability, problem-solving strategy, and cultural differences in ontology and ideology. Reaction-time data will be highly informative concerning the structures of modular, automatic systems, but of much more limited use in the investigation of deliberate processes. Protocol data could well be useful in the investigation of the presumably more introspectable central processes, but might well be useless in the study of the rapid, encapsulated modular processes. Each of these methodological implications of the modularity hypothesis is addressed by one or more of the chapters in part I.

Fodor's "Modules, Frames, Fridgeons, Sleeping Dogs, and the Music of the Spheres" (chapter 1) is primarily concerned with the last of the above-mentioned issues, and in particular with the difficulty of developing a theory of central processes. The problem Fodor highlights is the infamous frame problem of artificial intelligence—the problem of how to delimit the information that must be considered in any particular instance of reasoning. Fodor points out that encapsulated, modular systems are easily studied, and that they make for good cognitive theory just because they do not suffer from the frame problem. Their encapsulation, together with their rigid automaticity, ensures that the range of information available to them is severely limited. But the price of such artificial limitations on the range of available information, though it is the necessary cost of the speed requisite in such systems, is irrationality and fallibility (as is evidenced by the persistence of perceptual illusions in the face of contrary knowledge).

Fodor argues that a theory of rational activity, or an artificial-intelligence model of general-purpose cognition is, *ipso facto*, a theory of unencapsulated processes, or a model of inference in a domain where any piece of information could become relevant to reasoning about anything. But success in this domain, Fodor argues, requires a successful theory of non-demonstrative inference—a theory which we have been after for millennia, and which is arguably not in sight. The upshot of these considerations is the recommendation that experimental cognitive science should concentrate its efforts not on the investigation of central processes (including prominently inference, problem solving, and the fixation and modification of belief) but rather on the encapsulated—and hence, in virtue of their immunity from the frame problem, more easily studied—input and output modules.

As for artificial intelligence, the moral Fodor draws is that the pursuit of computational solutions to the frame problem is a hopeless quest, and that until such time as major breakthroughs in the philosophy of science are announced the best hope for progress rests in the study of knowledge and performance in highly informationally encapsulated domains (including not only input/output processes, but also inference in domains for which the relevant information is *de facto* encapsulated—the so-called expert domains, such as chess). One should be wary, however, if Fodor is correct, about generalizing results gleaned from research about reasoning in these constrained domains into theories about general-purpose, rational cognition.

This advice to study the input systems and to leave the central processes alone is taken, plus or minus a bit (perhaps more than a bit in the case of

Marslen-Wilson and Tyler), by every writer in part I. Forster (chapter 3) is most directly in this Fodorian tradition, concerned as he is with defending the thesis of the encapsulation of the language input system against the apparent penetration into its operation by general knowledge and with articulating the sequence of processing stages within the linguistic input system, and the information that becomes available to it at each stage.

The problem Forster confronts is this: There is considerable evidence that the grammaticality of target-sentence word strings facilitates their rapid matching (in comparison with nonsentence word strings), indicating that grammatically structured representations are available to the subject very early in the task. So, the ungrammatical strings

(17)   *Mary were writing a letter to her husband.

(18)   *To go to Disneyland John wanted.

(19)   *Lesley's parents are chemical engineers both.

(20)   *The girl behind you the subsequent discussion.

are all matched significantly more slowly than grammatical controls. But there are ungrammatical strings for which this is not true. So the difference in processing time between (15) and (14) is the same as that between (13) and (12):

(12)   The police believe that John shot Mary.

(13)   The police believe the claim that John shot Mary.

(14)   Who do the police believe that John shot?

(15)   *Who do the police believe the claim that John shot?

And, finally, there is evidence that matching is facilitated by semantic plausibility. So (21) is matched more rapidly than (22):

(21)   The workman repaired the factory slowly.

(22)   The florist disguised the composer daily.

Thus, two puzzles within the paradigm defined by the modularity hypothesis are created regarding the linguistic-processing module: What is the internal structure of the module that accounts for the processing costs in the violations represented in (17)–(20) but for the absence of cost for the subjacency violation in (15)? Is there a way to salvage the thesis of the informational encapsulation of the module in the face of the evidence provided by (21) and (22) that semantic representations of sentences affect processing time? Forster argues that these puzzles can be resolved squarely within the modularity framework by means of the construct he calls the *controlling level* for a task (for a subject, since the same task may have distinct controlling levels for distinct subjects). The controlling level represents the level of analysis in a multistage model of sentence analysis at which the comparison required in the matching task is made. On this model, a fixed sequence of processing stages is posited, each generating a level of representation. A task (such as matching) controlled for a subject at any level will be sensitive only to information available at or before that processing level. Since lexical, phrasal, S-structure, logical form, and interpretive levels succeed one another, matching could be sensitive to phrasal grammatical violations, but not to violations that become apparent only at S-structure. Furthermore, since lexical analysis has access to such information as the likelihood of two lexical items' being juxtaposed, so long as semantic implausibilities are coincident with implausible lexical juxtapositions, these implausibilities will be coincident with processing costs, but costs whose source is not in the penetration of the linguistic input system by semantic representations but rather in the lexicon, squarely within the linguistic input module.

Hence, Forster defends the thesis that the linguistic module has access only to specifically linguistic information, and that its operation is automatic in that the structure of linguistic processing is determined by a fixed architecture. (The Fodorian claim that the processing is also mandatory comes in for some implicit criticism, insofar as in the matching task subjects have some choice regarding controlling level, though performance in such matching tasks is, to be sure, a rather anomalous aspect of linguistic performance.) Forster also provides evidence regarding the details of the structure of the module and the locus of its interface with general, semantic knowledge, and demonstrates the efficacy of matching tasks as a research tool in probing the dimensions of modularity.

Marslen-Wilson and Tyler (chapter 2) are also concerned with the evidence regarding modularity provided by processing tasks in which subjects' performance is apparently sensitive to semantic information. Their evidence, however, leads them to conclude that the language-processing system, at least, is not a modular input system in Fodor's sense.

Marslen-Wilson and Tyler argue that the representation of discourse models (a semantic task that arguably must draw on nonmodular central resources) is as fast and mandatory as the representation of "shallower" linguistic representations such as LF or S-structure representations, whose construction, on the modularity hypothesis, requires only domain-specific linguistic knowledge. They also argue that nonmodular pragmatic inference is as fast as specifically linguistic inference, and that significant top-down effects are exerted by clearly nonmodular cognitive systems on linguistic processing. All these claims are clearly in conflict with central tenets of the modularity hypothesis. However, despite the significant critique of the modularity thesis this chapter represents, it does not constitute a rejection of all the theses bound up with modularism. Marslen-Wilson and Tyler argue that there *is* a domain-specific language-processing system with fixed properties, and that it is both fast and mandatory. They even argue that in normal cases, on first-pass processing, it is insensitive to top-down influences, and so it is relatively informationally encapsulated. However, on their account, this system fails to be modular in important respects, and the conclusion they draw is pessimistic with regard to the utility of the cluster of diagnostics proposed by modularists for distinguishing natural cognitive components.

Marslen-Wilson and Tyler diverge most sharply from Fodor and Forster in two quite specific respects. First, orthodox modularists are concerned to draw the boundaries of the language input module (and thus all specifically linguistic processing) somewhere below the level of semantic representation, claiming that that module delivers something like a LF representation to central processes, which then interpret it. Marslen-Wilson and Tyler argue that specifically linguistic processing prominently includes the construction of semantic representations, and that none of the members of the Fodorian quartet distinguishes semantic from other linguistic processing. Second, orthodox modularists claim that the linguistic module produces, at at least some intermediate level of processing, syntactic or logical representations of linguistic input, and that this module can be identified in terms of the bundle of processes responsible for generating and transforming these representations. Marslen-Wilson and Tyler argue that mapping is directly from lexical information to models, with no intermediate levels of representations, and that a wide range of general-purpose, unencapsulated cognitive resources are marshaled for this task.

Hence, Marslen-Wilson and Tyler conclude, while there are indeed fast, mandatory, domain-specific cognitive processes with bottom-up priority (the language-processing system comprising one cluster), there is no reason to believe that they are autonomous cognitive modules, and no reason to believe that speed, encapsulation, domain specificity, and mandatoriness are universally coincident among cognitive processes or that they are individually or collectively diagnostic of distinct, isolated cognitive subsystems.

Tanenhaus, Dell, and Carlson (chapter 4) consider the relationship between the connectionist and modularity paradigms in psycholinguistic theory, arguing that there is good reason to adjoin the two paradigms. Like Forster and Marslen-Wilson and Tyler, they are concerned with the possibility of both modular and nonmodular explanations of the effects of context on processing, which provide *prima facie* evidence of interaction between central and language input processes. They argue that one of the principal virtues of a marriage of the connectionist and modularity paradigms is that it would facilitate the computational testing, via easily constructed connectionist models, of rival hypotheses regarding the degree to which linguistic processing is informationally encapsulated and domain specific. Further methodological advantages to be achieved from this proposed marriage are the possibility of distinguishing the degrees of modularity enjoyed by various components of the language-processing system and the possibility of accounting for modularity or its absence by reference to the computational characteristics of the linguistic structures processed. (On connectionist models, some structures will be most efficiently processed via widely connected networks, some via highly modular networks.)

This methodological suggestion is surprising, as Tanenhaus et al. note, because modularism and connectionism have generally been regarded as antithetical, if not in substance, then at least in spirit. The principal explanatory burden of connectionist models is borne by the extensive connections between nodes in the system, and by the spread of activation and inhibition along these connections. Furthermore, it is typical of these systems that their processing is massively parallel. These features contrast dramatically with the lack of connection between information available to distinct modules and with the hierarchical models of modular processing posited by the modularity hypothesis.

However, Tanenhaus et al. argue, the flexibility of connectionist processing models is greater than might be thought. The explicitness and testability of these models, and the varieties of connection types and of ways of organizing nodes and spreading activation, permit one to construct a wide variety of linguistic-processing models. In some of these, networks might be strikingly nonmodular, but in others, because of the structures of the links among nodes, the networks might have highly modular properties, including hierarchical structure, encapsulation, and domain specificity. What is more, they argue, one can tell by constructing connectionist models just when one is driven to a modular structure and when one is not; this yields a better and a finer-grained research approach for the investigation of the causes and dimensions of modularity, as well as joining the insights of two independently plausible but heretofore disjoint research programs.

Taken collectively, these chapters reveal the theoretical and methodological fecundity of the modularity hypothesis. They also provide valuable insights into the nature of work to be done in the course of its empirical assessment and the variety of possible interpretations and developments, both orthodox and heterodox, of the paradigm.

1

Modules, Frames, Fridgeons, Sleeping Dogs, and the Music of the Spheres

Jerry A. Fodor

There are, it seems to me, two interesting ideas about modularity. The first is the idea that some of our cognitive faculties are modular. The second is the idea that some of our cognitive faculties are not.

By a modular cognitive faculty I mean—for present purposes—an "informationally encapsulated" cognitive faculty. By an informationally encapsulated cognitive faculty I mean one that has access, in the course of its computations, to less than all of the information at the disposal of the organism whose cognitive faculty it is, the restriction on informational access being imposed by relatively unlabile, "architectural" features of mental organization. For example, I think that the persistence of the Muller-Lyer illusion in spite of one's knowledge that it is an illusion strongly suggests that some of the cognitive mechanisms that mediate visual size perception must be informationally encapsulated. You know perfectly well that the lines are the same length, yet it continues to appear to you that they are not. It would seem to follow that some of what you know perfectly well is inaccessible to the cognitive mechanisms that are determining the appearances. If this is the right diagnosis, then it follows that some of those mechanisms are informationally encapsulated.

It is worth emphasizing a sense in which modular cognitive processing is *ipso facto* irrational. After all, by definition modular processing means arriving at conclusions by attending to arbitrarily less than all of the evidence that is relevant and/or by considering arbitrarily fewer than all of the hypotheses that might reasonably be true. Ignoring relevant evidence and overlooking reasonable hypotheses are, however, techniques of belief fixation that are notoriously likely to get you into trouble in the long run. Informational encapsulation is economical; it buys speed and the reduction of computational load by, in effect, delimiting *a priori* the data base and the space of candidate solutions that get surveyed in the course of problem solving. But the price of economy is warrant. The more encapsulated the cognitive mechanisms that mediate the fixation of your beliefs, the worse is your evidence for the beliefs that you have. And, barring skeptical worries of a boring sort, the worse your evidence for your beliefs is, the less the likelihood that your beliefs are true.

Rushing the hurdles and jumping to conclusions is, then, a characteristic pathology of irrational cognitive strategies, and a disease that modular processors have in spades. That, to repeat, is because the data that they consult and the solutions that they contemplate are determined arbitrarily by rigid features of cognitive architecture. But—and here is the point I want to emphasize for present purposes—rational processes have their debilities too; they have their characteristic hangups whose outbreaks are the symptoms of their very rationality. Suppose that, in pursuit of rational belief fixation, you undertake to subject whichever hypotheses might reasonably be true to scrutiny in light of whatever evidence might reasonably be relevant. You then have the problem of how to determine when demands of reason have been satisfied. You have, that is to say, Hamlet's problem: How to tell when to stop thinking.

The frame problem is just Hamlet's problem viewed from an engineer's perspective. You want to make a device that is rational in the sense that its mechanisms of belief fixation are unencapsulated. But you also want the device you make to actually succeed in fixing a belief or two from time to time; you don't want it to hang up the way that Hamlet did. So, on the one hand, you don't want to delimit its computations arbitrarily (as in encapsulated systems); on the other hand, you want these computations to come, somehow, to an end. How is this to be arranged? What is a nonarbitrary strategy for restricting the evidence that should be searched and the hypotheses that should be contemplated in the course of rational belief fixation? I don't know how to answer this question. If I did, I'd have solved the frame problem and I'd be rich and famous.

To be sure, the frame problem isn't always formulated quite so broadly. In the first instance it arises as a rather specialized issue in artificial intelligence: How could one get a robot to appreciate the consequences of its behavior? Action alters the world, and if a system is to perform coherently, it must be able to change its beliefs to accommodate the effects of its activities. But effecting this accommodation surely can't require a wholesale review of each and every prior cognitive commitment in consequence of each and every act the thing performs; a device caught up in thought to that extent would instantly be immobilized. There must be some way of delimiting those beliefs that the consequences of behavior can reasonably be supposed to put in jeopardy; there must be some way of deciding which beliefs should become, as one says, candidates for "updating," and in consequence of which actions.

It is easy to see that this way of putting the frame problem underestimates its generality badly. Despite its provenance in speculative robotology, the frame problem doesn't really have anything in particular to do with action. After all, one's standing cognitive commitments must rationally accommodate to each new state of affairs, whether or not it is a state of affairs that is consequent upon one's own behavior. And the principle holds quite generally that the demands of rationality must somehow be squared with those of feasibility. We must somehow contrive that most of our beliefs correspond to the facts about a changing world. But we must somehow manage to do so without having to put very many of our beliefs at risk at any given time. The frame problem is the problem of understanding how we bring this off; it is, one might say, the problem of how rationality is possible in practice. (If you are still tempted by the thought that the frame problem is interestingly restricted by construing it as specially concerned with how belief conforms to the consequences of behavior, consider the case where the robot we are trying to build is a mechanical scientist, the actions that it performs are experiments, and the design problem is to get the robot's beliefs to rationally accommodate the data that its experiments provide. Here the frame problem is transparently that of finding a general and feasible procedure for altering cognitive commitments in light of empirical contingencies; i.e., it is transparently the general problem of understanding feasible nondemonstrative inference. If experimenting counts as acting—and, after all, why shouldn't it?—then the problem of understanding how the consequences of action are rationally assessed is just the problem of understanding understanding.)

Here is what I have argued so far: Rational mechanisms of belief fixation are *ipso facto* unencapsulated. Unencapsulated mechanisms of belief fixation are *ipso facto* nonarbitrary in their selection of the hypotheses that they evaluate and the evidence that they consult. Mechanisms of belief fixation that are nonarbitrary in these ways are *ipso facto* confronted with Hamlet's problem, which is just the frame problem formulated in blank verse. So, two conclusions:

• The frame problem goes very deep; it goes as deep as the analysis of rationality.
• Outbreaks of the frame problem are symptoms or rational processing; if you are looking at a system that has the frame problem, you can assume that the system is rational at least to the extent of being unencapsulated.

The second of these conclusions is one that I particularly cherish. I used it in *The Modularity of Mind* (1983) as an argument against what I take to be modularity theory gone mad: the idea that modularity is the general case in cognitive architecture, that all cognitive processing is informationally encapsulated. Roughly, the argument went like this: The distinction between the encapsulated mental processes and the rest is—approximately but interestingly—coextensive with the distinction between perception and cognition. When we look at real, honest-to-God perceptual processes, we find real, honest-to-God informational encapsulation. In parsing, for example, we find a computational mechanism with access only to the acoustics of the input and the body of "background information" that can be formulated in a certain kind of grammar. That is why—in my view, and contrary to much of the received wisdom in psycholinguistics—there are no context effects in parsing. It is also why there is no frame problem in parsing. The question of what evidence the parser should consult in determining the structural description of an utterance is solved arbitrarily and architecturally: Only the acoustics of the input and the grammar are ever available. Because there is no frame problem in parsing, it is one of the few cognitive processes that we have had any serious success in understanding.

In contrast, when we try to build a really smart machine—not a machine that will parse sentences or play chess, but, say, one that will make the breakfast without burning down the house—we get the frame problem straight off. This, I argued in *MOM*, is precisely because smart processes aren't modular. Being smart, being nonmodular, and raising the frame problem all go together. That, in brief, is why, although we have mechanical parsing and mechanical chess playing, we have no machines that will make breakfast except stoves.[1]

In short, that the frame problem breaks out here and there but does not break out everywhere is itself an argument for differences in kind among cognitive mechanisms. We can understand the distribution of outbreaks of the frame problem on the hypothesis that it is the chronic infirmity of rational (hence unencapsulated, hence nonmodular) cognitive systems—so I argued in *MOM*, and so I am prepared to argue still.

Candor requires, however, that I report to you the following: This understanding of the frame problem is not universally shared. In AI especially, the frame problem is widely viewed as a sort of a glitch, for which heuristic processing is the appropriate patch. (The technical vocabulary deployed by analysts of the frame problem has become markedly less beautiful since Shakespeare discussed it in *Hamlet*.) How could this be so? How could the depth, beauty, and urgency of the frame problem have been so widely misperceived? That, really, is what this chapter is about.

What I am inclined to think is this: The frame problem is so ubiquitous, so polymorphous, and so intimately connected with every aspect of the attempt to understand rational nondemonstrative inference that it is quite possible for a practitioner to fail to notice when it is indeed the frame problem that he is working on. It is like the ancient doctrine about the music of the spheres: If you can't hear it, that's because it is everywhere. That would be OK, except that if you are unable to recognize the frame problem when as a matter of fact you are having it, you may suppose that you have solved the frame problem when as a matter of fact you are begging it. Much of the history of the frame problem in AI strikes me as having that character; the discussion that follows concerns a recent and painful example.

In a paper called "We've Been Framed: or, Why AI Is Innocent of the Frame Problem," Drew McDermott (1986) claims that "there is no one problem here; and hence no solution is possible or necessary" (p.1). The frame problem, it turns out, is a phantom that philosophers have unwittingly conjured up by making a variety of mistakes, which McDermott details and undertakes to rectify.

What philosophers particularly fail to realize, according to McDermott, is that, though no solution of the frame problem is "possible or necessary," nevertheless a solution is up and running in AI. (One wonders how many other impossible and unnecessary problems McDermott and his colleagues have recently solved.) McDermott writes: "In all systems since [1969] ... programs have used the 'sleeping dog' strategy. They keep track of each situation as a separate database. To reason about e, s, *i.e. about the result of an event in a situation*, they compute all the effects of e in situation s, make those changes, and leave the rest of s (the 'sleeping dogs') alone." In consequence of the discovery of this sleeping-dogs solution, since 1970 "*no working AI program has ever been bothered at all by the frame problem*" (emphasis in original).

It is, moreover, no accident that the sleeping-dogs strategy works. It is supported by a deep metaphysical truth, viz. that "most events leave most facts untouched" (p. 2): You can rely on metaphysical inertia to carry most of the facts along from one event to the next; being carried along in this way is, as you might say, the unmarked case for facts. Because this is so, you will usually do all right if you leave well enough alone when you update you data base. Given metaphysical inertia, the appropriate epistemic strategy is to assume that nothing changes unless you have a special reason for changing it. Sleeping dogs don't scratch where it doesn't itch, so doesn't the sleeping-dogs strategy solve the frame problem?

No; what it does is convert the frame problem from a problem about belief fixation into a problem about ontology (or, what comes to much the same thing for present purposes, from a problem about belief fixation into a problem about canonical notation.) This wants some spelling out.

As we have seen, the sleeping-dogs strategy depends on assuming that most of the facts don't change from one event to the next. The trouble with that assumption is that whether it is true depends on how you individuate facts. To put it a little more formally: If you want to use a sleeping-dogs algorithm to update you data base, you must first devise a system of canonical representation for the facts. (Algorithms work on facts as represented.) And this system of canonical representation will have to have the following properties:

- It will have to be rich enough to be able to represent all the facts that you propose to specify in the data base.
- The canonical representations of most of the facts must be unchanged by most events. By definition, a sleeping-dogs algorithm will not work unless the canonical notation has this property.

The problem is—indeed, the *frame* problem is—that such notations are a little hard to come by. Oh yes, indeed they are! Consider, for example, the following outbreak of the frame problem.

It has got to work out, on any acceptable model, that when I turn my refrigerator on, certain of my beliefs about the refrigerator and about other things become candidates for getting updated. For example, now that the refrigerator is on, I believe that putting the legumes in the vegetable compartment will keep them cool and crisp. (I did not believe that before I turned the refrigerator on because until I turned the refrigerator on I believed that the refrigerator was off—correctly, we may assume.) Similarly, now that the refrigerator is on, I believe that when the door is opened the light in the refrigerator will go on, that my electricity meter will run slightly faster than it did before, and so forth. On the other hand, it should also fall out of solution of the frame problem that a lot of my beliefs—indeed, most of my beliefs—do not become candidates for updating (and hence don't have to be actively reconsidered) in consequence of my plugging in the fridge: my belief that cats are animate, my belief that Granny was a Bulgarian, my belief that snow is white, and so forth. I want it that most of my beliefs do not become candidates for updating because what I primarily want of my beliefs is that they should correspond to the facts; and, as we have seen, metaphysical inertia guarantees me that most of the facts are unaffected by my turning on the fridge.

Or does it? Consider a certain relational property that physical particles have from time to time: the property of being a fridgeon. I define 'x is a fridgeon at t' as follows: x is a fridgeon at t iff x is a particle at t and my fridge is on at t. It is a consequence of this definition that, when I turn my fridge on, I change the state of every physical particle in the universe; viz., every physical particle becomes a fridgeon. (Turning the fridge off has the reverse effect.) I take it (as does McDermott, so far as I can tell) that talk about facts is intertranslatable with talk about instantiations of properties; thus, when I create ever so many new fridgeons, I also create ever so many new facts.

The point is that if you count all these facts about fridgeons, the principle of metaphysical inertia no longer holds even of such homely events as my turning on the fridge. To put the same point less metaphysically and more computationally: If I let the facts about fridgeons into my data base (along with the facts about the crisping compartment and the facts about Granny's ethnic affiliations), pursuing the sleeping-dogs strategy will no longer solve the frame problem. The sleeping-dogs strategy proposes to keep the computational load down by considering as candidates for updating only representations of such facts as an event changes. But now there are billions of facts that change when I plug in the fridge—one fact for each particle, more or less. And there is nothing special about the property of being a fridgeon; it is a triviality to think up as many more such kooky properties as you like.

I repeat the moral: Once you let representations of the kooky properties into the data base, a strategy that says "look just at the facts that change" will buy you nothing; it will commit you to looking at indefinitely many facts.

The moral is not that the sleeping-dogs strategy is wrong; it is that the sleeping-dogs strategy is empty unless we have, together with the strategy, some idea of what is to count as a fact for the purposes at hand. Moreover, this notion of (as we might call it) a *computationally relevant* fact will have to be formalized if we propose to implement the sleeping-dogs strategy as a computational algorithm. Algorithms act on facts only as represented—indeed, only in virtue of the form of their representations. Thus, if we want to keep the kooky facts out of the data base and keep the computationally relevant facts in, we have to find a way of distinguishing kooky facts from computationally relevant ones in virtue of the form of their canonical representations. The frame problem, in its current guise, is thus the problem of formalizing the distinction between kooky facts and kosher ones.

We do not know how to formalize this distinction. For that matter, we don't even known how to draw it. For example, the following ways of drawing it—or of getting out of drawing it—will quite clearly not work:

(a) Being a fridgeon is a relational property; rule it out on those grounds.

Answer: being a father is a relational property too, but we want to be able to come to believe that John is a father when we come to believe that his wife has had a child.

(b) *Fridgeon* is a made-up word. There is no such word as *fridgeon* in English.

Answer: You can't rely on the lexicon of English to solve your metaphysical problems for you. There used to be no such word as *meson* either. Moreover, though there is no such word as *fridgeon*, the expression *x is a particle at t and my fridge is on at t* is perfectly well formed. Since this expression is the definition of *fridgeon*, everything that can be said in English by using *fridgeon* can also be said in English without using it.

(c) Being a fridgeon isn't a real property.

Answer: I'll be damned if I see why not, but have it your way. The frame problem is now the problem of saying what a 'real property' is.

In this formulation, by the way, the frame problem has quite a respectable philosophical provenance. Here, for example, is a discussion of Hume's version of the frame problem:

> Two things are related by what Hume calls a 'philosophical' relation if any relational statement at all is true of them. All relations are 'philosophical' relations. But according to Hume there are also some 'natural' relations between things. One thing is naturally related to another if the thought of the first naturally leads the mind to the thought of the other. If we see no obvious connection between two things, e. g. my raising my arm now ... and the death of a particular man in Abyssinia 33,118 years ago, we are likely to say 'there is no relation at all between these two events.' [But] of course there are many 'philosophical' relations between these two events—spatial and temporal relations, for example. (Stroud 1977, p. 89)

Hume thought that the only natural relations are contiguity, causation, and resemblance. Since the relation between my closing the fridge and some particle's becoming a fridgeon is an instance of none of these, Hume would presumably have held that the fact that the particle becomes a fridgeon is a merely 'philosophical' fact, hence not a 'psychologically real' fact. (It is psychological rather than ontological reality that, according to Hume, merely philosophical relations lack.) So it would turn out, on Hume's story, that the fact that a particle becomes a fridgeon isn't the sort of fact that data bases should keep track of.

If Hume is right about which relations are the natural ones, this will do as a solution to the frame problem except that Hume has no workable account of the relations of causation, resemblance, and contiguity—certainly no account precise enough to formalize. If, however, Hume is in that bind, so are we.

(d) Nobody actually has concepts like 'fridgeon', so you don't have to worry about such concepts when you build your model of the mind.

Answer: This is another way of begging the frame problem, another way of mistaking a formulation of the problem for its solution.

Everybody has an infinity of concepts, corresponding roughly to the open sentences of English. According to all known theories, the way a person keeps an infinity of concepts in a finite head is this: He stores a finite primitive basis and a finite compositional mechanism, and the recursive application of the latter to the former specifies the infinite conceptual repertoire. The present problem is that there are arbitrarily many kooky concepts—like 'fridgeon'—which can be defined with the same apparatus that you use to define perfectly kosher concepts like 'vegetable crisper' or 'Bulgarian grandmother'. That is, the same basic concepts that I used to define *fridgeon*, and the same logical syntax, are needed to define nonkooky concepts that people actually do entertain. Thus, the problem—the frame problem—is to find a rule that will keep the kooky concepts out while letting the nonkooky concepts in.

Lacking a solution to this problem, you cannot implement a sleeping-dogs "solution" to the frame problem; it will not run. It will not run because, at each event, it will be required to update indefinitely many beliefs about the distribution of kooky properties.

(e) But McDermott says that solutions to the frame problem have actually been implemented; that nobody in AI has had to worry about the frame problem since way back in '69. So something must be wrong with your argument.

Answer: The programs run because the counterexamples are never confronted. The programmer decides, case by case, which properties get specified in the data base; but the decision is unsystematic and unprincipled. For example, no database will be allowed to include information about the distribution of fridgeons; however, as we have seen, there appears to be no disciplined way to justify the exclusion and no way to implement it that doesn't involve excluding indefinitely many computationally relevant concepts as well.

There is a price to be paid for failing to face the frame problem. The conceptual repertoires with which AI systems are allowed to operate exclude kooky and kosher concepts indiscriminately. They are therefore grossly impoverished in comparison with the conceptual repertoires of really intelligent systems like you and me. The result (one of the worst-kept secrets in the world, I should think) is that these artificially intelligent systems—the ones that have been running since 1970 "without ever being bothered by the frame problem"—are, by any reasonable standard, ludicrously stupid.

So, there is a dilemma: You build a canonical notation that is rich enough to express the concepts available to a smart system (a canonical notation as rich as English, say) and it will thereby let the fridgeons in. (*Fridgeon* is, as we've seen, definable in English.) Or you build a canonical notation that is restrictive enough to keep the fridgeons out, and it will thereby fail to express concepts that smart systems need. The frame problem now emerges as the problem of breaking this dilemma. In the absence of a solution to the frame problem, the practice in AI has been to opt, implicitly, for the second horn and live with the consequences, viz., dumb machines.

You may be beginning to wonder what is actually going on here. Well, because the frame problem is just the problem of nondemonstrative inference, a good way to see what is going on is to think about how the sleeping-dogs strategy works when it is applied to confirmation in science. Science is our best case of the systematic pursuit of knowledge through nondemonstrative inference; thus, if the frame problem were a normal symptom of rational practice, one would expect to find its traces "writ large" in the methodology of science—as indeed we do. Looked at from this perspective, the frame problem is that of making science cumulative; it is the problem of localizing, as much as possible, the impact of new data on previously received bodies of theory. In science, as in private practice, rationality gets nowhere if each new fact occasions a wholesale revision of prior commitments. So, corresponding to the sleeping-dogs strategy in AI, we have a principle of "conservatism" in scientific methodology, a principle that says "alter the minimum possible amount of prior theory as you go about trying to accommodate new data." [2]

While it is widely agreed that conservatism, in this sense, is constitutive of rational scientific practice, the maxim as I've just stated it doesn't amount to anything like a formal principle for theory choice (just as the sleeping-dogs strategy as McDermott states it doesn't constitute anything like an algorithm for updating data bases). You could, of course, *make* the principle of conservatism into a formal evaluation metric by specifying (a) a canonical notation for writing the scientific theories that you propose to evaluate in and (b) a costing system that formalizes the notion 'most conservative theory change' (e.g., the most conservative change in a theory is the one that alters the fewest symbols in its canonical representation). Given (a) and (b), we would have an important fragment of a mechanical evaluation procedure for science. That would be a nice thing for us to have, so why doesn't somebody go and build us one?

Well, not just any canonical notation will do the job. To do the job, you have to build a notation such that (relative to the costing system) the (intuitively) most conservative revision of a theory does indeed come out to be the simplest one when the theory is canonically represented. (For example, if your costing system says "choose the alteration that can be specified in the smallest number of canonical symbols," then your notation has to have the property that the intuitively most conservative alteration actually does come out shortest when the theory is in canonical form.) Of course, nobody knows how to construct a notation with that agreeable property—just as nobody knows how to construct a notation for facts such that, under that notation, most facts are unchanged by most events.

It is not surprising that such notation don't grow on trees. If somebody developed a vocabulary for writing scientific theories that had the property that the shortest description of the world in that vocabulary was always the intuitively best theory of the world available, that would mean that that notation would give formal expression to our most favored inductive estimate of the world's taxonomic structure by specifying the categories in terms of which we take it that the world should be described. Well, when we have an inductive estimate of the world's taxonomic structure that is good enough to permit formal expression, and a canonical vocabulary to formulate the taxonomy in, most of science will be finished.

Similarly, *mutatis mutandis*, in cognitive theory. A notation adequate to support an implemented sleeping-dogs algorithm would be one that would represent as facts only what we commonsensically take to really be facts (the ethnicity of grandmothers, the temperature in the vegetable crisper, but not the current distribution of fridgeons). In effect, the notation would give formal expression to our commonsense estimate of the world's taxonomic structure. Well, when we have a rigorous account of our commonsense estimate of the world's taxonomic structure, and a notation to express it in, most of *cognitive* science will be finished.

In short, there is no formal conservatism principle for science for much the same sort of reason that there is no workable sleeping-dogs algorithm for AI. Basically, the solution of both problems requires a notation that formalizes our intuitions about inductive relevance. There is, however, the following asymmetry: We can do science perfectly well without having a formal theory of nondemonstrative inference; that is, we can do science perfectly well without solving the frame problem. That is because doing science doesn't require mechanical scientists; we have us instead. However, we can't do AI perfectly well without having mechanical intelligence; doing AI perfectly well just *is* having mechanical intelligence. Thus, we can't do AI without solving the frame problem. But we don't know how to solve the frame problem. That, in a nutshell, is why, although science works, AI doesn't. Or, to put it more in the context of modularity theory, that is why, though we are sort of starting to have some ideas about encapsulated nondemonstrative inference, we have no ideas about unencapsulated nondemonstrative inference that one could ask an adult to take seriously.

I reiterate the main point: The frame problem and the problem of formalizing our intuitions about inductive relevance are, in every important respect, the same thing. It is just as well, perhaps, that people working on the frame problem in AI are unaware that this is so. One imagines the expression of horror that flickers across their CRT-illuminated faces as the awful facts sink in. What could they do but "down-tool" and become philosophers? One feels for them. Just think of the cut in pay!

God, according to Einstein, does not play dice with the world. Well, maybe; but He sure is into shell games. If you do not understand the logical geography of the frame problem, you will only succeed in pushing it around from one shell to the next, never managing to locate it for long enough to have a chance of solving it. This is, so far as I can see, pretty much the history of the frame problem in AI, which is a major reason why a lot of AI work, when viewed as cognitive theory, strikes one as so thin. The frame problem—to say it one last time—is just the problem of unencapsulated nondemonstrative inference, and the problem of unencapsulated nondemonstrative inference is, to all intents and purposes, the problem of how the cognitive mind works. I am sorry that MacDermott is out of temper with philosophers; but, frankly, the frame problem is too important to leave it to the hackers.

We are really going to have to learn to make progres working together; the alternative is to make fools of ourselves working separately.

Notes

1. Playing chess is not a perceptual process, so why is it modular? Some processes are modular by brute force and some are modular in the nature of things. Parsing is a case of the former kind; there is relevant information in the context, but the architecture of the mind doesn't let the parser use it. Chess playing, by contrast, is modular in the sense that only a very restricted body of background information (call it chess theory) is relevant to rational play even in principle. This second kind of modularity, precisely because it stems from the nature of the task rather than the architecture of the mind, isn't of much theoretical interest. It is interesting to the engineer, however, since informational encapsulation makes for feasible simulation regardless of what the source of the encapsulation may be.

   To put it in a nutshell: On the present view, the natural candidates for simulation are the modular systems and the expert systems. This is, however, cold comfort; I doubt that there are more than a handful of the first, and I think that there are hardly any of the second.

2. Nothing is perfect, analogies least of all. Philosophers of science usually view conservatism as a principle for evaluating scientific theories, not as tactic for inventing or revising them; it is part of the "logic of confirmation," as one says, rather than the "logic of discovery." I'll talk that way too in what follows, but if you want to understand how science works it is usually unwise to push this distinction very hard. In the present case, not only do we think it rational to prefer the most conservative revision of theory *ceteris paribus*; we also think it rational to try the conservative revisions first. When conservatism is viewed in this way, the analogy to the sleeping-dogs solution of the frame problem is seen to be very close indeed.

2

Against Modularity

William Marslen-Wilson and Lorraine Komisarjevsky Tyler

The fundamental claim of the modularity hypothesis (Fodor 1983) is that the process of language comprehension—of mapping from the speech signal onto a message-level interpretation—is not a single, unitary process but involves at least two different kinds of process.[1] There is a modular, highly constrained, automatized "input system" that operates blindly on its bottom-up input to deliver, as rapidly as neurally possible, a shallow linguistic representation to a second kind of process, labeled by Fodor a "central process." This second type of process relates the output of the modular input system to the listener's knowledge of the world, of the discourse content, and so on. In particular, these central processes are responsible for the fixation of perceptual belief.

To justify this dichotomy between kinds of mental process, Fodor marshals a list of properties that input systems have and that central processes do not have. These include domain specificity, mandatoriness, speed, informational encapsulation, and a number of less critical properties. We do not dispute that there are some "central processes" that do not share these properties. Our argument here, nonetheless, is that those processes that map onto discourse representations and that also participate in the fixation of perceptual belief in fact share many of the special properties that Fodor treats as diagnostic of modular input systems.

We will argue on this basis that the modularity hypothesis gives the wrong kind of account of the organization of the language-processing system. This system does have fixed properties, and it does seem to be domain specific, mandatory, and fast in its operations. It is also, in a restricted sense, informationally encapsulated, because top-down influences do not control its normal first-pass operations. But its boundaries do not neatly coincide, as Fodor and others would have us believe, with the boundaries conventionally drawn between the subject matter of linguistic theory (construed as formal syntax) and the subject matter of disciplines such as pragmatics and discourse analysis.

In other words, we will argue, Fodor has misidentified the basic phenomenon that needs to be explained. Our comprehension of language, as he repeatedly stresses, is of the same order of immediacy as our perception, say, of the visual world. The modularity hypothesis tries to explain this by arguing that the primary processes of language analysis must operate with the blindness and the immunity to conscious control of the traditional reflex. Only in this way can we buy the brute speed with which the system seems to work.

But what is compelling about our real-time comprehension of language is not so much the immediacy with which linguistic form becomes available as the immediacy with which interpreted meaning becomes available. It is this that is the target of the core processes of language comprehension, of the processes that map from sound onto meaning.

In the next section we will discuss the diagnostic properties assigned to input systems. We will then go on to present some experimental evidence for the encroachment of "modular" properties into processing territories reserved for central processes. This will be followed by a discussion of the implications of this failure of the diagnostic features to isolate a discontinuity in the system at the point where Fodor and others want to place it. We do not claim that there are no differences between input systems and central processes; but, the differences that do exist are not distributed in the way that the modularity hypothesis requires.

Diagnostic Features

Table 1 lists the principal diagnostic features that, according to Fodor, discriminate input systems from central processes.[2] We will go through these six features in order, showing how each one fails to support a qualitative discontinuity at the fracture point indicated by Fodor and by most other modularity theorists, e.g., Forster (1979 and this volume), Garrett (1978), and Frazier et al. (1983b). In each case the question is the same: Does the feature distinguish between a mapping process that terminates on a specifically linguistic, sentence-internal form of representation (labeled "logical form" in the table) and a process that terminates on some form of discourse representation or mental model?

Table 1
Diagnostic features for modularity.

Diagnostic feature	Target of mapping process	
	Logical form	Discourse model
Domain specificity	Yes	Yes
Mandatory	Yes	Yes
Limited access to intermediate representations	Yes	Yes
Speed	Yes	Yes
Informational encapsulation	No	No
Shallow output	—	—

Domain Specificity
The argument here is that when one is dealing with a specialized domain—
that is, a domain that has its own idiosyncratic computations to perform—
one would expect to find a specialized processor. However, as Fodor
himself points out (1983, p. 52), the inference from domain idiosyncracy to
modular processor is not by itself a strong one. Furthermore, he presents
neither evidence nor arguments that the process of mapping linguistic
representations onto discourse models is any less domain specific (i.e.,
less idiosyncratic or specialized) than the processes required to map onto
"shallow" linguistic representations.

Mandatory Processing
Mandatory processing is what we have called *obligatory processing* (Marslen-
Wilson and Tyler 1980a, 1981), and what others have called *automatic* (as
opposed to controlled) processing (e.g., Posner and Snyder 1975; Shiffrin
and Schneider 1977). The claim here is that modular processes apply
mandatorily and that central processes do not. Fodor's arguments for this
are entirely phenomenological. If we hear an utterance in a language we
know, we are are forced to perceive it as a meaningful, interpretable string,
and not as a sequence of meaningless noises.

But there is no reason to suppose that this mandatory projection onto
higher-level representations stops short at logical form. Indeed, one's phenomenological experience says quite distinctly otherwise. Consider the
following pair of utterances, uttered in normal conversation after a lecture:
"Jerry gave the first talk today. He was his usual ebullient self." Hearing
this, it seems just as cognitively mandatory to map the pronoun *He* at the
beginning of the second sentence onto the discourse representation of *Jerry*
set up in the course of the first sentence as it does, for example, to hear *All
Gaul is divided into three parts* as a sentence and not as an acoustic object
(see Fodor 1983, p. 55).

In other words, in what we call *normal first-pass processing* the projection
onto an interpretation in the discourse model can be just as mandatory as
the projection onto "shallower" levels of linguistic analysis.[3] And if there is
a distinction here between mapping onto logical form and mapping onto a
discourse model, it probably isn't going to be picked up by this kind of
introspective analysis.

Limited Central Access to Intermediate Representations
The underlying assumption here is that the perceptual process proceeds
through the assignment of a number of intermediate levels of representation, culminating in the final output of the system. Fodor claims that these
"interlevels" are relatively less accessible to central processes than the output representation. There are two points we can make here.

First, there is nothing in Fodor's discussion of this (1983, pp. 55–60) that specifically implicates a shallow linguistic level as *the* level of representation that is more accessible to central processes. Second, if one is dealing with a series of automatized processes, tracking obligatorily through the processing sequence, then one is surely going to get a form of overwriting of the perceptual representations at each level intermediate to the final one. This will make the interlevels less accessible to the perceiver, but without the need to assign a special status to this final level—other than that, because it is the final level, it will not be overwritten by subsequent levels.

At this point one is returned to the phenomenological issues raised in the preceding section: What is the level of perceptual representation onto which the process obligatorily maps, and is this the form of representation that is most readily accessible to other processes?

Speed

The speed of language processing is central to Fodor's argument. The projection from signal onto message seems to be carried out as rapidly as is either neurally or informationally possible. Close shadowers, as he points out, with repetition delays of around 250 msec, seem to be operating at the limit of the ability of the speech signal to deliver information. In fact (as we argue in Marslen-Wilson 1985), close shadowers are outrunning even the abilities of their processing system to deliver its products to conscious awareness; they start to initiate their repetition of what they hear before they are fully aware of what they are saying.

But why does this speed matter? How does it help to diagnose an input system with its boundaries somewhere in the region of logical form?

Fodor's argument is simply that speech processing can only be this fast if it is domain specific, mandatory, and informationally encapsulated—if, in other words, it is like a reflex.[4] And for a process to be reflexive it cannot also be reflective—or, as Fodor puts it, "sicklied o'er with the pale cast of thought" (p. 64). This means, in particular, that this primary rapid analysis process must be restricted to properties of utterances that can largely be computed from the bottom up and without reference to background knowledge, problem-solving mechanisms, and the like. These properties, Fodor believes, are the grammatical and logical structure of an utterance: the abstract representation of utterance *form*.

Fodor's argument fails on two counts: because the available evidence shows that mapping onto a discourse model can be at least as fast as any putative mapping onto logical form, and because discourse mapping is not necessarily slowed down even when it does involve pragmatic inference (which is just the kind of open-ended process that Fodor argues must be excluded from rapid first-pass processing).

Informational Encapsulation
Informational encapsulation is the claim that input systems are information-ally isolated from central processes, in the sense that information derived from these central processes cannot directly affect processing within the input system. This claim lies at the empirical core of Fodor's thesis.

Informational encapsulation is not a diagnostic feature that functions in the same way as the previous four we have discussed. Although it is a property that modular language processes are assumed to have and that central processes do not, it is definable as such only in terms of the relationship between the two of them. To defeat Fodor's argument, we do not need to show whether or not central and modular processes share the property of encapsulation, but simply that they are not isolated from each other in the ways the modularity hypothesis requires. Exactly what degree of isolation does the hypothesis require?

The notion of informational encapsulation, as deployed by Fodor, is significantly weaker than the general notion of autonomous processing, argued for by Forster (1979) and others. This general notion states that the output of each processing component in the system is determined solely by its bottom-up input. Fodor, however, makes no claims for autonomous processing within the language module. Top-down communication be-tween levels of linguistically specified representation does not violate the principle of informational encapsulation (Fodor 1983, pp. 76–77). The language module as a whole, however, is autonomous in the standard sense. No information that is not linguistically specified—at the linguistic levels up to and including logical form—can affect operations within the module. Fodor believes that the cost of fast, mandatory operation in the linguistic input system is isolation from everything else the perceiver knows.

As stated, this claim cannot be completely true. When listeners encounter syntactically ambiguous strings, where only pragmatic knowledge can re-solve the ambiguity, they nonetheless seem to end up with the structural analysis that best fits the context.[5] To cope with this, Fodor does allow a limited form of interaction at the syntactic interface between the language module and central processes. The central processes can give the syntactic parser feedback about the semantic and pragmatic acceptability of the structures it has computed (Fodor 1983, pp. 134–135). Thus, in cases of structural ambiguity, extramodular information does affect the outcome of linguistic analysis.

How is this limited form of interaction to be distinguished, empirically, from a fully interactive, unencapsulated system? Fodor's position is based on the exclusion of top-down predictive interaction: "What the context analyzer is *prohibited* from doing is telling the parser *which* line of analysis it ought to try next—i.e., semantic information can't be used predictively to guide the parse" (Fodor 1983, p. 135; emphases in original). What this means, in practice, is that context will not be able to guide the normal first-pass processing of the material; it will come into play only when the first-pass output of the syntactic parser becomes available for semantic and pragmatic interpretation. This, in turn, means that the claim for informational encapsulation depends empirically on the precise timing of the contextual resolution of syntactic ambiguities—not whether context can have such effects, but when. Is there an exhaustive computation of all readings compatible with the bottom-up input, among which context later selects, or does context intervene early in the process, so that only a single reading needs to be computed? Fodor presents no evidence that bears directly on this issue. But let us consider the arguments he does present, bearing in mind that he does not regard these arguments as proving his case, but simply as making it more plausible.

The first type of argument is frankly rhetorical. It is based on an analogy between input systems and reflexes. If (as Fodor suggests on pages 71–72) input systems are computationally specified reflexes, then, like reflexes, they will be fully encapsulated. The language module will spit out its representation of logical form as blindly and as impenetrably as your knee will respond to the neurologist's rubber hammer. But this is not in itself evidence that the language input system actually is informationally encapsulated. It simply illustrates what input systems might be like if they really were a kind of cognitive reflex. By the same token, the apparent cognitive impenetrability of certain phenomena in visual perception is also no evidence *per se* for the impenetrability of the language module (Fodor, pp. 66–67).

Fodor's second line of argument is teleological in nature: If an organism knows what is good for it, then it will undoubtedly want to have its input systems encapsulated. The organism needs to see or hear what is actually there rather than what it expects should be there, and it needs its first-pass perceptual assignments to be made available as rapidly as possible. And the only way to guarantee this kind of fast, unprejudiced access to the state of the world is to encapsulate one's input systems.

It is certainly true that organisms would do well to ensure themselves fast, unprejudiced input. But this is not evidence that encapsulation is the optimal mechanism for achieving this, nor, specifically, is it evidence that the language input system has these properties—or even that it is subject to this kind of stringent teleological constraint.

The third line of argument is more germane to the issues at hand, since it deals directly with the conventional psycholinguistic evidence for interaction and autonomy in the language-processing system. But even here, Fodor has no evidence that the relationship between syntactic parsing and central processes is restricted in the ways his analysis requires. What he does instead is show that many of the results that are usually cited as evidence for interaction need not be interpreted in this way—although, as noted above, it is only by significantly diluting the concept of autonomy that he can defend the modularity hypothesis against its major counter-examples.

In any case, despite Fodor's caveats, the evidence we will report below suggests that context does guide the parser on-line, and not solely in the "after-the-event" manner Fodor predicts. Hence the entry in table 1. Informational encapsulation does not separate the processes that map onto logical form from those that map onto discourse models.

Shallow Output
Fodor claims that the output of the language input system is restricted to whatever can be computed without reference to "background data." This, however, is not a diagnostic feature at all—it is the basic point at issue.

It is our position that the diagnostics discussed by Fodor, and briefly analyzed here, do not select out an output level corresponding to logical form. Rather, they select an output level that is at least partially non-linguistic in nature. Although the output of the class of mandatory, fast processes may be relatively "shallow," it does not fall at a level of the system that distinguishes either modular processes from central processes (as defined by Fodor) or the linguistic from the nonlinguistic.

Experimental Evidence

In this section we will review some of the evidence supporting our position. In particular, we will argue for three main claims, each of which is in conflict with one or more of the major assumptions upon which Fodor has based the modularity hypothesis. These claims are the following:

(i) that the mapping of the incoming utterance onto a discourse model is indistinguishable in its rapidity from the mapping onto "logical form" (or equivalently shallow levels)
(ii) that the discourse mapping process is not significantly slowed down even when the correct mapping onto discourse antecedents requires pragmatic inference (showing that speed *per se* does not distinguish processes involving only bottom-up linguistic computation from processes involving, at least potentially, "everything the perceiver knows")
(iii) that, if we do assume a representational difference in on-line processing between a level of logical form and a post-linguistic level situated in a discourse model, then there is clear evidence for top-down influences on syntactic choice during first-pass processing and not only after the event.

The evidence for these claims derives from a variety of different experiments. We will proceed here by describing each class of experiment separately, showing in each case how it bears on the three claims.

Word-Monitoring Experiments
This research provides evidence for the speed of discourse mapping and for the rapid on-line computation of pragmatic inferences. The first of these experiments (Marslen-Wilson and Tyler 1975, 1980a) was designed to track the availability of different types of processing information as these became available during the processing of an utterance.

The experiment used three types of prose materials (see table 2). The Normal Prose strings were normal sentences that could be analyzed both semantically and syntactically. The second prose type, Anomalous Prose, was syntactically still relatively normal but had no coherent semantic interpretation. The third condition, Scrambled Prose, could not be analyzed syntactically or semantically. Sentences of each of these three types were presented either in isolation or preceded by a lead-in sentence. This allowed us to observe the effects of the presence or absence of a discourse context. Each test sentence also contained a monitoring target word, such as *lead* in the sample set given in table 2. These target words occurred in different serial positions across the test sentences, varying from the second to the tenth position. By measuring the monitoring response time at different points across each type of test material, we could determine the time course with which syntactic and semantic processing information became available, and how this was affected by whether or not a discourse context was available.

We will concentrate here on the relationship between Normal Prose and the other two prose conditions at the early target positions as a function of the presence or absence of a discourse context. The upper panel of figure 1 gives the response curves for the discourse condition, where the lead-in

Table 2
Sample word-monitoring materials.

Normal prose
The church was broken into last night.
Some thieves stole most of the *lead* off the roof.

Anomalous prose
The power was located in great water.
No buns puzzle some in the *lead* off the text.

Scrambled prose
In was power water the great located.
Some the no puzzle buns in *lead* text the off.

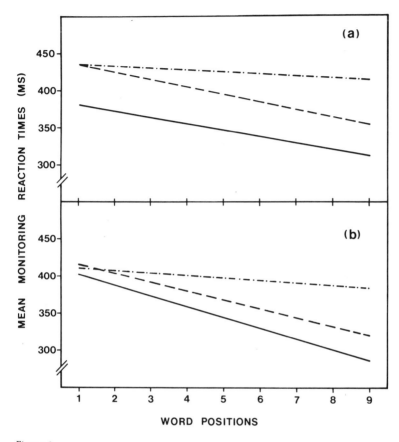

Figure 1
Mean reaction times (in milliseconds) for word monitoring in three prose contexts, presented either with a preceding context sentence (a) or without one (b) and plotted across
word positions 1–9. The unbroken lines represent responses in normal prose, the broken
lines responses in anomalous prose, and the dotted lines responses in scrambled prose.

sentence is present. Here, targets in Normal Prose are responded to faster than those in Anomalous or Scrambled Prose even at the earliest word positions. The average difference in intercept between Normal Prose and the other conditions (for Identical and Rhyme monitoring[6]) is 53 msec. This means that the extra processing information that Normal Prose provides is being developed by the listener right from the beginning of the utterance.

The critical point, illustrated by the lower panel of figure 1, is that this early advantage of Normal Prose depends on the presence of the lead-in sentence. When no lead-in sentence is present, the extra facilitation of monitoring responses in Normal Prose contexts develops later in the utterance, and the mean intercept difference between Normal Prose and the other two conditions falls to a nonsignificant 12 msec.

We can take for granted that the on-line interpretability of the early words of the test sentence depends on their syntactic well-formedness, so that the early advantage of Normal Prose reflects in part the speed and earliness with which a syntactic analysis of the incoming material is being computed. But the effects of removing the lead-in sentence show that the mapping onto a discourse model must be taking place at least as early and at least as rapidly as any putative mapping onto logical form. There is nothing in the data to suggest the sort of temporal lag in the accessibility of these two kinds of perceptual target that would support the modularity hypothesis.

It is possible to devise modular systems in which predictions about the differential speed of different types of process do not play a role, so that the absence of a difference here is not fatal. But what it does mean is that speed of processing cannot be used as a diagnostic criterion for distinguishing processes that map onto purely linguistic levels of representation from those that map onto mental models. This, in turn, undermines Fodor's basic assumption that speed requires modular processing. If you can map onto a discourse level as rapidly as you can map onto a shallow linguistic level, then modularity and encapsulation cannot be the prerequisites for very fast processing.

A second word-monitoring experiment (Brown, Marslen-Wilson, and Tyler, in preparation) again illustrates the speed of processing and, in particular, the rapidity with which pragmatic inferences can be made during on-line processing. Instead of the global disruption of prose context in the previous experiment, this experiment used only Normal Prose sentence pairs containing local anomalies of different types. A typical stimulus set, illustrated in table 3, shows a neutral lead-in sentence followed by four different continuation sentences. The same target word (*guitar*) occurs in all four sentences. Variation of the preceding verb creates four different context conditions.

In condition A there are no anomalies; the sentence is normal. In con-

Table 3
Sample materials for local-anomaly experiment.

Condition A
The crowd was waiting eagerly.
The young man carried the *guitar* . . . .

Condition B
The crowd was waiting eagerly.
The young man buried the *guitar* . . . .

Condition C
The crowd was waiting eagerly.
The young man drank the *guitar* . . . .

Condition D
The crowd was waiting eagerly.
The young man slept the *guitar* . . . .

---

dition B there is no syntactic or semantic violation, but the combination of critical verb and target is pragmatically anomalous—whatever one does with guitars, one does not normally bury them. Conditions C and D involve stronger violations—in C of semantic-selection restrictions, and in D of subcategorization constraints. Presented to subjects in a standard monitoring task, these materials produce a steady increase in mean response time across conditions, from 241 msec for targets in the normal sentences to 320 msec for the subcategorization violations.

We are concerned here with the significant effects of pragmatic anomaly (mean: 267 msec) and what these imply for the speed with which representations of different sorts can be computed. The point about condition B is that the relative slowness to respond to *guitar* in the context of burying, as opposed to the context of carrying in condition A, cannot be attributed to any *linguistic* differences between the two conditions. It must instead be attributed to the listeners' inferences about likely actions involving guitars. The implausibility of burying guitars as opposed to carrying them is something that needs to be deduced from other things that the listener knows about guitars, burying, carrying, and so on. And yet, despite the potential unboundedness of the inferences that might have to be drawn here, the listener can apparently compute sufficient consequences, in the interval between recognizing the verb and responding to the target, for these inferences to significantly affect response time.[7]

The possibility of very rapid pragmatic inferencing during language processing is also supported by the on-line performance of certain aphasic patients. In one case of classic agrammatism (Tyler 1985, 1986) we found a selective deficit in syntactic processing such that the patient could not construct global structural units. When this patient was tested on the set of contrasts described above, we found a much greater dependency on prag-

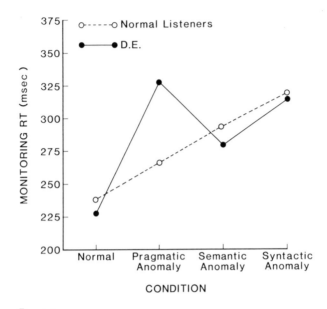

Figure 2
Mean word-monitoring reaction times for four experimental conditions for the patient D.E.
and for a group of normal controls.

matic information, as reflected in his greatly increased latencies to the
pragmatic anomaly condition relative to normal subjects and relative to his
own performance in the other conditions (see figure 2). Again, the pragmatically plausible relationship between verb and potential object was
being computed very rapidly as the utterance was being heard.

Resolution of Syntactic Ambiguity
The research described in this section bears on all three of the claims at
issue, but it speaks most directly to the on-line contextual guidance of
syntactic parsing. It does so by looing at the processing of phrasal fragments (such as *landing planes*) when they are placed in different kinds of
discourse contexts.

Ambiguous fragments of this type have two different readings, which
we will refer to here, following Townsend and Bever (1982), as the *adjectival* and the *gerund* reading. The question at issue is whether prior nonlinguistic context can resolve such ambiguities, and the timing with which
this contextual disambiguation might occur. The crucial claim for the
modularity hypothesis is that context cannot act predictively, so that the
first-pass analysis of such structures will be conducted on the basis of
purely linguistic considerations.

In our first examination of this question (Tyler and Marslen-Wilson 1977) we placed the ambiguous fragments in disambiguating contexts of the following types.

Adjectival bias: If you walk too near the runway, landing planes. . . .
Gerund bias: If you've been trained as a pilot, landing planes. . . .

The subjects heard one of the two context clauses, followed by the ambiguous fragment. Immediately after the acoustic offset of the fragments (e.g., at the end of the /s/ of *planes*), a visual probe was flashed up, which was either an appropriate or an inappropriate continuation of the fragment. The probe was always either the word *is* or the word *are*, and its appropriateness depended on the preceding context. For the cases above, *is* is an appropriate continuation of *landing planes* when this has the gerund reading, but not when it has the adjectival reading. The opposite holds for the probe *are*.

The results of the experiment seemed clear-cut. There was a significantly faster naming latency to appropriate probes. These on-line preferences, we argued at the time, could be explained only if we assumed that the listener was rapidly evaluating the structural readings of the ambiguous fragments relative to the meanings of the words involved and relative to the pragmatic plausibility of each reading in the given context. Furthermore, since the inappropriateness effects were just as strong for these ambiguous fragments as they were for a comparison group of unambiguous fragments (e.g., *smiling faces*), we argued in favor of a single computation. Instead of arguing that both analyses were being computed and that one was later selected, we argued that context affected the parsing process directly, so that only one reading was ever computed.

This first experiment was criticized, primarily on methodological grounds, by Townsend and Bever (1982) and by Cowart (1983), who pointed out that the stimuli contained a number of potential confounds, of which the most serious was the distribution of singular and plural cataphoric pronouns in the context sentences. Examination of the stimulus materials shows that the adjectival contexts tended to contain such pronouns as *they* and *them*, whereas the gerund contexts contained pronouns such as *it*. For example, for the ambiguous phrase *cooking apples*, the adjectival context was *Although they may be very tart* . . . ; the gerund context was *Although it doesn't require much work* . . . .

Given that these sentences appear in isolation, such pronouns tend to be treated as cataphoric—that is, as co-referential with an entity that has not yet been mentioned. They may create, therefore, the expectation that either singular or plural potential referents will be occurring later in the text. This is a type of contextual bias that could potentially be handled within the syntactic parser, without reference to pragmatic variables.

Although this pronoun effect can just as easily be attributed to an inter-action with discourse context, it is nonetheless important to show whether or not a discourse bias can still be observed when the pronoun effect is neutralized.

To this end, a further experiment was carried out (W. Marslen-Wilson and A. Young, manuscript in preparation) with pairs of context sentences having exactly parallel structures, containing identical pronouns, and differing only in their pragmatic implications—for example, the following.

Adjectival bias: If you want a cheap holiday, visiting relatives . . . .
Gerund bias: If you have a spare bedroom, visiting relatives . . . .

The results, summarized in figure 3, show that there was still a significant effect of contextual appropriateness on response times to the *is* and *are* probes. Responses were slower for *is* when it followed an ambiguous phrase heard in an adjectival context, and slower for *are* when the same phrase followed a gerund context. Even when all forms of potential syn-tactic or lexical bias were removed from the context clauses, we still saw an immediate effect on the structure assigned to these ambiguous fragments.

These results confirm that nonlinguistic context affects the assignment of a syntactic analysis, and they tell us that it does so very early. The probe word comes immediately after the end of the fragment, at the point where the ambiguity of the fragment first becomes fully established—note that the ambiguity of these sequences depends on knowing both words in the

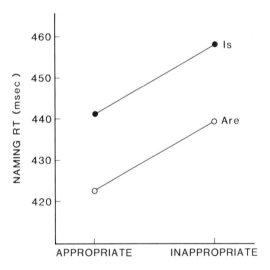

Figure 3
Mean naming latencies for appropriate and inappropriate *is* and *are* targets.

fragment; sequences like *landing lights* are not ambiguous in the same way. This means that we are finding significant context effects at what is effectively the earliest point at which we can measure.

What does this mean for the modularity hypothesis and its claims for informational encapsulation? The results do not force a single-computation account. No matter how early context effects are detected, it is always possible to argue that multiple readings were nonetheless computed, so that what we are picking up are after-the-event selection effects rather than direct control of the initial syntactic parse. But the cost of this move is that it makes it very difficult to discriminate the modular version of interaction from an account that allows continuous or even predictive interactions between levels. The modular account simply fails to make empirically distinct predictions. And if this is the case, then the claim for informational encapsulation cannot help us to distinguish modular from central processes.

Pragmatic Inference in Anaphor Resolution
A third class of experiments, using the same naming task, looked at the processing relationship between an utterance and its discourse context. They were specifically designed to test the claim that even when the linkage between an utterance and its discourse context can only be based on pragmatic inference, this will not slow down the on-line mapping process.

In the first of these experiments (Marslen-Wilson and Tyler 1980b; Tyler and Marslen-Wilson 1982), two context sentences were followed by one of three continuation fragments (see table 4). Each of these fragments contained an anaphoric device linking the fragments to the preceding discourse. In fragment 1 the device was the name of some individual previously mentioned; in fragment 2 it was an unambiguous personal pronoun; in fragment 3 (an example of zero anaphora) there were no explicit lexical cues at all.

In each case, to interpret the fragment, it is necessary to determine who is the agent of the action denoted by the verb, and to evaluate this with

Table 4
Sample materials for anaphora experiment.

Context sentences
As Philip was walking back from the shop he saw an old woman trip and fall flat on her face in the street. She seemed unable to get up again.

Continuation fragments
(1) Philip ran towards....
(2) He ran towards....
(3) Running towards....

respect to the preceding discourse. In fragments 1 and 2 the agent is directly lexically specified (*Philip; He*), and can be unambiguously related to possible antecedents on the basis of this lexical information alone. It is case 3 that concerns us here. The only way in which agency can be assigned is on the basis of differential pragmatic inference that matches the properties of *Running towards* ... to the properties of the potential antecedents in the discourse. It is necessary to infer who is most likely running towards whom.

To measure the timing of anaphoric linkage in these three conditions, we used the naming technique described in the preceding section. The subjects heard the context sentences together with one of the three continuation fragments. At the acoustic offset of the fragment (e.g., at the end of *towards*), a visual probe word was presented to them, which they had to name as quickly as possible. For the examples given in table 4, the probe word would have been either *him* or *her*. For each case, *her* is a more appropriate continuation than *him*. The critical experimental question was whether the size of the expected preference effect (slower naming of inappropriate probes) would be the same for all three continuations.

This bears upon the claims of the modularity hypothesis in two ways. First, it measures the speed and the on-line effectiveness of discourse linkages based on pragmatic inference, in direct comparison with linkages that can be based on less computationally costly search and matching processes. Second, it asks whether top-down context can act upon the syntactic parser in ways that are prohibited by the modularity hypothesis.[8] If the appropriateness effect is as strong in the zero case as in the other two, then, on our analysis, the missing subject of the verb will have been filled in, on-line, on the basis of a process of differential pragmatic inference. This will mean that contextual considerations can determine the assignment of predicate-argument relations in logical form. But the modularity hypothesis specifically excludes central processes from having this kind of influence on syntactic representations. Context can give the parser Yes/No feedback, but it can never directly tell the parser what the content of its analyses should be.

The results, summarized in table 5, show that there is a marked appropri-

Table 5
Results of anaphora experiment.

Type of anaphor	Mean naming latencies (msec)		
	Appropriate	Inappropriate	Difference
Repeated name	379	429	50
Pronoun	385	434	49
Zero anaphor	384	420	36

ateness effect in each condition, and that the size of the effect does not vary significantly. This confirms that utterances are immediately integrated with their discourse contexts, since the inappropriateness of *him* or *her*, in all three conditions, depends on the relationship between the discourse properties of the antecedent and the properties assigned to that antecedent in the continuation sentence. It also shows that when the linkage can depend only on pragmatic inference, as in the Zero Anaphor case, this does not significantly impair or slow down the on-line integration process.

The speed of these integration processes is underlined by the outcome of another manipulation in the experiment. This was a variation in the length of the verb phrase in the continuation fragment, so that, in the zero case, the probe could appear anywhere from the second to the fifth word of the fragment. These variations had no effect on the size of the inappropriateness effect for the Zero Anaphor conditions. The difference between appropriate and inappropriate probes averaged 36 msec for the shortest verb phrases and 33 msec for the longest verb phrases.

As we noted above, the effects for the zero condition suggest a form of top-down effect on syntactic representations that is incompatible with the claim for informational encapsulation. The appropriateness effect depends on the inferral of agency; to the extent that this leads to the top-down filling of the empty subject slot in the argument structure of the verb, then context is specifying the actual content of a representation within the linguistic input system.

The results of this first study were elaborated and confirmed in a subsequent experiment using similar materials and techniques. The first goal of this second experiment (Marslen-Wilson, Tyler, and Koster, in preparation) was to ensure that the effects we have attributed here to differential pragmatic inference had not been confounded with the effects of discourse focus. In a narrative discourse, a particular individual may become salient —or "in focus"—and this can lead listeners to expect that this individual will continue to be mentioned, especially as subject, in subsequent utterances (see Karmiloff-Smith 1980, 1985; Marslen-Wilson and Tyler 1980b; Marslen-Wilson, Levy, and Tyler 1982). This possibility was not fully controlled for in the first experiment.

To deal with this problem, and to look more specifically at how different sources of constraint were integrated to determine the mapping of an utterance onto its discourse context, the second experiment co-varied in a semi-factorial manner three different factors: discourse focus, the pragmatic implications of the verb, and the lexical specificity of anaphors. The subset of these contrasts that concern us here are given in table 6, which lists some sample context stories and (in capitals) their associated continuation fragments and visual probes.

For all three main conditions, a strong discourse bias was set up. Each

Table 6
Materials for factorial anaphora experiment.

Condition 1: Discourse bias with congruent verb bias

After the surgeon had examined the 12-year old girl with the badly broken leg, he decided he would have to take immediate action. He'd had a lot of experience with serious injuries. He knew what he had to do next.

A. He quickly injected...
B. She quickly injected...   HER/HIM
C. Quickly injecting...

Condition 2: Discourse bias with neutral verb

As Bill was buying popcorn at the movies, he saw an old girl-friend get in line for a ticket. He had arrived at the movies especially early. He wanted to be sure of getting a good seat.

A. He waved at...
B. She waved at...   HER/HIM
C. Waving at...

Condition 3: Discourse bias with opposing verb bias

Mary lost hope of winning the race to the ocean when she heard Andrew's footsteps approaching her from behind. The deep sand was slowing her down. She had trouble keeping her balance.

A. She overtook...
B. He overtook...   HIM/HER
C. Overtaking...

---

context story always contained two protagonists, with one foregrounded and the other not. The principal actor appeared in subject position in the first sentence and continued to function as the main actor for at least two subsequent sentences. Pretests of these materials showed that listeners expected the following sentence to have the main actor continuing in subject position. This was the manipulation of *discourse focus*.

The second manipulation, also applying to all three conditions, was the variation in the *lexical specificity* of the anaphor in subject position in the continuation fragments. The contrast here was between lexically unambiguous anaphors (for these examples, the pronouns *He* and *She*) and the lexically empty Zero Anaphor case. The two pronouns co-varied with discourse focus. For the A continuations, the pronoun was always consistent with the discourse bias, so that it selected as subject the individual who was salient in the preceding context. For the B continuations, the pronoun selected the individual who was not in discourse focus (the second of the two protagonists).

The third manipulation was the *pragmatic implications of the verb*—that is, the congruence of the actions denoted by the verb with what was already known in the discourse about the two protagonists. This was co-varied with the other two factors. Thus, in condition 1, the verb bias fitted the discourse bias. These two together were also congruent with the pronoun for continuation 1A, but not for 1B. In continuation 1C, verb bias and discourse bias worked together. In condition 2, the pragmatics of the verb were neutral and were designed to be equally compatible with both potential antecedents. This allowed us to measure, in continuation 2C, the effects of discourse bias when no other cues were available.

Finally, in condition 3, the verb bias was in conflict with discourse bias. The crucial test was in 3C, the Zero Anaphor condition. If verb semantics can be interpreted on-line to select the pragmatically appropriate antecedent, then we should detect this effect even here, where discourse focus favored a different antecedent in subject position.

To test for the effects of these variations, we again used the naming task. Subjects heard the context story together with one of the continuation fragments, and were asked to name as rapidly as possible a visual probe that appeared at the acoustic offset of the fragment. The relative speed of their responses to the probes—which were always unambiguously co-referential with one of the two protagonists in the preceding context story—were taken to reflect the way in which the listeners had linked the continuation fragment to the discourse context.

The probes were not labeled "appropriate" or "inappropriate" in advance, since for many conditions the appropriateness of a given probe was itelf the question at issue. Instead, we adopted the convention of referring to probe 1 and probe 2. Probe 1 was always the probe that was consistent with the discourse bias and with the subject pronoun in continuation A—in table 6, for example, probe 1 is *her* for conditions 1A and 2A, and *him* for 3A. The term *consistent* means here that a given pronoun probe in object position is consistent with a given assignment of an agent to subject position. A probe will be consistent with a source of constraint, such as discourse bias, if this favors the instantiation in subject position of a suitable agent.

The results of this experiment, listed in table 7, bear upon the modularity hypothesis in two ways. First, there is the confirmation that pragmatic inference, operating alone, can link utterances to discourses as effectively as pronouns and names. In condition 3C, where the pragmatic implications of the verb actually go against discourse bias—therefore ruling out any possibility of a confounding with discourse effects—there is an appropriateness effect of 48 msec.

Consider the example in table 6, where the discourse in condition 3 sets up the character Mary in discourse focus. In our pretests of this context, listeners produced continuation sentences that kept Mary in focus as subject and main actor. In the experimental materials, however, the verb in the

Table 7
Results of factorial anaphora experiment.

| | Mean naming latency (msec) | | |
Condition	Probe 1	Probe 2	Difference
Discourse bias and congruent verb			
1A: Congruent pronoun	481	535	+54
1B: Incongruent pronoun	532	506	−26
1C: Zero anaphor	500	536	+36
Discourse bias and neutral verb			
2A: Congruent pronoun	472	528	+56
2B: Incongruent pronoun	527	467	−60
2C: Zero anaphor	496	543	+47
Discourse bias and incongruent verb			
3A: Congruent pronoun	511	506	−5
3B: Incongruent pronoun	549	482	−67
3C: Zero anaphor	530	482	−48

continuation fragment (*Overtaking*) is inconsistent with the listener's mental model of the relationship between Mary and her competitor Andrew. Mary, slipping and stumbling, is in no position to be overtaking someone, and it is this that determines who the listener instantiates as agent of the action. It is probe 2 (*her*) that is treated as appropriate, and not the probe that is consistent with the discourse bias. The size of the effect compares favorably with cases like 1A and 2A, where a congruent pronoun is present as well.

Equally significant, the results show that discourse focus on its own can also control the on-line intepretation of utterance fragments. Discourse bias is the weakest of the three variables, and its effects are usually obscured by the other two sources of constraint. But when these other sources are neutralized (as in condition 2C, where there is no pronoun and the verb is pragmatically neutral) there is a clear discourse-based appropriateness effect, which is just as strong as the effects produced by pronouns or verbs in other conditions. Once again agency is being assigned under conditions where the parser could have no basis for doing so on purely linguistic grounds. It is only in the representation of the discourse that any basis exists for choosing between one actor or the other as subject of the verb in the continuation fragment. If the way the effect operates is by affecting the assignment of predicate-argument relations in logical form, then it is doing so in contradiction to the crucial predictions of the modularity hypothesis.

The effect of discourse bias in 2C demonstrates, in addition, that these assignment processes take place as the continuation fragment is being heard—in particular, before the presentation of the visual probe. If an assignment of agency had not already been made before the subject knew what the visual probe was, there would not have been any inappropriateness effect. The effects in 2A and 2B show that the assignment of either protagonist as agent is equally acceptable here—the probe *her* is named just as rapidly after *He waved at* . . . . as the probe *him* after *She waved at* . . . . Equally, there is nothing about the sequence *Waving at him* (with the female actor as agent) that makes it any less appropriate in the given discourse context than *Waving at her* (with the male as subject).

To explain the appropriateness effects, we have to assume a particular ordering of processing events. At the moment when the continuation fragment starts, the manipulation of discourse focus has led to the expectation that the actor in focus will continue in subject position. Unless the subject pronoun is inconsistent with this expectation (as in 2B), and unless the semantics of the verb select the other protagonist (as in 3C), the listener will go ahead and assign agency on this basis. He or she can do this as soon as the information becomes available that the verb is pragmatically neutral. Evidence from other studies (see the subsection on word-monitoring experiments) shows that this occurs while the verb is still being heard. Thus, by the time the visual probe appears, a commitment has already been made to the discourse mapping of the continuation fragment. Given this assignment, probe 2 will be perceived as inappropriate.

More generally, the results over the nine conditions reveal a pattern of dependencies between the discourse model and the current utterance that is difficult to handle within a system based on the rigidly bottom-up communication paths that characterize the modularity hypothesis. In particular, we are dealing here with a system that is highly flexible, even opportunistic, in its use of different types of processing information to achieve the perceptual goal of relating an utterance to its discourse context.

We see in the results that all three types of constraint—pronoun constraint, discourse bias, and pragmatic coherence—are equally capable, under the right conditions, of controlling the outcome of this process, and we see this occurring within the kind of on-line time frame that is supposed to characterize modular processes. This flexibility in using different sources of constraint, as and when they are available, means that the process of discourse linkage is not dependent on information being made available to it in a fixed order or in a fixed format. This stands in opposition to the central argument of the modularity thesis: that language comprehension is centered around a system that is entirely fixed in its properties and that is entirely insensitive to the changing informational circumstances within which utterances occur.

Implications

The evidence presented in the preceding section, and the analyses discussed earlier, lead to a view of language processing that is in many ways quite similar to the approach put forward by Fodor. It shares Fodor's emphasis on the remarkable speed and efficiency of real-time language processing, and it accepts that these processes normally operate in a mandatory fashion. It also accepts a certain degree of functional encapsulation, in the sense that contextual influences do not operate in a top-down manner in normal first-pass processing.

But it diverges from Fodor's approach in two major respects. First, it does not attempt to explain the special properties of language processing by postulating a distinct type of cognitive entity called an input system or a module. Second, it includes within the domain of these special processes the aspect of language comprehension that Fodor is most eager to exclude: the computing of inferences that draw upon nonlinguistic knowledge.

What is the nature of the approach we are advocating, and how does it accommodate the kinds of phenomena that Fodor hoped to explain with the concept of a module? How, in particular, does it accommodate the kinds of phenomena that behave as if they were modular, on Fodor's account, but nonetheless involve extramodular processes? We repeat below the view of language processing that we began to lay out in our 1980a, 1980b, and 1981 papers.

• We assume that language comprehension is mediated by a stable set of highly skilled, automatized processes that apply obligatorily to their characteristic inputs. Such a system has fixed properties in the sense that there is a mandatory sequence of operations that must always apply to a given input.

We leave open the question of whether this system has fixed properties in the sense intended by Fodor—that is, because its properties are in some way genetically specified and therefore "hardwired." At present there seems to be no very convincing way of discriminating those fixed properties of language processing that derive from genetic constraints on the system from those that derive from the automatization of highly practiced skills (see Jusczyk and Cohen 1985; Sternberg 1985).

• The function of this set of core processes is to project the speech input onto a representation in the world—onto, for example, a mental model in the sense defined by Johnson-Laird (1983). It achieves this as rapidly as is informationally and neurally possible. There is no processing hiatus, no detectable change of cognitive means of transport, that coincides with the transition from the strictly linguistic to the discourse-representation or mental model. Nor is there evidence of any lag that might correspond to the requirement to map onto some linguistic level before mapping onto the discourse model. On the contrary, there is evidence (see our subsection on pragmatic inference) that the input can be mapped onto the discourse level even when the assumed linguistic level is still incomplete.

• These obligatory core processes operate on the principle of *bottom-up priority*. It is the bottom-up input to the system that sets it into motion and that determines what its possible outputs can be. We see this very clearly in the behavior of the word-recognition process. The membership of the initial cohort of word candidates is determined by the sensory input alone, and it is this initial cohort that defines the universe of possible candidates (Marslen-Wilson 1984; Tyler and Wessels 1983). Such a system cannot produce an output that is incompatible with its bottom-up input.

This is not the same as informational encapsulation, although it has many of the same effects. So long as the bottom-up input is phonologically and morphosyntactically unambiguous, it will uniquely determine the output of the system, and contextual influences will be difficult to detect—in other words, the system will give the appearance of encapsulated modularity. But when the input to the system is ambiguous or incomplete (as in the *landing planes* experiments or the Zero Anaphora studies), one can see clearly the on-line consequences of contextual factors. (For a further discussion of the conditions under which "predictive" context effects can be observed, see chapter 12 of this volume.)

• Finally, and most controversial, these core processes permit no top-down effects in normal first-pass processing. This is because the concept of a top-down effect is defined in terms of a relationship between different representational levels arranged in a hierarchy. In Fodor's psycholinguistic ontology, a level of something like logical form exists as a representational level in the processing system, and this stands in a hierarchical relationship to some further level (or levels) of representation corresponding to the pragmatic interpretation of the utterance. The notion of informational encapsulation, forbidding certain kinds of top-down interaction, is defined by Fodor in terms of these ordered levels.

To be able to evaluate the modularity hypothesis on its own terms, and to construct tests that would be intelligible within its particular frame of reference, we have up to this point in the chapter gone along with these assumptions about levels of representation. We turn now to an alternative ontology, in which we recognize no distinct level of representation corresponding to logical form—or to any other purely syntactic analytic level.

We assume, instead, that there is no level of symbolic representation mediating between lexical representations and mental models. Instead, there are procedures and mechanisms for mapping the one onto the other; for using the information provided by what the speaker is saying to construct a representation of his intended message. The apparatus of syntactic theory is a description of the properties of this construction procedure—as Crain and Steedman (1985, p. 323) put it, the rules of syntax "describe what a processor *does* in assembling a semantic interpretation." Notions such as logical form, therefore, are part of a description of a process; they are not themselves the process they are describing.

Where does this leave the context effects, and the violations of informational encapsulation, that we discussed above? The answer is, in part, that the issue disappears. If there are not two levels standing in the necessary hierarchical relationship to each other, there cannot be interactions between them. The true implication of evidence for interaction may be, in the end, that there is no interaction.

In particular, it becomes meaningless to infer "interaction" from the filling in of insufficiencies at one level on the basis of information available at a higher level. For a two-level, hierarchical system, the implication of the Zero Anaphor effects discussed above was that the lower level was penetrable by the higher level. But where there is no lower level of structural representation, and where the basic processing act performed by the system is the mapping onto pragmatically coherent locations in the discourse model, then the concept of interaction simply fails to apply.

We have, instead, multiple potential sources of cues for correct mapping, one of which (in the experiment in question) is the explicit lexical cues provided by the subject pronouns, but which also include the expectations derived from the structure of the discourse, and the differential inferences drawn from the relationship between input semantics and the state of the discourse model and the entities it contains. If the subject slot is lexically empty, as in our Zero Anaphor cases, the listener will assume that the speaker intends him to recover the intended agent from some other property of the message and its discourse environment. The end result is the same: an instantiation of the appropriate agent in the discourse model. But this involves no top-down influences, no creation at a lower level of mental contents that are derivable only at a higher level. There is no lower level of the appropriate sort, only the ability to integrate diverse information in the construction of the discourse.

By the same token, the arguments for interaction based on the resolution of structural ambiguity will also dissolve. In a system of the type Fodor envisages, the existence of an early preference for the contextually appropriate reading of a phrase like *landing planes* is *prima facie* evidence for a top-down effect on the operation of the syntactic parser. But again, if there is no autonomous syntactic level of representation, and if the basic operation of the system is to construct coherent interpretations in the domain of the discourse model, then there is no "interaction" here, and in effect, no ambiguity either. In terms of the on-line functioning of the system, the bottom-up input is ambiguous only to the extent that the interpretative target in the discourse model permits it to be. And cooperative speakers will not present their addressees with irresolvable ambiguities.

In fact, we might speculate, it is the cooperativeness of speakers and listeners that goes the furthest in explaining how the speech process can be so rapid, and how, in particular, inputs can be projected with such immediacy onto the listener's discourse model: It is because speakers prepare their utterances so that they cohere with what has been said before, and because listeners run their processing systems on this assumption. This is what gives language processing its seemingly ballistic property—that the speaker constructs a communicative packet that is already configured to map onto the receptive configuration of the listener.[9]

Concluding Remarks

We end with some comments on what can be regarded as the hidden agenda of the modularity discussion—namely, the underlying question of the kind of role that syntactic theory should play in a psychological model of language processing. From this perspective, the modularity hypothesis can be regarded as the very strong psychological claim for the direct participation of the constructs of linguistic analysis in the process of language comprehension, up to and including the level of logical form. It saves a central role for syntactic analysis and representation, safely encapsulated within the language module.

This is one reason why it is so important for the modularity hypothesis that the dividing line between modular and extramodular processes falls at the interface between the linguistic and the nonlinguistic. Unfortunately, as we have tried to show here, the diagnostic features that are supposed to place the dividing line at just this crucial point fail to do so. The central processes of language comprehension do not conveniently stop dead at the level of logical form. This means not only that the hypothesis itself fails, but that so do the assumptions it tries to smuggle in about the role of linguistic theory in a model of psycholinguistic processing.

It is at this level of the discussion that we are "against modularity." We reject it as a claim about the relationship between linguistic construct and psychological process. The facts of psycholinguistic performance simply do not support the rigid dichotomy between the domains of the syntactic and the non-syntactic that is the central claim of the modularity thesis. The thesis is seductive, entertaining, perhaps even heuristically useful. But as a basis for the construction of explanatory theories of human psycholinguistic performance it is, we believe, fundamentally misleading. It misconstrues the nature of the problem that is set for us by the extraordinary speed and immediacy of on-line language comprehension, and it invites us to accept, as a solution to this problem, a view of the organization of the language-processing system that obscures rather than clarifies the questions we now need to be asking.

Notes

1. We exclude from consideration here the immediate sensory transducers.
2. We will not discuss here three additional features that Fodor mentions: neural hardwiring, characteristic breakdown patterns, and ontogenetic uniformity. The evidence in these domains is hardly crisp enough, at the moment, to seriously distinguish the opposing views we are contrasting.
3. This is not to say that all discourse mapping is phenomenologically mandatory. Consider the following discourse pair: *John couldn't decide whether to eat steak or hamburger. In the end he went for the less expensive meat.* Here one has to stop and think before deciding on the referent for *less expensive meat.* It is worth considering how this might differ from cases where the mapping goes more smoothly.
4. It is important, nonetheless, to keep clear the relationship between speed and automaticity. Very fast processes will almost certainly be mandatory processes, but the converse does not hold. Some mandatory processes—growing old, getting hungry—are really quite slow.
5. These are cases like *The detective watched the policeman with the walking-stick,* where the prepositional phrase *with the walking-stick* is more plausibly attached to *the policeman* than to *the detective.*
6. In Identical monitoring the actual target word is specified in advance to the subjects; in Rhyme monitoring the subjects listen for a target that rhymes with a cue word given in advance.
7. These arguments hold even if one tries to take the view of monitoring performance proposed by Tanenhaus, Carlson, and Seidenberg (1985), in which the effects of context on monitoring performance are written off as a form of sophisticated guessing. Even if this is the way context effects are mediated, the difference between conditions A and B still depends on the on-line computation of the differential pragmatic plausibility of the target appearing as the object of the different verbs in these two conditions. And it is the speed of pragmatic inferencing that is at issue here.
8. We are indebted to Jerry Fodor and Merrill Garrett for extensive discussions of this aspect of the research.
9. For a detailed illustration of the extent to which a speaker fits the design of his utterances to the informational requirements of his addressee, see Marslen-Wilson et al. 1982.

3

Binding, Plausibility, and Modularity

Kenneth I. Forster

It is a fundamental tenet of psycholinguistic research in sentence recognition that any processing task that is claimed to index the perceptual complexity of a sentence should at least be sensitive to the well-formedness of the input string. However, recent results have uncovered what appears to be an exception to this rule (Freedman and Forster 1985). The aim of this research was to investigate the processing costs associated with violations of movement constraints, partly to show that there were such costs and partly to investigate which constraints were the most important. We found no such processing costs, despite evidence that other types of ungrammaticality produced clear costs with the same task.

The task in question was the delayed same-different matching task, in which the subject is presented with two sequences of printed words and is required to decide as quickly as possible whether they are the same or different. To facilitate the comparison process, the two sentences are vertically aligned, as in (1).

(1) JOHN KNEW THAT MARY WAS COMING
     JOHN KNEW THAT MARY WAS COMING

To check that the subject is in fact performing the task accurately, half of the items contain a different pair of words, as in (2).

(2) JOHN KNEW THAT MARY WAS COMING
     JOHN FELT THAT MARY WAS COMING

Items such as (1) required a "same" decision, and items such as (2) required a "different" decision. Only the responses for "same" items are used for data analysis, since performance on "different" items depends on the location of the difference, and hence the entire sequence is not processed. To encourage the subject to read each sequence from left to right, a delay of 2 seconds was introduced between the first sequence and the second.

The idea behind this task is that the comparison process is aided by the presence of structure in the input sequence. For example, consider the relative difficulty of the following items. In each case, the correct response is "different."

(3)   ATFCDHMLORTEUODGAMCH
       ATFCDHMLORBEUODGAMCH

(4)   MKLP AFDM BRST KDBS HWRD
       MKLP AFDM BRKT KDBS HWRD

(5)   MELP KAST FLEN BERL HAST
       MELP KAST FLUN BERL HAST

It should be apparent that the perceptual grouping in (4) facilitates comparison compared with (3), where the sequences are totally unstructured. In (5) the comparison is easier still, owing to the fact that each subgroup is itself structured in the sense that the letter arrangements spell phonologically possible syllables. A further enhancement is produced if these pseudo-words are embedded in a pseudo-syntactic structure, as in (6).

(6)   THE JOLDER GINTS TO HIS GLOOB
       THE JOLDER GINTS TO HIS GLOOB

(7)   THE TO GLOOB JOLDER GINTS HIS
       THE TO GLOOB JOLDER GINTS HIS

The precise nature of the structural effect is not well understood. It may be that comparison is more efficient if the second sequence is compared with a memorized version of the first rather than with a visual representation. Since structured sequences are easier to store in short-term memory, the effect of structure could readily be explained in this way. Or, as Chambers and Forster (1975) have argued, it could be that structure changes the types of representations that get compared. At the lowest level, the sequences are represented purely in terms of a letter code, and comparison takes place letter by letter. At the highest level, where the sequences are well-formed sentences, the comparison objects are structural descriptions; this enables the subject to "chunk" his comparisons into, say, phrasal units.

For present purposes it may not matter why the effect occurs. It seems obvious that structured descriptions of various types are recruited in the matching task, and hence performance in this task can potentially index the availability of structural descriptions.

However, in the Freedman-Forster (1985) study the matching task appeared to be quite insensitive to the well-formedness of the structural description. This was shown by a comparison of the following four types of sentences:

(8)   You saw a painting of a bullfight.

(9)   You saw Leonardo's painting of a bullfight.

(10)   What did you see a painting of?

(11)   *What did you see Leonardo's painting of?

In (11), movement of *wh-* is blocked by the lexically specified subject *Leonardo*, and hence (11) is not well formed. So we must conclude that no complete structural description is available for (11), although partial descriptions of the individual phrases are available. This should make (11) harder to match than (10), where a complete representation is available. However, a direct comparison between these items would be confounded with lexical differences (*Leonardo's* versus *a*), and hence we need to include control conditions (8) and (9), where the same difference in lexical content is present but both are well formed.

The results of the experiment showed that items such as (11) took 38 msec longer to match than items such as (10), but the corresponding comparison between the control conditions (9) and (8) showed an even greater difference of 69 msec. Thus, the matching times are quite sensitive to the variation in lexical content but are quite insensitive to the fact that (11) is not well formed.

Similar results were obtained for violations of the subjacency constraint, as in (12)–(15). That is, the difference between (15) and (14) was the same as the difference between (13) and (12).

(12)   The police believe that John shot Mary.

(13)   The police believe the claim that John shot Mary.

(14)   Who do the police believe that John shot?

(15)   *Who do the police believe the claim that John shot?

This result is perhaps a little more surprising than the first, since (15) seem more grotesque than (11). An obvious question to ask at this point is whether the matching task really is sensitive to the presence of a well-formed structure. We know that it is highly sensitive to gross departures from grammaticality, such as (16), as was shown by Murray (1982), but we do not know that it is sensitive to (relatively) minor departures.

(16)   believe police that the John Mary shot

The following cases seem to indicate that the matching task does have the required sensitivity. In each case, significant increases in matching time were obtained in comparison with a fully grammatical control sentence.

(17)   *Mary were writing a letter to her husband.

(18)   *To go to Disneyland John wanted.

(19)   *Lesley's parents are chemical engineers both.

(20)   *The girl behind you the subsequent discussion.

Items such as (17) involve violations of number agreement; (18) is an example of phrase-order scrambling (or illegal movement of a VP). Illegal quantifier placement is involved in (19); (20) consists of two well-formed phrases that do not form a well-formed sentence.

Given these results, there appear to be three alternatives:

1. We accept that the matching task is sufficiently sensitive, and conclude that violations of movement constraints are cost-free.
2. We argue that the degree of ungrammaticality involved in violations of movement constraints is not as great as in (17)–(20). That is, violations of movement constraints are not cost-free, but the cost involved is not sufficient to produce a detectable effect with the matching task.
3. We argue that the effects of ungrammaticality in (17)–(20) are misleading, and that the matching task is insensitive to well-formedness *per se*.

The first alternative is the one adopted in Freedman and Forster 1985. To explain the absence of cost, it is proposed that the purely formal notion of overgeneration has psychological reality. Within an approach that assumes highly general and freely applied movement rules, as does Government and Binding theory (Chomsky 1981), it is difficult to prevent some structures from being generated; hence they must be filtered out at a later stage of the derivation. This means that at some level of description, overgenerated sequences are assigned a fully elaborated structural interpetation. If this level is the one normally recruited in the matching task, and performance of the task is not hampered by the unavailability of any higher-level description, then it is to be expected that constraint violations should be cost-free. This proposal creates something of a linguistic muddle, since the subjacency case is not normally treated as a case of overgeneration. For this account to work, it is necessary to argue that the ungrammaticality of both (11) and (15) stems from constraints on the interpretation of structures, not from their derivation.

The second alternative is much less interesting. Since it is possible that there is some threshold value of deviance, below which the matching task has zero sensitivity to deviance, one could always argue that constraint violations happen to fall below this threshold value whereas examples such as (17)–(20) happen to exceed it. As was reported in Freedman and Forster 1985 (p. 112), subjects do not rate sentences such as (11) as having the same degree of deviance as sentences such as (18), so this fact could be cited as support for this proposal. However, Freedman (1982) found that subjacency violations were far more comparable in their degree of deviance. On a four-point scale (where 4 indicates a totally unacceptable sentence), subjacency violations produced a mean rating of 3.18, whereas phrase-order scramblings such as (18) produced a mean rating of 3.30 and illegal quantifier placement items such as (19) produced a mean of 2.68. Hence, if subjacency violations are not sufficiently unacceptable to produce processing costs, items such as (18) and (19) should not be either.

The third alternative was advanced by Crain and Fodor (1985), who suggest that the matching task is sensitive only to gross departures from grammaticality, such as (16). They explain the processing costs observed for (17)–(20) in terms of the notion of *correctability*. Briefly, it is assumed that subjects correct such items to the nearest well-formed sentence. For example, if the first input string was X, it would be stored as $X' + C$, where X' is a well-formed sentence (but X is not) and C is the correction necessary to convert X' to X. When the second input string is presented, it will also be corrected to $X' + C$. Crain and Fodor suggest that confusion is now created because the corrected version of the second string matches the corrected version of the first but not the uncorrected version. However, this confusion is absent in the case of constraint violations, since these are usually not at all correctable. That is, subjects have difficulty in determining what the nearest well-formed sentence would be, and hence are forced to represent the input string in its uncorrected form. Thus, the variable that controls matching time is not grammaticality but correctability. For the moment, I will simply note that there are some cases that are not easily handled by this interpretation. For example, in Freedman and Forster 1985 it was shown that items such as (20) which consisted of two NPs or two VPs were more difficult to match than fully grammatical controls consisting of an NP and a VP. The point of this observation is that items such as (20) are not as readily corrected as items such as (17), or at least are not correctable in the same way. In (17), one's knowledge of syntax is sufficient to supply the correction automatically, but in (20) this knowledge indicates only that a correction is necessary. One could still argue that subjects supply the missing verb, and that this leads to subsequent confusion, although this argument seems distinctly less plausible in such cases.

The Shallow-Sensitivity Hypothesis

We return now to the first alternative in order to explore some of the implications of the overgeneration argument. In this case, I argue that there is a level of structural representation at which constraint-violation sentences are fully represented, and that the matching process has access to this level. Further, I argue that it is irrelevant to performance in the matching task that these sentences are marked as ungrammatical at some higher level of representation, such as Logical Form (LF). This latter assumption will be referred to as the *shallow-sensitivity hypothesis*.

The model of the matching process proposed in Chambers and Forster 1975 and Forster 1979 assumes that strings are matched at all available levels of description simultaneously. Thus sentences can be matched at a purely visual level (in which the elements being compared are lines, angles, etc.), a letter level, a syllable level, a word level, a phrase level, or a sentence level. Whichever level of comparison reaches a determinate outcome first is said to be the *controlling* level. The fact that pseudo-words such as CLANCH are matched more rapidly than letter strings such as CNACLH indicates that there must be a level of representation higher than that of letters but lower than that of words, and that this level can be a controlling level. The fact that words such as CLENCH are matched faster than pseudo-words such as CLANCH indicates that the lexical level can also be a controlling level, and so forth. Which level turns out to be the controlling level depends on whether a representation of the input at that level is available (e.g., there is no representation at the lexical level for CLANCH and on how efficiently the strings can be compared at that level. This in turn depends on how many elements must be compared (fewer elements need to be compared for "different" items) and on the conditions under which the materials are presented.

We have no way of specifying the efficiency parameters for each level, and hence there is no way to genuinely predict which level will turn out to be the controlling level in any particular situation. For example, it can be shown that the lexical level ceases to be a controlling level under special presentation conditions where the individual letters of the second string are displayed sequentially (Forster 1980), but there is no way in which this outcome could have been predicted in advance. Generally, however, it appears that efficiency increases as the level of representation becomes more abstract.

If this is really the case, why should the matching process for sentences be indifferent to the availability of higher-level representation? If matching could be carried out at the level of LF, then we might expect this to be a controlling level, since it is a more abstract level than, say, the level of S-structures. If constraint-violation sentences can be represented only at the level of S-structures and not at the level of LF, then these sentences should show a processing cost when compared with well-formed sentences that are represented at the level of LF[1].

Perhaps the answer is that we were wrong to believe that the efficiency of matching always increases as the level of abstraction increases. Or, perhaps we could argue that the S-structure level is the highest *syntactic* representation, and that the level of LF is concerned only with the semantic properties of propositions, which may be irrelevant to matching efficiency. However, both of these arguments appear to be blocked by the finding that matching is faster for semantically plausible sentences such as (21) than for implausible sentences such as (22), as shown by Murray (1982) and Ratcliff (1983).

(21)   The workman repaired the factory slowly.

(22)   The florist disguised the composer daily.

Clearly (or so it seems), the implausibility of (22) must arise at some interpretive level where questions of situational reference are involved. That is, it is not literally sentence (22) that is implausible; it is the situation described by the sentence that is implausible. However, it is difficult to imagine how this situational implausibility could exert an effect in a task that is insensitive to, say, the availability of a representation at the level of LF. To put it another way, recognizing implausibility requires at least that the literal meaning of the proposition expressed by the sentence has been computed, and this in turn requires LF.

This result does two things: It confirms the expectation that the controlling level will be the highest level of representation available for the input, and it refutes the claim that only syntactic representations are relevant to matching. In short, the shallow-sensitivity hypothesis appears to be incompatible with the data. Some new evidence that may provide a way out of this impasse will be presented shortly. But first, I will present the evidence that convinced us that a way out must exist.

Binding Effects

One way to look at the shallow-sensitivity hypothesis is as follows. Suppose that there is a psychological operation that is directly isomorphic with the linguistic operation of binding. Suppose further that this binding operation is not carried out until the entire sentence has been represented (say, at the level of S-structure). Since the constraint violations will be detected as soon as an attempt is made to bind *wh-* with its trace, it follows that either the matching process is completed before the binding operation is carried out or binding is not carried out at the controlling level. Either way, the efficiency of the matching operation is insulated from the failure to achieve binding. If this is the case, any implausibility that results from a binding operation should have no effect on matching performance. That is, matching times should not be any faster for (23) than for (24).

(23)   What did the mayor order them to unfurl?

(24)   Who did the mayor order them to unfurl?

On the other hand, there should be a difference between (25) and (26), since here the implausibility does not involve a moved element.

(25)   The mayor ordered them to unfurl it.

(26)   The mayor ordered them to unfurl her.

Such an experiment was carried out by Bruce Stevenson (1984), who used 40 examples of each type and tested 48 subjects with a delayed matching task. The delay was 2 seconds, and the mean correct "same" response times for items such as (23) and (24) were 1,523 and 1,518 msec respectively—a reverse plausibility effect of 5 msec. However, for items such as (25) and (26) the mean RTs were 1,353 and 1,418 msec, yielding a significant plausibility effect of 65 msec ($P < 0.05$ by minF′).

So, although the phrase *unfurl her* increases matching times (for whatever reason) compared with *unfurl it*, the phrase *unfurl t* does not lead to a corresponding increase when the trace *t* is bound with *who* rather than with *what*.

In a further experiment, Stevenson (1984) investigated whether adjacency was a critical variable. In the above examples, plausibility effects were obtained only when the implausible constituents were adjacent. One might imagine that adjacency is the critical variable, not binding. Similarly, in cases such as (17), the ungrammaticality produced by agreement violation is produced by two adjacent elements, whereas in constraint violations the ungrammatical elements are necessarily nonadjacent. The way to test this hypothesis is to produce nonadjacency without movement by placing another construction between the two critical elements. Stevenson contrasted two cases. In the first, ungrammaticality was produced by a number disagreement between the subject and the verb, as in (27)–(29).

(27)   *The man who bought the cars are rich.

(28)   *The sharks which inhabit the lagoon has sharp teeth.

(29)   *The rock which fell in the mine have ore in it.

Matching for items of this type took 148 msec longer than for grammatical controls, which were the same sentences with the appropriate inflections of the verbs. The second case involved agreement violations for reflexive and reciprocal constructions such as (30)–(32).

(30)   *John smiled for he knew herself to be innocent.

(31)   *She decided on a holiday for each other.

(32)   *The sparrows built the nest itself.

These items produced a significant increase in matching times of 93 msec compared with the appropriate grammatical controls (33)–(35).

(33)   John smiled for he knew himself to be innocent.

(34)   They decided on a holiday for each other.

(35)   The sparrow built the nest itself.

These results show clearly that nonadjacent elements are capable of producing processing costs. Hence the absence of costs in the constraint-violation conditions cannot be attributed to nonadjacency *per se*. This reinforces the notion that movement operations are critically involved. The results for (30)–(32) also raise an additional point: The interpretation of reflexives and reciprocals involves a binding operation. For example, in (30) the agreement violation would not be detected unless an attempt was made to bind *herself* with *he*. The fact that agreement violation produces a reliable cost in these cases rules out the argument that binding operations in general are not carried out at the controlling level for the matching task. It must be that only those bindings operations that involve moved elements are deferred to a higher level of processing.

This suggests a two-stage binding process. If the antecedent and the anaphoric element are both in their base-generated positions, then binding is carried out at the controlling level for the matching task (or at some lower level). However, if one of the elements is moved, then binding is deferred until some higher level is reached. Alternatively, we could say that binding of *wh-* with its trace is carried out at a higher level than other types of binding; this amounts to the same thing, since a trace implies that movement has occurred.

Global and Local Plausibility Effects

I argued above that the plausibility effect creates problems for the shallow-sensitivity hypothesis because plausibility can be assessed only by higher-level interpretive processes. But the absence of a plausibility effect for (23)–(24) throws some doubt on this argument. If it is the plausibility of the overall interpretation assigned to the entire sentence that matters, then these sentences should produce just as clear an effect as (25)–(26). The fact that they do not do so raises the possibility that in the matching task (and perhaps only in that task) plausibility may be a local phenomenon rather than a global one.

A similar suggestion was made in Freedman and Forster 1985 for slightly different reasons. There we were concerned with the fact that plausibility effects were apparent in constraint-violation sentences. For example, consider the following items taken from Freedman 1982:

(36)   *Who did the soldiers hate orders to kill?

(37)   *What did the pygmies like orders to smell?

Although not directly compared in the same experiment, it was clear that items such as (37) took far longer to match than their counterparts such as (36). To explain this effect in a manner consistent with the shallow-sensitivity hypothesis, it was necessary to postulate that the matching task is sensitive to plausibility at a phrasal level. So the implausibility of (37) may stem solely from the implausibility of the phrase *orders to smell*.

We are now in a position to suggest a stronger hypothesis: that the matching task is sensitive to plausibility only at a phrasal level. We thereby cope with the absence of any effect in (23)–(24). One way to test this hypothesis is to combine perfectly plausible phrases in an implausible way, as in (38).

(38)   The girl in the sweater was made of wool.

Such sentences can be constructed by exchanging VPs from pairs of plausible sentences with similar structure. Such sentences are implausible at a sentential (global) level, but not at a phrasal (local) level. For example, if (39)–(40) are the base sentences (plausible at both phrasal and sentential levels), then (41)–(42) are the corresponding sentences that are implausible at a global level only.

(39)   His extensive cellar contained many rare wines.

(40)   That part of the river is a good place to fish.

(41)   His extensive cellar is a good place to fish.

(42)   That part of the river contains many rare wines.

If the matching task is sensitive only to local plausibility, then matching performance for (39)–(40) should not be any faster than for (41)–(42).

Our first experiment to test this hypothesis used 32 sentences in each condition, with 40 subjects.[2] The mean matching time for plausible sentences was 1,435 msec, and that for implausible sentences was 1,464 msec; the difference was 29 msec. However, this difference was not significant (minF' < 1), and was due mainly to one subject who showed a very large plausibility effect in this condition. In an attempt to show that this experiment was sensitive to local plausibility, we included a further set of items in which single words were exchanged from each phrase. Sentences (43)–(44) are examples of the base sentences; (45)–(46) are the corresponding implausible versions.

(43)   That cheese in the refrigerator tastes like cheddar.

(44)   That lady in the library writes detective novels.

(45)   That cheese in the library tastes detective novels.

(46)   That lady in the refrigerator writes like cheddar.

Exchanging *cheese* for *lady* and *tastes* for *writes* produces sentences that are implausible at both a global and a local level. The plausible sentences in this set produced a mean matching time of 1,414 msec, versus 1,492 msec for the implausible versions—a difference of 78 msec, which proved to be significant.

The implication of these results is that plausibility is somehow relevant to the processing of local phrases but is irrelevant to the higher-level integration of those phrases. Thus we can reconcile the seemingly incompatible properties of the matching task by arguing that it is sensitive to plausibility manipulations but insensitive to violations of constraints on movement that must disrupt the process of interpreting the meaning of the sentence.

Inter-Task and Inter-Subject Differences
The remarks above apply only to the matching task. It is entirely possible that other tasks will be highly sensitive to manipulations of global plausibility. Indeed, it would be of value to discover such a task, because we could then ask whether it was also sensitive to constraint violations. The expectation would be that if the controlling level for the task was high enough to show global plausibility effects, it would also be high enough to show constraint-violation effects. This argument is illustrated by the following list of possible controlling levels and the types of effects that should be shown.

Control level	Observable effects
0: Visual	Stimulus quality
1: Letter	Letter familiarity
2: Syllable	Orthographic legality
3: Lexical	Word-nonword, word frequency
4: Phrasal	Phrasal grammaticality
5: S-structure	Sentential grammaticality
6: Logical form	Constraint violation
7: Interpretive	Global plausibility

The idea is that if the control level for a task is level N, that task should show level-N effects plus all effects at levels lower than N. Thus, if a task is found that is sensitive to global plausibility (level 7), it automatically follows that it must be sensitive to constraint violations (level 6) as well. However, the converse is not necessarily true; that is, a task could show constraint effects without showing global plausibility effects.

A further point to be considered is that the controlling level need not be constant across individuals. A normal subject may recognize in the matching task that identity of form entails identity of meaning, entailments, etc., and hence no further processing will be required once identity of form is established. But suppose, for example, that we test on the matching task an extremely conservative subject whose criterion for a match is set so high that the sentences are also checked for synonymy. This might have the effect of forcing the matching task for this subject up to level 7, in which case this subject would show global plausibility effects. To complicate matters still further, the control level may vary within the one individual from moment to moment. Suppose, for example, that some subjects occasionally "forget" the precise form of the initial string but remember its meaning. To achieve a match, they must either recover the form of the initial string (which may be time consuming) or rely on a comparison of meaning. If the latter course is adopted, then once again the controlling level is raised.

If this approach is correct, perhaps we should avoid terms such as "*the controlling level*" for a given task and think instead of statistical tendencies or probabilities. This way of thinking is not incompatible with the race-model assumptions outlined in Chambers and Forster 1975. In fact, it is very much in keeping with them, since the controlling level is defined merely as the level of processing that happens to be the most efficient for a given set of conditions. There are no good grounds for insisting that a particular level will always be the most efficient for all subjects on all occasions.

There is some indication that this analysis may be on the right track. For example, Stevenson (1984) found that the lexical decision task produced a constraint effect much larger than that produced by the matching task, which bordered on statistical significance by the minF' technique. In this task the subject is simply asked to decide whether the input string consists solely of words. (The entire string is presented simultaneously.) The fact that the constraint effect is larger for this task suggests that the controlling level is higher than in the matching task. However, if this were really the case we should find a statistically significant constraint effect—and we do not.

Sense can be made of this result if we argue merely in terms of probabilities. That is, the result shows that, for any given subject on any given trial, the probability that the controlling level is 6 or above is higher for the lexical decision task than for the matching task. In a pilot study using the lexical decision task, we found a global plausibility effect of 57 msec for items such as (39)–(42) that also hovered on the edge of statistical significance. This suggests that there may be correlation between constraint effects and global plausibility effects across tasks. The matching task is at one extreme, showing weak or nonexistent effects for both, and the lexical decision task is at an intermediate position, showing marginal effects for both. What we need is a task at the opposite extreme from the matching task. The only obvious candidate is the multiple-choice sentence-construction task described on page 127 of Freedman and Forster 1985, which shows very strong constraint effects. If this task also shows strong global plausibility effects (as seems very likely), a case for an intertask correlation can be made.

The most convincing way to support this type of analysis would be to demonstrate reliable individual differences. There may be some individuals who show reliable global plausibility effects in the matching task, but these subjects would be in a minority. If such individuals can be identified, then we would expect that they would also show constraint violation effects.

How Local Is Local?

We now consider the problem of deciding what would be a local effect and what would be a global effect of plausibility. As a first approximation, we might take the division between NP and VP. Sentences (39)–(42) were designed with this division in mind. If detecting implausibility requires integrating an NP with a VP, then as far as the matching procedure is concerned this implausibility will go unnoticed (which is not to say that subjects do not notice and remark on the implausibility). However, if the individual constituents of either an NP or a VP are implausibly related, then matching performance will be adversely affected.

An exceptionally strong test of this hypothesis is provided by a comparison of adjectival constructions of the form Adj-N and N-be-Adj. In the former case both Adj and N are elements of an NP and hence are locally related. Thus, if the adjective is inappropriate to the noun, we have a local case of implausibility, and hence we would expect to find an effect of plausibility on matching times. But in the latter case, Adj and N belong to different phrases and hence are only globally related. Therefore we would expect no effect of an inappropriate adjective. To test these expectations, we can compare performance on sentences such as (47) and (48), and (49) and (50).

(47)   The woman liked Peter's cotton shirt.

(48)   The woman liked Peter's timber shirt.

(49)   Peter's shirt was made of cotton.

(50)   Peter's shirt was made of timber.

The method of testing used in this experiment differed from that used in the previous experiments. Instead of testing large numbers of subjects, we tested ten subjects over four sessions. In each session the same set of 48 "same" items was used, so for each subject we got four different estimates of the matching time for each item. To prevent the subjects from learning which items to respond "Yes" to, the initial strings of these items also appeared as the initial strings of "different" items. By the end of the four testing sessions, it would be fair to say, each subject was highly familiar with all the test sentences. It was also the case that each subject was exposed to all four combinations shown above. The reason for adopting this testing procedure was to minimize any "surprise" factor in the plausibility effect. This was already achieved to a certain extent through the use of a delayed matching task in which the subject had 2 seconds to read the initial string before the second string was presented. Repeated testing with the same stimulus materials simply ensured that all sentences had a high degree of familiarity.

For the Adj-N cases the matching time for plausible sentences such as (47) was 1,097 msec; for implausible sentences such as (48) it was 1,153 msec. This 56-msec effect of plausibility proved to be significant. However, for the N-be-Adj cases, such as (49)–(50), the corresponding times were 1,097 and 1,117 msec, producing a nonsignificant 20-msec plausibility effect. This result supports the local-global distinction and is consistent with the notion that the NP-VP boundary is the right place to draw the distinction. Further, the result emphasizes that the plausibility effect does not stem from the strangeness of conceptual content, for it seems clear that the notion of a timber shirt is not markedly stranger than the notion of a shirt's being made of timber (indeed, the former comes close to entailing the latter).

Further support for this proposal has been provided by Ratcliff (1983), who used a simultaneous matching task and changed either the object NP or the subject NP to produce a variation in plausibility, as in (51)–(54).

(51)   The landlord helped the customer.

(52)   The landlord helped the insects.

(53)   The pilots shifted the tables.

(54)   The lambs shifted the tables.

Despite the fact that the variation in plausibility was approximately the same in both cases (as indicated by ratings), there was a corresponding difference in matching performance only for (51) and (52), where the plausibility of the V-NP relation was altered. The difference in this case was 50 msec, but for (53)–(54) there was no difference at all in matching times. This contrast can be interpreted in terms of the global-local distinction. The difference between (51) and (52) is local (a within-phrase effect), but that between (53) and (54) is global (a between-phrases effect).

However, there is also some evidence to suggest that the NP-VP boundary is not the place to separate local from global effects. In earlier experiments using a simultaneous matching task (no delay between strings), we noticed that plausibility effects could be obtained for two-word sentences such as (55)–(56).

(55)   dogs growl

(56)   dogs paint

In these cases the NP-VP boundary lies between the two words, and hence they are only globally related and should produce no effect. A potential weakness of items such as (55) is that there is a strong associative connection between the noun and the verb that is absent in the implausible versions, which means that the obtained effect might not be a sentential effect at all but rather a lexical-relatedness effect. For this reason we decided to repeat the experiment using a delayed matching task, and using materials with weaker associative links, as in (57)–(58). Naturally, the plausible pairs were not totally unrelated, since otherwise they would not be plausible. Once again, a repeated-testing procedure was used in which each subject completed six testing sessions with the same materials.

(57)   bears hunt

(58)   poets limp

These items also showed a significant effect of plausibility, confirming our initial suspicions. Hence it seems clear that the NP-VP boundary cannot be used in all cases to distinguish local from global effects. Either the notion of locality is altogether wrong (in which case we must find a nonstructural explanation) or we must find another way to draw the local-global distinction. One possibility is that at least one of the lexical items involved in the implausibility must c-command another (i.e., the first branching node dominating one must also dominate another). This would cover the N-V cases in (57)–(58) and the Adj-N cases in (47)–(48), since if the critical elements are adjacent to each other, and together form a constituent, then each must necessarily c-command the other. It would also explain the absence of effects for the N-be-Adj case (49)–(50), since in (50) the first branching node dominating *shirt* does not dominate *timber*.

Defining locality in terms of c-command also appears to cover the earlier examples. In (41), for example, the critical elements are *cellar* and *fish*, but neither c-commands the other and hence no plausibility effect is to be expected. However, in (45) the phrase *tastes detective novels* should produce an effect, since *taste* c-commands *novels*. This definition might also be extended to explain the contrast between (23)–(24) and (25)–(26): In (26) the verb c-commands the pronoun, but in (24) the verb does not c-command *wh-*.

But if the N-V relation matters in (56) and (58), why is it irrelevant in (54), where *lambs* c-commands *shifted*? One possible answer is that the notion of lambs' shifting something is not itself implausible; it is just the notion of lambs' shifting a table that is implausible. That is, three elements need to be combined before the implausibility becomes apparent. This approach implies that only pairwise combinations of lexical elements can produce a plausibility effect. Another possible answer is that, strictly, *lambs* does not c-command *shifted* in (54), since it is first combined with the determiner and therefore it is the phrase that c-commands the verb. This leads to the highly counterintuitive prediction that items such as *Lambs shifted the tables* should produce an effect.

Clearly, we are in no position to offer a resolution of these problems. Despite this, it does seem fair to conclude that there must be some structural condition that must be met before a plausibility effect will occur. We now consider why this might be the case.

Plausibility and Parsing

The argument to this point has been intended to show that there may be no incompatibility between the assumption that the matching task does not recruit structural descriptions higher than the level of S-structures (the shallow-sensitivity hypothesis) and the fact that plausibility effects can be observed with this task. The form of the argument is simply that the plausibility effect in the matching task does not seem to be the consequence of an interpretive process that has as its domain the entire sentence. Hence there is no need to involve representations higher than the level of S-structures.

But it still remains to provide an explanation of these low-level, local plausibility effects. What type of low-level processing is affected? One possibility is that the lexical identification process is affected by plausibility. In this case, one would argue that the left context of any word in the sentence is used in a predictive sense to limit the range of possible alternatives, which leads to faster identification. This is not an attractive option, since there are grounds for doubting that such effects exist (see Forster 1979, 1981 and Fodor 1983 for discussions of some of the issues involved). The typical method of demonstrating such an effect would be to require lexical decisions on the final word of a sentence to be displayed one word at a time. The problem with this approach is simply that we cannot be sure that the controlling level for the response is the lexical level. For example, lexical decision responses on the final words of (24), (41), (42), and (50) would almost certainly be longer than those for appropriate controls, since the left contexts in these cases are quite typical of the contexts normally used in such experiments. Yet the matching task fails to register these effects; this suggests that the controlling level for the lexical decision task may well be higher than that for the matching task.

The only other possibility seems to be that local plausibility affects the operation of the parser itself. Suppose that parsing is carried out in two stages along the lines proposed in Frazier and Fodor 1978. In the first stage, the preliminary phrase packager attempts to group lexical items into phrasal or clausal units. The second stage is assigned the task of deciding how these units are related. Obviously, the overall efficiency of this system depends on how accurately the first stage assembles the possible phrases. For example, in (47) the analysis of the overall structure of the sentence will be facilitated if an early decision can be made concerning the first NP. Is it *Peter's cotton*, or is it *Peter's cotton shirt*? One way to find out quickly might be to ask whether *cotton* is likely to be used as an adjective with *shirt*. If the answer is yes, the latter analysis might be adopted immediately. If the answer is no, no early decision is possible and both avenues will have to be explored.

If the answer to this question was provided by a consideration of the conceptual content of the phrase, we can no longer maintain the assumption of autonomous syntactic processing (Forster 1979). But suppose instead that the lexical entry for *shirt* points to a list of frequently used adjectives for that noun. If the adjective in question is on that list, the combination is marked as likely; otherwise it is not. Likely combinations will be adopted as first approximations; if they prove to be correct (as they will more often than not), the processing of the remainder of the sentence will be facilitated. If we could also imagine that the lexical entries of verbs might point to lists of possible nouns that frequently appear as objects, then we could extend the power of this heuristic device considerably.

It is conceded that this "lexical combination" mechanism is dangerously close to the notion that meaning influences syntactic analysis; hence we must attempt to make clear how the proposals differ. The important point is that we intend to limit the kind of information that the parser has access to—to "informationally encapsulate" the parser, in Fodor's (1983) terms. This means that the parser has access only to the formal properties of each word as specified in the lexicon, and is denied any real-world knowledge except for information about frequently used word combinations. So the pointer literally points to a list of lexical items, not to a semantic field. If *orange* is listed as a frequently used object of the verb *peel* but *tangerine* is not, then only the former should show an advantage, despite the conceptual similarities of oranges and tangerines. As Fodor would put it, this is a case of a dumb system pretending to be smart.

A second point is that the parser is presumed to have access only to distributional information about pairs of words. This means that the difference in plausibility between (59) and (60) should be irrelevant to the matching task.

(59)   The spider crawled onto my finger.

(60)   The spider crawled into my finger.

The point here is that the implausibility depends on the locative phrase as a unit, and there are no pairwise lexical combinations that are implausible. Hence, from a parsing point of view, there is no reason to suppose that (60) should be any harder to parse than (59). Of course, if *crawled into* and *crawled onto* were each represented in the lexicon as separate single lexical items, it would be possible to specify a list of nouns that could appear as objects; this, however, seems an unlikely possibility.

The relevant data for the matching task are not available, but we do have evidence that sentences such as (59)–(60) produce plausibility effects for tasks such as the grammaticality decision task, where the subject is asked whether a string forms a grammatical sentence or not. If the same effects are found for the matching task, it will be very difficult to maintain our position.

We do, however, have some preliminary indications that offer some support for this view (indeed, it was only because of these results that we even considered such a view). In the above-mentioned experiment with N-V sentences such as (57)–(58), subjects were tested repeatedly for six sessions with the same materials. The effect of plausibility referred to was obtained only in the first two testing sessions. In subsequent sessions the effect declined, and by the sixth session there was no effect at all. This "habituation" effect was not due to the fact that the subjects had memorized which items would be "same" and which would be "different," because the same initial strings occurred in both conditions. One way to explain this reduction in the plausibility effect is to assume that after many exposures to the sentence *poets limp*, the subjects simply included *limp* on their list of things that poets are often said to do. Of course, this is not the only explanation. Subjects may have been developing more efficient matching procedures, or learning to ignore plausibility. We tested for such effects by including a seventh testing session, in which the same words were presented in new combinations, such as (61)–(62).

(61)   bears growl

(62)   poets dodge

The result was that the plausibility effect reappeared, although perhaps in a slightly diminished form. This recovery from habituation provides quite strong support for the lexical-combination hypothesis, since the habituation effect would be restricted to specific lexical combinations. Any change in lexical content would be sufficient to produce a recovery effect, perhaps even if the new combination was very similar in meaning to the habituated combination.

These conclusions must be regarded as quite tentative. The experiments have not been replicated, and we have not yet considered a very wide range of cases. Indeed, my purpose in discussing the evidence at all is merely to raise the possibility that such effects exist.

The work of Ratcliff (1983) raises a critical problem for the lexical-combination hypothesis. She compared matching performance on sentences such as (63)–(65). Cases such as (63) were intended to be relatively stereotypical, in the sense that selling meat is a prototypical activity of butchers. Cases such as (64) were intended to be more "neutral." Although telephoning a dentist is a perfectly plausible thing to imagine a mother doing, it is not to be thought of as a prototypical activity. Cases such as (65) were intended to be outright implausible.

(63)   The butcher sold the meat.

(64)   The mother telephoned the dentist.

(65)   The butcher ate the uniform.

Ratcliff's results with a delayed matching task indicate that the contrast between (63) and (64) produced a strong effect on matching, whereas the difference between (64) and (65) was marginal at best. From the point of view proposed here, this seems to be the wrong result, for the following reason. If we adopt the view that only local plausibility effects are relevant to matching performance, then the subject noun is quite irrelevant, since in all three cases the noun is plausibly associated with the verb. This means that the variation in matching times must be controlled by the VPs. However, the sharpest contrast is provided by (65), since this is the only VP that is at all implausible. Hence one might expect no difference between (63) and (64), but both of them should differ markedly from (65).

However, the lexical-combination hypothesis predicts a difference only if the object noun is present on the list of typical objects of the verb in one case and not in the other. Hence we expect (64) and (65) to differ only if *dentist* is on the list specified by the verb *telephone* and *uniform* is not on the list specified by *eat*. The latter is surely true, but is the former? Possibly not, and hence there is very little effect. However, *meat* might well be on the list for *sell*, and hence (63) differs from both (64) and (65).

Ratcliff's analysis differed in the assumption that the important element in (63) was the word *butcher*. That is, one would expect *meat* only in the context of *butcher sold* —. If this is the correct analysis, then one ought to obtain a difference between items such as (66) and (67), whereas the locality principle would predict no difference, since it considers only pairwise combinations (and both are equally likely).

(66)   The butcher sold the meat.

(67)   The stockbroker sold the meat.

The important feature of these items is that the pairwise linkages are comparable. That is, *butcher-sell* is intended to match *stockbrocker-sell*. Hence,
it is only when all three terms are considered together that the two
cases can be distinguished in terms of plausibility. Unfortunately for the
present argument, Ratcliff did not contrast stereotyped and neutral cases
of this type in which the VP was held constant while the subject NP was
varied (although she did contrast neutral and implausible cases of this
type—see examples 53 and 54 above). If the data support Ratcliff's analysis, then it seems pointless to pursue the lexical combination view any
further, since any procedure that modifies the list of possible objects depending on the subject of the verb clearly requires a global process. To
attempt to store frequent combinations of the form N-V-N seems tantamount to storing a list of all possible sentences.

Conclusion

The suggestion that the plausibility effect in the matching task is somehow
governed by structural factors more or less demands an explanation in
terms of parsing operations. But providing such an explanation is not an
easy matter, especially if we wish to maintain autonomous levels. However, the alternative seems even more difficult. To suggest that the effect is
controlled by the propositional content of the sentence runs into the
problem of explaining why constraint violations are cost-free in this task,
why in (24) there is no plausibility effect when an inappropriate form of
wh- is bound with its trace, and why there are some cases where global
plausibility appears to exert little influence.

   However these problems are resolved, it seems clear that the matching
task raises interesting questions about the intermediate stages of sentence
processing. Such questions would normally addressed by means of "on-
line" tasks, in which a probe item is presented for response while the target sentence is being processed. The matching task appears to provide an
interesting "off-line" alternative that avoids the technical problem of deciding how to time the probe.

Notes

1. The force of this argument does not depend on specific assumptions about particular
   levels. For "the level of S-structures" we could read "level *X*," and for "the level of LF"
   we could read "level *Y*." Level *Y* is whatever level we assume the ungrammaticality of
   constraint-violation sentences to be marked at, and level *X* is the next level down.
2. The results of this experiment and subsequent experiments are reported here in preliminary form only. A more detailed presentation of the evidence is in preparation.

4

Context Effects in Lexical Processing: A Connectionist Approach to Modularity

Michael K. Tanenhaus, Gary S. Dell, and Greg Carlson

Our aim in this chapter is to bring together two controversial ideas in cognition: modularity (the claim the processing is divided among autonomous subsystems) and connectionism (an approach to cognitive modeling that emphasizes the parallel spread of activation among neuronlike processing units).[1]

To say the least, modularity and connectionism are strange bedfellows. They are both broad claims about cognitive structure, but beyond that most researchers see the two approaches as either orthogonal or antithetical. The view that modularity and connectionism are orthogonal stems from the observations that connectionism, with its emphasis on quasi-neural elements, is a claim about microstructure whereas modularity is a claim about macrostructure. The view that the two approaches are in opposition is due to the fact that connectionist modelers often have a commitment to interactive (that is, nonmodular) treatments of processing. Spreading activation, in which diverse sources of information are translated into the common coin of activation, is a natural mechanism to handle interaction (McClelland and Rumelhart 1981). Claims that the structure of cognition is highly modular are therefore claims that the connectionists' most potent mechanisms are only minimally useful.

Here we challenge both the idea that connectionism and modularity are irrelevant to each other and the view that they are incompatible. We will argue that connectionist microstructure offers some insights into the global structure of knowledge and that, with some kinds of knowledge, a connectionist approach leads one to expect modular processing. Moreover, we hope to illustrate that thinking in connectionist terms can provide a different and enlightening perspective on modularity. In order to develop our argument we will begin with some general considerations of the issues that surround the modularity of language. Our discussion then turns to connectionist models—in particular, connectionist models of language processing. We introduce some of the properties of these connectionist models and indicate why we believe that the connectionist framework is relevant to modularity. In the final section we provide a short review of the literature on context effects in word recognition and develop an explanation for the

data that is, in large part, inspired by the ideas developed in recent connectionist models of language.

Modularity and Language Processing

A dominant issue in psycholinguistics has been whether the language-
processing system is best characterized as a highly interactive system in
which different sources of knowledge communicate freely, or as a highly
modular system composed of autonomous subsystems which are blind to
each other's internal states and operations and which communicate only at
their input and output stages.[2] Much of the controversy about modularity
is due to the fact that researchers studying language have radically different
intuitions about the nature of language and the nature of perceptual systems. Researchers favoring the modularity perspective generally follow
Chomsky (see e.g., Chomsky 1980a) in assuming that the linguistic system
is a specialized multilevel system that can be distinguished from the more
general-purpose cognitive system. On this view it is natural to look for
language processing to reflect the special properties of the linguistic system.
The Chomskyan perspective may be contrasted with a *functionalist* view in
which the linguistic system is seen as relatively impoverished and much of
language structure is seen as a by-product of processing constraints and the
pragmatic function of language (see e.g. Bates and McWhinney 1982). On
this view it makes little sense to distinguish between linguistic and nonlinguistic representations; the same principles that determine other cognitive
behaviors underlie language. Functionalists are generally impressed by the
lack of invariance in the interpretation of linguistic expressions across
processing contexts. From this perspective, highly interactive processing
systems are attractive. They provide a mechanism for different sources of
knowledge to communicate during processing. They also provide a mechanism for contextual information, in the form of top-down knowledge, to
reduce the noise in bottom-up inputs. Perceptual inputs that are contextually
inappropriate tend to be filtered, whereas those that are contextually
appropriate are amplified. Although reducing the noise in perceptual
systems is clearly desirable, the potential cost to the processing system is
that some contextually inappropriate information will be lost. However,
this is a small price to pay on the view that language processing should be
heavily contextualized.

   Most proponents of richer, more articulated linguistic systems have been
suspicious of interactive models, generally because they seem to blur the
distinctions that these researchers find so interesting. Thus they have argued
against interactive models on the methodological ground that positing
autonomous systems is a stronger, more easily falsifiable hypothesis than
allowing unconstrained interaction (Cairns 1983). Fodor (1983) was the

first to present an argument for the autonomous position that offered a true counterpart to the functionalist case for interaction. He argued that modularity is a general property of input systems, designed to protect them from top-down contamination. The idea is that an organism with a powerful cognitive system needs to make sure that its perceptual systems stay tuned to the outside world. After all, one does not want to fail to recognize a tiger when it appears unexpectedly. However, modularity does not appear to be a property of higher-level cognitive systems (Fodor's "central systems"), and thus one expects the language-processing system to be modular only if it is a highly specialized biological system—a view that is clearly consistent with the Chomskyan view of language. Thus the idea that the linguistic system is a specialized system and the idea that input systems are insulated fit naturally together under the umbrella of modularity.

In short, nonmodular and modular views of processing are guided by different underlying intuitions. According to the nonmodular view, the noise in perceptual inputs can be reduced by bringing to bear other relevant sources of knowledge to amplify compatible inputs and to filter incompatible ones. The cost of doing this is relatively minor given that interpretation is seen as contextually conditioned. The modular viewpoint is that perceptual systems must be protected from highly developed inferential systems in order to keep them tuned to the environment.

Thinking in connectionist terms, we believe, can provide an alternative perspective on modularity. In particular, if we adopt a parallel processing system that is completely unconstrained as far as what interactions among levels are permissible and then build in the structure necessary to account for language processing, we may then find varying degrees of modular organization emerging for computational reasons. This would provide an alternative to the view that modularity, or the lack thereof, results from the design characteristics of the architecture of the language-processing system. In this chapter we present a preliminary attempt to develop this approach by applying ideas developed by connectionist modelers to the problem of context effects in lexical processing.

Connectionist Models of Language Processing

A connectionist model is a parallel computational model consisting of a network of simple processing units. Each unit, or node, sends simple numeric messages to those that it connects to. (See Rumelhart and McClelland 1986 and Feldman and Ballard 1982 for formal definitions of connectionist models and their components.)

Connectionist models, sometimes called spreading activation or interactive models, have appeared in several domains in addition to language, including vision (Feldman 1985), motor control (Rumelhart and Norman

1982), and knowledge representation (Shastri 1985). Much of the paradigm's popularity is due to its apparent success in providing new computational solutions to hard problems (e.g., Shastri's [1985] treatment of evidential reasoning; Hinton and Sejnowski's [1983] and Rumelhart, Hinton, and Williams's [1986] approach to learning) and in accounting for psychological data (e.g., McClelland and Rumelhart's [1981] word-recognition model). Further interest stems from claims that the models are biologically plausible in that processing units are supposed to work like neurons. These claims are important; however, we believe that the psycholinguistic adequacy of connectionist models of language processing can and should be evaluated independent of any biological-plausibility claims.

Our focus will be on connectionist models that have adopted a "localist" or "punctate" coding of concepts (Feldman 1986) in which each concept is represented by one unit or by a very few units. In such models one sees a fairly direct encoding of structure; e.g., if concept A is structurally related to concept B then the unit for A connects to the one for B. In contrast with localist coding stands the "distributed" or "diffuse" approach, in which a concept is represented by a pattern of activity across the network. (See the papers in Rumelhart and McClelland 1986 and McClelland and Rumelhart 1986 for details.) Connectionist models of language processing have for the most part adopted the localist approach. It is much easier to incorporate linguistic units and structure into the network when one can identify relatively small parts of the network with particular units or relationships. Because of our focus on these kinds of connectionist models, our conclusions regarding modularity with respect to these models will be restricted to the localist view.

In language processing, connectionist models have been developed in a number of areas: visual and auditory word recognition (McClelland and Rumelhart 1981; Rumelhart and McClelland 1982; Elman and McClelland 1984), production (Dell 1986; Stemberger 1985), lexical access (Cottrell and Small 1983; Cottrell 1985a), and parsing (Cottrell 1985b; Waltz and Pollack 1985; McClelland and Kawamoto 1986; Selman and Hirst 1985). As a means of presenting some of the important properties of connectionist models, we will first consider models of purely lexical phenomena, including word recognition and lexical access (lexical disambiguation). We then turn to parsing models, which must deal with linguistic rules.

Lexical Models
The connectionist model best known to psychologists is the model of visual word recognition developed by McClelland and Rumelhart (1981; see also Rumelhart and McClelland 1982). As shown in figure 1, this model contains a network of nodes with excitatory and inhibitory connections among them. Each node stands for either a word, a letter, or a feature. Associated with

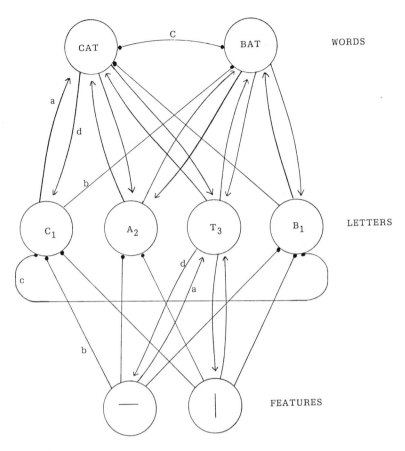

Figure 1
Word, letter, and feature nodes and their connections in the interactive-activation model.
Arrows indicate excitatory connections; dots indicate inhibitory connections. Letter sub-
scripts index the letters' word positions. Only the features of the letter T are shown.

each node is a real number—its activation level—reflecting the extent to which that unit is participating in the processing. Higher activation levels reflect greater degrees of involvement. The function of the connections is to transmit an input pattern of activated features to the word level in such a way as to identify the most likely word given the features. The connections in the model come in four types:

• *Excitatory bottom-up.* These connections (labeled a in figure 1) activate higher-level nodes that are consistent with activated lower-level nodes.
• *Inhibitory bottom-up* (b in figure 1). These work in the same way as the excitatory bottom-up ones, only in an inhibitory fashion; i.e., they decrease the activation level of connected nodes. They communicate the presence of a feature to those letters that don't have it.
• *Lateral inhibitory* (c in figure 1). In most connectionist networks the connections are arranged so that nodes representing incompatible hypotheses cannot be highly activated at the same time. Thus, in this model all competing nodes inhibit one another, creating a "winner-take-all" situation in which one unit from a competing group ends up with all or most of the activation.
• *Excitatory top-down* (d in figure 1). These connections deliver positive feedback from higher to lower levels. They mold the activation pattern of a lower level (e.g. the letter nodes) until it meshes with higher-level (e.g. lexical) information. The availability and the extent of top-down feedback help to define the degree to which the processing at a level is modular.[3]

We will not go into detail about how the units work other than to say that each computes its activation level from its input (activation sent from its neighbors) and sends activation to its neighbors depending on that level.

Another example of a connectionist model of lexical processes is Cottrell's (1985a) account of lexical access, presented in figure 2. The purpose of this model is to explain how lexical ambiguity is resolved. The model takes its input at the word level. Activation then spreads from word nodes to word senses. A word is disambiguated when only one sense is left activated. (Lateral inhibitory connections between competing senses ensure that this will be the case.) When a word such as *deck* comes in, all senses are initially activated via bottom-up excitatory connections. The word is eventually disambiguated as input from context comes in. Given the context 'The man walked on the ...', both syntactic contextual information (favoring noun senses) and semantic information (favoring senses of *deck* that a person can walk on) would provide inputs to the relevant senses. An interesting feature of the model is that it predicts that words (such as *deck*) that have several noun and verb meanings are disambiguated in such a way that when context biases for a particular noun meaning, other noun meanings are deactivated more

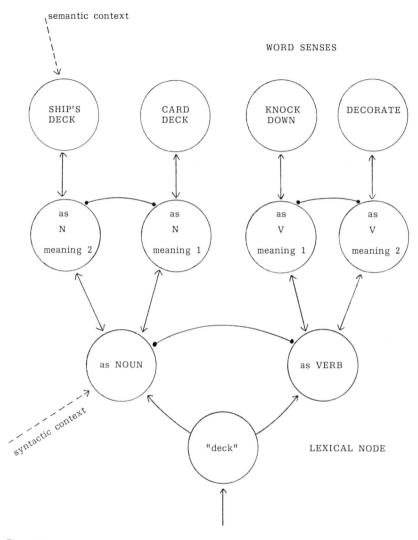

Figure 2
Cottrell's (1985a) model of lexical access. Arrows and dots indicate excitatory and inhibitory connections, respectively.

rapidly than the verb meanings. Seidenberg, Tanenhaus, Leiman, and Bien-kowski (1982) have presented experimental results consistent with this prediction.

Parsing Models
The two models presented so far illustrate a common feature of many connectionist models: They compute by matching an input pattern to a stored set of units. The idea is to pick out, or activate, the unit or coalition of units that best reflects the input. In the lexical models the goal of the processing has been to identify a single node; for the word-recognition model this is the word node that best matches the featural input, and for the lexical-access model this is the word-sense node that matches the lexical input and the context. This idea of having the "answer" be a single node is not going to work for processing a sentence, however. Even if sentences are limited in length, it is not plausible to imagine that the syntactic or semantic representation of a sentence would consist of a single node. A node for each possible sentence and its attendant connections would have to be available in the network beforehand. Clearly, the rule-governed, creative nature of language dictates that representations must be assembled out of an existing set of options rather than be already wired in.

    This brings us to models of semantic processing and parsing. Cottrell's (1985a) model can be used to illustrate a connectionist "semantic" represen-tation. The semantic representation in this model is a coalition of activated nodes that identifies the word senses (concepts) in the sentence and assigns thematic roles to them (figure 3). Some of the nodes in the model stand directly for word senses. The semantic representation of *Bob saw the cat* would include a node for BOB1 (the concept, not the word), CAT1 (the particular cat that Bob saw), and the action SEE. (We will ignore tense and aspect.) In addition there would be activated nodes representing the roles Agent and Patient. This set of nodes, however, does not constitute a complete representation; it lacks structural information specifying who is the Agent and who is the Patient. This information is supplied by special *binding nodes*, which are activated and participate in the representation. In-stead of presenting the details of Cottrell's binding process, which is quite complex, we will present a simplification of it that captures the features relevant to our discussion. In our simplification, binding nodes directly stand for links between word senses and thematic roles. So, for the sen-tence *Bob saw the cat* the representation would include a BOB1/Agent node and a CAT1/Patient node. (The model also includes "exploded-case" nodes, e.g. SEE/Agent and SEE/Patient, which can also be thought of as binding nodes linking the action and its roles.)

    Given that bindings between concepts and roles are necessary features of the representation, it follows that the network, if it is prepared to handle

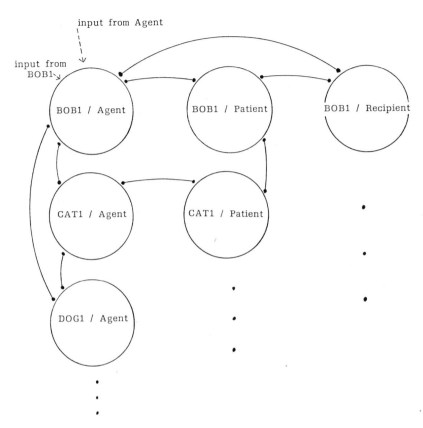

Figure 3
Two-dimensional binding space between concepts (e.g., BOB1) and thematic roles (e.g., Agent) from Cottrell 1985a. Dots indicate inhibitory connections.

"any" sentence, must contain binding nodes for every possible assignment of concepts to roles. Although this is a very large number of nodes, it is really nothing more than a listing of the semantic properties of all word senses.

In Cottrell's model the binding nodes between concepts and thematic roles are arranged in a two-dimensional binding space (figure 3). Each binder inhibits all other incompatible binders. For example, BOB1/Agent inhibits CAT1/Agent, the model assumes that there is only one agent for each action, and BOB1/Agent also inhibits BOB1/Patient, reflecting a constraint in the model that a particular *mention* of a concept can fill only one role in the proposition.[4] (Sentences like *Bob saw himself*, in which BOB has two roles, are not a problem because of a buffer system in which each mention of a concept occupies a different buffer position, i.e. is coded by a different node. For details see Cottrell 1985a.) The inhibitory connections in the binding spaces create winner-take-all subnetworks, within which sets of binders compete for activation. After the competition, each occurrence of a concept is bound to a single role.

Binding nodes are also crucial in connectionist syntactic representations. In Selman and Hirst's (1985) and Cottrell's (1985b) models, syntactic representations contain nodes for syntactic constituents and binding nodes that link the constituents (figure 4). For example, one binder in the figure represents the assignment of NOUN1 as the head of NP2. Thus, these binders identify the various syntactic relationships among constituents. Binding nodes are also required to link lexical items to nodes representing terminal syntactic categories. For example, a binder cat/NOUN1 would be required to encode the fact that the noun *cat* is assigned to the particular syntactic role played by NOUN1 in the sentence in the figure.

As was the case for binding nodes in the semantic representation, syntactic binders would have to exist to handle all possible bindings. Thus, there must be nodes to link all possible syntactically disambiguated lexical items to their possible syntactic functions, and each node for a constituent must, as well, have binders for every role that the constituent could play. Like the semantic binders, the syntactic binding nodes in the models inhibit one another when they stand for mutually incompatible bindings.

Thus we have seen that the way connectionist models deal with rule-governed linguistic behavior is to employ large numbers of binding nodes (arranged in mutually inhibitory subnetworks). The necessity of these nodes can be understood in two ways. First, the nodes are needed to specify relationships among items in the representation. (Nonconnectionist representations must code these relationships as well.) In the connectionist paradigm all aspects of representations are coded as activated nodes, so the representation of both items and the relationships among items is reduced to a common form. Second, the binders between lexical items and their

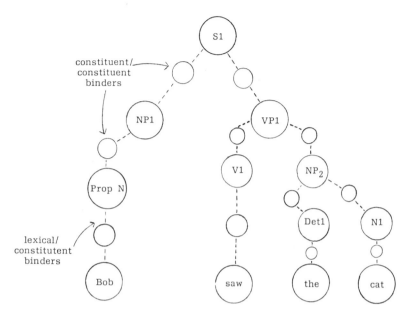

Figure 4
Nodes participating in the syntactic representation of the sentence *Bob saw the cat*. Adapted
from Selman and Hirst 1985 and Cottrell 1985b.

syntactic and semantic functions serve to link lexical processes with rule-
governed processes. Because the parts of the network that encode the rules
compute with nodes that represent categories of items rather than the items
themselves, the linking of particular items to their rule-governed roles is
essential.

Connectionism and Modularity

Any explicitly worked-out model of language processing makes claims
about modularity in the sense that it specifies what information is available
for decision making at various times. Connectionist models have the virtue
of being quite explicit in this respect. However, what makes them particularly useful in thinking about modularity is the fact that the models directly generate *activation-history functions*, and many modularity issues can
be couched in these terms.

An activation-history function represents the potential (or the availability) of some hypothetical mental entity to influence a response as a
function of the time from some instigating stimulus. Psycholinguistic experiments are, to a great extent, concerned with discovering these functions for linguistic entities and how the functions vary with experimental

conditions. For instance, tasks such as lexical decision, naming, and the detection of phonemes, letters, and words are all assumed to reflect the availability of a particular linguistic unit or set of units. If the availability of a linguistic unit is identified with the activation level of the node representing that unit in a connectionist model, the model can give a theoretical account of data of this kind.

In order to see how activation-history functions are relevant to modularity, consider two mutually exclusive hypotheses about linguistic input: A and B. In a localist connectionist model, A and B would be nodes at the same processing level (words, word senses, parsing options, etc.). Next assume that bottom-up input fails to distinguish between them. Given all this, there are several different activation functions that could result, some of which are listed below and pictured in figure 5. The zero time point is that point when bottom-up input just reaches nodes A and B. The alternatives include the following:

• *No feedback.* In this situation the activation functions for A and B are identical. No top-down feedback arrives to distinguish them. Although A and B are competing interpretations, the decision is made by nodes at a higher level. This pattern usually occurs in models only when A and B are unimportant intermediary nodes or are the lowest level of the model (e.g., the feature nodes in the word-recognition model).

• *Late feedback.* This situation is similar to the one above except that higher-level processes eventually feed back to A and B after a great deal of computation. Why is the feedback necessary? Because A and B may serve as inputs to other parts of the network, and these parts may need to know whether A or B won the competition. The late feedback pattern occurs in Cottrell's (1985a) lexical-access model, with A and B standing for competing word senses.

• *Early feedback.* The pattern here is similar to the preceding one, only the feedback arrives long before the nodes have reached their asymptotic activation levels. In some models, feedback is made quickly and preferentially available to one option (A) because of other units activated at A's level. Thus, if A and B are competing letters, other letters can activate the higher-level word units and the words can quickly send top-down feedback to the letters preferentially to the one that is consistent with the other letters (McClelland and Rumelhart 1981).

• *One option "primed."* Occasionally, connectionist modelers arrange things so that one of a set of alternatives is in a ready state so that the slightest input causes it to become activated or causes its activation level to grow very quickly. Such a unit is said to be *primed.* When one option is primed it gets an immediate head start on its competitors, and, if the options mutually inhibit, the nonprimed competitors may never get activated at all.

This occurs in Cottrell's (1985a) lexical-access model, in which A and B represent competing word senses and a previous word sense has an exceptionally strong semantic association to A.

• *One option already activated.* A unit that normally is activated when there is bottom-up input delivered to it could become activated purely through top-down feedback, creating a "hallucination." This situation should naturally be avoided in all but the most constraining contexts. It occurs in Elman and McClelland's (1984) auditory-word-recognition model, in which A and B are competing phonemes and enough phonemes have already come in to identify the word.

These five patterns can easily be seen as falling along a continuum of "feedback" time, with the more modular characterizations of A-B resolution associated with longer times (see figure 6). We will argue in the following discussion on context effects that connectionist models provide natural reasons to limit feedback in certain situations, but not in others.

Modularity and Lexical Processing

We now turn to the empirical literature on context effects in lexical processing—an area that has figured prominently in the debate about modularity. The empirical issue is whether or not contextual information can provide early feedback during word recognition. The modularity hypothesis makes two strong claims about the invariance of lexical processing across contexts (Tanenhaus, Carlson, and Seidenberg 1985; Tanenhaus and Lucas 1986): that the information made available as a consequence of lexical access should remain invariant across processing contexts, and that the speed with which information is made available should not be affected by processing context.

Evaluating evidence for and against context effects is complicated by a methodological problem: For every demonstration of a context effect in lexical processing, there is a feedback explanation (which violates modularity assumptions) and a decision-bias explanation (which is consistent with modularity). As an illustration of this point, consider an experiment in which subjects are timed as they decide whether or not a stimulus (either a word or a pseudo-word) begins with the phoneme /b/. Decision times are faster on word trials than on pseudo-word trials. Assume a simple model containing three levels of nodes: feature nodes, phoneme nodes, and lexical nodes. Phonemic nodes are activated by feature nodes, and lexical nodes by phonemic nodes. The mechanism for lexical context facilitating phoneme detection in a feedback explanation is positive feedback from an activated lexical node to its component phonemes. When a lexical node becomes activated, it sends positive feedback to its component phoneme

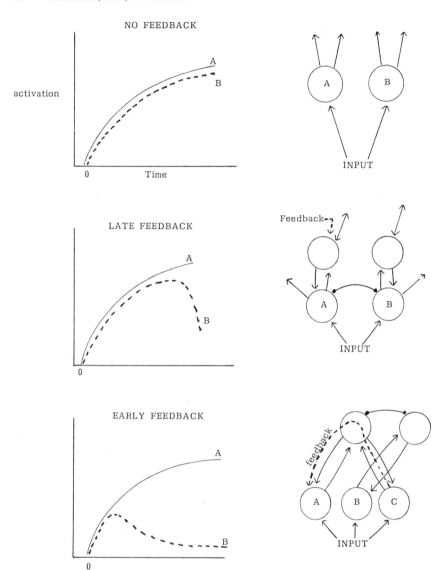

Figure 5
Activation history functions for two mutually exclusive hypotheses about linguistic input,
A and B, and corresponding network configurations. The pathway that feedback takes to
the preferred alternative, A, is indicated by a dashed line. Arrows and dots indicate excitatory and inhibitory connections, respectively.

ONE ALTERNATIVE "PRIMED"

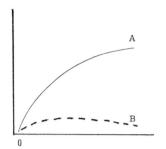

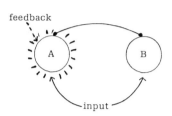

ONE ALTERNATIVE ACTIVATED

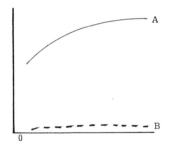

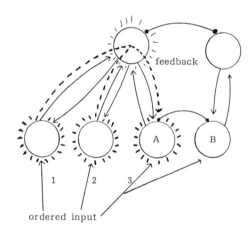

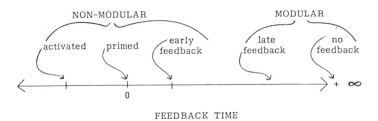

FEEDBACK TIME

Figure 6
The feedback-time continuum divided into modular and nonmodular parts.

nodes, thus increasing their activation levels. When activation at the lexical node or the phoneme node crosses a threshold, the concept represented by the node is available for recognition. Since phonemes in nonword stimuli do not connect to a single lexical node, phoneme nodes will receive less activation due to positive feedback when the carrier stimulus is a nonword.

In contrast, a decision-bias model accounts for context effects without postulating feedback by assuming that listeners can use information at higher levels to guide decisions at lower levels. Given the same sensory evidence that a phoneme has been presented, a listener might be more inclined to respond "yes" if he or she had reason to believe that a word containing the phoneme was being processed. This situation might arise when both the phonemic representation and the lexical representation of a word containing the phoneme were partially activated, or when the word was activated beyond threshold but the phoneme was not. The crucial difference between a feedback explanation and a decision-bias explanation is that in a feedback explanation the activated lexical node changes the activation level of the phoneme node, whereas in a decision-bias explanation the criteria for deciding that a phoneme was presented may be altered by the presence of an activated lexical node but the activation of the phoneme node itself is unaffected.

Although there is an extensive literature on context effects in word recognition, few studies have used methodologies that can distinguish between decision-bias and feedback explanations. A noteworthy exception is Samuel 1981. Samuel used a signal-detection analysis in a paradigm in which a phoneme in a word or a nonword was either replaced by noise or had noise added to it. Replacing a phoneme with noise reduces the bottom-up activation that the phoneme node representing the excised phoneme would recieve. The subject's task was to discriminate between noise-added and noise-replaced trials. Samuel reasoned that if feedback operated between the lexical and phonemic levels, then noise-replaced phonemes should often be restored in word stimuli, making them perceptually similar to the noise-added stimuli. The feedback provides activation to the phoneme that is indistinguishable from any activation it may have from the input. If, on the other hand, lexical knowledge were only influencing response bias, then the ability to discriminate noise-added from noise-replaced stimuli should not differ for word and nonword contexts. The results completely supported a feedback account. Discriminability, as measured by d', was poorer when the altered phoneme occurred in a word than when it occurred in a nonword, indicating that lexical context was perceptually restoring the altered phoneme.

Samuel also conducted an experiment in which he examined the effects of sentential context on phonemic restoration. Phonemes were altered in words that were either congruous or incongruous with the preceding context. Congruency had a large effect on response bias, with congruous words more likely to be judged as noise-added; however, congruency had no effect on discriminability. This is just the pattern of results predicted by a decision-bias model. Thus, Samuel's results suggest that different mechanisms underlie lexical-context effects on sublexical processing and sentential-context effects on lexical processing. There appears to be feedback between lexical and phonemic representations, but not between the sentential contexts and lexical representations.

To what extent is Samuel's conclusion that sentential context does not provide early feedback in word recognition consistent with the rest of the literature on sentential-context effects? We begin by considering syntactic context.

Syntactic Context
Evidence about the effects of syntactic context comes from three types of studies: studies of lexical ambiguity resolution; studies investigating the response time to recognize a word in a biasing context; and gating studies, in which the amount of sensory input required for a word to be recognized with a certain accuracy is measured.

Several studies have used a cross-modal priming paradigm in which an ambiguous word with a noun sense and a verb sense (e.g., *rose*) is preceded by a context in which only one sense is syntactically appropriate (e.g., *I bought a* or *They all*). Response time is measured to a target related to the contextually appropriate or inappropriate sense (e.g., *flower* or *stood*). Facilitation in responding to the target relative to an unrelated target provides evidence that the sense related to the target was accessed. The question of interest is whether senses of ambiguous words that are syntactically inappropriate are initially accessed. Tanenhaus, Leiman, and Seidenberg (1979) found that latency to name visually presented targets related to both syntactically appropriate and inappropriate senses of ambiguous words were facilitated when the targets were presented immediately after the ambiguous word. When a delay of 200 msec was introduced between the ambiguous word and the target, only targets related to appropriate meanings were facilitated. This result was replicated by Seidenberg, Tanenhaus, Leiman, and Bienkowski (1982). Tanenhaus and Donnenwerth-Nolan (1984) introduced a pause between the context and the ambiguous word to guarantee that subjects had completed the processing of the context before the presentation of the ambiguous word. Targets related to both the syntactically appropriate and inappropriate senses were still initially facilitated. Thus the ambiguity studies suggest that lexical access proceeds independent of syntactic context.

A somewhat more complex story emerges from studies examining response to words in syntactically appropriate and inappropriate contexts. Goodman, McClelland, and Gibbs (1981) found that lexical decisions to target words were faster when they were syntactically appropriate continuations of a prime word (e.g. *they laugh*) than when they were syntactically inappropriate continuations (e.g. *it laugh*). A similar effect of syntactic context was reported by Lukatela, Kostic, Feldman, and Turvey (1983), who found that lexical decisions to nouns in Serbo-Croatian were faster when the target was preceded by an appropriate preposition than when it was preceded by an inappropriate preposition. However, these lexical-decision results may be due to decision bias rather than to feedback. Goodman et al. (1981) also conducted an experiment in which syntactic primes were intermixed with semantic primes in which the prime and the target were semantically related. Under these conditions no effects of syntactic appropriateness obtained, leading the authors to conclude that their syntactic priming effects were strategic. This conclusion was supported by Seidenberg, Waters, Sanders, and Langer (1984), who compared naming and lexical decision in a range of different situations in which priming effects had been reported in the literature, including syntactic priming. They found no evidence for syntactic priming using the materials of Goodman et al. when the subject's task was to name the target word. This result is important because naming was, in general, found to be less sensitive to strategic priming (that is, decision bias) than lexical decision.

It could, however, be argued that the syntactic contexts (one word) in these studies were too impoverished to have activated normal mechanisms of syntactic processing. Wright and Garrett (1984) found syntactic context effects in lexical decision using full sentential contexts. These effects cannot be attributed to decision bias in the lexical decision task, because they have recently been replicated by West and Stanovich (1986) using the naming task. Although these results seem to suggest that syntactic context constrains initial lexical access, there is an alternative explanation. Motley, Baars, and Camden (1981) have demonstrated output-editing effects for syntactically ill-formed phrases. Thus, it is possible that output editing is inhibiting the pronunciation of syntactically inappropriate words in the West-Stanovich studies. This explanation places tha loci of the syntactic-context effect at an output stage rather than at a recognition stage.

Two empirical results suggest to us that the output-editing explanation may be correct. First, West and Stanovich (1986) found that their syntactic-context effects were purely inhibitory, and inhibitory effects are generally associated with later processes than facilitatory effects (Neely 1977). Second, we have recently completed a study that demonstrates syntactic-output editing in naming. Our materials were modifications of those used by Wright and Garrett (1984) and West and Stanovich (1986). We used syntactic contexts consisting of a phrase ending in a modal verb, such as *They thought that they might* .... Subjects read the context and then named a target. The target was a verb, either appropriately inflected (e.g. *compete*) or inappropriately inflected (e.g. *competes*). We also included appropriately and inappropriately inflected nonwords (e.g. *condete* and *condetes,*). As expected, inappropriately inflected words took longer to name than appropriately inflected words. The nonword conditions were of primary interest. If the syntactic contexts were having their effect during word recognition, then no effects of appropriateness should have obtained for the nonwords. However, the appropriateness effects in the nonword condition were similar in size to the effects in the word condition, indicating that the effects were not lexical. Although this result demonstrates that nonlexical grammaticality effects can occur in naming, our results are of limited generality in that we manipulated verb inflection and not the appropriateness of the syntactic class of the target word as Wright and Garrett and West and Stanovich did. Thus, we cannot rule out the possibility that the effects in these studies were lexical, although we think it unlikely.

Further evidence that syntactic context does not guide word recognition comes from a "gating" study in which Tyler and Wessels (1983) measured tha amount of sensory input necessary to identify a word with a certain accuracy. They found no significant effects of syntactic context. Although the gating paradigm does not distinguish between feedback and decision bias, it is a powerful global measure of context effects. Thus, the failure of Tyler and Wessels to observe syntactic-context effects provides compelling evidence against the claim that syntactic context guides lexical access.

A Connectionist Explanation

Why might feedback obtain between lexical and phonemic processing but not between syntactic and lexical processing? Let us examine how feedback might be implemented for each of these cases in the localist connectionist framework discussed above. Our analysis develops some ideas initially presented by Tanenhaus and Lucas (1986).

Lexical nodes and phonemic nodes are arranged in a part-whole relationship: Each word consists, in part, of an ordered set of phonemes, and an ordered set of phonemes constitutes a word. Levels of representation arranged in a part-whole relationship have several interesting properties. First, there are relatively direct connections between levels without any binding nodes. Second, the feedback is restricted; only those phonemes constituting a lexical item will receive direct feedback from that item. For example, if the unit representing the lexical item DOG is activated, only the D, O, and G nodes will receive direct feedback. Finally, the conditional probability than a lower-level unit (e.g. a phoneme) is present given the presence of a higher-level unit (e.g. a word) approaches 1.0. This is important because connectionist modelers are beginning to use conditional probabilities to set connection strengths (Hinton and Sejnowski 1983; Shastri 1985). Thus, the top-down connection strengths from a unit to its parts should be as strong as or stronger than the connections from the parts to the whole, as the probability of D given DOG is higher than the probability of DOG given D. Under these conditions, feedback will not only be effective in helping to clean up noisy perceptual input, it will do so practically without cost.

By way of contrast, consider how syntactic contexts might provide feedback to lexical items. In order for syntactic information to constrain lexical access, feedback must be provided to lexical items that would be appropriate grammatical continuations. Syntactic constraints are expressed in terms of syntactic categories. Therefore, in a localist connectionist model the feedback would come from a node representing a grammatical category to a lexical node. Unlike the part-whole relationship between phonemes and words, the relationship between a grammatical category and a lexical item is one of set membership. When nodes are in a set-membership relationship, the activation of the higher-level node will send activation to all members of the set. As the size of the set increases, feedback will generally become less efficient because it will fail to discriminate among possible alternatives. The number of syntactic categories in natural languages is quite small, whereas the number of lexical items that are members of these categories is extremely large (for major syntactic categories, at least). The size of the possible feedback set is increased even more because in a particular syntactic context several syntactic categories are usually grammatical possibilities, and because many lexical items can be members of more than one grammatical category. Thus, feedback from syntactic categories to lexical items would be relatively inefficient.

In addition, connections between nodes representing grammatical categories and lexical items will have to be mediated by other connections. Recall that binding nodes are necessary in order to connect nodes representing lexical items to nodes representing terminal syntactic categories. Without such nodes the assignment of lexical items to terminal syntactic categories would be indeterminate if any category were used twice. Recall that it is also necessary for incompatible binders to be mutually inhibitory. The result is that a pathway for syntactic-lexical feedback does not become established until the appropriate binding node receives enough activation to prevail in its winner-take-all network. It turns out that this does not happen until bottom-up input from lexical nodes has arrived.

To see why this should be true, consider a situation in which a single syntactic category is expected (for example, VERB following AUX). The expectation of a verb can be assumed to be coded in the network as a highly activated node (e.g. V3), representing a particular syntactic role for that category. This node would have the potential for providing relatively early feedback to all verbs, except that the binding nodes stand in the way blocking early feedback. When activation from V3 reaches all the V3 binders (V3/run, V3/see, etc.), it will stop because these binding nodes are all mutually inhibitory and prevent one another from accumulating activation. A winner will not emerge until bottom-up input arrives from an activated lexical item. It is likely that the time for one binder to win the competition will be related to the size of the syntactic category. With large categories, such as N, V, and Adj, a large amount of inhibition needs to be overcome, and feedback will be late. With minor categories, however, such as Det and Aux, these models may allow for somewhat earlier feedback to lexical nodes. However, as long as the category is larger than a very few words, the binding nodes will act as a barrier preventing feedback between syntactic and lexical nodes.

Thus far we have considered two extreme cases: lexical-phonemic feedback, where the conditions are optimal for early feedback, and syntactic-lexical feedback, where early feedback appears unlikely. We now turn to a consideration of sentential-lexical feedback, where the feedback is provided by nonsyntactic mechanisms.

Because the literature on sentential-context effects in lexical processing is extensive and somewhat disorderly, we will not attempt an extensive review. Instead we will highlight a few important results and then make some suggestions about how these results might be explained within the framework we have been developing.

One of the difficulties in evaluating sentential-lexical context effects is that researchers have generally not been explicit about the mechanism by which the sentential context exerts its influence. In part this is a general theoretical problem. While it is relatively easy to specify the syntactic constraints that a context places on a lexical item, it is much more difficult to specify how semantic and pragmatic context might constrain lexical access. Perhaps the most detailed study of sentential context effects on word recognition has been that of Stanovich and West (1983), who have explored the influence of context on latency to pronounce a target word that is presented as a completion of a sentence. They compared the recognition times for words that are contextually congruous, words that are contextually incongruous, and words that are neutral with respect to context. Their results can be summarized as follows:

• Facilitatory effects are obtained for words in congruous contexts relative to the neutral control when the target immediately follows its context.
• Inhibitory effects for words in incongruous contexts obtain only when a delay is introduced between the context and the target.

Stanovich and West argue that facilitatory effects are due to automatic spreading activation within the lexicon, whereas the slower inhibitory effects are due to a controlled attentional shift. Because word recognition is highly skilled and very fast in accomplished readers, Stanovich and West argue that only the rapid facilitatory effects normally influence word recognition. Whether or not this story holds for auditory word recognition is controversial. On the one hand, the cross-modal ambiguity studies, which have found that context does not constrain initial lexical access (see Simpson 1984 and Tanenhaus and Lucas 1986 for reviews), and Samuel's (1981) study are consistent with Stanovich and West's conclusion. On the other hand, there are a number of studies in which sentential context speeds word-recognition decisions (e.g. Marslen-Wilson and Welsh 1978; Marlsen-Wilson and Tyler 1980a; Tyler and Wessels 1983). However, the theoretical implications of many of these results are complicated by the difficulty of ruling out decision-bias interpretations. We will use the results of Stanovich and West as a starting point.

Following Forster (1979), Stanovich and West assume that facilitatory effects are due to spreading activation within the lexicon—the same mechanism that is assumed to account for lexical priming effects. Two kinds of connections could be used to explain these effects. The first would be connections between lexical nodes. Thus the lexical nodes representing *dog* and *cat* might be share facilitatory connections. As a result, activation of the *dog* node would partially activate the *cat* node. It is inappropriate to consider these kinds of lateral facilitatory connections to be a source of feedback (because they connect units at the same level of representation), but they could provide a brute-force source of contextual facilitation (Fodor 1983). However, these connections are insufficient to account for the range of priming effects observed in the literature. For example, they cannot account for why lexical priming is sensitive to ambiguity resolution, or for priming between semantically related words that are not associated (see Tanenhaus and Lucas 1986).

Results such as these would seem to indicate that facilitatory semantic effects in word recognition are due to conceptual-lexical feedback rather than lateral connections among lexical nodes. Assume that word senses activate semantic feature nodes and that these nodes can then send feedback to all words sharing the activated feature. Word senses can be directly connected to feature nodes, and vice versa—no binding nodes will be necessary. As is the case for phonemes and words, there is a part-whole relationship between conceptual features and word senses (at least on a componential analysis of lexical meaning). Thus feedback will be fast.[5] On the other hand, if it is assumed that the semantic feature vocabulary is small, the feedback set will often be fairly large, although not as large as the feedback set between a syntactic category and lexical nodes. In fact, conceptually mediated feedback is not a particularly useful mechanism for facilitating word recognition, since sentences do not usually contain related words (Gough, Alford, and Holly-Wilcox 1983). However, these kinds of connections would be necessary for choosing words in language production, assuming that during production one must map between conceptual features and lexical items.

We have thus far been considering only those sentential context effects where the recognition of a word is facilitated by the presence of a related word in the context. What about more general message-level context effects? Consider one case that appears to be instructive: feedback from a verb to possible nouns that could serve as arguments of a verb. Take, for example, the sentence *John petted the cat*. In the spirit of Cottrell's (1985a) model, we might have a *furry animal* thematic role, PET/RECIPIENT, activated by the verb *petted*. This node could then send feedback to all nouns sharing the feature *furry animal*, thus partially activating *cat*. However, this kind of feedback would likely have to be mediated by a binding node, because furry animals can play other thematic roles as well. The extent to which these binding nodes would slow feedback would depend in part on the specificity of semantic information associated with the case node. Clearly the set of furry animals is much smaller than the set of animate objects or even the set of touchable objects. The more specific the information associated with a case role, the smaller the set of nodes that could be bound to the case role. However, as was the case for the syntactic effects discussed earlier, the presence of competing binding nodes arranged in a winner-take-all network will act as a barrier to feedback until bottom-up activation from the lexical node supports the appropriate binder. How rapidly this barrier can be overcome may depend on the size of the competing set of nodes.

Conclusions

The conclusion that emerges from our analysis is that different feedback patterns will be associated with different types of contextual information. When the relationship between higher-level and lower-level information can be represented as a stored pattern, as in part-whole relationships, feedback will be rapid. Moreover, under certain circumstances the benefits of such feedback will far outweigh the costs. In contrast, when the re-lationship between the higher-level and the lower-level unit is mediated by units that enter into rules, such as syntactic categories, or case roles, feedback will be much slower.

More generally, our discussion has illustrated several points. First, mas-sively parallel processing systems that communicate by passing activa-tion among hierarchically organized processing levels are not incompati-ble with autonomous processing modules. This is not a trivial point, since connectionist-type models have many of the properties that one would like for modeling language processing and since connectionist models have generally been associated with strong interactionist positions. Second, it appears that the type of feedback that obtains between units representing different levels of representation differs depending upon the type of units and their relationship to one another. We have explored one such differ-ence: the difference between units that have a part-whole relationship and units that have a set membership relationship. This raises the more general hypothesis that neither interactive nor modular language-processing sys-tems emerge because of the design characteristics of the architecture of the language-processing system. Instead, some components of language pro-cessing will be modular and others interactive because of the computational characteristics of the structures that need to be processed.

Our claim has been that whether or not certain linguistic processing decisions can be carried out independent of context depends on the nature of the context. For "stored" part-whole contexts, rapid feedback is the rule; for more computed, categorically mediated contexts, feedback is late. This may, in fact, be a general rule about the modularity of perceptual processes. Consider, for example, the following anecdote. Recently one of us (GSD) experienced a perceptual illusion that paradoxically illustrated both the modularity and the nonmodularity of perceptual identification processes. GSD's cat, a small all-black cat named Ruth, was outside in the very cold and snowy Rochester winter. GSD knew this and was concerned. On the floor inside was a Ruth-size black purse. Although GSD knew Ruth was outside, every time the purse was in his peripheral vision he "saw" her. The illusion persisted in spite of the knowledge. One might think that this simply illustrates the insulation of perceptual processes from belief, which is a hallmark of modularity. The paradoxical aspect is that GSD had never been fooled by the purse before. It was his preoccupation with the cat that (in nonmodular fashion) provided the top-down input to create the illusion. The computational distinction outlined here provides an account of how the "cat thoughts" both leaked down and did not leak down. The belief that Ruth was outside, LOC(RUTH, OUTSIDE, NOW), is a computed representation in which Ruth must be bound to a location. As such, feedback about this state of the world is not available at an early time to the perceptual system. In contrast, the concept RUTH would be directly connected to a RUTH-as-perceptual-object node that stands in a part-whole relationship with the lower-level perceptual features that provide sensory evidence necessary for recognizing Ruth. Because the RUTH-object node was already activated (or at least primed), the sensory input from the black purse was sufficient to signal GSD that he was seeing Ruth.

The hypothesis that this anecdote illustrates is that thoughts (bound relations among concepts) do not contribute to lower-level processing, but the *components* of thoughts (their concepts) may contribute if the thought is important (i.e., activated). This hypothesis reminds us of the distinction between perceptual features and perceptual objects in Triesman and Gelade's (1980) feature-integration theory of attention. In this theory the features (components) of objects are directly available for responses. That is, subjects need not attend to them. Conjunctions of features require the focus of attention before a response contingent on the conjunction can be made. We can thus make an analogy between perceptual features and their conjunctions, on the one hand, and the components of thoughts and the thoughts themselves on the other hand. In both cases the components are easily available to other parts of the system, whereas the computed combination of these components is not automatically delivered elsewhere. We can speculate that this is precisely because the combination of components is computed (i.e., not previously stored) and hence there are no sets of connections in place designed for distributing that specific combination widely throughout the system.

Whether our analogy and our anecdote say anything substantial about processing will, of course, have to await further research. But regardless of the truth of our speculations, we can say that thinking about modularity in connectionist terms has proved useful to us both in clarifying specific hypotheses and in providing accounts of context effects.

Acknowledgments

This research was partially supported by NSF grants BNS-8217378 and BNS-8406886, ONR grant N00014-84-K0655, and NICHHD grant HD-18944. The authors are grateful to Gary Cottrell for discussions about the issues presented here and to Jerry Feldman and Susan Garnsey for comments on the paper.

Notes

1. The use of the term *connectionism* should not be taken to imply that there is a monolithic connectionist doctrine. We use the term, somewhat reluctantly, for stylistic reasons.

2. Our use of the term *modularity* is closely related to Fodor's (1983) notion, though not identical. Fodor's the notion of modularity depends heavily on the hypothesis that the "input systems" involve propositional representations. We, on the other hand, wish to define "modularity" operationally, in terms of the organization of processing systems. An entirely "modular" system would consist of a set of operations the internal structure of which would be unaffected by information in any form that lay outside the system proper. This would include a processing model based on Fodor's ideas, but it allows for other arrangements as well. (See Tanenhaus, Carlson, and Seidenberg 1985 for further discussion.)

3. Top-down inhibitory connections are permitted in the connectionist framework, but they have not been used in any models that we are familiar with.

4. We do not wish to claim that this is an adequate semantic representation. In particular, thematic roles should be assigned to noun phrases and not to nouns. However, the examples serve to illustrate the basic form of semantic representation within a connectionist network.

5. Patrizia Tabossi has recently demonstrated that only the contextually appropriate sense of an ambiguous word is activated when the context emphasizes a property that can be considered part of the definition (loosely speaking) of one of the senses of the ambiguous word. For instance, only the "harbor" sense of the ambiguous word *port* would be activated in a context that emphasized that a captain was looking for a safe place for his ship. According to the story we have outlined. Tabossi's contexts lead to early feedback effects through conceptually mediated priming in much the same way as in lexical contexts.

II

Semantics, Syntax, and Learnability

Introduction
Steven Weisler

The chapters in part II express different points of view with regard to modularity, and operate in two different analytic traditions. Higginbotham, Hornstein, and Weisler explore several issues arising within the framework of Chomsky's Extended Standard Theory as they bear on modularity in several distinct senses of the term. Grimshaw is concerned with language learning and modularity. Her discussion, which also assumes a version of the EST, considers work by Baker (1979), Wexler and Culicover (1980), and Pinker (1984) on learnability theory.

Flynn and Steedman investigate topics in modularity in the rather different framework of categorial grammar (Ajdukiewicz 1935; Montague 1973; Ades and Steedman 1982; Bach 1983). This welcome broadening of the debate on modularity is noteworthy—these are, to my knowledge, among the first papers on modularity to be published by linguists working outside the EST.

Here I will briefly discuss the major conclusions and locate the main arguments contained in these chapters. I will also highlight the implications of the theses developed therein for a theory of modularity, and hence their (sometimes indirect) connections to one another.

Higginbotham (chapter 5), on his way to defending the standard view that linguistic theory is a theory of linguistic knowledge in the light of Fodor's claim that language is an input module, first takes up the autonomy of syntax from semantics. After a brief discussion of the analysis of quantification islands in relative clauses developed in Rodman 1976, Higginbotham contrasts the style of explanation of this phenomenon that relies on conditions on representations at Logical Form (May 1977, 1985; Hornstein 1984) with the style that depends on conditions on the computation of meaning representations (Cooper 1983). Although these two rather different types of analyses are often taken to represent rival syntactic and semantic explanations for quantification, Higginbotham argues that what an analysis of quantifier scope (such as Cooper's) that places restrictions on the calculation of interpretations registers is "as much a syntactic fact as a semantic fact." He submits that analyses such as Cooper's or the allegedly semantic analysis of reflexive binding in Pollard and Sag 1983 do not threaten the autonomy of syntax, and suggests that only analyses that characterize well-formedness by appealing directly to meaning would constitute such a threat. Higginbotham then briefly considers linguistic analyses that seem to pose such problems (i.e., the patterns of distribution of *among* and *between* [Chomsky 1980a]), and concludes with a defense of autonomy.

Higginbotham's next point concerns the mental representation of grammars. On this topic, he is at pains to distinguish "representing what is known" from "representing how what is known is represented by the knower." He maintains that linguistic constructs such as sentences, nouns, and phrase markers are not themselves likely candidates for mental representations but rather are working characterizations of what is known that stop short of analyzing how the knowledge they represent is actually represented in the mind.

Higginbotham next turns to a discussion of the autonomy of syntax and semantics from other cognitive capacities or processes in which he addresses some of Fodor's (1983) claims about modularity. Part of Higginbotham's burden here is to argue that, given a characterization of modularity that depends on the familiar cluster of properties that Fodor has identified (e.g. informational encapsulation, mandatoriness of operation, speed), there is no reason to conclude that grammatical knowledge is solely manifest in a production/perception system. Rather, linguistic competence not only subserves fast, mandatory processing but also provides the basis for the formation of linguistic intuitions, fosters judgments that arise from reflection, and can aid in recovery from perceptual garden paths. All this is to be expected, Higginbotham contends, if the object of linguistic inquiry is taken to be linguistic knowledge.

Higginbotham next considers a position (which he identifies as Fodor's, with a caveat that it may be somewhat strongly stated) according to which a putative feature of language can be assigned by a linguistic theory in the description of a linguistic object if and only if its assignment follows from the action of the language-processing module. Principles of scope assignment would be counterexamples to this claim, given Fodor's view that such principles are not computed in the language input module, or so the recent practice of linguists as discussed above would suggest.

Higginbotham closes by suggesting—pace Fodor (1983; this volume) —that certain central systems may be modular and hence may be fruitfully explored within the purview of cognitive science. He considers two cases in point, the first being that of the module of knowledge of logic and the second having to do with our phenomonological knowledge of the world.

Thus, Higginbotham emphasizes rather different conclusions from the study of modularity for linguistic theory and cognition. Although he endorses the thesis of the autonomy of syntax from semantics, he defends this principle on internal methodological grounds rather than on the basis of the Fodorian assignment of syntactic analysis to an input system and semantics to a central system. There is disagreement about the range of phenomena analyzed by linguistic theory, about what a linguistic theory is a theory of, and about the architecture of the linguistic module and of the central systems.

Despite these differences of detail, Higginbotham's investigation of modularity is undertaken within the general conceptual framework developed by Fodor. Hornstein (chapter 6) pursues the topic of modularity from a rather different angle. Whereas Higginbotham analyzes the informational relationship between modules devoted to reason and perceptual and linguistic function, Hornstein explores the informational relations between the levels within a single module: the linguistic module. He is interested in the interpretive components of the grammar, and particularly in identifying the submodules within the linguistic module. In particular, he advances the hypothesis that semantic interpretation must proceed at two distinct levels of grammatical analysis: S-structure and LF. At the first of these levels, all non-NP/NP interactions (including opacity, modality, scope of negation, predication, and modification) are calculated primarily on the basis of government relations. Interactions between NPs (such as quantifier scope, reciprocal and pronoun binding, and PRO interpretation) are to be analyzed at LF on the basis of indexing and c-command relations in the familiar manner. Hornstein argues that these two different aspects of interpretation are informationally encapsulated from one another, and that together they constitute a complete interpretation.

Let us examine just one example of S-structure interpretation discussed by Hornstein to get the flavor of his argument. If we suppose for the sake of discussion that *anyone* must be in the scope of negation to be acceptable, the contrast between

(1)   *Anyone was not expected to leave

and

(2)   John does not expect anyone to leave

can be accounted for by a structure in which *not* is restricted to VP-scope, since only in the second case is *anyone* c-commanded by (and hence in the scope of) negation. If we establish the scope of negation at S-structure, such an account goes through. However, if we attempt to establish the scope of negation at LF, we run into difficulty.

The root of the problem has to do with the fact that, on a popular analysis, passivized subjects such as *anyone* in (1) must be lowered and adjoined to the lower clause to account for the correct range of interpretations (May 1977; Hornstein 1984; Aoun and Hornstein 1985). After lowering, this results in a structure like

(3)   e was [$_{VP}$ not expected [$_S$ anyone$_i$ [$_S$ t$_i$ to leave]]].

Unfortunately, after lowering, *anyone* is within the scope of negation, as (3) shows. Therefore, if we were to establish the scope of negation at LF, we would mistakenly predict that lowering can "save" (1). In contrast, an analysis of scope of negation that takes place at S-structure (and consequently prior to lowering) makes just the correct prediction.

On the basis of this and related arguments, Hornstein finds evidence for a bifurcated interpretive component for which both S-structure and LF provide the inputs. This forces him to give up the "Strong Consolidation Thesis," which holds that all interpretation takes place at the single level of LF. Hornstein also rejects the "weak consolidation" thesis, which holds that "all interpretive structures are derivationally related to one another." By this he means that S-structure interpretation goes on independent of LF interpretation. Furthermore, since each of these stages of interpretation involves different primitives and relations, Hornstein suggests that they are informationally encapsulated from one another, and consequently that the linguistic module contains other, separate modules within itself. This suggests that the mind may be hierarchically modular, and that the Fodorian characterization of modularity can be extended from a macroscopic to a more microscopic level of analysis.

In chapter 7 I examine Hornstein's analysis of opacity, with special attention to how it interacts with ellipsis. Hornstein's conclusion that (unlike quantifier scope ambiguities) the *de re*/*de dicto* distinction cannot be analyzed at Logical Form is accepted, but Hornstein's alternative in which the former are calculated at LF is argued against, and the latter is analyzed at S-structure. It is pointed out that, as Sag (1976) and Williams (1977) note, the operation of VP-ellipsis is sensitive to both kinds of relations, suggesting that both must be represented at a single stage of analysis although they are analyzed by distinct mechanisms. It is also contended that the two aspects of interpretation are not encapsulated but rather are both determined within a single module.

Grimshaw begins chapter 10 by distinguishing two mental modules (or cognitive capacities): the grammatical representation system and the grammar-selection system. She considers several different relations that might hold between these two systems, among which is the intriguing possibility that they are organized by fairly different principles. If so, the two systems pass the encapsulation criterion, as is required, in Fodor's view, for them to qualify as distinct modules. In general, it will be the interaction between the two systems that accounts for the nature of the acquired grammar and the process of acquisition. Although early work on formal learning theory (Baker 1979; Wexler and Culicover 1980) tended to pursue restrictions on grammars as the way of accounting for learnability, more recent work carried out by Wexler and his associates places a greater responsibility for its explanation on the grammar-selection mechanism. Grimshaw reconsiders the account of the acquisition of the English dative alternation presented in Baker 1979 from this new perspective, and concludes by suggesting several alternatives that depend more substantially on properties of the grammar-selection system than did Baker's analysis. Thus, Grimshaw seeks to extend our conception of the sort of cognitive processes that can constitute modules. Not only are mature capacities candidates, but we must also consider second-order capacities—in this case, the capacity to learn a language.

Flynn (chapter 8) and Steedman (chapter 9) develop their positions with regard to modularity in a grammatical framework that presumes that the syntactic component takes the form of a categorial grammar. Despite this common thread, they come to rather different conclusions with regard to the issue of modularity.

To examine the status of modularity in an alternative grammatical framework, Flynn begins by substituting a categorial base for the more common $\overline{X}$ syntax employing context-free rewriting rules. This produces a hybrid grammatical framework which is otherwise understood to conform to the principles of the Government and Binding theory. The version of the categorial base and corresponding semantics that Flynn adopts is inspired by recent work by Chierchia (1984, 1985). The syntax involves three types of categories: basic categories (e.g. S and NP), predicates (e.g $V_t(S/NP/NP)$ and $V_i(S/NP)$), and functors (e.g. VP adverbs (IV//IV) and DET(NP//CN)). Members of the first type of category (the basic category of expressions) denote things, which are here understood to include propositions as the *denotata* of sentences. Both types of "fractional" categories correspond to functions, but in the theory of the model that Flynn adopts only members of the class of predicates also "correspond to individuals in the ontology."

In addition to this categorial base, Flynn adopts the $AFFIX_n$ template of Chierchia (1985) as a substitute for the Theta-Criterion to handle concatenation and "wrapping" rules (Bach 1980), a condition on node admissability he calls *connection*, and a language-specific principle for left-to-right ordering.

Against this background, Flynn's main question then emerges: Does such a theory of grammar have the property of domain specificity? Given that Universal Grammar specifies the biologically necessary properties of human languages, the issue is focused by defining the "language organ" as the domain-specific part of Universal Grammar. We can then ask whether the language organ exhausts Universal Grammar, whether it is included in Universal Grammar, or whether it is null. Flynn identifies Chomsky's and

Piaget's positions on this topic as being at the respective extremes. His goal is to argue for the middle road.

The nub of Flynn's argument is that the tight connection between syntactic and semantic categories in his theory of grammar, and the corresponding and equally tight connection between semantic categories and the kinds of things in one's ontology, imply that "the way we organize the world and the way we hierarchically organize the expressions we use to speak of the world are, in a sense, two sides of the same coin." Flynn generalizes this argument into a picture of the architecture of the mind in which there may be distinct modules, each contributing to the functioning of a number of cognitive domains. In the case under consideration, the structure of our ontological and syntactic categories would be determined by a single defining principle located in a single module. As a consequence, the determination of our syntactic categories, based as it is on the nature of ontological categories, is inherently nonlinguistic but may nevertheless follow from universal principles which fall outside the language organ. This view challenges the position that the functions of the language module are executed without reference to information in other encapsulated modules.

Steedman presents a somewhat different version of categorial grammar, supplemented with combinators as employed in the combinatory logic of Curry and Feys (1958). The combinatory grammar that results handles the part of a language that can be generated by a standardly formulated context-free phrase-structure grammar with a rule of functional application similar to that in Montague 1973, but can also account for constructions involving long-distance dependencies which have traditionally been analyzed with transformational rules. For example, one of the combinatory operations that is introduced, called *composition*, allows a topicalized constituent to be directly combined with the sister clause from which it is dislocated. The adjacent constituents are construed as syntactic functions which can compose with one another to form an S/NP constituent, which in turn combines with the dislocated NP by the rule of functional application. A second combinator, substitution, allows parasitic gap sentences to be directly composed, again, without appeal to transformations.

After sketching how combinatory operations can facilitate syntactic description and tracing their history in mathematical logic, Steedman concludes by asking why natural languages include combinatory operations, and what implications such an analysis has for the theory of sentence processing. The latter question leads him to a discussion of the status of the claims that are made concerning the modular nature of linguistic theory, considered relative to his theory of grammar. Although Steedman asserts that "an unusually high degree of parallelism is claimed to hold between syntax, processing, semantics, and even the inference system," he goes on to point out that "these components are all formally and computationally autonomous and domain specific, with a distinct 'old look' about them." Thus, whereas Flynn takes the parallelism between cognitive systems to suggest an argument against domain specificity, Steedman does not.

In sum, although these six authors all use the Fodorian conception of modularity as a starting point, each of them extends the reach of these original ideas considerably. The identity of the modules is questioned, their relative shares in our cognitive function are reassessed, and the implications for modularity within the bounds of alternative syntactic theories are considered. Despite the fact that nothing like a shared view is yet emerging, this work collectively points to promising areas for further study which provide a coherent, exciting program. In this regard, the study of the modularity of mind continues to be auspicious.

5

The Autonomy of Syntax and Semantics

James Higginbotham

At this point in the study of linguistics I need not rehearse in detail the often unclear discussion or the historical fate of the thesis of the autonomy of syntax. The considerations in favor of syntactic autonomy that were advanced in Chomsky 1975a, for instance, seem to have been not refuted or vindicated but merely superseded by later developments. Despite analytic differences among contemporary researchers, debates over Chomsky's central examples (the semantics of adverb-preposing, restrictions on scope of quantifiers, the definiteness effect for *there*-insertion sentences, and others) are unlikely to lead to a call to methodological arms.

If the question of the autonomy of syntax has perished or been transformed, another question of autonomy persists in a form that is not markedly different from that in which it first arose: the question whether the human linguistic system constitutes a realm of knowledge having its own characteristic laws and principles.

The practice of syntacticians and semanticists, including those who work in comparative grammar and in developmental psycholinguistics, tentatively assumes that the answer to this question is affirmative. It assumes, that is, that the linguistic system is first of all a system of knowledge, put to use in manifold ways in behavior and mental processes, and that the structure of language and its course of maturation in the normal individual follow a distinctive path that justifies thinking of language as a faculty of the mind. The affirmative answer is a form of autonomy thesis about linguistics that has been questioned since the emergence of generative grammar and defended in different ways by Chomsky and others for many years.

Even in the simple form in which I have sketched it, the autonomy thesis is seen to be a conjunction, liable to objections of two different sorts (or both together). First, since the thesis affirms that language is a system of knowledge and not only of behavior or of inner processes, it is liable to the objection that, as a system of knowledge, it is not special; rather, it might be urged, the characteristic shape of human language is the result of the exercise of our general cognitive powers on a particular realm: that of significant speech. This sort of objection was voiced by Hilary Putnam and others early on. Second, it might be objected that, although language is "special," its peculiar features follow from its being a special system of behavior and mental processes, hence not a system of knowledge at all.

It is the second of these objections to the autonomy of linguistics that I see being advanced on at least one reading of Jerry Fodor's book *The Modularity of Mind*. In a striking passage in that work, Fodor suggests that the fundamental "input systems" for human beings are "the perceptual faculties *plus language*" (Fodor 1983, p. 44; emphasis in original). By this remark, as Fodor makes clear, he means much more than the commonplace that linguistic messages are often perceived with remarkable speed and accuracy. Rather, what is suggested in the passage, and pursued in detail in the subsequent pages, is the thesis that language is an "input module," or a system specially designed for the perception of linguistic objects, characterized by informational encapsulation, mandatoriness of operation, domain specificity, speed, and several other features that collectively make it a module in Fodor's sense of that term. These features indeed underscore the "special" character of language. But they also suggest that linguistic theory is, or ought to be, the theory of what is computed by the special input system—that is, the theory of the outputs of this system (though not of the computation itself).

Fodor's picture of linguistic theory contrasts with the standard picture, according to which grammars represent what people know by providing, for a range of available concepts, formal explications of those concepts or of other concepts in terms of which they may be characterized. Linguistic knowledge flows from the grasp or internalization of a grammar; that is, from the grasp of the very thing that linguistics, if successful, posits to account for that knowledge. Ignorant as we are of what the grasp of a grammar may amount to in terms of the organization of the nervous system, we suppose that it is among the things responsible for what people do, and say, and think.

Evidently, the standard picture is compatible with the existence of special systems for the perception of language (as it had better be, since some such systems are known). What I take to be distinctive about Fodor's proposal is the suggestion that the linguistic realm is exhausted, or exhaustively mirrored by, the action of these perceptual systems. It is this thesis—that language is indeed a special faculty, but that it is special only as a perceptual faculty—that clashes with the autonomy of linguistics in the standard picture as I have described it.

I will approach my topic in an indirect fashion. First, I will review some of the questions that were prominent in the discussion of the autonomy of syntax, and some points about contemporary work. These will serve, I hope, to show how the practice of generative grammarians is to be seen against the background of the autonomy thesis, and to indicate the variety and extent of the realm of linguistic knowledge assumed. Only then will I turn to some of the views in *The Modularity of Mind*, with the aim of clarifying what seems now to be at stake in some issues of language and psychology. One might look forward to a time when these issues will be superseded, as the issue of the autonomy of syntax was superseded, by detailed empirical research. If only to speed the time of supersession, however, some debate may be in order now.

In retrospect, the most interesting phenomena considered by those who questioned the autonomy of syntax had to do with formal conditions on interpretation that were analogous to conditions on well-formedness. Rodman (1976), for example, observed that ordinary quantifiers cannot escape relative clauses, so that (1) is unambiguous.

(1)   [A person who solved every problem] is here

He associated this fact with the prohibition of relativization within a relative clause. On this view, (1) is unambiguous for the same reason that (2) is ungrammatical.

(2)   *Which problem is [a person who solved ___] here?

A common explanation of the status of (1) and (2) might, therefore, seem to violate the thesis of the autonomy of syntax. Chomsky (1974) disagreed with Rodman's analogy; however, May (1977) endorsed it, finding both (2) and the wide-scope representation of the quantifier in (1), namely (3), in violation of a proposed subjacency condition at the level LF of Logical Form.

(3)   every problem [[a person who solved t] is here]

May, therefore, offered a straightforwardly syntactic account of the very facts (or association of facts) in question.

Now, Rodman's analogy between (2) and the absence of a wide-scope interpretation of (1) is rather questionable. The prohibition against relativization within a relative is a very strong one, found in languages that do not express relativization by *wh*-movement, such as Navajo (Barss et al. 1985). On the other hand, *wh*-expressions themselves can have wide scope even when they are in relative clauses, as noted in Cooper 1979 and Higginbotham 1980.[1] Nevertheless, data and explanations of the sort that Rodman proposed have become commonplace.

In a theory with LF, the clause-boundedness of ordinary quantification is rather naturally (though not inevitably) expressed in terms of conditions on well-formedness at that level. The alternative framework of Cooper would specify bounding in terms of the outputs of computations of representations of meaning (see especially pp. 136–137 of Cooper 1983). Whether Rodman's observation is to be explained in terms of conditions on LF or in terms of conditions on the computation of interpretations does not affect the syntactic character of the analysis; that a course of computation of the meanings of expressions in L is constrained to work in one way rather than another is a syntactic fact about L, or at least as much a syntactic fact as a semantic fact. Conversely, the ungrammaticality of (3) does not by itself explain why (1) is unambiguous; what we would need in addition is a semantics that, to put it counterfactually, has the consequence that if (1) were ambiguous, then (3) is the structure that would deliver the meaning that it does not in fact have.[2] The difference between the LF approach and Cooper's approach is just the difference between conditions on levels, or filters, and conditions on transformations. It is my impression that this point is sometimes obscured.[3]

Common to all approaches now being pursued is the assumption that conditions on such matters as the relative scopes of quantifiers belong to the linguistic system. These conditions connect form and meaning, and are therefore both syntactic and semantic in character. Under these circumstances, what can the "autonomy of syntax" amount to?

A version of the thesis of autonomy of syntax can indeed be stated, as the thesis that conditions on well-formedness are purely formal, and make no reference to meaning. However, apart from made-up examples, where one simply stipulates that well-formedness is to be sensitive to certain semantic conditions, I am not aware of any serious candidates for counterexamples to autonomy as just construed. Once we distinguish well-formedness from semantic coherence (both of these being theoretical notions, distinct from each other and distinct also from the intuitive notion of acceptability), things fall into place within ongoing research, without precipitating terminological quarrels.

Consider in this respect Chomsky's (1980a) example concerning the use of the prepositions *between* and *among* in the dialect of English where *between* is to be used when its object is a binary conjunction of singulars and *among* is not to be used when its object fails to denote at least three things. If, in this dialect, I say *There is no love lost among the Smiths*, there had better be at least three Smiths. What should be said about this sentence in a context where there are only two Smiths? More simply, how are mistakes like (4) to be evaluated?

(4)   There are no differences among this and that

This example is unacceptable; but, considering it as English, I see no reason to think of it as not well formed. The general principle that one can speak of what is going on *among* a bunch of things only if there are at least three things in question is like the principle than one can speak of a comestible as addled only if it is an egg (Quine 1951). It seems that (4) is best thought of as a category mistake, or a violation of what Quine (1951) calls "stage-directions for the use of language." Now we could, perhaps, stipulate a language having the property that (4) was not well formed. The stipulation would not be routine, since we would have to ensure that conditions on form and interpretation were simultaneously well defined. To identify the made-up language with English would require some argument. More significant, it seems that we would not learn anything more about the nature of grammar by such identification. Insofar as the phenomena are explained by the interpretation of *among* as something like *'in re* (said of groups of three things or more)', which is on a par with the interpretation of *addled* as *'spoiled* (said of eggs)', there does not seem to be any motivation for complications in the syntax.

The proper theory of semantic categories and the nature of category mistakes—widened (if I am right) to include the incoherencies of (4) and other incoherencies—still pose questions. These questions have long lain fallow, because of the decline of interest in analyticity. Perhaps they will become important again; however, they do not seem to raise problems of principle for linguistic research.

A native speaker of the English language knows the facts about the clause-boundedness of quantification, the facts about the meanings of words, and much more. How does linguistic theory characterize this knowledge? Consider a simple example of linguistic questions and answers at work: the issue of the unacceptability of the putative NP

(5)   a baker in ovens

as meaning a person x such that x bakes things in ovens. Sproat's (1985) analysis of this fact is that attachment of the affix -*er* to a verb, at the same time it selects the agent or actor position in that verb for predication (a baker is a thing that bakes, not a thing that is baked), has the effect of closing off the verbal position for events or states of affairs of the kind that the verb is true of.[4] The PP *in ovens*, however, is not subcategorized for by *bake*, and so must be licensed by predication of the position for events, as in fact it is in

(6)   He bakes in ovens

(which means that he typically bakes things in ovens, not in kilns; or that, when bakings by him take place, the bakings occur in ovens). Suppose that Sproat's answer to the question of the peculiar status of (5) is correct. Then a proposed grammar that incorporates this answer represents something that speakers of English know about (5)—in this case by having the property that the expression *baker in ovens* is not a well-formed N' true of persons x such that x bakes things in ovens.

English speakers of course reject (5). The explanation that Sproat's hypothesis provides for this phenomenon is the following: Knowing as they do that the English affix *-er* has the property described, knowing that the PP *in ovens* is not licensed by a position for events or states of affairs in the noun *baker*, and knowing that it must be so licensed if it is to be incorporated into the complex noun *baker in ovens*, they reject the NP *a baker in ovens* as bizarre. Explanations of their rejection of (4) or of the uniqueness of interpretation of (1) would proceed similarly.

The explanations just offered are of the form that Fodor calls *neo-Cartesian*. Fodor (1983, pp. 9 ff.) points out that in such explanations a gap between premises and conclusion goes unfilled; a simple neo-Cartesian explanation does not specify how a person who has the knowledge ascribed goes on to apply that knowledge in such a way that the judgment made emerges. In addition to the rules of grammar, we must have ways of applying the rules to particular cases and ways of conforming our perceptions and actions to what the rules deliver.

The point is a conceptual one, and it is independent of the "neo-Cartesian" character of linguistic explanation. Suppose I explain that Mary renewed her investment in AT&T because she believed that utilities do well in times of low inflation. Then Mary must have had, besides her general belief, a way of applying it to the case at hand and ways of conforming her actions to her rational conclusions. Explanations of judgment made by knowledge had always have gaps: whether explicit or tacit, and whether its application requires inference or not, knowledge alone does not bring forth behavior.

Yet knowledge of language manifests itself in judgment and in behavior. Students of linguistics apart, people do not often direct themselves to make judgments about the status of linguistic objects. But judgments that involve knowledge of language, even if not themselves linguistic judgments in the narrower sense, are very frequent. One thinks first of spontaneous interpretation, or of speaking. But thinking and planning what to say, and considering the different ways that one might interpret what someone has said, also involve knowledge of language. Suppose that I am on the point of speaking, and that—recognizing that what I was going to say would be ambiguous and therefore liable to misinterpretation—I switch at once to a more precise way of expressing myself. Then I have used my knowledge of language, even though nothing may have happened that my auditors could detect.

These observations suggest that the rules of grammar, being manifested in behavior and mental processes of the most diverse kinds, are not at the service of any particular mechanism. They are, in other words, a central resource, with many applications.

The conception of language as a central resource is seen also from the developmental point of view, at least in its "neo-Cartesian" manifestation. The methods and idealizations that are there standardly employed rely upon the correctness of two bets on the acquisition process. The first bet (whose most general expression is to be found in formal learning theory) is that the language that a person comes up with is a function of linguistic experience rather than of experience of other kinds. This bet would prove to have been misplaced if it should turn out, say, that the degree of parental affection a child receives has large consequences for the nature of the grammar that the child acquires. The second bet is that linguistic experience influences language projected in a way that is controlled by reason (that is, controlled by the principles of the language faculty, or the universal grammar in Chomsky's sense). From these principles, we assume, a grammar is deduced, given experience as evidence. (The principles themselves are, of course, not postulates of reason in any sense.) This bet would be wrong if linguistic experience affected grammar in ways that, although formally specifiable within the vocabulary of linguistics, did not stand to that grammar in the way of evidence at hand to hypothesis advanced. In other words, neo-Cartesianism is involved in linguistics both in explaining action and behavior on the basis of knowledge and in explaining how persons come to know the premises from which those explanations proceed. Now, it is not surprising that these bets should be correct if in fact the linguistic system is a system of knowledge.

A number of theorists speak of themselves as aiming to understand language as a system of mental representations. If only to preclude misunderstanding, it may be worthwhile to clarify this matter before proceeding. In constructing theories of knowledge, it is needful to distinguish representing what is known from representing how what is known is represented by the knower. A grammar, which represents what a person knows about language, does not in virtue of this power alone represent how the person represents that knowledge. Naturally, it is a good thing to know both what is represented and how it is represented; and it may seem that one can combine these aims by thinking of the elements of what is known as themselves mental representations. I think that this move breeds confusion. In the case of grammar in particular, I believe that a great deal of confusion has been caused by thinking of the typical notions of grammar, notions such as *noun* and *sentence*, as notions of mental representations. I assume that grammar is represented in the mind; to endorse that proposition is just to identify language as a faculty. But the way I see it, there is no more reason to say that nouns or sentences are mental representations than there is to say that numbers, or even chairs or human beings, are mental representations. What goes for parts of speech goes also for more complex objects such as phrase markers, conceived along any of the currently available models: The phrase markers are not representations, but rather what persons who know language have representations of. Now, as I have argued elsewhere (Higginbotham 1983), this circumstance does not deprive linguistic theory of its claim to be a chapter of epistemology or of psychology. We are not, in linguistics, interested in the abstract structures of possible languages for their own sakes; rather, we would like to know which of those structures are or can be the languages of human beings, and how come.

Confusion about mental representation can lead, and in my opinion has led, to an overemphasis on the power of notations to effect explanations in linguistics. If one thought that the objects of grammar were representations, then one might think that the importation of some notational feature, constrained to do the work one specified, was superior to a mere statement of the facts, and one might not distinguish the case where the notation does some work beyond what was put into it from the case where it doesn't.[5]

Above I contrasted Cooper's (1983) view of quantification in natural language with that of May (1977), and more generally with views that propose conditions on well-formedness at the hypothetical level LF. Now, Cooper's view was in part motivated by an emphasis on the autonomy of syntax.[6] But it should be clear that, if my comparison of Cooper's view with the LF view is correct, syntax is exactly as autonomous on the latter as it is on the former. So these views are neither notational variants nor representatives of incomparable frameworks; rather, they are hypotheses about grammar, at most one of which is true. (Of course, the likelihood is that both are false.) Again, they are not rival schemes of mental representation but rival theses about what is represented.

I have said that on one reading of *The Modularity of Mind* the contents of linguistic theory are said or implied to be confined to a particular aspect of the use of language—in fact, to the perception of linguistic objects, or perhaps to perception together with some production system.[7] The conceptual point that I have cited is meant by Fodor not as an argument for this view but merely as an indication of the need to supplement the neo-Cartesian theory if one is to get a full picture of linguistic activity. But the conceptual point, given the range of activity in which the rules of grammar are involved, casts doubt on the view.

It is time to try to specify more precisely what Fodor's view might be taken to be. His characterization of language as an "input system" invites the conclusion that linguistic theory just *is* the theory of the action of this system; however, Fodor clearly does not intend this consequence, if only because he suggests that a representation of grammar is internal to the parsing mechanism. The consequence, anyway, is dubious in the extreme, inasmuch as language is not just perceived but is also produced (under the same rules). Every English speaker knows that the expression *John's dog* refers to John's dog (if it refers to anything), and knows also that it does not express the proposition that John is a dog. Are these facts about that phrase just facts about how we parse it? Evidently not. It is not just that the words *John's dog* will spontaneously be understood in one way rather than another, for they will also be uttered with one intent rather than another, entertained in thought with one meaning and not another, and so forth. Despite the continued popularity of the question whether grammars are "psychologically real," and the conviction that their "reality" is to be shown (if at all) in the operations of "the parser," the idea that parsing is what the theory of grammar is about is not to be taken seriously; we don't just listen, we talk and think too.

Although Fodor does not think of grammar as just the theory of linguistic perception, he also does not, as I understand him, intend only to assert that the perception of language is accomplished by a special modular system. The latter thesis indeed fits with the cognitive impenetrability of perception (in the sense of Pylyshyn 1980), and in drawing a sharp line between perception and cognition it takes a stand on a controversial empirical question; however, that alone is not sufficient to warrant the picture of language as an input system. I should like to consider the thesis to be this: that all and only those features of language that figure in the structural descriptions of linguistic objects as given in linguistic theory are the features that attach to linguistic inputs as a result of the action of the perceptual module for language. Even if this thesis is stronger than Fodor intends or not carefully enough qualified, I think that it is significant enough in its own right to be worth further consideration. Because I think it is at any rate close to Fodor's intentions, I shall call it "Fodor's thesis," with I hope pardonable license.

Fodor's thesis is biconditional, and may be separated into its two parts. In one direction it says that what the perceptual module delivers is a linguistic description; i.e., that perception makes use only of those categories, principles of organization, and linguistic relations that are given in linguistic theory. This proposition is not so controversial, although it is hardly analytic; we could easily conceive of a perceptual device that yielded up interpretations of linguistic objects by means of various heuristic devices that bore only a distant relation to the descriptions of those objects in grammatical theory. In the other direction, Fodor's thesis is that only those categories, principles, and linguistic relations that figure in perception belong to grammatical theory. This half is more controversial, and critical.

Consider, for example, two features of language that Fodor suggests are, or may be, ruled out of properly linguistic description in virtue of his thesis. One of these is analytic definition, including the use of "semantic postulates," or other inferential principles connecting sentences to sentences (see Fodor 1983, especially pp. 91 ff.). Another is relative scopes of quantifiers (ibid., p. 135, note 29). Naturally, since native speakers do know about these inferential principles (whether or not they reflect analyticity, strictly so-called), and since they do know about scopal ambiguities, these features of language are reflected somewhere—perhaps in a "postcomprehensive inferential process," as Fodor suggests (p. 92). But knowledge about them is then not grammatical knowledge; such is the conclusion if the grammar is internal to the perceptual system, and that system does not show any use of inferential principles, or disambiguation by relative scopes.

I remarked above that principles governing relative scope have been studied in recent years, from different points of view, as part of the theory of grammar; and of course a number of authors, though differing among themselves, have made widespread use of inferential principles as part of linguistic theory. These researches cast doubt on Fodor's thesis.

To focus the issues better, I will elaborate on what I called the standard picture of linguistic theory, so as to bring it into connection with Fodor's conception of modularity. The standard picture views the theory of grammar as the theory of a context-independent cognitive resource—as, one might say, a clerk at a desk who is consulted from time to time on linguistic matters that come before the mind. This resource is made use of in perception, but also in other activities. We might imagine that perception, indeed, does not use all the information the clerk can deliver, and that such is the case in the mind's economy for the reasons that Fodor states as the rationale for "informational encapsulation" (see Fodor 1983, especially pp. 70 ff.). But on the standard picture it is grammatical theory, personified in the clerk, that is the "module" for language.

Recall that modularity in Fodor's sense is a cluster concept, construed as the possession of some significant number, in some significant degree, of characteristic features, including informational encapsulation, mandatoriness of operation, domain specificity, and several others. Throughout his discussion, Fodor is concerned with the modularity of mechanisms, for which the question of "speed of operation" arises. Contrasting mechanisms with what I am calling cognitive resources, it is noteworthy, I believe, that almost all the characteristics of modularity may be applied to them. A cognitive resource is domain specific by definition; it may exhibit "limited access" in the sense that persons are in general aware only of the answers that are provided through the resource, not of how the answers were obtained. It may show characteristic breakdown patterns and paths of maturation in the normal individual, and it may be associated with a fixed neural architecture. It may even be mandatory in operation, in the sense that questions about its domain are referred only to it, if to anywhere. It is less clear whether the notions of speed and depth of output apply, but the general moral is, I hope, plain enough.

It is significant that aspects of meaning may dawn slowly, as Chomsky notes in connection with examples like *John is too clever to expect us to catch*. You don't (or at least I didn't) at first hear it the right way, as *John is too clever for one to expect us to catch him, John.* But you can be brought to hear it the right way, and so to recognize it as grammatical, by thinking of analogous structures, such as *This movie is too good (for one) to expect us to miss.* These aspects of meaning impose themselves, context-independently, and so belong to the language faculty. But they are not therefore perceptual; on the contrary, since they arise from reflection, they probably aren't perceptual.[8]

What goes for aspects of meaning goes also, and inextricably, for aspects of syntactic structure. Derailment of the perceptual system in various garden-path phenomena, and subsequent recovery in virtue of thinking things through (perhaps with pencil and paper), seems to show that what belongs to the linguistic module is not confined to perception, although it is of course used in perception.

One can conceive various modifications of Fodor's thesis that will be consistent with above phenomena, and also with the inclusion of inferential and relative scope relations in linguistic systems. If I have interpreted Fodor in a strong, unmodified fashion, that is because I assume that he is not advancing a view that is consistent with whatever might be discovered about language and perception.

In *The Modularity of Mind*, Fodor contrasts input systems with central systems. The former receive information; the latter act on information received. In a way, the, I have suggested that language is a central system and is modular. In the last chapter of his book, Fodor is skeptical about the modularity of central systems. In concluding the present chapter, my burden will be that, whatever the truth about their modularity may turn out to be, some of the considerations that Fodor advances against it are rather weak, inasmuch as some obvious candidates seem to have been passed over.

Consider the principle of reason that true thoughts to the effect that q if p are such that q is true provided that p is true. This principle is a candidate for inclusion in a hypothetical module of knowledge of logic. If you know it then you know, for instance, that it is irrational to persist in denying q if you have the steady belief that q if p and have come to acknowledge that p. The principle is context-independent, since the thoughts in question may have any contents whatever; and it is domain-specific, in that it treats of thoughts, or things that are evaluable for truth and falsehood, and not of sensations or actions. Furthermore, it would be wrong to object, on the ground that the logically grounded principles of truth and rational belief apply to information of all sorts, that they are therefore not "encapsulated," and that one cannot appropriate Fodor's notion of a module here. On the contrary, encapsulation is a matter not of range of application but of the range of information consulted, which in the case of logic is very narrow.

More tendentious, consider the central, organized knowledge that I and all other humans have about the place of their minds, sensations, and thoughts—the phenomena that were classically called the unity of consciousness—in the objective world. I know that my beliefs about the world, my representations of it, may be false, and that I can be led to false beliefs by the ways things in the objective world have of appearing to me through their effects on my sensory organs, which are themselves part of that world, and are therefore to be explained by the laws that apply to it. I standardly explain how things appear to me by reference to the properties of the world, including the properties of my sensory organs, and I am prepared to alter my ways of doing so if it should be demonstrated to me that my notions about how things cause those appearances is mistaken. However, I know that others are not *a priori* in any better position than I am to judge how the world is, and I modulate my concern for my errors with criticism and examination of other opinions, insofar as they may be rational. Finally, I know that everybody knows what I know, and does what I do, with respect to these matters.

It is not as if the statements that I just made about the nature of the objective world and my place in it were in any sense mere hypotheses, or were subject to fluctuating degrees of belief depending on the local context. On the contrary, they are among the general, systematic presuppositions that I bring to apprehending the world, in all contexts, and thus they may constitute a module in Fodor's sense of that term.

In the later chapters of *The Modularity of Mind*, Fodor argues against the modularity of ordinary nondemonstrative inference and conjectures that the global character of such inference is what is responsible for its being a relatively intractable object of study. Assuming that he is correct in this, I still think it would be incautious to infer that no feature of general cognition is modular. Indeed, just those elements of cognition that range, context-independently, over all of knowledge would seem to be good candidates for modularity.

Acknowledgment

I am indebted to Jerry Fodor for discussions both during and after the conference, and have also been helped particularly by the comments of Sylvain Bromberger, Noam Chomsky, Gabriel Segal, and Scott Weinstein.

Notes

1. A simple example would be *Who likes [people who live where]?*, whose interpretation shows that *where* must have matrix scope.
2. For a more precise formulation see Higginbotham 1985.
3. For example, I should fault Pollard and Sag (1983) for maintaining that their proposal on English reflexives is a "semantic explanation" of the data, of a different character from

"binding theory" in the sense of Chomsky. In fact, their proposal is a binding theory, and an interesting competitor with other accounts.

4. Or at least of closing them off provided that the thematic role of the object is not assigned; thus *a baker of cookies in ovens* is better than (5), although still somewhat degraded.

5. As an example I would cite the popular idea that the pronoun *his* should be split into two formatives in order to account for the ambiguity of *John scratched his arm, but Bill didn't*. The discussions of Sag (1976), Williams (1977), and Reinhart (1983a, 1983b), who use observations first made by Lasnik (1976), assume that one of the interpretations (the one where Bill scratched his own arm) is secured by taking the pronoun as a variable. At the Hampshire College conference, Weisler pointed out a serious limitation of this idea due to examples like *I scratched my arm, but you didn't* (meaning that I scratched my arm, but you didn't scratch yours). My conjecture is that, apart from the empirical difficulties pointed out by Weisler, the pronoun-as-variable idea is far less plausible when questions of notation are seen in the light of the distinction above.

6. I am indebted here to discussions with R. Cooper.

7. See, for instance, Fodor 1983, p. 135, note 29 for the added feature of production.

8. The observations and discussion in Nagel 1969 also bear on this point.

6
Levels of Meaning
Norbert Hornstein

Except for a short period of time around 1972, when Jackendoff published *Semantic Interpretation in Generative Grammar*, generative grammarians have assumed, quite often tacitly, that the linguistically determined interpretive properties of a sentence are reflected in the structural properties of a single annotated phrase marker at some level of derivation. In the mid 1960s the Katz-Postal hypothesis reigned supreme. Deep structure was singled out as the relevant level of semantic interpretation, and transformations were taken to be "meaning preserving."[1] The grammar was structured as follows:

(1)   Deep Structure → Semantic Interpretation
    ↓ Transformations
    Surface Structure → Phonetic Interpretation

The initial Deep Structure phrase marker in this diagram—PM(DS)—was taken to contain whatever linguistically relevant information was needed for semantic interpretation.

Jackendoff's 1972 theory treated S-structure (the intermediate phrase markers), as well as D-structure, as relevant input to interpretation rules. On this theory, it is the set of phrase markers, starting from PM(DS) to PM(SS) and including the phrase markers in between, that feed semantic interpretation.

(2)   D-structure → Theta role
    ↓ Transformations → Reflexives
    S-Structure → Modal scope, opacity, scope of negation, etc

The major difference between Chomsky's (1965) theory (exemplified in diagram 1 above) and Jackendoff's theory (diagram 2) was the existence in the latter of multiple levels of semantic interpretation keyed to phrase markers of different levels of derivation. Theta-role assignment was defined over PM(DS), as in Chomsky's theory; modal scope, opacity, etc. were defined over PM(SS); and anaphora was defined over the intermediate PMs produced in the course of transformationally deriving PM(SS) from PM(DS).

The major theoretical change between diagram 2 and the Extended Standard Theory (diagram 3) was the introduction of traces.

(3)   D-structure
       ↓ Transformations
       S-structure → Semantic Interpretation

Trace theory makes it possible to read the history of derivation from the S-structure phrase marker. Traces, in effect, preserve the relevant structural information needed for interpretation by encoding the history of derivation in an annotated S-structure PM. Consider examples 4.

(4)   a. Who (did) Tom see
       b. John was hit

In both the standard theory and Jackendoff's theory (theories without traces), it is PM(DS) that tells us that *who* in (4a) is linked to the object position despite its being in adjunct position at S-structure, and that *John* is the logical object of (4b) even though it is the surface subject.

Given trace theory, this sort of information is recoverable at S-structure. The PM(SS) of (4a) is (5a), and that of (4b) is (5b).

(5)   a. [Who$_i$ [Tom see t$_i$]]
       b. [John$_i$ [was hit t$_i$]]

The traces—t$_i$—left behind by the movement of *who* and *John* mark the positions from which these elements derivationally originated. As this is all that is needed to recover the relevant D-structure information, the interpretation of (4a) and (4b) can proceed with PM(SS) taken as the sole input. As Jackendoff and others showed PM(SS) to be necessary as well, it seemed reasonable to think that, given traces, all that was required to feed semantic interpretation rules was PM(SS).

However, the long march from D-structure to S-structure did not end at S-structure. In the mid 1970s, as a consequence of work on what Chomsky (1976) dubbed Logical Form (LF)[2] and especially as a result of work on languages such as Chinese (see Huang 1982), LF rather than S-structure was determined to be the right level at which to state significant interpretive generalizations. At LF the rule of Quantifier Raising (QR) operates and adjoins quantified phrases to S, leaving indexed traces behind. *Wh-* raising applies to move *wh- in situ* to COMP positions, and the binding theory applies to weed out ill-formed representations. As in the earlier move from D-structure to S-structure, it is assumed that traces conserve the relevant D-structure and S-structure information so that all the necessary interpretive information from these prior levels of derivation can be consolidated at PM(LF), the phrase marker that is the output of LF rules and processes. A glance at diagram 6 should make apparent the parallel with the earlier move in which all relevant semantic information was consolidated at PM(SS).

(6)   D-structure
        ↓ Transformations
        S-structure

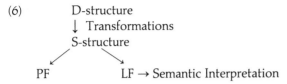

        PF   LF → Semantic Interpretation

On the assumption that traces are not "erased" as the derivation moves down the right branch of the grammar (i.e., that the Projection Principle holds), PM(LF) should suffice for purposes of semantic interpretation. I dub the claim that all semantic interpretation proceeds off PM(LF) the Consolidation Thesis. In what follows I will argue against it.

To be more specific, I believe that both strong consolidationism (the thesis that interpretation rules operate on a unique PM) and weak consolidationism (the thesis that all interpretive strucures are derivationally related to one another) are incorrect. Rather, interpretation in natural language is modularized. There are two distinct kinds of interpretive processes, which branch with respect to one another, which are not defined over the same sorts of primitives, and which demand different types of structural relations among the elements that they attend to. The model I will argue for is (roughly) the one shown in diagram 7.[3]

(7)   D-structure
        ↓ Transformations
        S-structure → Semantic Interpretation (SI-1)

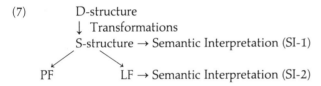

        PF   LF → Semantic Interpretation (SI-2)

As diagram 7 indicates, I want to argue here that there are two distinct interpretive processes.[4] SI-2 is read off PM(LF). It is concerned with NP/NP interactions, i.e., internominal relations.[5] These include quantifier interactions (e.g. relative quantifier scope) and NP/NP interactions (anaphora, reciprocals, pronoun binding, PRO interpretation, etc.). The characteristic interactions in LF are determined via indexing and c-command, so the antecedent of an anaphor must be coindexed and c-commanded by it. One quantifier has scope over another just in case it c-commands it in LF. In short, SI-2 interpretation is keyed to the c-command and indexing properties of sets of noun phrases.

What about SI-1? For now, let us assume that it is done off PM(SS) (see note 3). It deals with non-NP/NP interactions. Examples include opacity (V/NP or V/S′ interactions), modality (A/S′ interactions), scope of negation, prediction (NP/VP or NP/S′ interactions), adverbial modification, and adjectival modification.[6] Interpretation in SI-1 is keyed to the government relations of the interacting elements.

SI-1 does not feed into SI-2. They constitute distinct, noninteracting modules. Both PM(SS) and PM(LF) are input to semantic interpretation in natural language. In short, strong consolidationism is incorrect.

This bifurcation of the interpretive process may strike some as unintuitive, perhaps even bizarre. Before considering the empirical evidence in favor of diagram 7, let me say a few words about the intuition that informs the approach.

A central feature of meaning in natural language is that it is compositional. That is, the meanings of complex units are functions of the meanings of their subparts. In the case of sentences, the subparts are words, which combine into phrases, which combine to form sentences. How this combining occurs is indicated by the structure of the relevant sentence. The main objective of a theory of meaning for natural language is to determine the basic subunits of the clause and the rules for combining them into phrases and ultimately into sentences. In the context of current Government and Binding (GB) theory, this problem reduces to two others: finding out how semantic information is represented grammatically, and identifying the correct level of representation at which the structural organization of the phrase marker is suitable for compositional interpretation.

Consider the question of grammatical representation. In current theory it is assumed that certain kinds of interpretive information are organized in certain specific ways. Heads govern their arguments, and modified elements govern their modifiers.[7] In effect, the branching structure of the phrase marker encodes via the government relation how elements are to combine. That is, they yield the relevant notion of compositionality. Well, almost.

The caveat is necessary because there is a second way in which interpretive interdependencies are encoded: by c-command and coindexation at LF. The issue for a theory of meaning is to determine the functions of these two ways of representing information and to determine how each relates to the basic requirement of compositionality. Diagram 7 suggests that S-structure is the correct level for compositional processes such as function/argument relations, and that LF can be viewed as a grid superimposed on this basically compositional base whose function it is to determine internominal dependencies.[8] Insofar as the relations among linguistic units relevant for semantic interpretation are represented via government, the compositional account of meaning is straightforward. Meaning is compositional in the sense that elements that govern one another combine to form larger and larger interpretive units. LF operations represent NP/NP interactions over this fundamental compositional core.

There is another way of looking at the model in diagram 7 historically.

Before Frege, predicate/argument structure was taken to be the core semantical relation in the clause. What Frege showed was that quantification
could be treated more adequately if predicate argument/structure was replaced by operators and variables. Diagram 7 suggests that, as far as natural language is concerned, both these approaches are appropriate when
suitably restricted. Operator/variable relations are just a special case of
internominal dependency, while predicate/argument relations are a special
case of SI-1 processes. Both are important, albeit in different parts of the
grammar.

In the remainder of this chapter I will present evidence supporting
diagram 7. I will pay particular attention to SI-1. I will argue that there are
generalizations correctly described at PM(SS) that are missed at PM(LF).
Moreover, I will argue that apparent intransitivities arise if one tries to
maintain the strong consolidationist position. These are easily resolved if
one assumes that both SI-1 and SI-2 exist and are read off S-structure and
LF, respectively.

Adverbs

There are three types of adverbs: manner adverbials, speaker-oriented
adverbs, and subject-oriented adverbs.

(8)   a. John left the party quickly
       b. Happily, John left the party
       c. John, cleverly, has left the party

In (8a) *quickly* modifies the verb *left*. In (8b) *happily* does not modify the
verb; rather it modifies the sentence *John left the party*. Sentence 8b can be
paraphrased roughly as *I am happy to say that John left the party* or *It was
good that John left the party*. In (8c) the adverb *cleverly* plays yet a third kind
of semantic role. As Jackendoff observed, *cleverly* is a two-place modifier
that takes both the subject of the clause (*John*) and the whole phrase *John
left the party* as arguments. Sentence 8c can be roughly paraphrased as *It
was clever of John to have left the party*. Other subject-oriented adverbs are
rudely, intentionally, carefully, advantageously, deliberately, and *clumsily*.

As Jackendoff (1972, p. 49) observes, it is an adverb's S-structure position that determines what it modifies. Rougly speaking, an adverb can
modify only those elements that it governs at S-structure. The clearest
demonstration of this comes from considering the subject-oriented adverbs.
In this section I will show that it is indeed the S-structure government
relations that are crucial for this purpose. Consider examples 9.[9]

(9)   a. John intentionally has seduced Mary
       b. Mary intentionally has been seduced by John
       c. Mary cleverly/advantageously was believed to be a nut

d. *It cleverly/advantageously was believed that Harry was a nut

e. *Harry was believed cleverly/advantageously to be a nut

Sentences 9a and 9b are not paraphrases of one another. They can be paraphrased respectively as *It was intentional of John to seduce Mary* and *It was intentional of Mary to be seduced by John*. Their respective S-structures are shown in (10).

(10)   a.   [$_S$ [$_{NP}$ John] intentionally [$_{Aux}$ has] [$_{VP}$ seduced Mary]]

b.   [$_S$ [$_{NP}$ Mary]$_i$ intentionally [$_{Aux}$ has] [$_{VP}$ been seduced t$_i$ [b6 John]]]

In (10a) *intentionally* governs *John* but not *Mary*; in (10b) it is the other way around. On the assumption that adverb/argument relations are read off S-structure and must be in a government relation to interact interpretively, these facts follow. As adverb/argument relations are instances of non-NP/NP interactions, diagram 7 requires S-structure to be the relevant level for interpretation and government to be the relevant relation.

Similar remarks hold for (9c)–(9e).[10] In (9c) *cleverly/advantageously* modifies *Harry*, the S-structure matrix subject, which was moved from embedded subject position in D-structure. In (9d) and (9e) the adverbs cannot modify *Harry*, as they do not govern it at S-structure. The respective S-structures are (11a) and (11b).[11]

(11)   a.   It cleverly/advantageously [$_X$ was believed [$_X$ that [$_X$ Harry was a nut]]]

b.   [$_S$ Harry$_i$ [$_{VP}$ was believed [$_S$ t$_i$ cleverly/advantageously to be a nut]]]

The government requirement explains the unacceptability of (9d) and (9e) as paraphrases of (9c).[12]

To this point we have traversed well-trod ground. Consider now sentences 12a and 12b.

(12)   a.   A senator cleverly/advantageously appeared to speak at every rally

b.   A senator cleverly/advantageously seemed to speak at every rally

c.   It seemed/appeared to be clever of/ advantageous for a senator at every rally to have spoken

These can be interpreted as sentence 12c. In other words, sentences 11 can have *a senator* modified by the subject-oriented adverb while at the same time it can be interpreted as whitin the scope of the universally quantified NP *every rally*.[13] What makes this interesting is that the latter interpretive fact is best accounted for by having QR lower *a senator* and attach it to the embedded clause.[14] Thus, (13a) has the LF structure (13b) under this interpretation.

(13) a. A senator seemed to speak at every rally

b. [$_S$ t$_i$ seemed [$_S$ Every rally$_i$ [$_S$ a senator$_j$ [t$_j$ speak at t$_i$]]]]

In fact, it has been argued (Hornstein 1984; Aoun and Hornstein 1985) that lowering the matrix QP is the only way to get the reading with *a senator* in the scope of *every rally*. Raising *every rally* to matrix position would leave us with no explanation as to why such raising is permitted if and only if the embedded subject has been raised (May 1977).

Thus in (14a) *a senator* must be interpreted with scope over *every rally* though in (14b) we get the ambiguity observed in (13). In (14b) but not in (14a) the embedded subject position is filled by a trace left behind after *a senator* moves to the matrix subject as in (14c).

(14) a. A senator expects Bill to speak at every rally

b. A senator is expected to speak at every rally

c. A senator is expected t to speak at every rally

These sorts of facts suggest that structures such as (15a) are, in general, ill formed.[15] Moreover, it suggests that (12a) and (12b) have LF structures analogous to (13b). In particular, they have LF phrase markers such as (15b).

(15) a. *[$_S$ Every Rally$_i$ [$_S$ a senator$_j$ [$_S$ t$_j$ seemed [$_S$ t$_j$ to speak at t$_i$]]]]

b. [$_S$ t$_j$ (cleverly/advantageously) (seemed/appeared) [$_S$ Every rally$_i$ [$_S$ a senator$_j$ [$_S$ t$_j$ speak at t$_i$]]]]

Observe that in (15b) the subject-oriented adverb does not govern *a senator*.[16] In short, the LF structure required to represent the relative scopes of *a senator* and *every rally* cannot simultaneously represent the fact that *cleverly/advantageously* govern, and hence can modify, *a senator*. Thus, if we assume that all interpretation is done off PM(LF), we have no account for the data in (11).[17]

On the other hand, if we assume the model in diagram 7, then PM(SS) is the phrase marker relevant for determining what the adverb modifies. At PM(SS), *cleverly/advantageously* does govern *a senator* and so can modify it. The fact that *a senator* may lower in LF is irrelevant for the adverb/subject NP relationship, because this is carried out in SI-1, which is fed by PM(SS). Thus, despite the fact that the adverbs in (12) do not govern the subjects in the LF phrase marker (15b), adverbial modification is possible—just as diagram 7 predicts.

The converse appears to be true as well. Note that (9d) and (9e) sound quite odd, presumably because the adverb must modify something but there is no suitable subject NP around at S-structure that it governs. Consider now (16).

(16) *? A senator appears/seems to cleverly have spoken at every rally

At PM(SS), *a senator* is not governed by *cleverly*. Parallel to (9d) and (9e), it sounds odd if interpreted as *it was clever of a senator at every rally to have spoken*. In fact, the preferred reading has *cleverly* acting as a manner adverb modifying *speak* rather than as a subject-oriented adverb; that is, (16) is preferably interpreted as *a senator appears/seems to have spoken cleverly at every rally*.[18] However, (16) sounds odd with the subject-oriented interpretation, although there is an LF phrase marker with *a senator* governed by the embedded adverb:

(17) $[_S$ t_j seems/appears $[_S$ every rally$_i$ $[_S$ a senator$_j$ $[_S$ t_j to cleverly [have spoken at t_i]]]]]

In short, the LF representation cannot "save" the unacceptable sentence. It seems that if the sentence is out at S-structure then it remains bad regardless of what happens at LF. This is just what a modular approach such as that of diagram 7 predicts on the assumptions that adverbial modification is an SI-1 process and that relative QP scope is determined in SI-2.

Negation

Similar effects can be seen if one considers phenomena relating to scope of negation. Like adverbial modification, this is an SI-1 process (i.e., one .involving interactions between NPs and non-NPs). Like adverbial modification, it is an interpretive proceedure sensitive to a sentence's S-structure configuration.

In (18a) the negation element governs the VP.[19]

(18) a. Many arrows did not hit the target
      b. The target was not hit by many arrows
      c. Not many arrows hit the target

The structure of (18a) is (19).

(19) $[_S$ Many arrows $[_{Aux}$ did] $[_{VP}$ not hit the target]]

In (19) the subject position fails to be governed by *not*, and so *many arrows* falls outside its scope.[20] On the other hand, the S-structure of (18b) is (20).

(20) $[_S$ [the target] was $[_{VP}$ not hit by many arrows]]

In this case, *many arrows* hangs from VP and so is interpreted as within the scope of *not*. In fact, (18b) is paraphraseable as (18c) whereas (18a) is not. In (18c) *not* governs *many arrows*; hence its similarity to (18a). In (18c) *not* is part of the subject NP, as indicated in (21). Hence, it governs the quantifier *many*, and an interpretation similar to (18b) results.

(21) $[_{NP}$ not [many arrows]] hit the target

Similar conclusions come from considering how *any* operates.

(22) a. *Anyone did not leave
      b. *? John expects anyone to leave
      c. John does not expect anyone to leave
      d. *Anyone was not expected to leave

As is well known, *anyone* must be in the scope of a negative-polarity item. In (22a) *not* fails to govern the matrix subject, and so (22a) is unacceptable. Similarly for (22d). At S-structure, *anyone* is in matrix subject position, having been raised by "Move alpha" from the embedded matrix position. The structure is illustrated in (23).

(23) [Anyone was [not expected [t to leave]]]

In (23) *not* fails to govern *anyone*, and so it cannot be interpreted as within the scope of the negation. Hence its unacceptability.

More important for our purposes are sentences such as (24).

(24) Sheila did not introduce every student to his home room teacher

The interpretation of (24) has the quantified NP 'every student' construed as within the scope of *not*. Sentence 24 has the LF structure shown in (25a) and the S-structure shown in (25b).

(25) a. $[_S$ Every student$_i$ $[_S$ Sheila $[_{VP}$ not introduce t_i to his$_i$ teacher]]]
      b. $[_S$ Sheila $[_{VP}$ not introduce every student to his teacher]]

In (25b) *every student* is in the scope domain of *not*. However, after QR has applied in LF *every student* is adjoined to S and is no longer governed by *not*. In short, at LF *not* fails to be in the domain of *not*. Consequently (25a) does not explain why *every student* must be read as within the scope of negation.[21] Sentence 25b, the PM(SS) of sentence 24, serves this purpose admirably. Moreover, this is just what we would expect if diagram 7 is correct.

There is one last argument for separating SI-1 and SI-2 processes as diagram 7 suggests.[22] As mentioned above, it is possible to lower a quantified subject Noun Phrase to embedded sentential position if it was raised from there by "Move NP" earlier in the derivation. See the discussion of (13)–(15). Consider now sentences such as (26).

(26) a. Everyone was not expected to leave
      b. *Anyone was not expected to leave
      c. $[_S$ t_i was $[_{VP}$ not expected $[_S$ everyone$_i$ [t_i to leave]]]]
      d. $[_S$ t_i was $[_{VP}$ not expected $[_S$ anyone$_i$ [t_i to leave]]]]

In (26a) *everyone* is interpreted with scope over the negation *not*, and (26b) is unacceptable as *anyone* must be in the scope of the negation. However, if one assumes that one can lower the matrix phrase in LF, then (26a) and (26b) should have structures analogous to (26c) and (26d).[23]

In (26c) and (26d) *everyone* and *anyone* are in the scope of negation. Given the actual interpretation of (26), this is a problem for a theory that takes LF to be the sole input to semantic interpretation, as it appears that LF movement does not affect the scope of negation processes. A theory such as that of diagram 7 has no difficulty with such cases. Scope of negation is an SI-1 process read off S-structure, and QR is an LF process that feeds SI-2. The two-track theory outlined in diagram 7 makes the right distinctions.

Opacity

In some earlier work I argued that the typical opacity data were not correctly accounted for by a theory that read interpretations off LF representations. In fact, I argued that grammatically these aspects of a sentence's interpretation were not mirrored in disambiguated LF structures. Consider why not.

Sentence 27a, as is well known, seems capable of being interpreted with *someone* either outside or inside the scope of *believes*. If this ambiguity were disambiguated at LF, the two readings would be represented as in (27b) and (27c).

(27) a. John believes (that) someone loves Mary
      b. [Someone$_i$ [John believes [(that) [t$_i$ loves Mary]]]]
      c. [John believes [(that) [someone$_i$ [t$_i$ loves Mary]]]]

Sentence 27b would represent the *de re* reading, as *someone* is outside the scope of *believe*. Sentence 27c, with *someone* inside the scope of *believe*, represents the *de dicto* interpretation. The problem with this is that (27b) is an ill-formed phrase marker. Owing to the empty-category principle (ECP),[24] *someone* cannot be pulled out of the embedded clause by QR and adjoined to the matrix clause.

However, in view of diagram 7 none of this should surprise us. Opacity is another example of an SI-1 effect. As such it should not be mirrored in LF structures and should not be sensitive to QR. Rather, the possibility that a phrase has a *de dicto* or *de re* reading is determined by the S-structure properties of the phrase marker.[25] Let's say that (28) holds.[26]

(28) An element can be given the nonspecific *de dicto* interpretation just in case it is in the domain of an opaque element.

For our purposes, (28) implies that an opaque verb (such as *believe* or *expect*) creates an opaque domain and that an element within this domain can be given a *de dicto* interpretation. The opaque domain of a verb is whatever it governs—typically a clause, but occasionally an NP. S-structure is where such interpretive possibilities are determined.

Before I give the details, please observe one point. Sentence 28 does not say whether a lexical element carries a *de dicto* or a *de re* interpretation, but whether it can. In this way (28) structurally parallels principle B of the binding theory. It rules out certain interpretive possibilities, but it does not further specify interpretation. In effect a rule like (28) applying in SI-1 says that if an NP is in a domain governed by an opaque verb at S-structure it can be given a *de dicto* interpretation, [27] and that otherwise it cannot.

If we adopt this sort of approach then in examples such as (26) we expect ambiguity regardless of what happens in LF. At S-structure *someone* is in a clause governed by the opaque verb *believe*.[28] Therefore (28) applies and *someone* can be given either interpretation.[29] The same applies to cases such as (29).

(29)   a. John is hunting a unicorn
        b. A unicorn is being hunted by John

Sentence 29a can carry the *de dicto* interpretation, as is well known. Sentence 29b, on the other hand, does not. *There* insertion highlights the difference in interpretation; (29b) can be naturally paraphrased as (30) but (29a) cannot.

(30)   There is a unicorn that John is hunting

Consider now pronominal coreference and *one* substitution. In (29a) we can treat *a unicorn* referentially if we choose. Thus, it can be linked to a suitable pronoun or to *one*.

(31)   John is hunting a unicorn and
        a. Harry is hunting one as well
        b. Harry is hunting it too

Here (31b) carries the referential interpretation, (31a) the nonspecific *de dicto* reading.

In (32), on the other hand, *a unicorn* is not governed by *hunt* at S-structure. Consequently it carries only the specific reading; hence the odd sound of (32a).

(32)   A unicorn was hunted by John and
        a. ?? Harry is hunting one too
        b. Harry is hunting him too

Similar observations hold for *believe*.

(33)   a. John believed someone on the boat was/to be a murderer
        b. John believed someone on the boat was/to be a murderer but he
           didn't know who

c. ?? Someone on the boat is believed by John to be a murderer but he doesn't know who

Sentence 33a is ambiguous, with *someone on the boat* either specific or nonspecific. In (33b) the tag *he didn't know who* forces the nonspecific reading. However, in (33c) this reading is not available, as *someone on the boat* is not in the opaque domain of *believe* as the subject position of the matrix is not governed by the verb. This leads to the anomalous sound of (33c).

Consider one last case.

(34) a. John expects someone to arrange every match
      b. John expects someone arranged every match

Here *someone* can have a *de dicto* or a *de re* interpretation and can be interpreted as within or outside the scope of *every* match.[30] In short, (34a) and (34b) can be paraphrased in one of four ways:

(35) a. There is someone who John expects to arrange every match
      b. For every match there is someone who John expects to arrange it
      c. John expects that there is someone who will arrange every match
      d. John expects that for every match there is someone who will arrange it

These four readings arise from the fact that at S-structure *someone* is in the opaque domain of *expect*, which governs the entire embedded clause. Furthermore, at LF, QR can apply first either to *every match* or to *someone*, yielding either (36a) or (36b).

(36) a. John expects [someone$_i$ [every match$_j$ [t$_i$ arrange t$_j$]]]
      b. John expects [every match$_j$ [someone$_i$ [t$_i$ arrange t$_j$]]]

Thus, (28) plus the two LF representations in (36) yield the four readings in (35). Furthermore, adding the tag *but he doesn't know who* to (34a) and (34b) forces the elimination of (35a) and (35b).

Sentence 37 can be paraphrased as in (38), but not as in (39).

(37) John expects someone to arrange/arranged every match but he doesn't know who

(38) a. John expects that there is someone who arranged every match but he doesn't known who
      b. John expects that for every match there was someone who arranged it but he doesn't know who

(39) a. There is someone who John expects arranged every match but he doesn't know who

b. For every match there is someone who John expects arranged it but he doesn't know who

What happens if we passivize *expect* and raise the embedded subject? By raising the embedded subject to matrix subject position we remove it from the opaque domain of *expect*. However, as in all such raising cases, as we have seen above, we should be able to lower the subject QP in LF to get it interpreted within the scope of the universally quantified NP *every match*. In short, we expect to interpret *someone* as outside the scope of *expect* but inside the scope of *every match*.

(40)   Someone was expected by John to arranged every match (* but he doesn't know who)

As the unacceptability of adding the tag in (40) indicates, *someone* is indeed interpreted *de re*. Moreover, (40) can be interpreted with *someone* in the scope of *every match*. Sentence 40 is paraphraseable as (41).

(41)   For every match there is a specific person who John expects to arrange it (i.e. Mansour match 1, Norbert match 2, etc.)

Now the punch line. These facts are inexplicable if all interpretation is done off PM(LF). The reason is that, on this view, *someone* must be represented as simultaneously inside and outside the scope of *expect*. To account for the fact that *someone* can be interpreted within the scope of *every match*, we lower it by QR to yield (42).

(42)   [t_i was expected by John [every match$_j$ [someone$_i$ [t_i arrange t_j]]]]

But (42) puts *someone* in the scope domain of *expect*. Example 40 shows that this reading is not in fact available. In sum, we appear to have a transitivity problem.

Diagram 7 has no such problem. To determine opacity we consult S-structure. Here *someone* is outside the opaque domain of *expect*, as *expect* does not govern the subject position. Consequently, (28) cannot apply and *someone* can receive only the *de re* interpretation.

To determine relative QP scope we consult LF. Here *someone* can be lowered to the embedded clause. Therefore it can be interpreted as within the scope of *every match*.

In short, modularizing interpretation enables us to avoid the transitivity problem noted above.[31] Unlike a consolidationist approach to interpretation, the two-level theory outlined in diagram 7 has no difficlty explaining how sentences such as (40) can come to have interpretations such as (41). As scope of opacity is determined at a different linguistic level than relative quantifier scope, we have no difficulty in explaining how *someone* can at the same time be interpreted as inside the scope of an element inside the scope of *expect* (viz. *every match*) and also outside the scope of *expect*. Where opacity interpretation applies it is outside the scope of *expect*; when it is within the scope of *expect* (at LF), only relative QP scope is determined, so this structural fact is of no consequence. Thus we are able to avoid the apparent contradiction.

Conclusion

The aim of this chapter has been to outline a modular theory of linguistic interpretation. The model described in diagram 7 and defended in the body of the chapter is modular in the sense that SI-1 and SI-2 operations are informationally encapsulated from one another. This is vital to the model's success. To see this, consider example 40 once again.

As was observed, (40) had the interpretation (41) in which *someone* was interpreted *de re*. To explain how this was possible despite our being able to interpret *someone* as within the scope of *every match* required us to say that SI-1 processes were independent of SI-2 processes. What happens at SI-1 does not constrain SI-2, and vice versa. In particular, the fact that *someone* is interpreted *de re* does not prevent its being lowered to the embedded S position in LF, nor does the fact that *someone* can be construed as within the scope of *every match* allow it to receive a nonspecific *de dicto* interpretation. In short, SI-1 and SI-2 processes do not share information. Moreover, they cannot do so if the above account is correct, for if they could we would expect a nonspecific reading for *someone* to be possible. As the unacceptability of (40) with the tag *but he doesn't know who* indicates, this is not possible. Thus, the informational encapsulation of SI-1 and SI-2 from one another is a crucial feature of our model's account of sentences such as (40). To the degree that informational encapsulation is a mark of modularity, this seems to suggest that SI-1 and SI-2 are separate interpretive modules within the more comprehensive linguistic faculty.

There has been a second thrust to the chapter as well. Much work in linguistic semantics draws considerable inspiration from work in philosophical logic. Concepts and techniques are often transplanted from the latter to the former quite uncritically. The notion that there is something philosophers might call "the logical form" of a sentence becomes the notion that PM(LF) is the sole input to semantic interpretation. The treatment of opacity phenomena as similar to relative quantifier scope is accepted because this is the way that Frege, Russell, and Quine treated it. There is no reason for linguists to abstain from intellectual opportunism. We should borrow from whatever other research might be useful. However, we should not forget that our aims and concerns are different from those of philosphers and logicians. Many of the concepts and techniques that the latter have elaborated might have to be substantially altered, if not wholly rejected, when they are applied to the study of the language faculty. Further, many notions that would seem foreign to the conerns of philosphers and logicians might well prove to be of great importance if one's aim is to adnumbrate the principles of Universal Grammar. It would be difficult to find a better example than modularity. It is hoped that the model limned above provides an extended argument for taking seriously the idea that such aphilosophical notions might well lie at the center of theories of meaning for natural language.

Acknowledgments

This paper grew out of another paper, co-authored with David Lightfoot, called "Predication and PRO." I would like to thank him as well as Elan Dresher and Amy Weinberg for helpful comments and discussion. I would also like to thank the colloquia at USC and UC Irvine for inviting me to present drafts of this material. In particular I would like to thank Joseph Aoun, Mürvet Enç, Neil Elliott, and Mario Montalbetti. Last but not least, I would like to thank Steve Weisler, whose comments at the Hampshire Conference were greatly appreciated.

Notes

1. In what follows I will ignore the distinction between Deep Structure and D-structure as well as the distinction between Surface Structure and S-structure. The differences be-tween these distinct notions will be of relative little importance in what follows.
2. See also Williams 1977 and May 1977.
3. I say roughly because there is interesting evidence to suggest that SI-1 is carried out after certain morpho-syntactic operations are carried out. SI-1 is keyed to a PM derived from S-structure after S-structure branches into PF and LF; see Hornstein 1986. This PM feeds PF, unlike LF which feeds SI-2. Thus SI-1 is not really read off S-structure but is read off this PF interpretive level. The issues that pertain to this elaboration of the present proposal are what make weak consolidationism untenable. In this chapter the stronger thesis will be the focus of discussion. The evidence against the weaker thesis will be developed in the paper cited above.

   If diagram 7 is correct then this will have implications for the analysis of VP deletion, which, it has been argued (Williams 1977), is fed by LF. If diagram 7 is correct, more than LF structures might be involved; S-structure might be relevant as well. I would like to thank Steve Weisler for bringing this to my attention.
4. The similarity that this approach has with Jackendoff's earlier model should be obvious. I have borrowed liberally from his work both in overall conception and in fine detail.
5. I say NP interactions. NP is a syntactic notion. It is these syntactic individuals that are the concern of SI-2, not the semantic values that may be associated with them. I have argued elsewhere that it is these syntactic entities that are the proper concern of a theory of linguistic interpretation; see Hornstein 1984.
6. See Higginbotham 1985 for discussions of adjectives and of the role of government in determining how they are to be interpreted. On predication within the theory of grammar see Williams 1980.
7. On government see Aoun and Sportiche 1983 and Chomsky 1981.

8. There are some similarities behind the intuition being explored here and the device in Montague Grammar known as Cooper Storage. The latter is the device required to bring quantifier scope within the reach of a compositional semantics of the Montague style. If one generalizes Cooper storage to treat all NP/NP interactions, I think that a theory like that of diagram 7 results.

9. These examples are from Jackendoff 1972 (examples 3.146 and 3.147 on p. 82).

10. Jackendoff (1972, p. 75) points out that one gets subject-oriented interpretations unambiguously only if the adverb is in pre-aspect position. In other positions one can get this interpretation but it also allows the simple manner reading: *John clumsily has dropped the dish* versus *John has clumsily dropped the dish*. I will generally place these adverbs in pre-aspect position in the examples that follow.

11. Sentence 11a appears to have a marginally possible reading where the adverb modifies the "implicit" agent argument of the missing *by* phrase, i.e. *it was clever of everyone to believe that Harry was a milquetoast*. If this is correct, it would be interesting to determine where implicit arguments become represented in the grammar and how they are added onto the representation. Offhand, it seems reasonable that this would get done where other morphological processes were accomplished, as implicit arguments seem tied to the morpho-syntactic properties of particular lexical items. At any rate, it does not seem farfetched to think that this too might be a SI-1 process. If so we would expect implicit arguments to be subject to SI-1 operations but not to SI-2 processes. The latter claim seems to be correct if processes such as PRO interpretation and anaphora are examined. The first part of the claim requires further study.

12. Indeed, these sentences seem to be simply unacceptable.

13. I owe this observation to Neil Elliot—thanks again!

14. For details see May 1977 and Hornstein 1984.

15. For details see Aoun and Hornstein 1985.

16. Nor is the trace of the matrix subject a variable. It is not operator bound. It has no semantic signingicance at all. Its role seems indistinguishable from the expletive *it* in English or the Italian *pro* of the null subject parameter. On the assumption that the null parameter is governed by PF conditions (Manzini 1983b), the possibility of *pro* in LF is expected.

17. This assumes that after lowering has applied the matrix trace cannot "transmit" the fact that it is modified adverbially to the embedded variable position. In short, the NP-t here and in (11) cannot go surrogate for the NP indexed with it. This makes sense when one realizes that NP-t bears no theta role in such cases and so cannot be modified. The adverb must govern a lexical theta marked NP at S-structure.

18. Even with this reading the sentence sounds odd, because the verb does not govern *cleverly*.

19. Examples 18a and 18b are taken from Jackendoff 1972 (pp. 302–303, examples 7.46 and 7.47).

20. The scope of negation is the phrase that the negation element governs. Elements within this domain are within scope of negation. For example, in *It does not seem that anyone is home, anyone* is in the negation domain of *not* though it is not governed by *not* directly. The VP position of *not* in (19) is argued for in Hornstein 1977, among other places.

21. All theories agree that QR can adjoin to S. Thus we should be able to get a reading with *everyone* having wide scope. As pointed out in Hornstein 1984, this is not in general possible. Where it seems best is where we get a species of verbal negation. So in sentences such as *John did not like everyone* it seems possible to read this with *everyone* enjoying scope over the negation. However, I suspect that this is because *not like* is the same as *dislike* or *hate—John disliked everyone*. Where this neg incorporation is not possible, the apparent wide-scope reading disappears; e.g. (24). Another confounding

effect comes from the fact that the negation can cliticize onto the dummy auxiliary *did*. When this happens it seems far easier to give *everyone* scope over negation. Compare *John didn't like everyone* with *John did not like everyone*. It is quite reasonable to analyze cliticization as incorporating the negation into the word *did*. If so it should then interact with *everyone* the way that the *dis* in *dislike* does. As we saw above, *everyone* easily moves across this negation element. For further discussion of negation effects see Hornstein 1986.

22. I owe this point to Ken Safire, who brought Linebarger's discussion to my attention.
23. This assumes that *any* is in fact moved by QR. If not, then (26b) is no problem though (26a) remains a difficulty. For arguments against QR's applying to *any* see Hornstein 1984.
24. Generalized Binding, to be more exact. See Aoun and Hornstein 1985.
25. See Hornstein 1984, chapter 3, where I argued that not all QPs move in LF; indeed some are interpreted *in situ*. *Anyone* is such a QP. Consider *John doesn't expect anyone to come*. At LF *anyone* is governed by *expect*. It can, however, be interpreted as either in the scope of the verb or outside it. If it does not move, however, this suggests that these interpretive aspects of the clause must be accounted for in terms different than whether or not in LF the QP hangs from the embedded clause or the matrix.
26. This is essentially Jackendoff's rule.
27. An element can always be interpreted objectively.
28. See Jackendoff 1975, 1980 for arguments showing that more than just the NPs can be construed opaquely.
29. Actually it is a range of interpretations; see Hornstein 1984, chapter 3. Note as well that the problem regarding *any* in note 25 is resolved if one adopts this approach.
30. *John* in this example is John Caughey, who was captain of the C-ladder UMCP squash team.
31. It seems that modals might be a problem for the analysis presented here. However, if modals hang from AUX, then they will govern the subject position given standard assumptions. Thus the ambiguity of

(i) A unicorn might be in the garden

is expected given a rule for models analogous to (28).

The more interesting issue is how to handle cases such as

(ii) A unicorn seemed to be in the garden.

Here, it has been argued, *a unicorn* can be either specific of nonspecific. Two responses are possible. First, it is not clear that *seems* is a regular verb. It has copula-like properties (Hornstein and Lightfoot, forthcoming), and this may indicate that it moves to AUX, thereby governing the subject. It may be raised by a rule like *have/be* raising. Second, the ambiguity of (ii) is a bit misleading. Consider the following sentences:

(iii) *A unicorn seemed to be approaching but it was really a moose.
(iv) It seems that a unicorn was approaching but it was really a moose.
(v) John believed that a unicorn was approaching but it was really a moose.
(vi) *A unicorn was believed to be approaching but it was really a moose.

When one adds *it was really a moose* one cannot get the *de re* meaning any longer, as (iii) and (iv) show. After all, a unicorn cannot be a moose. Thus, it seems that in (iii) *a unicorn* must be interpreted *de re*. What then of (ii)?

I think that what is happening here is that the embedded VP is being interpreted differently. Note that one can say *A unicorn seemed to be standing still but it was really sitting*. The embedded VP is still in the scope of *seem* in (ii), and so its interpretation can be affected. Thus, (ii) means that there is a unicorn that had the property of seeming to be in the garden. In a sense, *a unicorn* in this case is being interpreted just as it would be in *A unicorn does not exist*. At any rate, I think that the apparent difficulties that modal constructions appear to cause should be handled in this way. I would like to thank Mürvet Enç for bring this problem to my attention and for subsequent discussion.

7

Quantification, Ellipsis, and Logical Form

Steven Weisler

As linguists working in the Extended Standard Theory became more interested in phenomena such as quantification and opacity, which previously had been studied primarily by philosophers and logicians, the language of linguistic theory came (once again) to look, in parts and to a degree, like a more or less traditional logical language. For example, the level of representation LF (read "logical form") in the analyses of Williams (1977) and Sag (1976) involved quantification theory and the lambda calculus, and seemed, in certain regards, rather like a simplified, extensional version of the language IL (Montague 1973).

These two approaches were, of course, distinguished by differences in both conception and execution. Montague viewed IL as dispensable—although English expressions were first translated into expressions of IL, which were then interpreted model-theoretically, interpretations could be assigned directly to English expressions. Thus, Montague thought of IL as a convenience rather than as a necessity. Furthermore, the motivation for the devices Montague employed in IL was to facilitate interpretation and to accommodate a theory of deduction. The goals of his work included assigning truth conditions and accounting for entailments. Williams and Sag, on the other hand, are primarily interested in accounting for elliptical constructions such as VP-deletion, Sluicing, and Gapping, and posit a level of LF in order to accurately state the principle of identity presupposed by the principle of recoverability of deletion. In this regard, for these theorists, LF is an indispensable level of representation encoding structures which must be checked before ellipsis rules can apply.

Aside from the issues of goals and dispensability, it is of interest that the form of logical form is so similar in the Sag-Williams and Montague systems. They share a common notion of bound variable, they both rely on the construct of scope, they each involve the lambda calculus, and so on. Some of the more glaring differences between the two styles of approach, such as the treatment of proper names and tense, turn out not to be deeply ingrained, as later work on VP-deletion (Sag and Weisler 1979) has shown. Thus, despite the fact that, as Chomsky (1975a) has argued, the investigation of LF was an empirical endeavor, and despite the fact that there was no guarantee that linguists would find logicans' devices useful, they did. For a time, at least, it looked as if there might be a convergence in the field.

More recent developments in the study of LF, however, have greatly broadened the gap between it and IL. For example, Hornstein (1984) argues that the assignment of quantifier scope is accomplished by a syntactic transformation applying at LF whose operation is indirectly constrained by the binding theory, and May (1985) claims that quantifier ambiguities are not always represented in terms of relative quantifier scope. This and much other ongoing work is reevaluating the form and scope of LF within the EST. It is in this vein that Hornstein's chapter in the present volume, "Levels of Meaning," explores LF. Hornstein provides an in-depth analysis of quantification, negation, adverbial modification, and opacity which he takes to argue for splitting semantic interpretation into two parts, so that inter-NP relations such as relative quantifier scope will continue to be formally represented at LF but other semantic relations, including opacity, will be calculated from S-structure representations. If we accept these modifications of our conception of LF, the convergence between logical and syntactic investigations of LF slips away and some of the assumptions of the Williams-Sag framework are called into question. It is this second point that will be the focus of attention in the present chapter.

In the first section, after summarizing Hornstein's arguments and conclusions, I will reconsider some of the deletion phenomena that motivated the Sag-Williams theory of LF and examine them in the light of Hornstein's work. The problems that arise are addressed in the following section, where I propose an alternative to Hornstein's theory of interpretation that better accommodates the deletion facts. The resulting account does provide separate mechanisms to account for opacity and inter-nominal NP relations, and is in this regard similar to Hornstein's account. However, the present account denies the strict modularity of these two classes of phenomena for which Hornstein argues, and instead characterizes the relationship between them in terms of a more general type of derivational relation. In the next section I discuss some of the remaining problems and implications of the alternative analysis.

Levels of Interpretation

Most work in contemporary linguistic theory holds that there is at most one level of semantic representation. Indeed, if we ignore the issue of the dispensability of logical form, virtually all recent accounts (i.e., those since Jackendoff 1972) agree that a single level of representation can provide the input for semantic interpretation, and there has been little initiative for the position that there are multiple semantic levels. An interesting exception to this tendency is Hornstein, who argues in this volume against what he calls strong consolidationism ("the thesis that interpretative rules operate on a unique P[hrase] M[arker]"). On Hornstein's analysis, both S-structure and LF provide input to the process of interpretation, although the semantic relations that are analyzed at each level are distinct. In keeping with much contemporary work, NP/NP interactions such as quantifier scope, PRO-interpretation, and reciprocal binding are represented at LF. On the other hand, non-NP/NP interactions such as modality, opacity, and scope of negation are analyzed at S-structure.

The bifurcation is not at all random. Those relations analyzed at LF involve co-indexing and C-command, whereas those analyzed at S-structure depend crucially on government. Hornstein's idea, then, is that these inherently different types of relations are represented at distinct levels in the grammar. This conclusion, although sensible, is not unavoidable. If both S-structure and LF are levels of representation that express information in terms of phrase markers defined over the same primitives and encoding the same types of relations, it is possible to try to consolidate all semantic information at a single representational level. Indeed, most work on LF has presumed this minimal position. Thus, the rationale for distinct levels of representation is just that, and empirical arguments are needed.

Hornstein's first two arguments concern the scope of adverbs and the scope of negation. In each case he argues that the relevant scope domain must be established at S-structure and not at LF. To consider the case of adverbs first, Hornstein, building on work by Jackendoff (1972), notes that subject-oriented adverbs such as *cleverly* and *advantageously* must govern the subjects they modify, and that this explains why (1) can be paraphrased as (2) but (3) cannot.

(1)   John cleverly has seduced Harry.

(2)   It was clever of John to seduce Harry.

(3)   Harry cleverly has been seduced by John.

In (1) *cleverly* governs and hence can modify (in its subject-oriented sense) *John*; in (3) it governs *Harry* but not *John*. Thus, we would expect (3) to be paraphasable as (4), as it is.

(4)   It was clever of Harry to have been seduced by John.

In examples such as (5), in which *cleverly* fails to govern a modifiable NP, the resulting sentence does not have a subject-oriented reading.

(5)   It cleverly was believed that Harry was crazy. ($\neq$ It was clever of Harry to be believed to be crazy.)

Against this background, Hornstein discusses the following crucial pair of facts:

(6)   A senator cleverly appeared to speak at every rally.

(7)   *? A senator appears to cleverly have spoken at every rally.

Although (6) is grammatical on the reading involving a subject-oriented interpretation of the adverb, if adverbial interpretation were to take place at LF we would fail to predict this fact. As Hornstein points out, this is because the LF for (6) scopes the quantifier phrase *A senator* in the lower clause, since raised NPs participate in quantifier lowering at LF (Aoun and Hornstein 1985; May 1977):

(8)   [t_i cleverly [$_{VP}$ appeared [$_S$ every rally$_j$ [a senator$_i$ [$_S$ t_i to speak at t_j]]]]]

As a consequence of quantifier lowering, the NP *every rally* is not governed by *cleverly*, and therefore does not qualify for the subject-oriented interpretation it receives, at LF. Example 7, on the other hand, is an example of a sentence that does not allow for a subject-oriented interpretation of *cleverly* carrying the interpretation of (9).

(9)   It appeared to have been clever of a senator to speak at every rally.

After quantifier lowering, the LF for (7) is (10).

(10)   [t_i appeared [every rally$_j$ [$_S$ a senator$_i$ [$_S$ t_i to cleverly [$_{VP}$ have spoken at t_j]]]]]

Hornstein maintains that lowering *A senator* into the modification domain of *cleverly* at LF is not sufficient to save the subject-oriented interpretation, and that, since no other interpretation is possible, (7) is ungrammatical. Again, we have an argument that the modification domain for subject-oriented adverbs must be calculated prior to LF.

Hornstein presents a parallel argument concerning the scope of negation. The key example he discusses is repeated as (11).

(11)   Sheila did not introduce every student to his home room teacher.

After motivating the claim that a quantifier must be inside the scope of negation (i.e. in the governing domain of negation) to be interpreted inside the scope of negation, Hornstein points out that in (11), after QR takes place at LF, *every student* will have been moved outside the scope of negation:

(12)   [every student$_i$ [Sheila did [not introduce t_i to his home room teacher]]]

Since according to his argument (11) can only be interpreted with *every student* in the scope of *not*, Hornstein concludes that the scope of negation must be determined prior to LF. Consequently, he identifies S-structure (after the application of morphosyntactic rules) as the level of representation that provides the input to the processes of semantic interpretation that construe adverbial modification and scope of negation.

Both of these arguments have their share of complications. At bottom, the arguments show that QR cannot precede the calculation of various modification domains, but not necessarily that that calculation cannot take place at LF. It is also not clear that taking the traces of movement at LF into consideration might not allow us to capture the relevant generalizations about scope of modification after QR. Finally, Hornstein's assumptions concerning the scope-boundedness of quantifiers that occur within the government domain of negation appear to run into difficulty when one considers that sentences like (13) appear to freely admit of a wide-scope *every* reading.

(13)   This product is not available in every area.
        (i.e., You cannot buy it anywhere.)

Hornstein is aware of this issue, and he provides some interesting discussion of what might distinguish cases that allow VP quantifiers to leak out from those that do not.

Putting aside these concerns, and accepting the above arguments for the conclusion that the scope of negation and the scope of adverbial modification are calculated off S-structure, we turn now to Hornstein's third argument for distinguishing S-structure and LF interpretation. This argument concerns opacity. As in the case of adverbials and negation, Hornstein comes to the conclusion that the process of semantic interpretation that accounts for opacity phenomena takes place at S-structure and not at LF. Since NP/NP quantifier scope interactions are represented at LF, it follows that opacity and inter-NP scope relations will not receive a uniform treatment. This is, of course, at odds with the semantic program of Montague (1973) and with the Williams-Sag conception of LF.

Thus, the particular version of the semantic theory that Hornstein adopts in the face of his rejection of strong consolidationism raises some fundamental questions about the unity of scope phenomena. If Hornstein is correct, opacity and quantifier scope are distinct phenomena. His first argument for this conclusion retraces the discussion of quantification and the binding theory presented in Hornstein 1984. The argument turns on examples such as (14).

(14)   John believes that someone loves Mary.

Although (14) clearly has a *de re* interpretation, which is often thought to involve assigning *someone* wider scope than *believes*, if we represent this interpretation with wide-scope quantification of *someone* at LF the resulting structure violates the binding theory, since the trace of QR (an anaphor) is then free in its minimal governing category (Hornstein 1984; Aoun and Hornstein 1985):

(15)   [someone$_i$ [$_S$ John believes [$_{S'}$ that [t$_i$ loves Mary]]]]

Hornstein concludes that the distinction between *de re* and *de dicto* is not represented at LF—an unsurprising outcome for him, since it does not involve an NP/NP interaction. However, since his alternative is to represent the distinction at S-structure, Hornstein is forced to abandon the mechanism of scope as the representation of choice. There are two reasons for this. First, on theoretical grounds, all scope relations are to be marked at LF, and all S-structure semantic phenomena are to turn on government relations. Second, since S-structure feeds the phonology, if QR were to apply at S-structure to assign wide scope to *someone* in (14), the reordering effects of QR would be reflected in obvious error in the phonological representation.

In an attempt to analyze the *de re* / *de dicto* distinction without appealing to scope, Hornstein (this volume) proposes the following principle:

D   An element can be given the nonspecific *de dicto* interpretation just in case it is in the domain of an opaque element.

We are to assume that the *de re* interpretation of an element is the default interpretation, and that (D) adds additional possibilities if its domain requirements are met. Thus, in the case of (14), the *de dicto* interpretation of *someone* is available because *someone* is in the scope of *believes* at S-structure (see example 16) with the corresponding LF (after QR) as given in example 17.

(16)   [$_S$ John [$_{VP}$ believes [$_{S'}$ that [$_S$ someone [$_{VP}$ loves Mary]]]]]

(17)   [$_S$ John [$_{VP}$ believes [$_{S'}$ that [$_S$ someone$_i$ [$_S$ t$_i$ [$_{VP}$ loves Mary]]]]]]

Hornstein (this volume) concludes with a discussion of some of the implications of his account of opacity. He points out that his analysis predicts that although (18a) should support a *de dicto* interpretation on which John is seeking no honest man in particular, (18b) ought not to allow this sort of interpretation, since *John* is outside the domain of *sought* at S-structure.

(18a)   John is seeking an honest man.

(18b)   An honest man is being sought by John.

The claim about (18b) seems to me mistaken. In general, passivized subjects seem to admit of *de dicto* interpretations quite freely. Consider (19) as a report of the desire of a frustrated committee that is unclear about what will fix some problem, and (20) as an ad for a boat.

(19)   A workable solution was desperately needed.

(20)   (Wanted:) A sloop is desired by a S.W.M. for ocean travel.

Surely one reading of (20) suggests slooplessness of the classic variety. Hornstein applies a *one*-pronominalization test to support his reported intuitions, but again I do not agree with his intuitions. He predicts, for example, that (19′) ought not to be well formed, since the use of *one* presupposes the *de dicto* interpretation of *a workable solution*, which is alleged not to be available.

(19′)   A workable solution was desperately needed. The committee must find one before midnight or face financial disaster.

It seems clear, however, that (19′) is perfectly well formed, and the fact that passivized subjects may appear outside the governing domain of an intensional verb for which they function as the logical object does not deprive them of the possibility of a *de dicto* interpretation with respect to that verb.

These examples are reminiscent of the raising cases discussed in Montague 1973 in which a raised NP subject can receive a *de dicto* interpretation despite the fact that it appears outside the normal opaque domain of the intensional verb:

(21)   A unicorn appears to be approaching.

If we assume that the *de re* / *de dicto* distinction is marked at LF, by adopting the quantifier-lowering analysis of quantifiers moved by NP-movement (i.e. raising or passive), we can assign a *de dicto* interpretation to *a unicorn* in (21) or *a sloop* in (20) if we apply Hornstein's principle (D) at LF. The LF for (21), given for illustrative purposes,[1] is (22).

(22)   [t_i appears [$_S$ a unicorn$_i$[$_S$ t_i to be approaching]]]

The discussion thus far can be summarized as follows: Hornstein has presented arguments to the effect that scope of negation and scope of adverbial modification are calculated at S-structure, whereas NP/NP quantifier scope phenomena are analyzed at LF. He has also presented evidence that *de re* readings of quantifiers cannot be analyzed via wide scope at LF on pain of violating the binding theory. On the other hand, the *de dicto* interpretation principle (D) that Hornstein proposes does not seem to work well at S-structure, foundering as it does on sentences, such as (19) and (21), that involve the NP-movement of quantifiers out of intensional contexts. Thus, if we are to use principle D, the *de dicto* interpretations of these sentences cannot be determined at S-structure and seem to be better calculated at LF. This is not only at odds with Hornstein's theoretical stance; it is also in conflict with his conclusion that the *de re / de dicto* distinction cannot be analyzed at LF on pain of violating the binding theory. After considering some data involving VP-ellipsis, I shall return to this paradox.

Montague's commitment to a treatment of quantifier interactions and opacity phenomena that depends in part on quantifier scope is, no doubt, historically connected to related treatments in the logical tradition. Nevertheless, as Hornstein's work emphasizes, decisions about which grammatical levels feed semantic interpretation raise what are, at bottom, empirical questions. In this regard, the work of Williams (1977) and Sag (1976) on VP-ellipsis is of considerable interest.[2] This work shows that the identity condition on VP-ellipsis is sensitive to properties having to do with variable binding. Consider first the following contrasts.

(23) a. The book which John read and Bill didn't was boring.
      b. *The book which John read and the book which Bill didn't were boring.

(24) a. What John read but Bill didn't is *War and Peace*.
      b. *What John read but what Bill didn't is *War and Peace*.

Presuming a deletion analysis of VP-ellipsis, the S-structure of the source for (23a) and the putative source for (23b) would be the following.

(25) a. [$_S$ [$_{NP}$ the book [$_{S'}$ which$_i$ [$_S$ [$_S$ John [$_{VP}$ read t$_i$]] and [$_S$ Bill did not [$_{VP}$ read t$_i$]]]]]] was boring]
      b. [$_S$ [$_{NP}$ the book [$_{S'}$ which$_i$ [$_S$ John [$_{VP}$ read t$_i$]]]] and [$_{NP}$ the book [$_{S'}$ which$_j$ [$_S$ Bill did not [$_{VP}$ read t$_j$]]]]] was boring]

When the subject NPs in these structures are mapped into LF (which in the Williams-Sag system is a version of the lambda calculus), roughly the following formulas result.

(26) $\exists!x[book(x) \land [John:y, \lambda y(\underline{read}\ y, x)] \land \sim[Bill:z, \lambda z(\underline{read}\ (z, x))]$
(27) $\exists!x[book(x) \land [John:y, \lambda y(\underline{read}\ y, x)] \land \exists!q[book(q) \land \sim[Bill:w, \lambda w(\underline{read}\ (w, q))]$

In (26), the underlined $\lambda y(\dots)$ and $\lambda z(\dots)$ expressions, which translate the VPs involved in VP-deletion in (25a) (cf. 23) express the same meanings: the property of reading the book in question. They qualify as alphabetic variants (Sag 1976), since they are identical except for the choice of variables bound within the lambda expressions, and the free (within the lambda expression) variable x in each expression is bound by the same quantifier. Because the two lambda expressions are alphabetic variants, they count as identical for the purposes of VP-deletion, accounting for why VP-deletion may be applied to the S-structure in (25a) to derive (23). In contrast, the $\lambda y(\ldots)$ and $\lambda w(\ldots)$ expressions in (27) are not alphabetic variants, owing to the fact that each contains a variable free within it that is bound by a distinct quantifier. This accounts for why the VPs in (25b) that correspond to $\lambda y(\ldots)$ and $\lambda w(\ldots)$ are not eligible to participate in VP-deletion, explaining why (23b) is ungrammatical. A parallel explanation is available for (24a) and (24b) (Sag 1976).

The condition on VP-deletion we are considering—alphabetic variance—entails, as we have seen, that occurrences of free variables in the lambda expressions that represent VPs involved in VP-deletion must be bound by the same quantifier. Thus far we have considered only variables that are the result of wh-movement (i.e., relativization in the case of examples 23). One of the important contributions of the work of Williams and Sag is that the variables of quantification appear to fall under the same principle of alphabetic variance for the purposes of VP-ellipsis. Consider the following example discussed by Williams and Sag (see also Sag and Weisler 1979).

(28)   Somebody loves everybody but Bill doesn't.

(29)   Somebody loves everybody but Bill doesn't love everybody.

The puzzle here is why it is that (29), the S-structure source for (28), has a reading that (28) lacks: the reading in which *everybody* takes widest scope in the left conjunct meaning that everybody is loved by a (potentially) different lover and Bill doesn't love anybody. Although this is one of the readings for (29), (28) has only the other reading of (29): the linear-scope reading in which there is one person who loves everybody but Bill doesn't love anybody. The representations for the two readings of (29) are given in examples 30.

(30)   a. $\exists x:x, \lambda y(\forall z[(y \text{ loves } z)] \wedge \sim \text{Bill}, \lambda q(\forall s[(q \text{ loves } s)])$
       b. $\forall z[\exists x:x, \lambda y(y \text{ loves } z)] \wedge \sim \forall s[\text{Bill}, \lambda q(q \text{ loves } s)]$

In (30a), the linear-scope reading, the $\lambda y(\ldots)$ and $\lambda q(\ldots)$ expressions that translate the two VPs in (29) involved in VP-deletion are alphabetic variants, accounting for why the output of VP-deletion in (28) preserves this reading. In (30b), however, the $\lambda y(\ldots)$ and $\lambda q(\ldots)$ expressions that translate the two VPs in question are not alphabetic variants, since each contains an occurrence of a free variable (z in $\lambda y(\ldots)$ and s in $\lambda q(\ldots)$) that is bound by a distinct quantifier. Thus, the wide-scope *every* reading of (29), which (30b) represents, is not supported by (28).

The explanation for the missing reading in (28) is parallel to that for the ungrammaticality of (23b) and (24b). In these latter cases a trace of wh-movement translated into a variable that was free within the VP translation at LF, and in the case under discussion a variable of quantification was free in a VP-translation at LF. What this suggests is that VP-deletion is sensitive to two "kinds" of scopal phenomena in precisely the same way. The uniformity in the manner in which quantifier scope and wh-word scope interact with the principle of alphabetic variance is explained in the Williams-Sag framework by analyzing both as instances of variable binding operators. Thus, we predict the parallelism between examples such as (28), (29) and (23), (24) in a principled way.[3]

For one final example (which will prove to be crucial below), consider the following instance of antecedent-contained deletion.

(31)   a. John [$_{VP1}$ read [$_{NP}$[$_{NP}$ [every book]$_i$ [$_{S'}$ that Bill [$_{VP2}$ read t$_i$]]]]
       b. John [$_{VP1}$ read [$_{NP}$ every book [$_{S'}$ that Bill did [$_{VP2}$ ∅]]]]

These sorts of sentences are called antecedent-contained because the deletion target (VP2) is contained within the deletion controller (VP1) at S-structure. Williams and Sag have argued that the LF for examples 31 would be on the order of (32).

(32) $\forall x(\text{book } (x) \land \text{Bill, } \lambda y(y \text{ read } x)) \supset \text{John, } \lambda z(z \text{ read } x)]$

Note that $\lambda y(\ldots)$ and $\lambda z(\ldots)$, which translate VP2 and VP1, respectively, are neither of them contained within the other, and are alphabetic variants. In this case, the essentially coordinate (i.e., implicational) structure of the translation of (31) at LF is critical to explaining the possibility of VP-ellipsis.

May (1985) adopts this analysis in its essentials, and offers it as one of the important arguments for quantifier raising at LF, although he does no more than allude to the complications that prompt Sag and Williams to introduce representations in the lambda calculus. On this analysis, Quantifier Raising applies to the S-structure of (31a) to derive the LF (33).[4]

(33)   [$_S$[$_{NP}$ [$_{NP}$ Every book]$_i$ [$_{S'}$ that Bill [$_{VP2}$ read t$_i$]]]$_i$ [$_S$ Bill [$_{VP1}$ real t$_i$]]]

After Quantifier Raising has applied, VP2 is "pulled out" of VP1, and the VPs are distinct, with a structure (lambda abstraction and logical notation aside) that is parallel to the representation assigned within the Sag-Williams framework.

To this point, there is little in my conclusions that is incompatible with Hornstein's position, since he is free to adopt a version of the Sag-Williams analysis of VP-ellipsis. A conflict will, however, emerge in the next subsection when we consider how opacity and VP-ellipsis interact.

Let us return, once again, to Montague's (1973) conclusion that it is possible to give a uniform, principled account of opacity and quantifier interactions that depends, in part, on scope. This conclusion finds additional support in work on VP-ellipsis. The following example, discussed in Sag 1976, is crucial.

(34) Betsy's father wants her to read every book that her boss
   a. wants her to read t_i.
   b. wants her to $\emptyset$.
   c. does $\emptyset$.

The unelided version, (34a), has both a *de re* and a *de dicto* reading. It means either that Betsy's father wants her to read books that turn out to be the same books that her boss wants her to read (*de re*) or that Betsy's father wants her to take her boss's advice and read whatever books the boss suggests (*de dicto*). Although (34b) maintains this ambiguity, (34c) does not. These curious facts may be explained as follows, with the *de re* reading of (34b) illustrated in (35) and the *de dicto* reading in (36).

(35) $\forall y[\text{book } (y) \wedge \text{Betsy's boss}, \lambda z(z \text{ wants (Betsy}, \lambda q(q \text{ read } y))) \supset \text{Betsy's father}, \lambda x(x \text{ wants Betsy}, \lambda r(r \text{ reads } y))]$

(36) Betsy's father, $\lambda x(x \text{ wants } (\forall y[\text{book } (y) \wedge \text{her boss}, \lambda z(z \text{ wants (Betsy}, \lambda q(q \text{ read } y))) \supset \text{Betsy}, \lambda r(r \text{ reads } y)])$

If VP-deletion is applied with respect to the representation in (35), there are two possible deletion targets. The $\lambda q(\ldots)$ and $\lambda r(\ldots)$ expressions are alphabetic variants sanctioning the deletion of the "small" VP *read t_i*, which results in (34b). In addition, $\lambda z(\ldots)$ and $\lambda x(\ldots)$ are alphabetic variants legitimating the deletion of the larger VP as in (34c). Consequently, both of these elliptical examples support a *de re* interpretation.

In the representation of the *de dicto* interpretation of (34a) in (36), again we find that the $\lambda q(\ldots)$ and $\lambda r(\ldots)$ expressions are alphabetic variants, accounting for the possibility of deleting the small VP in (34b) while maintaining a *de dicto* interpretation. On the other hand, $\lambda z(\ldots)$ and $\lambda x(\ldots)$ are not alphabetic variants; $\lambda z(\ldots)$ is a part of $\lambda x(\ldots)$. Furthermore, there are no other VP interpretations available to sanction the deletion of the larger VP in this representation. This accounts for why (34c) cannot support the *de dicto* interpretation of (34a).

The key to this analysis is representing the *de re* interpretation of (34a) with wide-scope quantification at LF. Within a framework that relies on movement to assign scope at LF, quantifier raising would seem to be the rule of choice, mapping the S-structure in (37) into the LF in (38).

(37) $[_S \text{Betsy's father } [_{VP1} \text{wants } [_S \text{her to read } [_{NP}[_{NP} \text{every book}]_i [_{S'} \text{that } [_S \text{her boss } [_{VP2} \text{wants } [_S \text{her to read } t_i]]]]]]]]$

(38) $[_S [_{NP}[_{NP} \text{every book}]_i [_{S'} \text{that } [_S \text{her boss } [_{VP2} \text{wants } [_S \text{her to read } t_i]]]]]_j] [_S \text{Betsy's father } [_{VP1} \text{wants } [_S \text{her to read } t_j]]]]$

After lambda abstracting over the subject of each clause, we can produce a structure that is essentially isomorphic to the translation of the *de re* reading of (34a) in the Sag-Williams system; see (35). This application of quantifier raising, however, is highly problematic from Hornstein's point of view.

To begin with, as was discussed above, quantifier raising cannot apply to the derivation of *de re* interpretations if—as in (38)—it involves raising a quantifier out of its clause on pain of violating the binding theory. (See the discussion of example 14, above.) This application of quantifier raising also flies in the face of Hornstein's conclusion that *de re* interpretations are calculated by principle D, which does not involve a scopal representation and is applied at S-structure. Under those assumptions, quantifier raising would not feed VP-deletion, as we have been assuming. Finally, since VP-deletion is sensitive to a level of representation that distinguishes *de re* from *de dicto* interpretation, as well as (on the basis of our previous discussion) to a level of representation that indicates variable binding, it is important to notice that, on Hornstein's analysis, these cannot be the same level of representation, since opacity is indicated at S-structure and variable binding is indicated at LF. This entails that the identity condition for VP-deletion must check two levels of the grammar, which seems an unwelcome complication.

There are more problems with this analysis, even if we are willing to accept these global consequences. For example, on Hornstein's account both the S-structure and the LF of an example like (34a) will be consistent with either a *de re* or a *de dicto* interpretation, since principle D only provides for the possibility of a *de re* interpretation. Consequently, if we check the S-structure and the LF of (34a) for identity of interpretation for the purposes of applying VP-deletion, we will fail to predict that an application of VP-deletion that results in (34c) disambiguates in favor of a *de re* interpretation.

Most important, it is not clear how one could check the S-structure and/or the LF of (34a) for VP identity, since, on the assumption that quantifier raising does not apply to derive the *de re* interpretation, the two VPs involved in the rule will be antecedent-contained at both levels of analysis—in this example, with VP1 containing VP2. To put this point more strongly: Because (37) has an antecedent-contained structure, it seems that quantifier raising must apply to "pull" VP2 out from within VP1 in order to account for the possibility of VP-ellipsis at all. (See the above discussion of May 1985.) However, in Hornstein's framework quantifier raising could not derive (38), since the trace of quantifier raising would be free in its minimal governing category (the lower S), constituting a violation of the binding theory. In fact, quantifier raising would move the quantifier phrase up to the front of the embedded S, but such a structure is still antecedent-contained:

(39)   [$_S$ Betsy's father [$_{VP1}$ wants [$_S$ [$_{NP}$[$_{NP}$ every book]$_i$ [$_{S'}$ that [$_S$ her boss [$_{VP2}$ wants [$_S$ her to read t$_i$]]]]]]]] [$_S$ her to [$_{VP2}$ read t$_i$]]]

From the Sag-Williams viewpoint, it is easy to see what has gone wrong: (39) would be the representation of the *de dicto* reading of (34a) (again, lambda abstraction and logical notation aside; see example 36), and consequently it ought not to sanction VP-ellipsis. Only the *de re* translation, which is structurally parallel to (38) in a quantifier-raising framework, supports deletion. For Hornstein, however, (39) is supposed to be neutral between a *de re* and a *de dicto* construal (both possibilities, recalling principle D, having been registered at S-structure), and (38) is underivable. This incorrectly predicts that neither the deletion in (34b) nor that in (34c) ought to be possible, and fails to account for the disambiguation effect of VP-ellipsis. Finally, recalling that there were independent problems with principle D regarding the prospects of applying the principle at S-structure (see the discussion of examples 18–21 above), let us briefly consider a alternative, suggested earlier, that involves applying principle D at LF (and consequently giving up Hornstein's principled distinction between S-structure interpretation and LF-interpretation). Such an analysis of the *de re / de dicto* distinction could be consistent with the binding theory and with an account of ellipsis that allows the identity condition to be checked at a single level of analysis (LF). Nevertheless, in the case of examples such as (34), it does not accommodate a successful analysis of VP-deletion, since it would still involve checking ambiguous LF representations in which the VPs involved in VP-deletion were antecedent-contained (e.g. example 39). In this regard, an analysis that applies principle D at LF runs into the same difficulties as one that applies it at S-structure. As a consequence, this minimal alternative to Hornstein's original proposal also cannot account for the disambiguation effect of VP-deletion when applied to examples such as (34a) to derive (34c).

To sum up: VP-deletion has been demonstrated to be sensitive to quantifier/variable dependencies, *wh*-word/variable dependencies, and the *de re / de dicto* distinction. In the framework of Williams and Sag, the representations of all three of these dependencies involve variable binding and scope, and the principled interaction of VP-deletion, quantifier scope, and opacity follows from the principle of alphabetic variance. This triple sensitivity suggests that a strictly modular analysis of quantifier scope and opacity such as Hornstein's modular theory runs the risk of failing to account for the observed interactions by separating out phenomena that must be uniformly analyzed—*de re* interpretations cannot be mediated by quantifier raising, since the binding theory prohibits the long-distance rule application that would be involved. Furthermore, over and above its globality, this alternative account of opacity makes incorrect predictions concerning the interpretation of raised and passivized NPs, thereby undermining the conclusion that opacity is analyzed at S-structure in terms of principle D. Furthermore, principle D cannot be applied at LF, because such an analysis leaves us unprepared to cope with antecedent-contained deletion and the interaction between opacity and VP-deletion.

In addition to calling into question Hornstein's attempt to draw a principled distinction between the range of semantic phenomena that are interpreted at S-structure and those that are interpreted at LF, we are left with the following problem. If we use relative (in this case, wide) quantifier scope to represent the *de re* reading of examples such as (34a) as well as to represent quantifier-quantifier interactions and other instances of variable binding, we pave the way for a uniform treatment of the semantics of quantification while at the same time allowing for a successful account of VP-deletion. Such an approach, which is essentially that of Sag and Williams and which has much in common with the system developed by Montague (1973), is inconsistent with the binding theory. Thus, from the point of view of the analysis of VP-deletion, *de re* interpretation, like the crossed-scope interpretation of quantificationally ambiguous sentences, involves wide-scope quantification. From the point of view of the binding theory, it cannot. Although Hornstein's account of quantification honors the second consideration, it ignores the first. The following subsection suggests another alternative which modifies certain of Hornstein's assumptions about modularity of interpretation and the analysis of quantification.

Any account of quantification that is consistent with the binding theory as typically stated must forbear dependence on long-distance applications of quantifier raising at LF. Suppose, then, that we adopt Hornstein's suggestion that *de re* interpretations are not marked by wide-scope quantification at LF. If the discussion in the preceding subsections is correct, Hornstein's own alternative of assigning *de re* and *de dicto* interpretations on the basis of S-structure representations is problematic. Furthermore, since (generative semantics aside) D-structure does not offer much to recommend it as the grammatical level at which opacity is analyzed, we appear to be out of grammatical levels to consider.

We are not, however, out of alternatives if we consider the possibility that the interpretation of LF has linguistic properties. We shall construe LF as an ambiguous level of representation, with the consequence that some properties of a sentence are determined after disambiguation and on the basis of the meaning of the sentence. In the case of a sentence manifesting a *de re* / *de dicto* ambiguity, the sentence will be associated with a single LF which itself is associated with the two meanings the sentence expresses.

We can think of LF as fixing the range of interpretations that a given sentence can support. The separate meanings of a sentence must be consistent with its LF and are therefore partially determined by it. Let us reconsider example 14 as a case in point in order lay out the proposed analysis, and then turn to some of the more complicated cases.

(14)   John believes that someone loves Mary.

The S-structure for (14) will be (40), and the LF will be (41).

(40)   John believes [$_{S'}$ that [$_S$ someone loves Mary]]

(41)   [$_S$ John believes [$_{S'}$ that [$_S$ someone$_i$ [$_S$ t$_i$ loves Mary]]]]

The LF in (41) must now be associated with its interpretations. This could be accomplished by associating each terminal node in (41) with a meaning and by composing the meaning of the phrasal categories (and, ultimately, the sentence) compositionally. If, for convenience, we use a logical language as a representation of meaning, we shall require a translation of (41) into the logic—in this case, into two distinct formulas, one capturing the *de re* reading of (14) and the other capturing the *de dicto* reading. Although this is not the place to present detail, we can assume that Cooper's (1983) storage device[5] is optionally available to provide *de re* interpretations in cases in which quantifiers are represented inside the scope of intensional verbs at LF—in this case, assigning *someone* higher scope than *believes*. In the case of (14), with the lambda-calculus version assumed for reasons that will become clear presently, the two formulas that would be ultimately produced are, roughly, (42) and (43).

(42) $\exists x[$ John, $\lambda y(y$ believes $[x, \lambda z(z$ loves Mary$)])]$

(43)   John, $\lambda y(y$ believes $[\exists x:x, \lambda z(z$ loves Mary$)])$

The principle that assigns scope to the existential quantifier (here assumed to be Cooper storage) does not fall under the binding theory. Indeed, if we remind ourselves that the interpretation of LF involves mapping LF representations into meanings, it is clear that the binding theory cannot apply at this level. This accounts for why the wide-scope representation in (42) is not ruled out by a grammatical principle such as the binding theory. It is crucial that this scope-assignment device is reserved for disambiguating *de re* / *de dicto* ambiguities and cannot introduce new quantifier/quantifier scope relationships which must be mediated by QR at LF. Otherwise, the binding theory would have no impact in limiting the interactions between quantifiers to those that are essentially clausemates.

This idea that there are two separate mechanisms to account for quantifier/quantifier interactions and opacity phenomena finds inspiration in Hornstein's proposals. Indeed, given his observation that the wide-scope quantification traditionally needed to represent *de re* interpretation would violate the binding theory, we seem to be forced to this conclusion. We are not, however, thereby forced to the conclusion that the *de re* / *de dicto* distinction is not represented in terms of scope (or its interpretive reflection). Pending other possible complications, the meaning of a sentence can be represented in a quantificational language, as long as we allow quantifier scope to be assigned at two different stages of the derivation. The stages are not fully encapsulated, however, and the range of meanings calculable at the second "level" (i.e. in the interpretation) is limited by the range of interpretations that are established at the first level (LF).

Such an analysis has many benefits when VP-ellipsis and (especially) antecedent-contained deletion are considered. To begin with, we will need to make a modification to one assumption made in the Williams-Sag approach to VP-ellipsis. The modification (which is, for the most part, conceptual) is this: We cannot treat the identity condition on VP-ellipsis as a condition on representations at LF. Among other reasons is that our decision to treat LF as an ambiguous level of representation precludes this option, since the *de re / de dicto* distinction will not have been resolved by LF, and VP-ellipsis is demonstrably sensitive to the distinction, as we have seen. We can, however, adopt an interpretive version of alphabetic variance that is calculated directly on meanings.[6] Such a condition requires that a potential controller VP and a potential target VP must express identical meanings in order be involved in the rule of VP-ellipsis. If we continue to use the lambda calculus as a representation of meaning, this amounts to applying the principle of alphabetic variance to meaning representations that are expressed in terms of the lambda calculus, in the familiar way.

The LFs of examples such as 23 and 24 (which are isomorphic to their S-structures, given in examples 25a and 25b) will be associated with meanings that can be represented just as they were in the Sag-Williams framework (see examples 26 and 27), and the relevant distinctions can be drawn in the same manner. The quantificationally ambiguous example 29 and the univocal, elliptical version 28 will also receive a parallel analysis, but in cases of this type the scope of the operator binding the trace of QR in each reading will be fixed at LF. The LF for the wide-scope *every* reading of (29) is (44a), and that for linear-scope reading is (44b).[7]

(44)   a. $[_S [_S \text{everybody}_i [_S \text{somebody}_j [_S t_j \text{ loves } t_i]]]$ but $[_S \text{everybody}_k [_S \text{Bill doesn't love } t_k]]]$

        b. $[_S[_S \text{somebody}_j [_S t_j [_{VP} \text{everybody}_i [_{VP} \text{loves } t_i]]]]$ but $[_S \text{everybody}_k [_S \text{Bill doesn't love } t_k]]]]$

The interpretations for (44a) and (44b) will be the meanings that can be represented by (30a) and (30b), respectively. The reading represented by (30b) and (44a) is not expressed by (28) because the VPs involved in VP-ellipsis do not express the same meaning (each of them involves a free variable); this is reflected by the fact that the representations of these VPs in (30b) are not alphabetic variants.

Finally, let us consider the antecedent-contained deletion cases which proved problematic for Hornstein's analysis. Examples such as 31a and 31b will first involve mapping the S-structure for the undeleted source (31a) into LF—in this case, (33). Then (33) is interpreted, with the representation in (32) expressing the relevant meaning. The deletion of the VP in (31b) is sanctioned since the meaning it expresses is "redundant." This is reflected by the fact that $\lambda y(\ldots)$ and $\lambda z(\ldots)$ are alphabetic variants in (32).

The analysis of more complicated cases of antecedent-contained deletion, such as (34), make crucial use of the storage mechanism to account for the fact that (34c) is missing a *de dicto* reading.

(34)   Betsy's father wants her to read every book that her boss
    a.   wants her to read t_i.
    b.   wants her to $\emptyset$.
    c.   does $\emptyset$.

As was discussed above for example 39, the LF for these examples will involve applying QR to the NP *every book that her boss wants her to read,* but the NP will be adjoined to the intermediate S-bracket.

(39)   [$_S$ Betsy's father [$_{VP1}$ wants [$_S$ [$_{NP}$ [$_{NP}$ every book] [$_{S'}$ that [$_S$ her boss [$_{VP2}$ wants [$_S$ her to read t_i]]]]]]]] [$_S$ her to [$_{VP2}$ read t_i]]]

The next step is to provide an interpretation of (39). Since the NP *every book that* ... is inside the scope of the intensional verb *wants,* its meaning can be optionally stored and can be figured into the meaning of the sentence after the rest of the matrix clause meaning is composed, resulting in a *de re* interpretation. If the NP meaning is not stored, the resulting interpretation is *de dicto.* As before, (35) and (36) provide representations of these two meanings.

(35) $\forall y$[book $(y) \wedge$ Betsy's boss, $\lambda z(z$ wants (Betsy, $\lambda q(q$ read $y))) \supset$ Betsy's father, $\lambda x(x$ wants Betsy, $\lambda r(r$ reads $y))$]

(36)   Betsy's father, $\lambda x(x$ wants ($\forall y$[book $(y) \wedge$ her boss, $\lambda z(z$ wants (Betsy, $\lambda q(q$ read $y))) \supset$ Betsy, $\lambda r(r$ reads $y)]$))

At the level of LF, QR has already pulled the lower VP *read t_i* out of its antecedent, but the larger VP introduced by *want* remains antecedent-contained. Consequently, if we attempt to delete the little VP (see example 34b) we should expect either the *de re* or the *de dicto* reading to be available whether or not the meaning of the *every book that* ... NP is stored in composing the interpretation. This follows because the meanings of the VPs involved in the rule are appropriately redundant, as is reflected by the fact that $\lambda q(\ldots)$ and $\lambda r(\ldots)$ are alphabetic variants in both (34) and (35). On the other hand, if the meaning of the NP *every book that* ... is not stored, then the meanings of the two larger VPs introduced by *want* will not be redundant, since one remains a part of the other. Again, this is represented by the fact that $\lambda z(\ldots)$ is contained within $\lambda x(\ldots)$ in (36). In (35), however, $\lambda z(\ldots)$ and $\lambda x(\ldots)$ are alphabetic variants; this accounts for why the *de re* reading, which involves storage of the *every book that* . . . NP, is available for (34c). In essence, this is the explanation provided originally by Sag (1976), with the conceptual difference that the antecedent-containedness that accounts for the missing reading is construed as involving a meaning contained within another meaning rather than as the antecedent-containedness of lambda expressions at LF.

To sum up this subsection: By partitioning our account of quantification into two parts, we are able to accomodate the binding theory as well as a satisfactory account of ellipsis. QR falls under the binding theory; storage does not. Both mechanisms of quantification are, however, essentially scopal although the analysis of opacity can be accomplished in the process of interpretation. Although the two mechanisms are separate, they are not encapsulated in the way Hornstein has suggested. Quantification seems to be best analyzed by formal devices operating at two different stages within a single module.

Conclusion

The present proposal is different in important respects from virtually all its alternatives. It departs from the Government and Binding tradition in viewing the level of meaning as the basis for significant linguistic generalization. In this regard it resembles model-theoretic approaches to meaning, but unlike those approaches it posits an indispensable syntactically motivated level of LF. Furthermore, LF is not a disambiguated level of representation but a syntactic level that provides input to the process of interpretation.

Perhaps the most surprising aspect of the present approach is its reliance on two mechanisms—storage and QR—to mediate the interpretation of quantifiers. These have typically been taken to be roughly equivalent devices in alternative frameworks designed to accomplish the same purpose. In the present proposal, however, both are recruited to analyze separate aspects of quantification. The intuition behind this decision springs from Hornstein's (1984) observation that analysis of interpretation *de re* in terms of QR violates the binding theory. Pace Montague (1973), the conditions on quantifying in cannot be stated uniformly to cover all cases of quantifying in. Nevertheless, the data from VP-ellipsis indicate that the quantification involved in opaque constructions requires an essentially scopal analysis, justifying the inclusion of both QR and storage.

Two independent empirical arguments can be given that more strongly support the conclusion that the analysis of quantification must be dichoto-mous. The second of these arguments raises some interesting issues for future research. First, consider the following two examples.

(46)   Someone read every book and every magazine.

(47)   John was looking for a sloop and a lost dog.

In (46), there are just two readings available, depending on whether the coordinate NP *every book and every magazine* takes wide or narrow scope with respect to the subject quantifier. In particular, it is not possible to construe the quantifier *every book* as having wider scope than *someone* at the same time as *every magazine* is construed as taking narrowest scope. Working from standard assumptions, if QR is sensitive to the coordinate-structure constraint, the range of possible interpretations will be appro-priately limited at LF.

However, (47) has four readings—*a sloop* and *a lost dog* can be construed *de re* or *de dicto*, and either NP can be construed *de re* while the other is construed *de dicto*. In other words, it is possible to assign a "wide-scope" interpretation to each of the coordinate NPs independently, in apparent violation of the coordinate-structure constraint. From the present point of view, this is all to be expected. Unlike the interpretation of quantifier/ quantifier scope ambiguities, which falls under QR, the possibility of *de re* interpretation is mediated by the storage device—a purely interpretive mechanism that is not constrained by grammatical conditions such as the coordinate-structure constraint (or the binding theory) which constraint applies exclusively to syntactic levels of the derivation. Thus, while it is difficult to see how a uniform analysis of quantification could account for these facts, the present analysis provides a natural account for the observed clustering of properties.

The second argument[8] turns on example 48.

(48)   John knew [$_{S'}$ that [$_S$ someone wanted [$_S$ Betsy to read every book that her boss wanted her to read]]]

The reading of (48) in which we are interested is the *de re* reading, which asserts that, with respect to the books that Betsy's boss wants her to read, John knows someone who also wants her to read them.[9] This is the reading on which *every book that her boss wanted her to read* is taken to have wider scope than *knew* (and *wanted*). Curiously, though, the *every book* NP cannot take wider scope than *someone* even though *knew* takes scope over *someone*. Thus, we have an example of what Hornstein has dubbed an *intransitivity*.

The binding theory can readily explain the absence of quantifier inter-action, since the higher quantifier *someone* is outside the governing domain (in this case, the clause) in which the lower quantifier *every book that* ... appears. Consequently, moving the lower quantifier over the higher quantifier would entail leaving the trace of QR free in its governing category, in violation of the binding theory. The LF that is derived is (49), in which *someone* takes scope over *every book that*. . . .

(49)   John knew [$_{S'}$ that [$_S$ someone$_j$ [$_S$ t$_j$ wanted [$_S$ [every book that her boss wanted her to read]$_i$ [$_S$ Betsy to read t$_i$]]]]]]

In the interpretation of (49), we can (optionally) store the meaning of *every book that* ... and introduce it into the sentence's meaning after the meaning of the rest of the sentence is composed to get the desired *de re* interpretation. Although it appears that this "wide-scope" interpretation of *every book that* ... gives it wider scope than *someone* by virtue of giving it wider scope that *knew*, our conception of LF will correctly avoid this result. LF provides a range of possible interpretations for a given sentence, with the quantifier-quantifier relationships fixed. Consequently, the "wide-scope" construal of *every book that* ... has an impact on its interpretation with respect to the subordinating verbs but cannot establish new quantifier-quantifier relationships that are interdicted at LF. Thus, although the two mechanisms that account for quantifier interpretation are distinct, the information determined at LF must be available to the interpretation procedure. The two mechanisms are not encapsulated, nor are they derivationally related in the usual way. Rather, the representations at LF underdetermine the interpretation by prescribing its bounds.

This evidence for independent mechanisms of quantification provides support for the present model, but it also raises important questions of representation. In particular, it is not possible to represent the *de re* reading of (49) in Montague's IL or in any other logical language that preserves scopal transitivity. That is, if the order of verbs and quantifiers is represented linearly, it is impossible to scope *every book that* ... higher than *knew* at the same time that it is scoped lower than *someone*, given that *someone* is scoped lower than *knew*. Thus, an alternative logical language (or interpretive algorithm) is needed to compose meanings. The answer may lie in the domain of branching quantifiers (Hintikka 1974) or independent interpretation (May 1985), but the details remain to be worked out (Rucker 1986).

Notes

1. It is not clear that the passive cases will also receive a lowering analysis. Since this proposed solution will be rejected below, I will not pursue the point here.
2. Sag's (1976) analysis of VP-ellipsis differs from Williams's (1977) in that the former employs a deletion rule whereas the latter employs an interpretive approach. The conception of the form of LF, however, is the same.

3. There are numerous complications pertaining to the quantificational examples that have been discussed by Hirschbühler (1982), Fodor and Sag (1982), May (1985), and Rucker (1986). So far as I know, none of these undermine the argument presented.

4. Although May (1985) does not discuss this point, it is crucial that the index on the moved quantificational phrase and the index on the trace of relativization be the same. If we assume that heads of relative clauses are co-indexed with relative pronouns and with the NP node that dominates the whole relative clause, we get this result.

5. The Cooper storage device allows the meaning of a quantifier to be held on a "stack" and figured into a sentence meaning after the meanings of other syntactically dominant nodes are composed. It has the effect of quantifying in in Montague grammar.

6. This proposal has been made previously for independent reasons; see Weisler 1979 and Sag and Hankamer 1980.

7. Notice that (44b) involves VP-adjunction of the raised quantifier. S-adjunction would move the quantifier outside the VP-deletion target, leaving a free variable. For arguments that VP-adjunction of quantifiers is available, see Sag and Weisler 1979 and May 1985.

8. In chapter 6 of the present volume Hornstein gives a related argument, which is complicated by his intuition (discussed above) that subjects of intensional passive verbs cannot receive *de dicto* interpretations.

9. *Someone* can be interpreted *de re* or *de dicto* with respect to *knew*. The point that follows can be made with either of these readings.

8

Categorial Grammar and the Domain Specificity of Universal Grammar

Michael Flynn

It is a commonplace that judgments about an object's properties are influenced by the point of view from which it is considered. For example, differences between theories of grammar that sometimes loom so large in the daily lives of linguists are for the most part invisible to just about everyone else, often even to colleagues in closely related disciplines. The observation of the distinction between a star and a planet, crucial for some purposes, on other occasions would be quite impertinent or downright rude.

The object I want to consider in this chapter is Universal Grammar, in Noam Chomsky's sense. What I am going to suggest is that if assignment of structure to sentences of natural languages is done with a categorial grammar along certain lines, then a widely adopted attitude about a property of Universal Grammar namely its domain specificity, shifts a bit. Before I turn to that, though, I want to add a little perspective to the discussion and outline the instantiation of categorial grammars I have in mind.

Once upon a time, the hierarchical organization of a sentence's constituents and their relative ordering were simultaneously specified by a context-free phrase-structure grammar, that is, by rules of the form $A \rightarrow \psi$, where A is a single nonterminal symbol and ψ is a finite ordered sequence of symbols of any sort. The resulting derivations can be associated with trees in the familiar way. As far as I know, these approaches were rarely contrasted with alternative procedures (at least not in print and with explanatory adequacy in mind; however, see McCawley 1968 for an exception). Besides, phrase-structure rules were straw men anyway. Chomsky forcefully argued that the important and influential work of many American Structuralists presupposed these sorts of rules, and that they (I mean the rules) don't do what they are intended to do, at least not by themselves. By a venerable strategy that dates back at least as far as the time of Ptolemy, new technical devices were grafted onto the old, improving, it came to be widely agreed, the empirical adequacy of the theory.

Later on, as the perception of linguistics as a branch of human psychology began to reemerge in a new form,[1] the question of how a child abducts structure-assigning rules from data that underdetermine them became prominent. The story here is complex and, I think, fascinating, even (maybe especially) from a sociological point of view. (For more details, see Newmeyer 1980.) For example, one could regard these rules as universal and hence innate, thus shifting the explanation for their complexity (or, at any rate, their character) to another science, such as psychobiology. What I'd like to emphasize now, though, is the very important work in which Jackendoff (1977) gave an explicit instantation of the $\overline{X}$ theory, some version of which (as we say) is today widely assumed. Much of the technical apparatus of Jackendoff's deployment, such as the symbol counting evaluation metric, has now, it appears, faded from the scene, but aspects of the spirit of the theory live on, particularly in the theory of government and binding. I'll display this by giving a simple example of how several components of the grammar interact to assign structure to phrases. These principles are under intensive investigation and are continuously being modified and elaborated, but I will overlook much of this here, as my goal is to highlight general features of the approach.

Consider how the principles in (1) assign the structure to the VP *loves a fish* in (2).

(1)   a. X-bar theory: Predictable phrasal categories are projected from lexical categories.
  b. θ criterion: Each argument bears one and only one θ-role, and each θ-role is assigned to one and only one argument, under (perhaps proper) government.
  c. Head Parameter: English is head initial.
  d. *Loves*, a verb, assigns a θ-role to an NP.

(2)

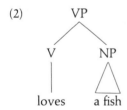

That V is dominated by VP follows from the $\overline{X}$ theory. That VP also dominates NP follows from the θ criterion, given (1d).[2] That the NP appears to the right of the verb follows from the setting on the Head Parameter.

The $\overline{X}$ theory and the θ criterion are a part of Universal Grammar (UG). The setting of the Head Parameter requires some input data. Notice that dominance and order, once inseparable, are now specified by independent principles. Other components may be involved as well, for example the theory of abstract case (Stowell 1981; Pesetsky 1983). And the head-initial setting may actually be a parameter on the directionality of case and θ-role assignment (Koopman 1984; Travis 1984). I won't elaborate on any of this here; the main point is that in the Government and Binding framework (or, for that matter, in just about any theory of grammar that comes to mind these days[3]) hierarchical organization and left-right order are specified by independent principles. Innate principles of UG, given minimal lexical information, determine dominance. Ordering principles, be they settings on the position of the head or parameter settings on the directionality of case and θ-role assignment, require some data to determine. Dominance, then, is largely universal, whereas order is language-particular (but not rule-particular, as in Montague 1973 and Chomsky 1965). Ordering principles, once they are determined, are presumably intended to apply language-wide.[4] It is exactly this way of slicing up the pie that I will now sketch by using a categorial grammar.

I take the following characterization of categorial grammars to be essential: In categorial grammar, dominance relations are explicitly encoded in the assignment of lexical items to categories, there is a functional correspondence between the syntactic categories and the logical type expressions in that category denote, and primitive syntactic categories correspond to primitive semantic entities whereas fractional categories correspond to functions. (For a particularly clear exposition of the basic idea, see Lewis 1970.) What I'm going to suggest is that the $\overline{X}$ theory and the θ criterion can be replaced by a categorial grammar. Now, what I'd like to do is simply surgically excise these two principles and the categories they presuppose, put in the replacement part, stitch the edges back together, and see how the patient gets along. The trouble is that things go badly, as Williams (1984) has pointed out.

   Rather than go into this here, I will embed a revised version of an idea I had about categorial grammars a few years ago (part of which appears in Flynn 1983) in a slightly modified form of the approach taken by Chierchia (1984, 1985) as influenced by the work of McConnell-Ginet (1982). The modifications I'll make are intended to factor our responsibilities in the grammar so that the organization will come as closely as possible to what I take to be the Government and Binding framework. (This is in part a rhetorical strategy. Since it is Chomsky's view of UG that I want to examine, I want to minimize the damage done to the framework that prompts the view. I also want to leave open the possibility of embracing the other insights articulated within the framework.) Then I'll be in a position to make the observations I promised about the domain specificity of UG.

   One important innovation in Chierchia's work is the adoption of Nino

Cocchiarella's theory of properties, deployed by means of the syntax and semantics of a family of second-order systems, prominently including Chierchia's IL_*. I can't do justice to this system here, but I will try to outline aspects of it that are important for my purpose.

The ontology of a natural model for IL_* consists of two basic kinds of entities: propositions (the nature of which is intentionally left open) and individuals. Individuals are of many a spot and stripe. They include not only ordinary things, such as Bertrand Russell's favorite necktie, but also what Chierchia (following the lead of many others) calls kinds, qualities, locations, periods, eventualities, and other things, many of which correspond to properties by means of what Cocchiarella calls a Fregean embedding (a map from properties to individuals). Properties themselves are n-place functions from individuals to properties. Propositions can be regarded as 0-place properties.

Expressions of natural languages fall into three broad classes, depending on the sorts of things they denote. First, there are the *basic* categories, as in (3).

(3)   S, NP, CN, $Pred_{pp}$, $Pred_{ADJ}$

Expressions of these basic categories denote basic entities. The type-assignment function (τ) for them is as in (4).

(4) $\tau(S) = p$; $\tau(\alpha) = e$ for all primitive categories α, where $\alpha \neq S$

p is the type of propositions, e the type of individuals.

There are two kinds of expressions assigned to fractional categories: predicates and functors. Predicates denote properties. Examples of these are given in (5).

$$(5) \quad IV\left(\frac{S}{NP}\right) \quad TV\left(\frac{S}{\frac{NP}{NP}}\right) \quad \frac{IV}{S} \quad \left(\frac{\frac{S}{NP}}{S}\right)$$

The "official" specifications for these commonly used abbreviations appear in parentheses. The type assignment for these is given in (6).

$$(6) \quad \tau\left(\frac{A}{B}\right) = \langle e, \tau(A) \rangle$$

For example, the type assignment for transitive verbs is $\langle e, \langle e, p \rangle \rangle$, i.e., a two-place predicate interpreted as a two-place property. Also to be included among the predicates in (5) are what McConnell-Ginet calls an admissible argumentation of an n-place predicate. Basically, McConnell-Ginet argued that certain restrictive modifiers, instead of being functions in, say, **IV/IV**, are actually arguments of the verb. She writes: "If $\langle X, V \rangle$ is a cover symbol denoting any category whose lexical members are verbs ... then I will propose a category of the form $\langle X, V \rangle / $**AD-V**." (1982, p. 164) In our terms, if *runs* is in category **S/NP** then an admissible argumentation for *runs* is a member of

$$\frac{\dfrac{S}{NP}}{AD\text{-}V}.$$

The type assignment here will be $\langle e, \langle e, p \rangle \rangle$, and the first argument of the function which the admissible argumentation of *runs* denotes will be the individual corresponding to the predicate denoted by the **AD-V**.

Chierchia also admits a third broad category (the second class of fractional categories), which he calls functors. Functors, like prediates, correspond to functions, but they are unlike predicates in that the objects they denote are not in the domain of the Fregean embedding, (i.e., they do not correspond to individuals in the ontology). Chierchia indicates this difference with a double slash, as in (7).

(7) $\dfrac{IV}{IV} \quad \left(\dfrac{\dfrac{S}{NP}}{\dfrac{S}{NP}} \right) \quad DET\left(\dfrac{NP}{CN} \right) \quad Prep\left(\dfrac{PRED_{PP}}{NP} \right)$

The type assignment for functors is as in (8).

(8) $\tau\left(\dfrac{A}{B} \right) = \langle \tau(B), \tau(A) \rangle$

The important point for my purpose about all this is that this system conforms to what I said earlier about the essential characteristics of categorial grammar. There is a functional correspondence between the syntactic category an expression belongs to and the logical type of thing the expression denotes, and primitive categories correspond to primitive semantic entities (individuals or propositions) whereas fractional categories correspond to functions. (Chierchia calls this the Principle of Functional Correspondence.) I'll now turn to the claim that dominance relations are encoded in the assignment of lexical items to categories.

Chierchia specifies the core combinatorial part of the syntax of the object language by means of a parametrized template he calls $AFFIX_n(\alpha, \beta)$.

(9) $AFFIX_n(\alpha, \beta)$: Affix α after the nth constituent of β.

He writes: "The parameter n and the level of constituenthood that $AFFIX_n(\alpha, \beta)$ has access to are severely restricted by an independent set of principles determining how such parameters may covary with a particular categorial base, the configurational characteristics of the language, etc. [Here Chierchia cites Ades and Steedman 1982 and Bach 1980, 1983 as examples.—M.F.] Right concatenation and Bach's 'Rightwrap' ('Affix α after the head of β') are the only instances of the core operation that have been argued to be active in the grammar of English." (Chierchia 1985, p. 427)

In line with my goal here, I'd like to reformulate this a bit. Suppose instead that we regard the grammar as a system of principles that structures assigned to sentences must satisfy in order to be generated by the grammar. So, corresponding to the items in (1a)–(1d), I'll reformulate our grammar so that one aspect of UG takes over the role played by the $\overline{X}$ theory and the θ criterion, and a language-particular setting on a parameter plays the role of the head-initial property of English.

Let us think of this in terms of node-admissibility conditions. The grammar will contain, say, functions from (sub)trees to $\{\sqrt{},*\}$ ($\sqrt{}$ for admitted, $*$ for rejected), and a tree is admitted only if every nonterminal node in the tree is admitted. I'll take the lexicon to be a set of ordered pairs of the form $\langle \alpha, \mathbf{W} \rangle$, where α is a lexical item and $\mathbf{W}$ is a category, and regard such specifications as licensing trees of the form

$$\mathbf{W}$$
$$|$$
$$\alpha$$

I confine myself here to those functions whose role is to check dominance and order. All these will conform to the provisional principle in (10), which I'll call Connection after the title of Ajdukiewicz's seminal paper (1935).[5]

(10)   Connection
       A node $\mathbf{W}$ is admitted only if it immediately and exhaustively dominates a node labeled with a fractional category of the form $\mathbf{W/Y}$ (or $\mathbf{W//Y}$) and a node labeled with the category $\mathbf{Y}$.

Connection will play a role corresponding to the $\overline{X}$ theory and the θ criterion in a way that will become obvious momentarily. The role of the Head Parameter will be played by what I call an Ordering Convention. Here, too, it is anticipated that UG will make available a number of options from which languages select, and, as with the setting of the head parameter, it is intended to apply language-wide. (See Flynn 1983 for some discussion of this in slightly different setting.)

For the purpose of illustration, I propose the principle in (11) as the language-particular principle to which functions in the grammar of English conform.

(11)   Ordering Convention for English
An S node is admitted only if its main functor is to the right of its argument. For all other nodes, the main functor must be to the left of the argument.

The term "main functor" here is from Ajdukiewicz (1935), who attributes it to Leśniewski. Basically, the main functor is that unique expression (perhaps I should say "tree" here) which can be analyzed as the fractional category **W/Y** in Connection. Before giving an example of how this works, let me be clear about its status. The convention in (11) is simpler that the one I had proposed for English in previous work because restrictive modification is handled differently in the Chierchia-McConnell-Ginet system than it was in the framework (i.e. Montague's) that I was assuming before. I regard this new convention as quite programmatic. It does, however, handle correctly all the cases displayed in (5) and (7). Whether or not it or something like it will work in general, especially when "wrapping" constructions are considered in detail, will I hope become clear as the investigation proceeds. The condition on wrapping proposed in Flynn (1983) will work to get the correct relative ordering between object **NP**s and restrictive modifiers under McConnell-Ginet's revision, but I still regard these cases as far from closed.

At any rate, for now I will serenely presuppose that (11) works perfectly. To see how it works, consider the tree in (12).

(12)

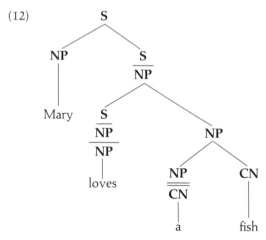

As the reader can easily verify, each node satisfies both Connection and the ordering convention for English. Among the consequences of the ordering convention are that English is SVO and that it is prepositional.

Though further details remain somewhat murky, especially to those a bit unfamiliar with the work I am relying on, the general approach is, I hope, fairly clear. I regard it as quite reasonable to suppose that a framework roughly isomorphic to the Government and Binding theory can be erected using a categorial grammar. Connection plays the role of the $\bar{X}$ theory and the θ criterion. The ordering convention plays the role of the setting on the Head Parameter (or, perhaps, the directionality of Case and θ-role assignment).[6] Conditions on the Wrap function will play the role of the Case Adjacency Principle. I said "roughly isomorphic" because it is to be hoped, and it appears, that there are empirical considerations that will choose between the two frameworks. (See, for example, Chierchia 1985.)

I now turn to the central conditional of this paper: If the approach outlined here can be sustained, what happens to our judgment about the domain specificity of properties in UG? This topic is a terminological minefield, and I will try to avoid lengthy textual exegesis. But I do want to be clear about what I think the empirical questions are, and about how the approach just outlined bears on one of them.

There are a number of attitudes one can adopt toward the lay of the mental land, approximations of some of which can be seen by considering the alternatives that arise in (13) by choosing one from column A and one from column B.

(13)   Most things of interest to us about the mind are

$$\left\{ \begin{array}{c} A \\ \text{innate} \\ \text{acquired} \end{array} \right\} \text{ and } \left\{ \begin{array}{c} B \\ \text{domain-specific} \\ \text{general} \end{array} \right\}.$$

The Procrustean beds induced here do not exactly characterize anyone's position that I know of, but I do think it fair to say that the dominant view in generative circles tends toward some variation of the top line selection in (13).

Chomsky's view of the matter is, I think, pretty clear, at least as far as language goes. During the famous debate with Jean Piaget, he put it this way:

> I would say, then, that a rational approach would be to assume that in the domain where we have some nontrivial results concerning the structure of language,[7] the principles of organization that determine the specific structures of language are simply part of the initial state of the organism [i.e., they are innate—M.F.]. So far as we know, these principles don't generalize, that is, there are no known analogues in other domains of intelligence (it is possible that such analogues are partially there, but this remains to be seen). (Piattelli-Palmarini 1980, p. 172)

Let me elaborate here by saying how I'm going to take the prevailing terminology. First, let's take the "domain of language" or "language domain." As Chomsky has noted (1975, pp. 15–16), pretheoretically we make a guess about the domains. Further investigation may indicate that our first approximations of domain boundaries (chosen usually on teleological grounds; e.g., face recognition, chess-playing) have to be altered somewhat to achieve a tolerable degree of coherence. But we do not want to *define*, say, the domain of language in terms of specific properties; if we do, Chomsky's claim becomes a tautology. After all, if the only properties a domain can (rather than happens to) have are those that are domain specific, then it is a trivial and uninteresting observation that properties that domains have are domain specific. In what follows, then, I will regard the domain of language to be the strictly formal (syntactic) properties; though this is still rather fuzzy, nothing really hangs on it. Thus, I take it that it is at least logically possible that factors determining grammaticality, no matter how refined we take this notion to be, are not specific to the domain of language.[8]

I will construe Universal Grammar in what I take to be the standard sense—namely, that system of principles, conditions, rules, and whatnot that are elements of properties of all human languages by biological, not logical, necessity (Chomsky 1975, p. 29; Chomsky 1980a, p. 28).

Now consider what Chomsky has called "the language organ." I'm not completely sure how he wants to define this notion, but I will take it as follows: The language organ is that part of UG that is domain specific. So UG is a set of principles or whatever, $P_1, \ldots, P_n$, that determine the formal properties of languages and are determined by human biology. The language organ (LO) is the collection of those principles P_i that are (contingently) domain specific.

I will assume that UG is non-empty, by the standard poverty-of-the-stimulus argument. The possibilities for LO, as I see it, are those given in (14).

(14)　a.　LO = UG
　　　　b.　LO ⊂ UG (proper inclusion)
　　　　c.　LO = ∅

I take Chomsky's view to be that expressed in (14a). Piaget, on the other hand, I regard as having endorsed the view expressed in (14c). (I read him as agreeing with Chomsky that UG is non-empty.) The view I want to urge here is the one in (14b); that is to say, I want to suggest that there is at least one property in UG that is not specific to the domain of language. (Notice that 14b does not preclude 14c, but I don't want to argue for the stronger 14c.)

As the reader can probably guess, the property I have in mind is Connection and the categories it presupposes. Another domain in which I think it plays an important role is what I sometimes think Chomsky (1975, pp. 48 ff.; 1980a, pp. 55, 92) is referring to when he speaks of "common sense understanding." In other words, our inventory of category indices and a principle that regulates admissible combinations of expressions assigned to these categories are in part determined by our semantics, and this is determined by our ontology (i.e., the way we categorize, to borrow Quine's charming phrase, "the passing scene"). Chierchia also writes in this vein. At one point he says: "If, as many philosophers seem to think, the role of a logical grammar should be to display somehow the structure of the world, then one of the theses of HST* [one of the systems that instantiate Chocchiarella's theory of properties—M.F.] seem to be that properties may be looked at from two points of view. *Qua* predicable entities they appear to be essentially incomplete or 'unsaturated' structures.... Properties however, can also be 'nominalized' and nominalized predicative expression can be subjects in predication acts." (Chierchia 1984, p. 53) (This is the role of the Fregean embedding I mentioned earlier.) Later Chierchia writes: "There is a certain hypothesis about possible semantic universes built into IL_x, namely, the three layers hypothesis ... syntactic categories fall into three natural classes, determined by the semantic type associated with them: arguments, predicates, and functors." (1984, p. 151)

Thus, the view is that the categories that play such a major role in the formal syntax of languages are determined, broadly speaking, nonlinguistically, as a reflex of how we categorize the world, i.e., our ability to analyze and manipulate abstract objects. By the way, we would probably not want to say that this ability is inherited from or attributable solely to natural language. As Fodor puts it (1975, p. 56), "either we abandon such preverbal and infrahuman psychology as we have so far pieced together, or we admit that some thinking, at least, isn't done in English." Like Fodor, I regard the latter as far more attractive. During the Chomsky-Piaget debate (Piattelli-Palmarini 1980, p. 173) Fodor remarks: "I take for granted that thinking is a domain that is quite different from language, even though language is used for the expression of thought, and for a good deal of thinking we really need the mediation of language." (See also Fodor 1975, pp. 83 ff., where it is argued that there must be some mental representation, independent of natural language, the terms of which are coextensive or perhaps synonymous with predicates of natural language.)

The view I am arguing for here may have been shared by the young Wittgenstein. For some discussion see Küng 1966,[9] chapters 4 and 6. Küng writes: "It is important to notice how for Wittgenstein the so-called logical form is not merely the syntactical form of sentences but at the same time the ontological form of the world of facts. He calls it explicitly 'the form of reality' (Wittgenstein 1922:2.18)."

I don't think that this sort of view comes as any news to those who have have been working on categorial grammars, especially those working in the very rich tradition of Polish philosophy. For example, Roman Suszko, in a paper about categorial grammars, writes: "It may be a reasonable conjecture that the content of this paper is connected with structural inquiries in linguistics and with some problems of the philosophy of language and thinking. But we do not discuss here these connections." [10] (Suszko 1958)

Recapitulating, I will now try to express the fundamental point here as succinctly as I can. In categorial grammar, the combinatorial possibilities of expressions in a language are explicitly encoded in the labels of the expressions' categories. The empirical claim is that the categories are functionally related to what one might call classes of objects in the language user's semantic universe—that primitive categories correspond to primitive objects and that fractional categories correspond to functions. These classes of objects are determined by the language user's classification of the world. Thus, the way we organize the world and the way we hierarchically organize the expressions we use to speak of the world are, in a sense, two sides of the same coin.

I see this not simply as a matter of two components "interacting" (Chomsky 1980, pp. 55, 123). It is, rather, a case of a principle and the objects the principle refers to in linguistic theory being homomorphic to a subsystem of a quite distinct domain. For a discussion along similar lines, see the transcript of the discussion between Chomsky and David Premack in Piattelli-Palmarini 1980.[11]

To conclude, I'd like to briefly articulate the view of the mind I think is suggested by (14b), generalizing now a bit. First, consider the view, suggested by (14a), that all properties of Universal Grammar are domain specific. Each species (humans, for example) has a set of domains in each of which (or at least in many of which) normal members of that species achieve a system of knowledge and/or belief. The boundaries of each of these domains are clarified as research proceeds, and are determined on grounds of coherency, not specificity. Suppose that what (14a) says for language is true for all domains. Without question, this would be an empirical discovery. In each case, the character of the domain is determined by domain-specific principles in the organism's initial state. Each of these principles has a biological explanation (in principle, at least) but no independent psychological explanation. The messy, fuzzy, difficult-to-classify activity we observe in the organism in question results from the interaction of the organ/domains. I believe this is the view that Chomsky has in mind when he writes of the "modularity of mind" in *Rules and Representation* (1980). (The sense of the phrase here is quite distinct from that discussed in Fodor 1983 and presupposed through much of the present volume.)

The picture painted by (14b) is somewhat different. Here we have the same domains, their interaction is responsible for the unwieldly behavior we observe, and we have what might be called a modular mind. The difference is that the modules don't correspond so closely to the domains. In other words, there need not be a unique module for every domain—or, indeed, for any domain.

Looking at things this way takes the bite out of what I think is a rather vexed question: the determination of domain. For example, is the ability to swat a fly in the same domain as the ability to hit a curve ball? A lot seems to hang on what abstractions we wish to make. Either way seems to lead to conceptual confusion when it comes to discussing the organ(s) on which the domain(s) is (are) based. But if we think of an organ, or module, as contributing to but not determining a domain, the number of modules (which, I am assuming, is biologically determined, i.e. an empirical question) can stay pretty small—say, under a thousand. But the number of domains we might be concerned with can be very much higher, and can be determined by what we take the organism to be doing and what we are interested in. (This is, I gather, a familiar strategy in ethology; see, for example, Morris 1958.)

Thus, (14b) suggests that the mind does consist of genetically determined modules, but that these do not match the domains in a one-to-one fashion. Each domain makes what might be called a selection, either ontogenetically or phylogenetically,[12] from the modules in constructing itself, perhaps adding genetically determined special-purpose properties. In particular, the language domain shares its categories with the independent domain that characterizes the world.

However, the language domain may also have special-purpose genetically determined properties. For example, suppose that Principle A in (15) is true and domain specific.[13]

(15)   An anaphor is bound in its governing category

It is indeed difficult to imagine another domain that has this property. If there is no other such domain, the resulting picture we get is something like figure 1. (The leftmost compartment may well by empty.)

The way I have set things up here runs the (empirical) risk of termino-

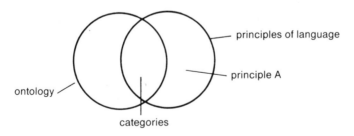

Figure 1

logical misrepresentation. That is, suppose it turns out, as more and more features of the description of the formal properties of language become known, that in fact many of these features are shared by other domains or are selected from more general, more abstract, genetically determined modules. The situation I'm envisioning here is one in which several distinct, higher-order modules contribute formal properties to the language domain. It would begin to seem very odd to speak of "the language organ." It would perhaps be better to speak of "the language organs" much as we speak of the speech organs (which in this case would be quite analogous), adding that one of these organs is domain specific. I need hardly mention that what I have said in this paragraph is rather speculative, yet it seems worth keeping the possibility in mind.

To sum up: I have suggested that the $\overline{X}$ theory and the θ criterion can be replaced by a categorial grammar embedded within a very promising general theory of language. I have argued that if this view is correct, our view of the impact of linguistic theory on the organization of the human mind is altered a bit. However, there should be heavy emphasis on the *if* in the last sentence. I hope I've contributed to the conceptual issues involved. Many intriguing and quite difficult empirical issues remain.

Acknowledgments

I would like to express thanks to Dan Finer, who gave me patient advice concerning several topics in the first section, to Gennaro Chierchia for checking parts of the second section for accuracy, and to the Max Planck Institute for Psycholinguistics in Nijmegen, The Netherlands, for providing me with the opportunity, in the fall of 1982, to begin thinking about some of the topics in the third section. Thanks also to Richard Oehrle for reading an earlier draft and making several suggestions.

Notes

1. In particular, the goals of general-process learning theory were abandoned. For a clear discussion of this, though not with reference to linguistics, see the introduction to Seligman and Hager 1972. I'd like to thank Randy Cornelius for recommending this book to me.
2. Perhaps not quite. The NP must also be strictly subcategorized by *love*, so that the position is obligatory. For discussion of this, see Chomsky 1981, pp. 40–41. Of course the argument remains an enthymeme, but the additional premises, including the one mentioned in this note, don't matter for the point I wish to make.
3. See also Gazdar and Pullum 1981.
4. Somewhat less strict requirements have been proposed by Huang (1982) and others.
5. This statement of Connection is provisional because it will no doubt have to be revised when wrapping operations and functional composition are added to the grammar. Though people working with categorial grammars have a clear intuition of what Connection will have to do in these cases, I have found an elegant articulation of the principle oddly elusive.

6. Curry (1963; written much earlier) writes that "we may conceive of the grammatical structure of a language as something independent of the way it is represented in terms of expressions." The grammatical structure, or what Curry calls the *tectogrammatics*, is the hierarchical organization of the phrases without the terminal elements; the *phenogrammatics* are the terminal elements plus their lieft-eight ordering. For further discussion of this distinction see Dowty 1982.

7. A nontrivial result for Chomsky is "one that has some explanatory force over a range of empirical facts and that can be refuted." It has been widely appreciated, at least since Quine 1951, that unpacking the notions of explanatory force and refutability is not entirely straightforward (see for example the introduction to Piattelli-Palmarini 1980.) But I will assume, as I think Chomsky intends, that if the principles at the "hard core" have general applicability and if it is reasonably clear when these in conjunction with "protective belt" hypotheses would make false predictions, then the principles at the core are nontrivial. For some further discussion of this, see Koster 1978, pp. 8–11.

8. I am avoiding the phrase "the language faculty." Chomsky sometimes seems to identify this notion with UG, as in the following passage:

> Suppose further that the operation of rules of grammar is in part determined by semantic properties of lexical items; ... These are by no means implausible ideas. If they are correct, the language faculty does not fix a grammar in isolation, even in principle. The theory of UG remains as a component of the theory of the mind, but as an abstraction. Note that this conclusion, if correct, does not imply that the language faculty does not exist as an autonomous component of mental structure. Rather, the position we are now considering postulates that this faculty does exist, with a physical realization yet to be discovered, and places it within the system of mental faculties in a fixed way. (Chomsky 1975, pp. 42–43)

However in the paragraph following the one just quoted, Chomsky writes: "My own, quite tentative, belief is that there is an autonomous system of formal grammar, determined in principle by the language faculty and its *component* UG" (footnote supressed, emphasis added). My own inclination runs to a broad and nontechnical use of the phrase "language faculty" (broader even than that of "language domain"); however, in order to minimize confusion, I will not use the term. I think Chomsky is using "UG" here in a sense different from and narrower than the one articulated in the next paragraph of the present chapter. In the interests of clarity I should remark that, were the paragraph quoted in this footnote to be rewritten using the terminology as it is employed in the present chapter, I could make an empirical claim of it only by replacing "language faculty" and "UG" with "the language organ" (a phrase to be introduced momentarily). To slightly modify a plea Jerry Fodor made (in a different context) at the conference at which the papers in this volume were presented: I will be happy to give away the words if I can keep the distinctions. Readers may have alternative (and equally, if not more, reasonable) appelative proclivities, and I hope that the sympathetic among them will make the required glosses, something I will henceforth eschew.

9. I'd like to thank Ron van Zonneveld for bringing this book to my attention.

10. This paper is translated, somewhat awkwardly in spots, from Polish. My quotation is altered slightly to improve readability. The original reads: "It may be a reasonable conjecture the content of this paper to be connected ...," with the rest as above.

11. See also Papert's (1980) and Putnam's (1980) discussions in the same volume.

12. To say "ontogenetically" here would be to begin moving a bit closer (but not much closer, I think) to Piaget's view; see Papert 1980. To say "phylogenetically" is, it seems, to move closer to the work of Konrad Lorenz; see Bischof 1980.

13. This principle is from Chomsky 1982.

9
Combinatory Grammars and Human Language Processing
Mark Steedman

What would we expect natural languages to be like if we had never seen one before? I suggest that we would expect the following properties:

1. We would expect them to exhibit the "rule-to-rule" relation between semantics and syntax that is exhibited by well-behaved artificial languages, such as predicate calculus and arithmetic. Such languages exhibit a functional relation—often one-to-one—between rules of semantics and rules of syntax. The reason is obvious enough: All that syntax is *for* is to tell you which semantic rule is to be applied, and what it is to be applied to. To have rules that do not map onto semantic rules, such as semantically vacuous transformations, would complicate these languages to no apparent purpose. There seems no obvious reason why human languages should be any different.

2. We would also expect a transparent relation between the rule-to-rule grammar and the computation performed by the processor of a natural language—that is, we would expect them to adhere to the "strong competence hypothesis" of Bresnan and Kaplan (Bresnan 1982). Such a relation is not a requirement for efficient processing as such. The operations of a processor may be quite unrelated to the rules of the grammar that it processes, as Berwick and Weinberg (1982, 1983) have noted. Indeed, Berwick and Weinberg point out that compilers for programming languages may parse according to a "covering grammar" whose syntax is quite different from that of the "competence" grammar that appears in the manual for the language in question. However, such "nontransparent" processors are necessary only when the properties of the grammar are not well suited to the computing machinery. Such is often the case with programming languages. There are all manner of constraints upon programming languages. Because these constraints stem from the purposes of their human users rather than from the machines that run them, they are typically somewhat at odds with the functional architecture of the von Neumann machines that most of them run on. But in the absence of any reason to suppose that natural languages are constrained by any external authority of this kind, parsimony suggests that there is likely to be a transparent

relation between their grammars and the operations of the processor. So does any kind of gradual evolution of the language faculty.

3. Ambiguity in the expressions of a language, whether local or global, cannot help but interfere with its primary purpose, which is to convey meanings. However, here there are some considerations that might make us expect such ambiguities in human languages. Limitations on long-term or short-term memory might force some degree of local ambiguity—for example, large lexicons might be intolerable, so that some words would have to do semantic double duty. Such lexical ambiguities are likely to engender local syntactic ambiguity. But we can be pretty sure that these ambiguities must be locally resolvable if the search-space for the correct analysis is kept within computationally reasonable bounds.

Of course, natural language gives every appearance of flying in the face of all these expectations. The existence of a wide variety of "discontinuous" constructions, in which elements that belong together in semantics are separated in syntax, has been taken to mean that natural languages are not "well behaved" under the first count. And the theories that have been proposed to capture the constructions that are so problematic under the first count have sometimes proved hard to reconcile with transparent processing. They have been particularly hard to reconcile with the intuition that people interpret utterances *incrementally*, word by word, without apparently needing to wait for the sentence or the constituent they are processing to be syntactically closed. Natural languages also exhibit a remarkably high degree of local and global ambiguity, much of which is not obviously susceptible to local resolution by the methods that are familiar from compiler construction.

What do we do when faced with a phenomenon that runs so very much counter to expectation? One possibility is to try to find factors that have been neglected, whose inclusion will make us revise our expectations. It may be that we have incompletely grasped the semantics of natural languages, or that some arcane requirement of natural processing machinery requires the anomalous constructions. It may be that evolution was less plastic—or that the mechanisms of variation were smarter—than we think, allowing the parallel development of grammars and covering grammars. It may be that the consequences of proliferating analyses can be contained by a more ingenious deployment of the methods used by compiler writers.

Or it may be that our expectations are in fact correct, and that it is our theories of syntax, semantics, and ambiguity resolution that make natural languages look ill behaved. A number of recent papers within the frameworks of Montague grammar (MG), Generalized Phrase-Structure Grammar (GPSG), and Lexical-Functional Grammar (LFG) have proposed grammars that are rule-to-rule (Bach 1979, 1980, 1983; Dowty 1982; Gazdar et al. 1985) and/or compatible with the strong competence hypothesis. One such theory of grammar is the one advanced by Ades and Steedman (1982 [hereafter "A&S"]), Steedman (1985a ["D&C"] and 1985b ["CGPG"]), and Szabolsci (1983). It seems appropriate to call this theory Combinatory Grammar, because it augments the context-free apparatus of Categorial Grammar (Ajdukiewicz 1935; Bar Hillel 1953; Lyons 1968) with operations corresponding to the "combinators" used in Combinatory Logic (Curry and Feys 1958). Categorial Grammar distinguishes constituents as functions or arguments, and in its original form the sole operation for combining these elements is the operation of functional application. Combinators are operations that combine functions to produce other functions. Their distinctive property is that they strictly eschew the use of bound variables. They are used by mathematical logicians to define the foundations of applicative systems such as the lambda calculus, and by computer scientists to define the semantics of the related programming languages. Combinatory grammar imports a few of these semantically primitive operations into natural-language grammar, in order to capture well-known problematic constructions that have given rise to unbounded and bounded movement transformations in theories stemming from the work of Chomsky (1965). Foremost among these combinatory rules is the operation of functional composition.

The question I address here is: Why should natural languages look like this? I shall argue that such an appearance is entirely consistent with the simplifying assumptions with which I began this chapter. Natural-language syntax looks like a raw combinatory system because it is a transparent rule-to-rule reflection of a semantics that is expressed using the combinators as primitives rather than some other primitive operations (such as the more familiar lambda abstraction).

But then why should natural-language semantics be that way? I shall argue that work on the efficient evaluation of "applicative" or "functional" programming languages suggests that there are considerable computational advantages to a semantics expressed in this form, and that in this respect there is a certain similarity between natural languages and functional programming languages.

Finally, why should local ambiguities be so much more widespread in natural languages than in functional programming languages? I shall argue that the incorporation of composition and other combinators allows the kind of constructions used in natural languages to be evaluated incrementally, left to right, even when their right-branching character under traditional assumptions makes incremental evaluation seem impossible without the invocation of some additional machinery. The availability of an interpretation at every stage means that this interpretation can be evaluated with respect to the context, and that the results can be used to choose among alternative analyses on grounds of plausibility rather than on purely structural grounds.

The argument will go as follows. The next section will introduce the basic assumptions of Categorial Grammar, and the intuitive and liguistic bases for its augmentation by function-combining operations. The following section contains a brief introduction to the combinators and combinatory logic, which provides the theoretical basis for these innovations and acts as a preparation for the subsequent section, in which I turn to the central question of the chapter and argue that combinatory grammars are well adapted to efficient semantic evaluation and incremental interactive processing under the strong-competence hypothesis. I conclude with a brief argument that, provided the nature of this interaction is confined to the variety that Crain and Steedman (1985) have called "weak," the theory is entirely consistent with the modularity hypothesis.

Combinatory Grammars and Unbounded Dependency

Categorial Grammar and Functional Application
What follows is a brief description of the bare bones of Categorial Grammar (CG), as a basis for the combinatory grammars developed in A&S, D&C, and CGPG and discussed below. The version of CG set out here is very general indeed. In particular, unlike CGPG, it uses *nondirectional lexical categories* and *nondirectional combinatory rules*. This unconstrained form is appropriate in the present context, where we are discussing general properties of categorial/combinatory grammars and reasons why human grammars should take this form. However, it follows that the rules given here generalize beyond the constructions that illustrate their use here. More restricted grammars for specific languages (such as Dutch and English) that have comparatively fixed word order can easily be produced; the interested reader is referred to those earlier papers for examples.

A Categorial Grammar can be thought of as consisting of two components: a categorial lexicon, which distinguishes the words of the language as either functions or arguments, and a set of "combinatory rules," which define the ways in which these elements can combine. In its original form, in which CG is merely a version of context-free (CF) grammar, there is only one combinatory rule, namely a rule of functional application which allows a function category to combine with an argument of an appropriate type. While the "combinatory" incarnation of CG extends the number of combinatory rules to include such rules as functional composition, it is an important restriction that these new combinatory rules preserve a crucial property of functional application: All such rules apply to *adjacent* elements of the string only.

The Categorial Lexicon

The categorial base is defined as a lexicon, in which each entry includes a "category" defining the kind of constituent (if any) with which the word in question can combine and the kind of constituent that results. The category of a pronoun like *me* or *that* is simply NP. The category of a transitive verb like *eat* is written as VP/NP, which identifies it as combining with an (object) NP to yield a VP. Similarly, the category of a ditransitive verb like *give* is (VP/NP)/NP—a thing that combines with an (indirect object) NP to yield a thing which still needs an (object) NP to yield a complete VP. (Naturally, any word, including the verbs mentioned above, is free to have more than one lexical entry.)

Items having categories of the form X/Y, $(W/X)/Y$, and so on are to be thought of as functions over Y. For example, the category VP/NP of transitive verbs identifies them as functions from NPs into VPs, and the category (VP/NP)/NP of ditransitive verbs identifies them as functions from NPs into functions-from-NPs-into-VPs. In the first place, such functions can be thought of as mapping between entirely syntactic domains. However, the categories can also be thought of as a shorthand for the semantics of the entities in question. Although in the present chapter I will remain entirely uncommitted concerning the nature of the semantic representations of the categories themselves (as opposed to the combinatory rules), the assumption is parallel to the basic "rule-to-rule" assumption prevalent in Montague grammar. The shorthand in question is very elliptical, in the interests of simplifying the syntactic rules. However, it is assumed that the semantic categories are related to the syntactic ones under the more restricted version of the rule-to-rule relation which Klein and Sag (1985) have called "type driven translation." The function categories can therefore be thought of as mapping between semantic representations. It is further assumed that it is this semantic function that defines the functional role of its argument. For example, it is the semantics of a ditransitive verb (VP/NP)/NP that means that the first argument with which it combines is the indirect object and the second is the direct object.

Functional Application

A function category can combine with an adjacent argument of the appropriate type according to the following rule:

(1)   Functional Application
       A function of category X/Y and interpretation F can combine with an adjacent argument of category Y and interpretation y to yield a result of category X and interpretation Fy, the result of applying F to y.

X and Y are variables that range over any category, including functions, so the rule allows the following combinations:

(2)   a. $\underbrace{\underbrace{\underbrace{\text{Eat}}_{\text{VP/NP}}\ \ \underbrace{\underbrace{\text{the}}_{\text{NP/N}}\ \ \underbrace{\text{cake}}_{\text{N}}}_{\text{NP}}\text{ apply}}_{\text{VP}}\text{ apply}$

b. $\underbrace{\underbrace{\underbrace{\text{Give}}_{\text{(VP/NP)/NP}}\ \ \underbrace{\text{me}}_{\text{NP}}\ \ \underbrace{\text{that}}_{\text{NP}}}_{\text{VP/NP}}\text{ apply}$

The verb phrases in the examples are each accepted by two successive function applications. (Combination of two entities is indicated by an underline indexed with a mnemonic identifying the rule, with the resulting category written underneath. In combination a, the categories that match X and Y in rule 1 are atomic. In combination b, X matches VP/NP in the first combination.) Because the categories and the general functional application rule (1) impose no restriction on the order of function and argument, they will also allow sequences like *the cake eat*, which are not allowed in English. However, they are allowed in other languages, and it is easy enough to restrict word order for given languages, so that is all right.

Such diagrams are in every way equivalent to the more familar trees associated with phrase-structure grammars, and the apparatus introduced so far is merely context free. Thus, for example, the following derivation merely reflects traditional notions of constituency and structure for the example in question.

(3)   Harry   must   have   been   eating   these apples
S/VP + fin VP + fin/VP VP/Cen Cen/Cing Cing/NP NP

(The nonce symbols VP + fin, Cen, and Cing stand for Finite VP, *-en*-complement, and *-ing*-complement, respectively.) The only difference is that CG identifies the function-argument structure, and in this respect the above tree needs further comment. No one would argue with the proposal that *eating* is a function over (object) NPs, but it is surprising to be told that the subject *Harry* is a function over the VP + fin, or predicate. Semantics would suggest it is the other way round. The assumption is justified at some length in the earlier papers, but for present purposes I shall for the most part treat it as a stipulation to make the wheels go round. However, it is worth noting that the categories S/VP + fin and VP + fin for subject and predicate arise, semantically speaking, from type-raising of the kind used by Montague (1973). That is, we have turned the subject NP into a function over predicates. Semantically, the predicate is a function over NP interpretations of type $\langle e, t \rangle$, which, if realized transparently in syntax, would bear the category S/NP. We have merely encoded the semantic category as the atomic syntactic category VP + fin, so that the type-raised subject, a function of type $\langle\langle e, t \rangle, t \rangle$ over such functions into their result, is written as S/VP + fin rather than as the transparent category S/(S/NP).

The central problem for categorial grammar, as for any theory of grammar, is the presence in natural languages of discontinuous constituents— that is, constructions in which elements that belong together in semantics are separated. It is these discontinuous constituents that gave rise to the addition of further combinatory rules in the earlier papers, whose main findings are reviewed next (with a great deal of language-specific detail omitted).

Extraction and Functional Composition
Consider example 4, in which the object has been "extracted to the left." [1]

(4)

These apples	Harry	must	have	been	eating
NP	S/VP + fin	VP + fin/VP	VP/Cen	Cen/Cing	Cing/NP

The rule of functional application that we inherit from categorial grammar will not do anything for us here. But there is another well-known operation that we can perform on functions, besides applying them: We can compose them, by rule 5.

(5) Functional Composition
A "main" function of category X/Y and interpretation F may combine with an adjacent "argument" function of category Y/Z and interpretation G to yield a function of category X/Z and interpretation $\lambda x[F(Gx)]$, the composition of F and G.

(There is are precedents for such rules of natural-language grammar in Lambeck 1958 and in Geach 1972.) The above rule allows the main and argument function to be in either left-to-right or right-to-left order, but in a right-branching language such as English the predominant pattern of composition is the "forward version" illustrated by (6).

(6) Forward Composition
$X/Y : F \ Y/Z : G \Rightarrow X/Z : \lambda x[F(Gx)]$

A&S showed that the repeated application of this rule in examples like (4) allows extraction, as illustrated by (7).

(7)

These apples	Harry	must	have	been	eating
NP	S/VP+fin	VP+fin/VP	VP/Cen	Cen/Cing	Cing/NP

```
                 ─────────────────── compose
                        S/VP
                 ─────────────────────────── compose
                            S/Cen
                 ──────────────────────────────────── compose
                                S/Cing
                 ─────────────────────────────────────────────── compose
                                    S/NP
 ────────────────────────────────────────────────────────────── apply
                               S
```

(Again, the completely general rules of application and composition give us lots of other word orders. Again, the reader is directed to earlier papers for examples of language-specific grammars.[2]) Because of the semantics of the composition rule (5), the result has the same semantics as the corresponding canonical sentence assembled without benefit of the new rule. As (8) illustrates, it handles unbounded dependency the same way (see A&S, p. 546).

(8)

Those cakes	I	can	believe that	she	will	eat
NP	S/VP+fin	VP+fin/VP	VP/S′	S′/S	S/VP+fin	VP+fin/VP	VP/NP

```
                ──────────────── compose
                      S/VP
                ──────────────────────── compose
                          S/S′
                ──────────────────────────────── compose
                             S/S
                ───────────────────────────────────────── compose
                           S/VP+fin
                ─────────────────────────────────────────────────── compose
                               S/VP
                ───────────────────────────────────────────────────────────── compose
                                   S/NP
 ──────────────────────────────────────────────────────────────────────────── apply
                                S
```

(The somewhat startling implications of this analysis as far as surface structure goes are discussed extensively in D&C and below.)

A&S and D&C "generalize" the rule of functional composition, using a "$" notational device, to include "higher-order" compositions like the following:

(9)   Forward Composition′
       $X/Y:F (Y/W)/Z:G \Rightarrow (X/W)/Z: \lambda z[\lambda w[F(Gzw)]]$

They argue that the generalization is required for the extraction of the NP in English sentences like (10), which involve a verb subcategorized for more than one complement and which therefore bears a "higher-order" functor category.

(10)

This cake	I	put	on the table
NP	S/VP+fin	(VP+fin/PP)/NP	PP

```
                 ─────────────────────────── compose′
                        (S/PP)/NP
                 ──────────────────────────────── apply
                      S/PP
 ──────────────────────────────────────────────────── apply
                          S
```

The generalization is an extremely simple one in terms of the theory of combinators.

Crossing Dependencies
The inclusion of functional composition accounts for the notorious incidence of crossing dependencies in Dutch sentences like (11) (see the extensive discussions in Bresnan et al. 1982 and D&C).

(11)   . . . omdat ik$_1$ Cecilia$_2$ Henk$_3$ de nijlpaarden$_3$ zag$_1$ helpen$_2$ voeren$_3$
       . . . because I Cecilia Henk the hippos saw help feed
       . . . because I saw Cecilia help Henk feed the hippos

The following categories for the verbs are implied by the semantics.

(12)   *zag*:   VP + fin/Sinf
       zien, helpen: (Sinf/NP)/Sinf
       voeren: (Sinf/NP)/NP

The surface orders of Dutch clauses like (11) including nested infinitival complements can be accepted on the basis of just these categories when functional composition is included. (The generalized Forward Composition rule 9 is required. The dependencies between NPs and the functions that take them as arguments are indicated by subscripts, which are included purely for the reader's convenience, the grammar itself does not include or require them.)

(13)   . . . omdat   ik   Cecilia Henk de nijlpaarden   zag   helpen   voeren
               S/VP + fin NP$_1$ NP$_2$ NP$_3$ VP + fin/Sinf (Sinf/NP$_1$)/Sinf (Sinf/NP$_2$)/NP$_3$
                                                        ――――――――――――――――――― compose'
                                                         (VP + fin/NP$_1$)/Sinf
                                                                            ――――――――――――――――― compose'
                                                                             ((VP + fin/NP$_1$)/NP$_2$)/NP$_3$
                                                                            ――――――――――――――――――――― apply
                                                         (VP + fin/NP$_1$)/NP$_2$
                                                        ―――――――――――――――――――― apply
                                              VP + fin/NP$_1$
                                             ―――――――――――――――― apply
                                              VP + fin
                             ―――――――――――――――――――― apply
                                     S

Such surface orders are accepted because the grammar includes the composition rule, which was expressly introduced on the basis of apparently unrelated extraction phenomena in English in order to glue functions such as verbs together in advance of their combination with any other arguments. Verbal functions that combine under this rule will necessarily produce as their composition a function that, if it is to find its arguments to the left, demands them in the crossed rather than the nested order.

It will be clear at this point that function composition is performing a role very much like that of "slash percolation" or slash feature-passing in GPSG. Indeed, in more recent incarnations of GPSG (Gazdar et al. 1985; Pollard 1985), the semantics of this operation amounts to functional composition. The present proposal simply amounts to the stronger claim that this mechanism is directly reflected in syntax. In D&C, the rule of functional composition is shown to capture and extend Gazdar's (1981) generalization concerning the relation of unbounded dependency and coordinate structure. However, the following type of multiple dependency is not explicable in terms of functional composition alone.

Multiple Dependencies and Functional Substitution
Construction 14 is of a type which Taraldsen (1979) and Engdahl (1981) have talked of as including a "parasitic gap."[3]

(14)   (articles) which I will file __ without reading __p

The term *gap* (which has nothing to do with the kind of gapping found in coordinate sentences) refers here to what a transformationalist would regard as extraction sites or "empty categories." The important properties of sentence 14 are that it has more than one gap corresponding to a single extracted item, *which articles*, and that one of these gaps (indicated by subscript p) is in a position from which extraction would not normally be permitted.

Szabolcsi (1983) pointed out that if we had one additional operation to construct such predicates, indexed as "substitute" in (15), then application and composition would do the rest.

(15)   (articles) which I will   file   without   reading

$$
\frac{\displaystyle \frac{\displaystyle \frac{\displaystyle \frac{\text{NP} \quad \text{S/VP} \quad \text{VP/NP} \quad \frac{\text{(VP/VP)/Cing} \quad \text{Cing/NP}}{\text{(VP/VP)/NP}}\,\text{compose}}{\text{VP/NP}}\,\text{substitute}}{\text{S/NP}}\,\text{compose}}{\text{S}}\,\text{apply}
$$

The rule in question can be seen as a special case of the combinatory rule given in (16), which is parallel to the earlier functional application and composition rules (1) and (5).

(16)   Functional Substitution
   A second-order "main" function of category $(X/Y)/Z$ and interpretation F may combine with an adjacent first-order "argument" function of category Y/Z and interpretation G to yield a function X/Z with interpretation $\lambda x[(Fx)(Gx)]$.

This rule allows combinations on the following pattern, as in derivation 15:

(17)   Backward substitution
   $Y/Z:G\ (X/Y)/Z:G \Rightarrow X/Z:\lambda x[(Fx)(Gx)]$

Extraction of the first gap alone is allowed under the earlier analysis, of course. But extraction from the second site alone is not allowed by the expanded grammar, because even the new combinatory rule cannot combine *read your instructions*$_{VP}$ with *before filing*$_{(VP\backslash VP)/NP}$:

(18)   *(articles) which I will   read   your instructions before filing
$$\underline{}\underline{\text{NP}}\underline{\text{S/VP}}\underline{\text{VP/NP}}\underline{\text{NP}}\underline{\text{(VP/VP)/NP}}$$

$$\underline{\text{VP}}\text{apply}$$
$$\underline{}\ *$$

At the same time, the new rule will not permit arbitrary double deletions, such as (19).

(19)   *(a man) who(m) I showed t t$_p$
$$\underline{\text{NP}\underline{\text{(S/NP)/NP}}}\ *$$

The implications of this rule for the grammar of English are explored more fully in CGPG.

It would be nice to have some independent linguistic support for the introduction of combinatory rules such as functional substitution. An obvious constellation of multiple dependency phenomena to which we can turn for this support is provided by "raising," "equi," and other such control phenomena, and Steedman (1985c) argues that these constructions reveal that the same set of combinators is at work in the lexicon as in syntax proper. However, it is more important for present purposes to ask what it means to introduce these combinatory operations to natural-language grammars, and what the consequences for processing are. To answer these questions, we shall have to leave linguistics for a while and turn to combinatory logic.

Combinatory Logics and Applicative Systems

The operations of functional composition and substitution introduced above bear a striking resemblance to the "combinators" of Curry and Feys (1958, especially chapter 5). Curry and Feys use combinators to define the foundations of logic in terms of "applicative systems," of which the lambda calculus is one example. Combinators are operations on functions that can be used to define applicative systems up to the full power of the lambda calculus—in particular, to define the fundamental operation of *abstraction*, or definition of a function. Their distinctive characteristic is that, unlike the λ operator, they do not invoke bound variables.

The intuitively most basic set of combinators, in terms of which Curry's first versions of Combinatory Logic were developed, consisted of four combinators called **B**, **C**, **W**, and **I**. The first three of these are intuitively simple. The most important one for present purposes is **B**, which is the combinatory logicians' rather un-mnemonic name for the functional-composition combinator. It takes two functions of syntactic type X/Y and Y/Z and semantics F and G respectively, and yields a composite function of syntactic type X/Z whose semantics is given by the identity (20).

(20) $\mathbf{B}FG = \lambda x\,[F(Gx)]$

A convention of "left associativity" for function application is assumed here—that is, the application of a second-order function ϕ to an argument x. The application of the result ϕx to a further argument y—that is, $(\phi x)y$—is written (somewhat tersely) as ϕxy. Thus, the left-hand side of (20) is an abbreviation for $((\mathbf{B}F)G)$.

The Functional Composition rule (5) of the theory presented above is simply a typed version of the combinator $\mathbf{B}$.[4] **C** is a "commuting" operator that maps second-order functions such as $(X/Y)/Z$ onto the corresponding function $(X/Z)/Y$ with the arguments reversed. Its semantics is expressed as in (13).

(21) $\mathbf{C}F = \lambda x\,[\lambda y\,[Fyx]]$

No related syntactic combinatory rule is used in the present chapter. However, such operations have been widely used in the Montague literature, in the form of rules like Bach's (1979, 1980) "Right-wrap," and **C** is shown in Steedman 1985c to be possibly implicated in the lexicon.

The "doubling" combinator **W** takes a function of two arguments onto a function of one argument which identifies the two arguments. Its semantics is given by (22).

(22) $\mathbf{W}F = \lambda x\,[Fxx]$

Again, no related syntactic combinatory rule is used in the present theory, but it is shown elsewhere to be implicated in the lexicon.

A less obvious but immensely useful "substitution" combinator **S** (which can be defined in terms of the preceding three) was first proposed by Schönfinkel (1924) and later incorporated into the combinatory schemes of Curry and his colleagues (see Curry and Feys 1958, especially the "historical statement" on pp. 184–185). Its semantics is defined by the equivalence

(23) $\mathbf{S}FG = \lambda x\,[Fx(Gx)]$.

This equivalence reveals that the syntactic rule 16, which we have been calling Functional Substitution, is merely an incarnation (again typed) of the combinator **S**.

The "identity" combinator **I** is rather different from the ones that we have encountered so far. It simply maps an argument onto itself, where

(24) I$x = x$.

This combinator should be considered in relation to another combinator, called **K**, which was also introduced by Schönfinkel and adopted by Curry. The "canceling" combinator **K** creates a constant function, and its semantics is given by (25).

(25) **K**$xy = x$

Applicative systems up to and including the full generality of the lambda calculus can be constructed from various subsets of these few primitive combinators. A number of results are proved by Curry and Feys (1958, chapter 5) for various systems of combinators. They note that the combinators fall into two groups, one including **I** and **K** and the other including **B**, **C**, **W**, and **S**. Curry and Feys show that for a system to be equivalent to the lambda calculus, it must contain at least one combinator from each group. The minimal system equivalent to the full lambda calculus consists of **S** and **K** alone. (The other combinators that are under discussion here can be considered as special cases of **S**. In particular, **B**FGx is equivalent to **S**(**K**F)Gx. Similarly, **C**Fxy is equivalent to **S**F(**K**x)y.[5]

The combinators we require include **B** and **S**, and possibly **C** and **W**, but that neither **I** nor **K** appears to be required. However, the operation of "type raising" must be included. This operation can be represented as a further combinator, **C***, defined by (26).

(26) **C***$x = \lambda F [Fx]$

This operation is related to **I**, and cannot be defined in terms of **B**, **C**, **S** and **W** alone, in a typed system.

Combinatory Grammars and Modularity in Human Language Processing

The theory presents two rather different question at this point. First, why should natural-language grammars include combinators at all (and why these particular combinators)? Second, what are the consequences for processing of introducing these operations?

Combinators and Efficiency in Evaluation

The distinctive characteristic of the combinators is that they allow us to define such operations as the function-defining operation of abstraction without using bound variables. Thus, one might suspect that they appear in natural grammars because there is an advantage in their doing so. The formation of a relative clause like (27a) is in fact very reminiscent of the lambda abstraction (27b), except for the lack of any explicit linguistic realization of the λ operator and the bound variable.

(27)   a. . . . (whom)   Mary likes
        b. λx [(LIKES x) MARY]

The work that the combinators do in the grammar of English is simply to achieve the equivalent of lambda abstraction without the variable x, in a manner strikingly reminiscent of Curry and Feys (1958, chapter 6), yielding an interpretation for the relative clause of the following sort, which is equivalent to (27b):

(27)   c. **B(C*MARY)LIKES**

But what is the advantage of doing without bound variables?

The use of bound variables is a major source of computational costs in running computer programs. Turner (1979a, 1979b) has shown that major savings can be made in the costs of evaluating expressions in LISP-like functional programming languages if one first strips variables out of them by compiling them into equivalent variable-free combinatory expressions and then evaluating the latter. Moreover, combinatory systems using non-minimal sets of combinators, particularly ones including **B** and **C** as well as **S**, produce much terser combinatory "code," and reduce to a minimum the use of the combinators **I** and **K**. To take an example adapted from Turner, consider the following definition of the factorial function in an imaginary programming language related to the lambda calculus:

(28)   *fact* = (lambda x (cond (equal 0 x) 1 (times x (*fact* (minus x)))))

("(cond A B C)" is to be read as "If A then B else C." As always, expressions associate to the left.) This expression can be converted (via an algorithm defined by Curry and Feys) into the following equivalent combinatory expression in the minimal **S-K** system:

(29)   **S(S(S(K** cond) **(S(S(K** equal) **(K** 0))**SKK)) (K** 1))
        (S(S(K times)**SKK) (S(K** *fact*)
        (S(S(K minus)**SKK) (K** 1))))

However, in a **B-S-C** system it converts (via an algorithm again defined by Curry and Feys and improved by Turner [1979b]) into the much more economical expression (30).

(30)   **S(C(B** cond (equal 0)) 1)**(S** times **(B** *fact* **(C** minus 1)))

In Steedman 1985c (to which the reader is referred for further explication) it is pointed out that the use of the combinators **S** (for abstraction over both function and argument terms of an applicative expression), **B** (for abstraction over the argument term alone), and **C** (for abstraction over the function term alone), together with the elimination of the combinators **I** and **K**, is strikingly similar to the use of the combinators in the earlier linguistic examples. In other words, combinatory grammars are of a form which one would expect natural syntax to take if it were a transparent reflection of a semantics expressed in a computationally efficient applicative language using combinators to perform abstraction without using bound variables.

Combinators, Incremental Evaluation, and Syntactic Processing
There is one respect in which combinatory grammars might appear to be much less reconcilable with the demands of efficient sentence processing. The introduction of functional composition to the grammar in the above subsection "Extraction and Functional Composition," in order to explain extraction, implies that the surface syntax of natural sentences is much more ambiguous than under traditional accounts. It will be recalled that many strings which in classical terms would not be regarded as constituents have that status in the present grammar. For example, the unbounded extraction in example 8 implies the claim that the surface structure of the sentence *those cakes I can believe that she will eat* includes constituents corresponding to the substrings *I can, I can believe, I can believe that, I can believe that she, I can believe that she will,* and *I can believe that she will eat.* In fact, since there are other possible sequences of application and composition combination that will accept the sentence, the theory implies that such sequences as *can believe that she will eat, believe that she will eat, that she will eat, she will eat,* and *will eat* may also on occasion be constituents. Since these constituents are defined in the grammar, it necessarily follows that the surface structure of the canonical *I can believe she will eat those cakes* may also include them, so that diagram 31 represents only one of several possible surface-structure alternatives to the orthodox right-branching tree.

(31)

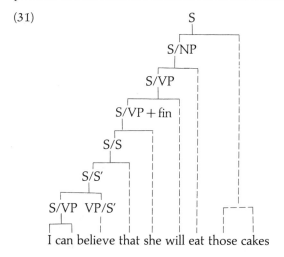

The proliferation of possible analyses that is induced by the inclusion of function composition seems at first glance to have disastrous implications for processing efficiency, because it exacerbates the degree of local ambiguity in the grammar. However, it is important note that the Functional Composition rule has the effect of converting the right-branching structure that would result from simple functional application of the categories in diagram 31 into a left-branching structure. In a grammar that maintains a rule-to-rule relation between syntactic rules and semantic rules, left-branching allows incremental interpretation of the sentence by a left-to-right processor. In the example, such a processor would, as it encountered each word of the sentence, build a single constituent corresponding to the prior string up to that point. And since the composition rule corresponds to semantic as well as syntactic composition, each of these constituents can immediately be interpreted. Indeed, as A&S and D&C point out, there is no reason for any autonomous syntactic representation, as distinct from the interpretation itself, to be built at all. Introspection strongly supports the "incremental interpretation hypothesis" that our own comprehension of such sentences proceeds in this fashion, despite the right-branching structures that they traditionally involve.

But if such fragments can be interpreted, then the results of evaluating them with respect to the context can be used to resolve local syntactic ambiguities. Crain (1980) and Altmann (1985; this volume), in experiments on the effect of referential context on traditional "garden path" effects in sentences analogous to Bever's famous *the horse raced past the barn fell*, have provided suggestive evidence that incremental interpretation and evaluation with respect to a referential context may be a very important factor in the resolution of local ambiguities by the human sentence processor.

Although nobody knows how human beings can reason so effectively and rapidly over such vast knowledge domains, there is no doubt that they do so. Such a basis for ambiguity resolution under the weak interaction is potentially so powerful that it would certainly explain both the extravagant amount of local ambiguity in natural languages and the fact that human users are rarely aware of it. If that is the way the job is done, then combinatory grammars provide a formalism for natural-language grammar that is directly compatible with such processing, under the Strong Competence hypothesis, without the addition of any extra apparatus.

In Crain and Steedman 1985 (originally written in 1981) it is argued that the only coherent manner in which such an interaction can occur is in the form called the "weak" interaction, in which the results of evaluation can suspend a line of analysis on the grounds that its interpretation is contextually inappropriate but cannot predispose syntactic processing toward any particular construction.[6] For example, it is argued that the presence in a hearer's mind of several potential referents (say several horses) will cause a simple NP analysis (e.g. *the horse*) to be rejected in favor of a complex NP analysis (*the horse [which was] raced past the barn*), while other contexts that do not support the presuppositions of restrictive adjuncts, including the so-called null context, will support the simple NP analysis. Crain and I argue on metatheoretical grounds against the alternative "strong"-interaction hypothesis, according to which the referential context might predispose the processor toward certain constructions. However, we note on page 326 that, while some versions of the strong-interaction hypothesis are empirically distinguishable from the weak variety, some are not. A version that says that the presence in a hearer's mind of several horses predisposes him toward complex NP analyses throughout a whole sentence—not just *horses raced past barns* but also *boats floated down rivers*—is so absurd as to be hardly worthy of experimental investigation. But a version that says that on encountering the word *horse* the presence of several referent horses "switches on" the complex NP analysis and switches off the simple one could probably not be distinguished experimentally from the alternative weak hypothesis, according to which the analyses would be developed first and then adjudicated by appeal to the context. The arguments against this version of the strong hypothesis rest on its theoretical complexity, and its probable computational costliness, in comparison with the weak interaction.[7]

Nothing in the above proposal conflicts in any way with the modularity hypothesis. While an unusually high degree of parallelism is claimed to hold between rules of syntax, processing, semantics, and even the inference system, with a consequent reduction of the theoretical burden upon innate specification (not to mention the practical developmental burden of all that hardwiring), these components are all formally and computationally autonomous and domain specific, with a distinct "old look" about them. While these modules can communicate, their communication is restricted to a channel of the narrowest possible bandwidth. One bit, the capacity to say yes or no, is all that the interpretive component needs under the weak interactive hypothesis in order to direct the syntactic processor to continue or abandon a particular analysis. Now, nobody has ever seriously proposed that any less communication than this was implicated between syntax and semantics in human language processing. Rather, the controversy has centered on when in the course of an analysis this channel could be used. The present claim that interpretation can deliver a verdict to the syntactic processor with great frequency, say after every word, does not compromise the informational encapsulation and consequent theoretical wholesomeness of that processor any more than a theory which says that the same information can be delivered only at the closure of a clause.

However, once we allow this minimal, weak interaction (as Fodor is clearly prepared to do) and realize that the modularity hypothesis does not impose any limit on the frequency with which the interaction can occur, it is not clear that there is any empirical content to the modularity hypothesis and the claim of informational encapsulation. As was pointed out in Crain and Steedman 1985, if one can continue to appeal to semantics at virtually every point in the sentence, it becomes very hard to distinguish experimentally between the weak interaction, which does not contravene the modularity principle, and the strong interaction, which does. The force of the concept of modularity lies in delineating the class of mental mechanisms that we can aspire to understand and that evolution might be capable of producing, rather than in predicting the detailed behavior of the mechanisms themselves.

Conclusions

The inclusion in the grammar of English and other natural languages of combinatory rules corresponding to functional composition and substitution appears to have a number of desirable consequences, which go beyond mere descriptive adequacy. Such operations are among the simplest of a class in terms of which applicative languages and related logics and inference systems can be defined, so that the grammar can maintain the most intimate of relations between syntax and semantics. This property promises to simplify considerably the task of explaining language acquisition and the evolution of the language faculty. These operations also provide a computationally efficient form for the evaluation of the interpretations of expressions in such languages. They also induce a grammar in which many fragmentary strings have the status of constituents, complete with an interpretation. While this property increases the degree of local syntactic ambiguity in the grammar, and therefore threatens to complicate the task of syntactic processing, it also makes it transparently compatible with incremental interpretation, which can be used via the weak interaction as a powerful means of resolving such ambiguities without contravening the principle of modularity.

Acknowledgments

This chapter has benefited from conversations with Peter Buneman, Kit Fine, Nick Haddock, Einar Jowsey, David McCarty, Remo Pareschi, Ken Safir, Anna Szabolcsi, and Henry Thompson, and from the comments and criticisms of the conference participants.

Notes

1. Such transformationalist terms are of course used with purely descriptive force.
2. In D&C and CGPG, fronted categories (e.g. relative pronouns and topics) are type-raised, like subjects, so that they are the function, and the residue of the sentence is their argument. This detail is glossed over in the present chapter.

3. As usual, the generative grammarians' vocabulary is used for descriptive purposes only. The example is adapted from Engdahl 1983. I replace a *wh*-question by a relative clause, so as to finesse the question of subject-aux inversion within the present theory.

4. The generalization of composition 9 corresponds to the combinator $\mathbf{B}^2$, which can be defined as **BBB**.

5. These equivalences are given in their most transparent form. The definitions of **B** and **C** can be reduced to less perspicuous combinatorial expressions not requiring the use of variables (Curry and Feys 1958, chapter 5).

6. This proposal is tentatively endorsed in a note to page 78 of Fodor 1983.

7. This proposal, in turn, suggests a variety of processing strategies which may reduce the proliferation of semantically equivalent analyses induced by the combinatory rules. For example, in the obvious implementation of the present grammars as "shift and reduce" parsers, a (nondeterministic) "reduce first" strategy will tend to produce an interpretation for the entire prior string, which can be checked against the context in this way. Such strategies are currently under investigation by Nick Haddock and Remo Pareschi in the Department of Artificial Intelligence at the University of Edinburgh (Haddock 1985; Pareschi 1985).

10

The Components of Learnability Theory

Jane Grimshaw

Current work on learnability is based on the assumption that learnability involves a theory of grammatical representation or "Universal Grammar" and a set of principles which choose among alternative grammars for a given set of data. Learnability is a function of the interaction between these two systems, the system of representation and the system of evaluation or grammar selection. The theory of grammatical representation is modular in the sense that it consists of interacting autonomous components. Grammar-selection procedures may be modular in the sense that they may be different for different components. It is often thought, for example, that grammar selection is conservative for lexical learning (lexical entries being learned case by case) but not for acquisition in the syntactic component, where generalization rather than conservativism is apparently the rule. (This claim is hard to evaluate because the selection system chooses grammars only from the set allowed by the theory of representation. If the representation theory allows only general rules in the syntax and only lists in the lexicon, the different characteristics of the learning profile would follow without appeal to grammar evaluation.) It is also possible that the grammar-selection system may not observe the same compartmentalization as the theory of representation. This will be the case if, for example, the preferred grammar is one in which syntax and semantics correspond in particular ways, even though the representation theory allows for divergencies between them. (For discussion of some proposals along these lines see Grimshaw 1981, Pinker 1984, Lasnik 1983, and Wexler 1985.) In general, the issue of modularity for selection procedures is independent of the question for Universal Grammar. Similarly, the question of domain specificity arises for both systems, and may be answered differently for each.

A fundamental goal of learnability research is to develop a theory of linguistic generalization. When do speakers generalize, and along what representational dimensions? Generalization is necessary if an infinite set of sentences is to be projected from a finite corpus; it is desirable, since making generalizations means that more can be learned on the basis of the same amount of evidence; it is problematic in that many apparently possi-

ble generalizations are incorrect (they lead to the generation of too many
forms and therefore seem to require negative evidence for correction) and
cannot be unlearned.

Early work (e.g. Wexler and Culicover 1980) has placed the burden of
accounting for learning squarely on linguistic theory by attempting to
constrain linguistic representations so that learnability is guaranteed. A
classic work in this genre is Baker's (1979) study of lexical exceptions to
transformations. Baker's argument can be summarized as follows: Suppose
that there is a transformation ("Dative Movement") which maps examples
like (1a) onto (1b) when the verb concerned is one like *give*.

(1)   a. We gave our books to the library.
      b. We gave the library our books.

What is to be said about verbs like *donate*, which do not undergo this
alternation?

(2)   a. We donated our books to the library.
      b. *We donated the library our books.

If there is a general transformation of dative movement at work in (1), then
verbs like *donate* must be exceptions to it. A description of the phenomenon
which was standard in the mid 1970s marked such verbs in the lexicon as
not allowing the rule—for example, by annotating their lexical entries with
a negative feature: [−Dative Movement]. Baker showed that a system like
this is unlearnable. A child who hypothesizes the general transformation
will require negative evidence to determine that *donate* does not undergo
the rule. Since negative evidence is unavailable, it follows that this child
(and all other children trying to learn the language) should maintain the
general form of the rule and never learn to speak English.

Baker's conclusion was that this must be the wrong representation for
the adult state of knowledge, which should rather be represented in a list
format. The grammar has two subcategorization frames for *give* (with no
general rule relating them), and only one for *donate*. (To complete the
picture, the theory must be constrained so as to rule out the Dative
Movement solution in principle—for example, by outlawing specified
deletion rules, as Baker suggests. It is not enough just to allow the list
representation; it must be forced on the learner.) The essence of Baker's
proposal was that the source of the learnability problem lay in the theory
of grammatical representation, which allowed the child to construct an
overgeneral characterization of the phenomenon.

It is an important property of current learnability models, such as the
one developed by Wexler and his colleagues and discussed in Wexler
1985, that they rest on a richer set of assumptions about the evaluation
system and therefore shift some of the burden of explaining learnability

onto grammar evaluation and away from the theory of grammatical representation, strictly construed. Examples include the ordering of hypotheses in parameter-setting models and Wexler's treatment of "markedness." As Baker himself explicitly recognized, the diagnosis of the dative problem that he offered was founded on an evaluation metric that picks the formally simplest solution.

Presumably in all models, a child first constructs multiple subcategorizations for dative verbs. Suppose that a child has heard 15 verbs of the *give* type, each of them occurring in two contexts, and 8 verbs of the *donate* type, which occur only before NP-PP. So far, all these contexts have simply been listed. Under the compulsion of the formal evaluation metric, the child then cashes these in for a general rule, driven by the evaluation system to choose this solution as the formally simplest.

However, other evaluation mechanisms, not based on complexity alone, will give quite different results. Here are a few that will illustrate the general point.

• Suppose that when the threshold is reached and the learner formulates a rule, the grammar-evaluation system dictates the addition of a positive rule feature, [+ Dative Movement], to verbs that have double subcategorizations, and no feature at all to the others. [+ DM] can then be conservatively added to verbs as they are heard in the double-NP version. In this case a learner could learn English but still have a lexically governed transformation (or general lexical rule) for datives.

• Suppose the grammar-selection procedure simply adds the feature [− Dative Movement] to every verb that has only one of the subcategorizations associated with it. [− DM] can then be conservatively deleted from the entry for verbs as they are heard in the double-NP version. The learner will construct the classical description of the phenomenon.

• Suppose that every time the learner formulates a rule R he marks every verb [− R] until he gets positive evidence that the verb is [+ R]. This will result in a learnable grammar that contains a general rule with exceptions to it.

I am not advocating any of these solutions; the real character of the problem is still being determined. Indeed, the question whether children do overgeneralize rules like dative is the focus of considerable research (see e.g. Pinker 1984; Mazurkewitch and White 1984, as is the correct characterization of the adult representation for datives (Stowell 1981; Grimshaw and Prince, in preparation). The point I'm making is more abstract and concerns the logic of the learnability situation when rich evaluation procedures are invoked. A grammar that consists of general rules with exceptions is neither learnable nor unlearnable *per se*. Learnability depends upon the selection system paired with the grammar, which determines what the learner actually does in the face of the available evidence. Learnability, then, is a function of the interaction between Universal Grammar and a set of selection principles, and cannot be evaluated for the theory of grammatical representation alone. The implications of a particular theory of grammar for learnability cannot be assessed without regard to those principles that mediate between the theory of grammar and the input to language learning.

Acknowledgments

The research reported here was supported by grant IST-8120403 from the National Science Foundation to Brandeis University and by grant BRSG S07 RR0744 awarded by the Biomedical Research Support Grant Program, Division of Research Resources, National Institutes of Health.

III

On-Line Processing

Introduction
Mark Feinstein

We must remind ourselves that the scientific study of language is conducted on (at least) two levels. Linguists *per se* go about constructing theories of competence, of abstract linguistic knowledge. Psycholinguists are in the business of building theories of performance, or on-line processing. The language input system that Fodor (1983) envisions is clearly one in which the performance mechanism incorporates a competence grammar, or some device that is explicitly characterized by the competence grammar; a linguistic theory is not, in and of itself, an account of an input system. But there is good reason to think that the architectural characteristics of linguistic-competence theory have had, and ought to have, a profound effect on the work of psycholinguists, and on their view of the modular (or nonmodular) nature of the language-processing system.

It is clear that much of contemporary linguistics (certainly the school of generative grammar influenced by Chomsky's work) is strongly committed to the hypothesis that the properties of competence grammars are domain specific. Although there have been many significant attempts to characterize linguistic knowledge and behavior in terms of general properties of cognition or elemental characteristics of behavior, none have stood up well to the generative grammarians' arguments that linguistic principles and properties are extraordinarily peculiar to the domain of language. Although some characteristics of linguistic structure are probably not exclusively linguistic (e.g., hierarchical structure), one is hard pressed to find analogues (let along homologues) of constraints on structure on the order of the Subjacency Condition, or conditions on the form of phonological representations. The longer linguists have looked, the more it appears that even the conventional subdomains of grammar involve highly specialized vocabularies, structures, and processes; taken as a whole, grammars do look "eccentric" and hence have the flavor of modular systems in Fodor's sense (1983, p. 51).

Something along these lines can also be said with regard to information encapsulation, though with less fervor. There is a long tradition within linguistic theory of pressing for (or at least arguing about) the autonomy of "levels." It is claimed not only that the subdomains of a grammar (syntax, phonology, morphology, semantics) operate over distinct vocabularies, but also that the vocabularies are encapsulated—that only phonological information is relevant to formulations within phonology, only syntactic properties are relevant within the syntactic component, and so forth. The earlier structuralists held forth for the position that every level was sacrosanct in just this way, and dictated against the "mixing of levels"; generative grammar has taken a more mixed view of things. Halle's (1959) celebrated argument against the structuralist phoneme was essentially a demonstration that the morphological and phonological levels are inextricably bound together, that the characterization of phonological generalizations requires access to morphological information. In contrast, one of Chomsky's strongest arguments has been that syntax is strictly autonomous, divorced from semantics, with much relegated to an autonomous morphological (lexical) component. There are, of course, competing views that are less friendly to the strict modular motif. The generative semanticists, though doomed to relative failure, represent an early rejection of Chomsky's autonomy theory. More recently, Montague grammarians have argued, with more success, for common syntactic/semantic representations. But virtually all current linguistic models, regardless of position with regard to the internal "modularity" of grammatical subsystems, are committed to the view that the proper business of the theory of grammar is grammar—that there is no place in grammars for nongrammatical (i.e., nonlinguistic) information. (The generative semanticists represent an aberration among linguists, having briefly and unsuccessfully fought to allow grammatical rules to have access to speakers' general knowledge about the world.)

The first four chapters in this part of the book confront questions that have arisen within this historical context; that is, the particular debates about modularity which they embody have been profoundly affected by the prevailing winds within linguistic theory. All of them presume that the language-processing mechanism incorporates a significant, if not dominant, role for the syntactic component of the grammar. This line of approach to the problem of language processing is not universally held, of course. Much of the work on language processing within the framework of artificial intelligence explicitly rejects the central role, or any special role, of grammar. The early work of Winograd (1972) is well known in this regard; other exemplars are Schank (1975), Waltz and Pollack (1985), and Lehnert (1981). There is considerable variation among AI workers in this domain, but it is fair to say that the dominant flavor is nonmodular in the extreme, strongly relying on powerful common problem-solving mechanisms with central access to general knowledge representations. There is no inherent reason for computationally explicit approaches to take this view; Marcus (1980, 1984) and Berwick, and Weinberg (1984) have presented models in which the grammar plays a separate and powerful role, and which have much of the flavor of the proposals of Clifton and Ferreira, Frazier, and Weinberg in the present volume. But the explicitly antimodular and non-grammatical stance of much AI work is simply not represented here. What is represented is the general view that syntactic principles are relevant and important to language processing. At this point, the present authors part company. Clifton and Ferreira (chapter 14) and Frazier (chapter 15) present a theoretical framework, and much empirical evidence, in support of the view that the sentence-processing mechanism involves a strictly modular syntactic component whose properties are, at heart, those of the syntactic component of the competence grammar (recruited in the service of processing). Both of these chapters defend the thesis that there is a discrete stage of processing at which grammatical mechanisms offer up a single syntactic analysis of the utterance; the vocabulary of the representation that emerges is purely syntactic, and only syntactic information is recruited in the course of arriving at this analysis. The focus of their work is the ambiguous utterance, whose ultimate meaningful interpretation in real discourse may well depend on many factors, including information about the discourse itself (beyond the sentence and its structure), its context, and general knowledge about the real world. But, they argue, there is a crucial level of processing at which none of that information is brought to bear—only information specific to the syntactic domain, insulated from other domains, is relevant at the point where an initial syntactic analysis is carried out.

Frazier also tentatively advances the view that, at later stages of processing, sentences are construed in terms of the thematic properties of relevant lexical items (information about roles such as agent and instrument); the vocabulary of this thematic processor, Frazier, suggests, may be shared by parts of the general knowledge system in the central processor, and thus may provide a direct interface between the grammatical module and other components of cognition. Grammatical theory has long debated the role of thematic relations; the case grammar of Fillmore (1968) is typical of early work, and Chomsky's recent work on the so-called theta criterion represents a major shift back to a special role for thematic notions (see Chomsky 1981). Thus, the work of Clifton and Ferreira and that of Frazier remains very close to, if not isomorphic with, autonomous view of the syntactic component within grammatical theory.

In much the same spirit, Weinberg's contribution (chapter 13) is entitled "Modularity in the Syntactic Parser," with an emphasis on the *in*. She is concerned with the internal structure of that component, and she argues that syntactic parsing (modular with respect to nonlinguistic information) is a two-stage process. In the first stage, the parser constructs a representation in the form of a phrase-structure tree, utillizing phrase-structure rules and lexical (selectional and subcategorizational) information. In the second stage, the parser takes account of binding relationships between syntactic elements (in the sense of Chomsky's theory of government and binding). First-stage parsing has no access to information about binding relationships, and in this sense it represents a distinct submodule, informationally encapsulated with respect to the second-stage binding representation. Weinberg presents experimental evidence from Freedman and Forster (1985) that tends to support the view that syntactic processing contains two modular subcomponents, and she argues that general considerations of computational efficiency militate in favor of this particular architecture.

Altmann (chapter 12) assigns an essentially nonmodular role to syntax (though it is a significant role, in contrast to some of the stronger anti-modular, central-processing views within AI). For Altmann, the construction of syntactic representations takes place roughly within (or at least compatible with) the framework of competence grammar. However, for Altmann (following the work of Crain and Steedman (1985), the syntactic representation of an utterance does not have an autonomous, informationally encapsulated status. It is presumed to be part of a larger construction of the sentence within a model of discourse that incorporates information about the real world in which the discourse occurs; ambiguities are resolved by nonlinguistic principles of construal of reference to real-world objects. In the case of ambiguity, there is no point at which the processor offers up a purely syntactic analysis that is not affected by these extragrammatical principles and this extragrammatical information.

Put another way, the proposals of Clifton and Ferreira, Frazier, and Weinberg all suggest a very close fit between the architecture of the competence grammar and that of the language processor at large; for Altmann, there is no direct fit. One hesitates to make any strong judgments on this difference, but it is suggestive of a fundamentally different (if inexplicit) stance with respect to modularity in general. Why, one may well ask, should *any* cognitive system, grammar or processor, be modular in nature? We may well speculate (with Clifton and Ferreira) that modularity follows from "evolutionary pressures toward specialization for important tasks." It is quite plausible to think that the evolutionary course of the language capacity (the basis for acquisition of competence grammars) and that of the ability to use that capacity were very closely intertwined. If grammar and processor essentially co-evolved, and if grammars have the form that the generativists propose, we might well expect the close architectural fit that characterizes the models of Clifton and Ferreira, Frazier, and Weinberg rather than the looser fit characteristic of Altmann's approach. On the other hand, if it should turn out (on empirical grounds) that grammars are not characterized by the kind of syntactic autonomy that generative grammar suggests, then Altmann's nonautonomous model gains in plausibility in this evolutionary perspective.

The remaining two defining traits of modularity—speed and mandatoriness—cannot be construed as properties of grammar, as there is nothing fast or automatic about abstract knowledge. But they are quite commonly held, on fairly firm empirical grounds, to be generally characteristic of linguistic performance—and, by extension, of the mechanisms that recruit grammatical knowledge in the service or processing. As Fodor (1983) points out, we cannot help but process linguistic input as language, and the overall speed of linguistic processing is impressive (at least, it is rapid enough to sustain effective heavy-duty communication of an order that has no doubt been of significant adaptive advantage to the species). But the language input system (incorporating some form of grammar) is a highly complex object, and there is room to question the modularity (the speed and automaticity) of particular subparts of the system. Miller (chapter 16) and Carroll and Slowiaczek (chapter 11) address questions within this arena.

Carroll and Slowiaczek (henceforth C&S) addresses domain specificity (and "architectural fit" in evolutionary terms) as well as rate and automaticity. C&S are concerned with differences in processing in two distinct modes: the auditory mode associated with normal speech processing and the visual mode characteristic of reading. Orthographically represented language is, of course, a very late (cultural) development in the development of the organism; to the extent that biological evolution determined the form of the language processor, and to the extent that it is modular in Fodor's terms, it is reasonable to assume that the processor is particularly designed to support auditory processing. The visual processing of the written form, we may presume, was not anticipated in the early course of the organism's evolution; nor has there been sufficient biological time since the development of writing for the processor to evolve any specialized mechanism for the processing of visual linguistic representation of the orthographic kind. Only if the processor were not domain specific (in the sense that the normal language domain is auditorily based) might we expect visual/orthographic and auditory processing to proceed identically. C&S provide experimental evidence that auditory (prosodic) information is normally and regularly recruited by the processor in constructing a syntactic analysis of the utterance; they argue that there is a direct pathway between auditory perception and the language processor that facilitates rapid and automatic processing. By contrast, C&S suggest that in the reading mode the general visual input system does not normally interact with the language processor until a difficulty in processing is encountered. At such points the language processor may redirect the visual system, inducing a reanalysis; on this view, they argue, "localized on-line language-processing effects should appear in eye movements [under control of the visual input system] only when normal untroubled comprehension breaks down." Their experiments provide evidence that supports this conclusion.

Miller is most directly concerned with the "front end" of auditory processing. She addresses the notion that there is a self-contained phonetic-processing submodule, independent (in the usual Fodorian sense of modularity) of the language processor at large, including the components of the grammar that are recruited by the processor. Miller is concerned primarily with the significant variation in rate of production that is characteristic of normal speech. She shows that listeners must be able to take rate differences into account when computing phonetic representations, and, furthermore, that listeners cannot avoid doing so—that it is mandatory aspect of the process of phonetic perception. Indeed, she and others have argued that phonetic processing as a whole is mandatory; listeners cannot avoid hearing speech events as language. Moreover, it is clear that speech perception is a relative rapid phenomenon. But although automaticity and rapidity are necessary, they are not sufficient conditions by which to determine that phonetic processing constitutes a module in its own right.

The question of the domain specificity of auditory processing remains open. There is some good evidence that aspects of phonetic processing are not specific to language (see, e.g., Cutting and Rosner 1974) and also that certain mechanisms of auditory perception recruited for speech processing (categorical perception of voicing distinctions) are common to humans and other (non-language-using) organisms (see Kuhl and Miller 1975). More important, there is reason to think that the level of phonetic processing is not informationally encapsulated. Were the phonetic processor a module, strictly speaking, we should not expect it to have access to information at later levels of processing. Miller suggests that rate-dependent processing is sensitive to the lexical status of words. Her experiments utilized only monosyllabic stimuli; since there is no difficulty in analyzing monosyllables as whole words in their own right, her experiments did not place the burden of word parsing on the phonetic processor.

But in more complex utterances, the processor is confronted with relatively long stretches of acoustic material which typically include no direct acoustic manifestations of word boundaries. Moreover, in rapid natural speech we find not only the kind of rate compression of segment and syllable duration that Miller discusses, but also dramatic compressions and deformations of segmental structure itself that occur partly as a function of rate of speech and partly as a consequence of morphophonemic processes. I have in mind here the kind of fast-speech forms of sentences like *Do you want to?* in which vowel deletion, palatalization, afffrication, vowel reduction, and contraction interact to produce phonetic representations like [jəwanə]. If the phonetic processor can access the lexicon in the

case of simple monosyllables, as in Miller's study, it is reasonable to conclude that it does so with the usual larger stretches of natural speech. In
order for the processor to be able to use the resources of the lexicon in
making decisions about lexical identity, it must, arguably, have access to
information beyond the physical-acoustic properties of the input signal—
the vocabulary one presumes would be uniquely available were the phonetic processor an informationally encapsulated module. Specifically, the
processor would seem to need information about language-particular syllable constraints, constraints on segmental sequences, and stress patterns,
and, in general, access to at least some phonological rules (and possibly
even information about higher-order morphological and syntactic structures)
of the sort that would assist in the unpacking of the highly deformed and
compressed events of normal rapid speech. In short, it would appear that,
even at very early levels of processing, information about the acoustic
properties of speech must be conjoined with higher-order information that
will ultimately determine the phonological representation of acoustic signals. For these reasons it may be incorrect to view the phonetic processor
as a modular acoustic analyzer.

   Miller raises the question of whether the mandatory rate-dependent
effect is a consequence of psychophysiological properties of the auditory
system rather than a characteristic of processing (modular or otherwise). As
she reports, McGurk and McDonald (1976) have shown that visual information about articulation can integrate with auditory information to create
hybrid perceptual effects; she then reports on work by Green (1984) which
demonstrates that visual rate information has an effect on simultaneous
perception of auditory rate information. Hence it cannot be the case that
the mandatory rate effect arises from very-low-level properties of the
auditory system alone. This intriguing result might at first blush seem to
provide additional reason to think that the phonetic processor is nonmodular, since it can utilize information from an apparently distinct domain; compare the results reported by Carroll and Slowiaczek.

   However, there are some essential differences between the two cases. As
was noted above, there is obvious reason to believe that reading does not
recruit a visual mechanism specially evolved to support the task in conjunction with normal linguistic processing. Hence, that component of the
visual processor is not expected to have modular characteristics with
respect to language. But one can make very good evolutionary sense of the
interconnection between visual-phonetic and auditory-phonetic perception.
Not only do the visual states of the articulators provide potential cues for
phonetic interpretation, but complex interlocking constellations of visual
and auditory signals are commonly found in the natural communicative
systems of all primates. If phonetic processing began to arise early in the
phylogenetic history of *Homo sapiens*, it is not at all surprising that it

should have supported a strong potential interaction of visual and auditory information of the sort that Miller reports. Were there other compelling reasons to believe that the phonetic processor is modular in nature, the fact that it has access to information in distinct perceptual modalities would not seem to be a convincing counterargument.

These chapters address issues in modularity and language processing at both "macro" and "micro" levels. Altmann, Clifton and Ferreira, and Frazier ask whether the macro language processor as a whole, incorporating a grammar, is modular with respect to general knowledge and general inferential ability; Altmann's answers No, the others Yes. Weinberg poses the finer-grained question of whether the (modular) syntactic processor itself is organized into submodules. Carroll and Slowiaczek, and Miller, are concerned with the modularity of specific microcomponents of linguistic performance: C&S argue that the reading mode engages a modular linguistic processor operating independent of the regular visual system; Miller claims that the low-level phonetic processor, the front end of any language processor, itself has a modular character.

11

Modes and Modules: Multiple Pathways to the Language Processor

Patrick J. Carroll and Maria L. Slowiaczek

When a listener tries to comprehend a spoken sentence, the stream of information must be organized quickly so that it can be maintained in working memory while the comprehension processes take place. Many years of psycholinguistic research have demonstrated that the initial perception of a sentence, and memory for the verbatim string of words, depend on the syntactic constituent structure (Fodor and Bever 1965; Garrett, Bever, and Fodor 1966; Fodor, Bever, and Garrett 1974). This has led to a model of sentence processing in which the words are rapidly identified and categorized so that they can be syntactically organized. It has been assumed that this process is identical to the one that occurs in reading, with the exception that in reading the words must be identified from visual information.

There is good reason to believe that the differences between reading and listening go beyond the obvious difference in the translation of words from visual or auditory signals to an abstract form. Table 1 lists some of the differences between reading and listening. First, in listening the sensory information is presented rapidly and decays quickly; in reading the words are permanently represented in print on the page. Second, in listening the producer controls the rate of presentation of the information; in reading the perceiver has control of how quickly the information is processed. Third, in listening one is often presented with ungrammatical strings of words and sentence fragments; in reading one usually encounters complete grammatical sentences. Finally, in listening there is a richly organized prosodic structure, composed of rhythm, intonation, and stress, that can provide additional information about the sentence; in reading this information is missing (although some of it is conveyed by punctuation).

As a result of these differences, the initial stages of organizing and interpreting spoken and written sentences differ. In the first half of this chapter we will discuss how sentences are initially organized in listening comprehension. We will present evidence that spoken sentences are structured using both prosodic and syntactic information, and that the sensory information is incorporated as part of the representation rather than simply

Table 1
Differences between reading and listening.

Listening	Reading
Quickly decaying signal	Permanence of information
Rate of information controlled by producer	Rate of information controlled by the perceiver
Incomplete sentence fragments	Grammatical sentences
Prosodic information	No prosodic infomation (except for punctuation)

Table 2
An example sentence from experiment 1.

EARLY CLOSURE
[BECAUSE HER GRANDMOTHER KNITTED] [PULLOVERS] [KEPT CATHY WARM IN THE WINTERTIME]

late closure
[because her grandmother knitted] [pullovers] [cathy kept warm in the wintertime]

translated into a modality-free abstract language form. In the second half, we will describe how the input system works in reading comprehension.

Prosodic Structure and Language Processing

We believe that the prosodic structure in spoken sentences is used to organize the representation of the sentence in working memory (Nooteboom, Brokx, and de Rooij 1978). There are several reasons that prosody can provide a useful structure for the working-memory representation. First, the speaker must produce sentences within the limits of the same processing system that the listener uses to comprehend them. Therefore, the prosodic structure will provide an organization that works within those processing limits. Second, since speakers often make false starts and hesitations in producing sentences, prosodic information can help to compensate for some of the syntactic structure that is lacking when an auditory string is not syntactically well formed.

Even with grammatical strings, temporary syntactic ambiguities often occur, which make it difficult to structure the sentence immediately on the basis of syntactic information alone. In some cases, prosodic information can be used as a cue to resolve the syntactic ambiguity. Consider the two sentences presented in table 2. These sentences are temporarily ambiguous at the word *pullovers*. Since the verb *knitted* can be optionally transitive or intransitive, pullovers might be the direct object of the verb in the first clause or the subject noun phrase of the second clause. Frazier (1978) has studied how people parse sentences with this kind of ambiguity. Using a variety of sentence-processing measures, she has found that people initially follow a syntactic parsing preference called the Late Closure strategy, by which ambiguous constituents are attached to the preceding phrase. According to this strategy, *pullovers* is attached as the direct object of *knitted*. This leads to a "garden path" in the first sentence, since *pullovers* must be the subject of the verb *kept*. When such sentences are spoken, speakers use prosodic information to indicate how the ambiguity should be resolved. In the early-closure sentence, a prosodic boundary (a pause and intonation boundary) would occur after *knitted: Because her grandmother knitted, pullovers kept Cathy warm in the wintertime*. We will refer to this as an early boundary. In the late-closure sentence, the prosodic boundary would occur after *pullovers: Because her grandmother knitted pullovers, Cathy kept warm in the wintertime*. We will refer to this as a late boundary.

We tested a set of sentences similar to those above to find out how much people use the prosodic information to structure the sentence (Slowiaczek 1981). In our experiment, an early-closure and a late-closure form of each of 40 sentences was spoken naturally and recorded. These sentences were then spliced into three segments: the sentence beginning, the ambiguous region, and the disambiguating region. The segments of the two versions of the sentence were recombined to form the eight conditions shown in table 3. The segments in upper-case letters came from the original early-closure sentence. The segments in lower-case letters came from the original late-closure sentence. The top four conditions, labeled "late closure," end with the same disambiguating segment: *Cathy kept warm in the wintertime*. This segment resolves the ambiguity with *pullovers* as the direct object in the first clause. The bottom four conditions, labeled "early closure," end with the disambiguating segment *kept Cathy warm in the wintertime*. This segment resolves the ambiguity with *pullovers* as the subject of the second clause. The four prosodic-boundary conditions are listed to the left of the sentences. Prosodic boundaries are marked in the sentences by a slash. In the late-boundary conditions, a prosodic boundary occurred after *pullovers*. For the late-closure sentence, the prosodic information was consistent with the correct syntactic grouping. For the early-closure/late-boundary sentence, the prosodic boundary was inconsistent. In the early-boundary conditions, a prosodic boundary occurred after *knitted*. For the late-closure/early-boundary sentence, the prosodic information was inconsistent with the correct syntactic grouping. However, for the early-closure/early-boundary sentence it was consistent. The both-boundaries condition had a prosodic boundary after *knitted* and another after *pullovers*; in the no-boundary condition there were no prosodic boundaries. Subjects

Table 3
An example sentence in the eight conditions in experiment 1.

	late closure
late boundary	because her grandmother knitted pullovers/ cathy kept warm in the wintertime
early boundary	BECAUSE HER GRANDMOTHER KNITTED/ PULLOVERS cathy kept warm in the wintertime
both boundaries	BECAUSE HER GRANDMOTHER KNITTED/ pullovers/ cathy kept warm in the wintertime
no boundary	because her grandmother knitted PULLOVERS cathy kept warm in the wintertime
	EARLY CLOSURE
late boundary	because her grandmother knitted pullovers/ KEPT CATHY WARM IN THE WINTERTIME
early boundary	BECAUSE HER GRANDMOTHER KNITTED/ PULLOVERS KEPT CATHY WARM IN THE WINTERTIME
both boundaries	BECAUSE HER GRANDMOTHER KNITTED/ PULLOVERS/ KEPT CATHY WARM IN THE WINTERTIME
no boundary	because her grandmother knitted PULLOVERS KEPT CATHY WARM IN THE WINTERTIME

Table 4
Mean response times (in milliseconds) for experiment 1.

	Late boundary (knitted pullovers/)	Early boundary (KNITTED/ PULLOVERS)	Both boundaries (KNITTED/ pullovers/)	No boundary (knitted PULLOVERS)
late closure (cathy kept)	1,132	1,536	1,142	1,243
EARLY CLOSURE (KEPT CATHY)	1,798	1,282	1,537	1,386

listened to each sentence and pressed a button when the sentence was understood. Response time to comprehend the sentence was measured.

The results presented in table 4 show that the prosodic information had an important impact on how quickly the sentences were understood. For the purposes of this chapter we will concentrate on the late- and early-boundary conditions. When the prosodic information was inconsistent with the syntactic information (i.e., in the late-closure/early-boundary condition or the early-closure/late-boundary condition), response time was slower than in the consistent conditions. In addition, the late-closure sentences were generally comprehended more rapidly than the early-closure sentences. This experiment shows that prosodic information can influence how a sentence is organized for comprehension. Although syntactic preference was still a major determinant of the difficulty of parsing these sentences, prosodic information was able to inform the syntactic decision.

On the basis of this and subsequent experiments, we believe that prosody has a more fundamental role than occasionally serving as a cue when syntactic information is insufficient. In the later experiments, we explicitly tested how prosodic structure is used in the working memory representation. We used an auditory version of the successor-naming task, a memory-probe technique developed by Sternberg (1969). In this task, subjects listen to a string of words. Shortly after the presentation of the last word in the list, a probe item is presented and the subject responds as quickly as possible by saying the word immediately subsequent to the probe in the original string. In prior research, response time to name the successor item was shown to be influenced by characteristics of the input string as well as by the search processes used by the subject to retrieve information from working memory.

In our experiments, as in naturally spoken sentences, prosodic properties of speech provide the string with an internal organization. Our critical hypothesis is that the temporal structure of the input string will determine the prosodic representation, which in turn will determine the response time to name the successor.

In the first experiment, we used strings of digits to remove any potential effects of syntactic structure or meaning that might occur in sentences. Prosodic structure was manipulated by varying the lengths of the pauses that occurred between the digits in the string. The digits were natural speech sounds that were digitized and resynthesized to remove the other prosodic features. Each digit was 350 msec in duration with a monotone fundamental frequency of 100 Hz.

Three pause patterns were used, as shown in table 5. The effect of these pause patterns was to create a grouping of the digits in the string into subgroups, mostly pairs. The numbers 1 through 5 in the table indicate the positions in the list, not the actual stimulus digits. In the experiment, these

Table 5
Pause patterns in experiment 1.

List length: 5	Long pause = 300 msec
	Short pause = 100 msec

Long-short pattern (LS)
1   2 3   4 5

Probe = 2 or 4: Same-group trial
Probe = 1 or 3: Different-group trial

Short-long pattern (SL)
1 2   3 4   5

Probe = 1 or 3: same-group trial
Probe = 2 or 4: different-group trial

Short-short pattern (SS)
1 2 3 4 5

Note: Digits in the patterns indicate serial position, not actual stimulus items.

Table 6
Outline of a single trial.

*Warning Tone + 500-msec delay
  *Spoken digit string presented (e.g., "5   37   21   4")
    *2,000-msec delay
      *Probe digit presented (e.g., "3")
        *RT to spoken response (correct answer: "7")

positions were filled by a different set of randomly selected digits on each trial. In the long-short pause pattern, the pauses between digits alternated between a long pause of 300 msec and a short pause of 100 msec, starting with a long pause and alternating throughout the string. In the short-long pattern, the pauses between digits alternated from short to long, starting with a short pause and alternating throughout the string. When the probe and the response are separated by a short pause, we say that they are in the same group. In the long-short pattern this is true for probe positions 2 and 4. When the probe and the response are separated by a long pause, they are in different groups, as is the case with probe positions 1 and 3 in the long-short pattern. If the temporal structure of these strings provides the organization in working memory, we expect that response times will be faster for same-group trials than for different-group trials. Digit strings were three, four, five, or six digits in length. The digits in the strings occurred randomly, and each probe position was tested equally often.

Table 6 shows the progress of an individual trial in the experiment. On

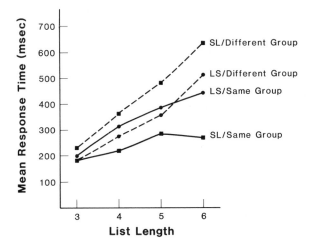

Figure 1
Mean response times in experiment 2 averaged across subjects for the two grouping conditions and the two experimental pause patterns (LS and SL) plotted by list length.

each trial, subjects heard a warning tone followed by a 500-msec interval. Then a spoken list of randomly selected digits was presented. A two-second delay was followed by a spoken probe. The subject responded by naming the digit that followed the probe in the presented list, and the response time was measured.

In figure 1 response time to name the probe is plotted as a function of list length. The results show that the internal structure of the string did affect retrieval time. Response times were faster when the probe and the response were in the same group than when they were in different groups. This grouping effect was consistent across various probe positions and list lengths. However, as figure 1 shows, the grouping information was not equally effective for the long-short and the short-long patterns. The difference in response times for the same-group and the different-group conditions was much larger for the short-long pattern than for the long-short pattern.[1]

In the next experiment, we used word strings that formed grammatical sentences to see if the prosodic grouping was still used when syntactic-structuring information was available. In all other aspects, the experiment was identical to the digit experiment. Words were presented in long-short or short-long patterns with list length equal to three, four, five, or six words. A set of adjectives, nouns, and verbs were digitized to a monotone fundamental frequency of 100 Hz. The stimulus words and the syntactic structures are presented in table 7.

Table 7
Example materials from experiment 3.

Adjectives	Nouns	Verbs
Angry	Artists	Admire
Bashful	Athletes	Amuse
Clever	Authors	Attack
Friendly	Coaches	Attract
Funny	Doctors	Convert
Jealous	Judges	Dislike
Nasty	Lawyers	Follow
Quiet	Plumbers	Marry
Sneaky	Singers	Notice
Wealthy	Teachers	Tickle

List length	Syntactic structure
3	N V N
4	A N V N
5	A N V A N
	N V A A N
6	A N V A A N
	A A N V A N

For each trial, words were randomly selected from the proper syntactic category to fit the syntactic frames presented at the lower half of table 7. For example, a stimulus sentence of list length 4 might be *Funny teachers marry plumbers*; one of list length 5 might be *Funny teachers marry bashful plumbers*; one of list length 6 might be *Funny teachers tickle bashful, wealthy plumbers*.

Table 8 shows examples of list length 4. In each example, the probe word is underlined. For the short-long pattern, pauses alternate from a short pause to a long pause. For the long-short pattern, the alternation begins with a long pause. In the first example (for the same-group trial), the probe *tickle* and the response *plumbers* are separated by a short pause. For the different-group trials, the probe and the response are separated by a long pause.

The results are presented in figure 2. Although the results are not as clear as in the digit experiment, the pattern is quite consistent with the prosody hypothesis, especially at longer list lengths. The line with the fastest response times shows the same-group trials for the short-long pattern. The slowest responses occurred in the different-group trials for the short-long pattern. The same-group trials were consistently faster than the different-group trials. As in the digit experiment, temporal grouping was less effective in the long-short pattern than in the short-long pattern. We suspect

Table 8
Examples of prosodic patterns and same-group
or different-group probes in experiment 3.

Short-long pattern

Same group:

(BASHFUL LAWYERS) (TICKLE PLUMBERS)

Different group:

(BASHFUL LAWYERS) (TICKLE PLUMBERS)

Long-short pattern

Same group:

(BASHFUL) (LAWYERS TICKLE) (PLUMBERS)

Different group:

(BASHFUL) (LAWYERS TICKLE) (PLUMBERS)

Note: The probe is underlined in the examples.

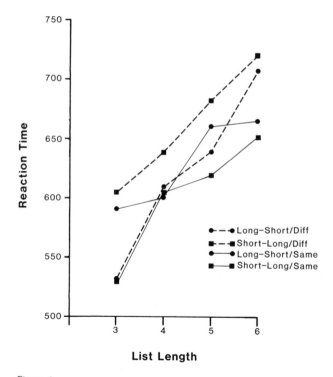

Figure 2
Mean response times in experiment 3 averaged across subjects for the two grouping
conditions (Same and Different) and the two experimental pause patterns plotted by list
length.

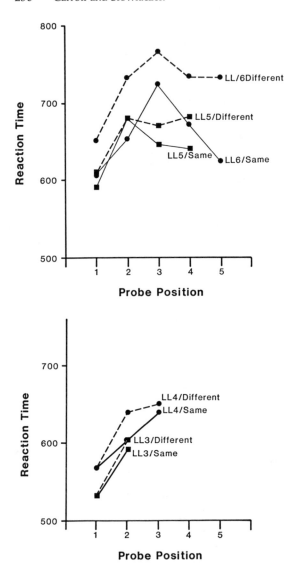

Figure 3
Mean response times in experiment 2 averaged across subjects.

Table 9
Examples of good and
bad temporal patterns for
list length 6 in experi-
ment 4.

Good pattern

1 2 3   4 5 6

1 2   3 4   5 6

1 2   3   4 5   6

Bad pattern

1 2 3 4   5 6

1   2 3 4 5   6

1   2 3   4 5   6

that the irregularities in this pattern reflect the contribution of the syntactic structure in these strings. Even so, temporal grouping still made a considerable difference, as figure 3 shows. Same-group trials were consistently faster than different-group trials across probe positions and list lengths.

The results of these experiments suggest that retrieval of an item from working memory is affected by prosodic information such as pauses. However, the size of the effect was determined by the overall pattern of the string. Subjects used the temporal grouping in their memory representations more when the string was a short-long pattern than when it was a long-short pattern. This suggests that the short-long pattern is a good temporal pattern for structuring information in memory and the long-short pattern is not.

In the next experiment, we outlined some criteria that might allow us to distinguish between "good" and "bad" patterns. Some examples can be seen in table 9. In general, good patterns were defined as patterns that were temporally predictable. This was accomplished either by making each group equal in size or by using a cyclic pattern such as the pattern in the third example: 12 3 45 6. Bad patterns could contain groups of unequal size (e.g. 1 2345 6) or mirror-image patterns (e.g. 1 23 45 6). We used digit strings and manipulated the goodness of the pattern. Strings contained 4, 6, or 8 randomly selected digits.

The results, presented in figure 4, showed that the temporal structure of the string again affected retrieval time. Response times were faster when the probe and the response were in the same group than when they were in different groups. This grouping effect was consistent across various probe positions and list lengths. However, the grouping effect was not equally effective for the good and the bad patterns. The difference in response time for the same-group and different-group conditions was much larger for the

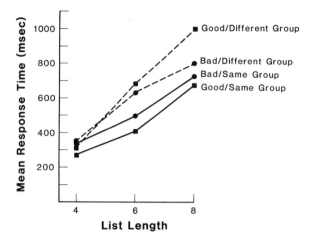

List Length

Figure 4
Mean response times in experiment 3 averaged across subjects for the two grouping conditions and the two kinds of pause patterns (good and bad) plotted by list length.

good patterns than for the bad patterns. This difference was especially apparent for the longer list lengths.

The grouping effect found in this experiment is not simply a local effect of pause length. The global property of the goodness of the patterns influenced how well the patterns were encoded and consequently how much of an impact the structure had on memory retrieval. Although our criteria of pattern goodness are intuitive, we suspect that a good pattern shares many properties with naturally spoken sentences.

We are currently investigating how the goodness of the temporal pattern affects the organization of sentence strings. We expect that if prosodic factors are used to organize the working memory representation, the goodness of the temporal pattern will not depend on how well it signals syntactic information alone. In the sentence experiment we reported above, the difference between the long-short and the short-long patterns occurred even though these patterns were arbitrary with respect to the syntax. Syntax will undoubtedly affect how the sentence string is structured, but we expect that the goodness of the prosodic pattern will affect the structure of the string as well. Table 10 shows the conditions in our current experiment, with examples taken from list length 6.

The goodness of the prosodic pattern is manipulated by the same criteria as in the previous study. In addition, we are manipulating how informative the temporal structure is with regard to the syntactic structure of the string. In our consistent patterns, the long pauses do not separate elements that belong in the same syntactic constituent. In our inconsistent patterns, long

Table 10
Stimulus conditions for experiment 5.

	Good pattern	Bad pattern
Consistent	(A N)(V)(A A)(N)	(A A A N)(V)(N)
Inconsistent	(A A)(N)(V A)(N)	(A N V A)(A)(N)
No syntax	(V A)(N)(A N)(N)	(N A N N)(A)(V)

Note: A means adjective; N means noun; and V means verb.

pauses separate syntactic constituents, creating a conflict between prosodic and syntactic information. In our no-syntax pattern, the words are randomly ordered. The goodness of the prosodic patterns is arbitrary with respect to the syntactic information that must be conveyed. Nonetheless, we expect prosodic-pattern goodness to influence how easily these sentences are structured.

The stimuli in this experiment, as in the sentence experiment we reported earlier, are composed of strings of words with legitimate syntax but little semantic content. More important, they are extremely impoverished prosodically, containing only a fraction of the timing information and none of the intonation that would occur in normal speech. This should make syntax the most salient organizing characteristic of the string.

Even under these conditions, the single available prosodic feature is used by the listener to organize the working-memory representation. In future experiments we will investigate the role of other prosodic features and of a full, natural prosody in structuring the incoming speech signal.

We have argued that the representation of a sentence by a listener is affected by modality-specific information: prosodic structure in speech. To the extent that the language-processing system has evolved to accept information from the speech modality, we will not be able to define a language-processing module that is distinct from the auditory input pathway. The relationship between the visual input pathway and the language processor appears to be quite different.

Reading and Language Processing

In reading, the eyes move along the page in a series of jumps or saccades, interrupted by pauses or fixations during which the reader can accumulate visual information. Research in eye movements in reading since 1977 has suggested that the movements of the eyes are closely related to the mental processes used to comprehend the sentences (Frazier and Rayner 1982; Just and Carpenter 1980). Naive introspection will convince you that the eyes move back or regress to previous parts of the text when a passage is confusing, or move along the page more slowly for difficult texts. When you encounter an unfamiliar word, you stop and try to make sense of it.

Some researchers have come to believe that eye-movement patterns and fixation durations can give a moment-by-moment measure of the cognitive processes used in comprehension. Most notable, Just and Carpenter (1980) have developed a theory that states that all comprehension processes are completed immediately and that the eyes will fixate a word in a sentence until the processing of that word is complete. This kind of theory of the language processor minimizes the impact of system architecture and supposes that disparate parts of the system are transparent to one another. More to the current point, it assumes that the working of the mind can be measured in a simply way from the length of the pauses of the eyes, if only we identify the proper cognitive variables.

When we began our current research on eye movements and discourse processing, our thinking was, for the most part, compatible with this view. We would like to outline the reasons that our thinking in this matter has changed considerably.

The existing data have led us to consider a model of reading in which control of eye movements is usually independent of momentary, on-line parsing and comprehension processes. First, under normal reading circumstances, eye movements are guided by perceptual characteristics of the text and by word-recognition processes. A syntactic representation of the text is constructed as the words are recognized, but fixation durations do not typically reflect each syntactic decision. Higher-level processors represent the information in the text and connect the discourse as a coherent propositional base. These processes do not affect the normal timing or pattern of eye movements. Thus, this model argues that the structure of the language-processing system produces effects that will not appear in the fixation-time measure. Not all information is immediately available to control the timing of eye movements.

Of course, the eyes, unlike the ears, are not slaves to the temporal flow of events. When the language processor detects a problem from the information that the visual input system has conveyed, the eye-movement-control system interrupts the word-recognition processor and switches into reanalysis mode, under the control of the language processor. It is not yet clear whether reanalysis is a resetting of normal processes or a special mode of processing akin to problem solving. Nevertheless, this hypothesis predicts that localized on-line language-processing effects should appear in eye movements only when normal untroubled comprehension breaks down. We will present four kinds of evidence for this two-state model.

First, there is strong evidence for word-recognition effects in fixation durations. Many studies report evidence for immediate changes in fixation time due to properties of lexical items, and we will add corroborating evidence from our own studies.

Second, there are effects on the global processing load that can be understood by analysis of the syntactic constituent structure of the sentence currently being fixated. Sentences are processed in a constituent-by-constituent fashion, and the timing of eye movements reflects changes in the processing load.

Third, we find little support for effects due to high-level integrative processes in our own work, and we believe that the effects of discourse variables reported by others may have a more complex cause than the theory of a homogenized processing system would suggest.

Finally, we will present some anecdotal evidence that disruption patterns in reading are not anomalies but are part of the complex solution the mind has worked out to connect two systems that are biologically and functionally distinct: vision and language processing.

Word-Recognition Effects

The properties of words that have been shown to influence word-recognition time are also reliable predictors of word-fixation time in reading sentences. Perceptual characteristics of the text, such as the size and legibility of the characters, as well as lexical characteristics, such as word length and word frequency, are frequently reported as powerful determinants of fixation duration. Reviews of these effects can be found in Mitchell 1982, Rayner 1978, and Tinker 1958.

A convincing source of support for the power of these low-level factors is Just and Carpenter's (1980) regression analysis of fixation times during extended text processing. They showed that simple lexical properties of words account for approximately 70% of the variance in reading times, while eleven other text-processing features can account for only 10% more variance.

Our own work, though still in an early stage of analysis, strongly supports these findings. Word length is a very robust predictor of processing time. This relationship is not a simple monotonic one, but rather a U-shaped function (see O'Regan 1981). Very short words and very long words receive longer processing times than do words of fours to ten letters. Word-frequency effects are somewhat variable, but in general there is a negative correlation between log frequency of a word and fixation duration. Less common words take longer to process than familiar lexical items.

In summary: Word recognition seems to have a strong influence on fixation time. However, not all of the variability in fixations can be accounted for by such simple measures. To make sense of reading times, we must look deeper into the processing system.

Table 11
Example sentence from experiment 6.

Physically near / syntactically near

Cathy Walters remained calm during the heated debate, but she could not persuade the committee to change the policy.

Physically near / syntactically far

Cathy Walters remained calm. The debate was heated, but she could not persuade the committee to change the policy.

Physically far / syntactically near

Cathy Walters remained calm about the blatant sexism during the heated debate, but she could not persuade the committee to change the policy.

Physically far / syntactically far

Cathy Walters remained calm about the blatant sexism. The debate was heated, but she could not persuade the committee to change the policy.

Syntactic Effects on Global Processing Load

In order to describe the evidence for syntactic effects and the lack of semantic integration effects, we will outline some of the experiments we have conducted. Our central experimental work is a study of pronoun processing under various conditions that might affect the availability of the referent in memory.

In our experiments, we present a series of sentences for subjects to read while their eye movements are being recorded. Each passage contained a pronoun, for which a referent occurred earlier in the passage. If it is true that the eyes await the complete processing of each word before they move on to a new place, the fixation time on the pronoun should reflect how difficult it is to find the referent of the pronoun in the text. We had some reason to believe that this process should be reflected in fixation durations. In a prior study, Ehrlich and Rayner (1983) found that pronoun processing time was longer when the pronoun was farther from the referent in the text. However, their materials suggested that the pronoun effects may have been produced by disruptions in the normal reading pattern due to anomalies detected when the pronoun was encountered.

In experiment 6, we created a set of sentences like those in table 11. Physical distance was manipulated by changing the number of words that occurred between the pronoun and the referent. As can be seen by comparing the upper two sentences and the lower two, we generally did this by adding prepositional phrases to the direct object of the initial sentence. On the average, eight additional words distinguished the long from the short versions.

Table 12
Mean total reading times (msec) for the passages in experiment 6.

	Syntactic distance	
Physical distance	Near	Far
Near	5,729	5,974
Far	7,433	7,611
$\overline{X}$	6,581	6,793

Syntactic distance was manipulated orthogonally by changing whether or not there was an intervening clause and a sentence boundary between the pronoun and the referent. This can be seen by comparing the first and the second sentence in the examples. The same number of words intervene between the pronoun and the referent, but there are more syntactically complete units in the Syntactically Far condition than in the Syntactically Near condition. Forty college students each saw ten different passages in each condition. In accordance with previous research, we predicted that increasing either physical distance or structural distance or both would lead to longer fixation durations on and around the pronoun.

The results from this experiment did not show the expected effects of time to resolve the anaphoric relationship, although they did show an influence of syntactic constituent structure on processing time. Table 12 shows the total time (in milliseconds) spent reading the passages. There is a large physical distance effect, but that is just due to the number of words (and, hence, the number of fixations) in the passages. The interesting result is the syntactic distance effect: When the sentence was composed of three clauses with a sentence boundary separating pronoun and referent, the passage took longer to read than when the sentence was composed of only two clauses without a sentence boundary.

Table 13 shows fixation durations in the region around the pronoun. The first column of data shows the cumulative fixation duration, called the gaze duration, in the area immediately around the pronoun. The second column is the duration of the first fixation after leaving the pronoun. Both sets of data show a clear syntactic-distance effect, but it is in the opposite direction from that predicted by the availability of the referent for the pronoun assignment. When the referent was syntactically near, fixation durations were longer throughout the remainder of the sentence then when the referent was syntactically far. This effect must be due to the syntactic structure of the sentence and not to the process of integration of the pronoun and referent. As the example in table 11 shows, in the Syntactically Near condition the clause that precedes the pronoun is longer and

Table 13
Summary statistics from experiment 6.

Distance				Fixation time:	Total time:	Gaze time:
			Gaze time:	first fixation	pronoun to end	last word
Phys.	Synt.	Condition	pronoun	after pronoun	of sentence	in sentence
Near	Near	1	454	208	1,913	456
	Far	2	434	188	1,814	436
Far	Near	3	449	195	1,794	425
	Far	4	421	192	1,736	405

contains more information; in the Syntactically Far condition the same information is separated into two sentences. We believe that the longer clause from the same sentence in the Syntactically Near condition is still active in memory until the end of the sentence is encountered and parsing is completed. This appears as an increase in the general processing load determined by the structure of the Syntactically Near sentences.

The syntactic-distance effect is evident in the total reading time to the end of the sentence (shown in the third column in table 13) and in the gaze duration at the end of the sentence (shown in the fourth column). Since the text is identical in all conditions from the pronoun to the end of the sentence, this effect must be due to the processing demands created before the pronoun is encountered.

There is also a physical-distance effect, but again it is in the reverse direction of what would be predicted for pronoun processing time. The Physically Far condition is faster than the Physically Near condition, and this effect shows up consistently throughout the end of the sentence, though it is significant only for the Total Time measure. In the Physically Far condition, there were extra words earlier in the passage, at the end of the referent clause. We believe that these filler phrases allow the reader to complete more of the processing of the first clause before reading the pronoun clause, thus reducing the general processing load later in the sentence.

We conducted three other experiments to look at the problem of syntactic distance. In general, the results suggest that a preceding clause in the same sentence increases fixation times, possibly through an increase in processing load, whereas a preceding clause in a previous sentence does not influence fixation times. Further evidence for increased processing load due to the syntactic connection between two clauses was found by contrasting subordinate and main clauses. Fixation times were longer in the second clause if the previous clause was subordinate than if it was a main clause, but this was true only if both clauses were in the same sentence. There were no reading-time differences if they were in different sentences.

There was also evidence that the syntactic processor regularly interrupts the word-recognition-based eye-movement control. Readers fixate for longer at times at the ends of syntactic clauses and especially at the ends of sentences. Table 14 compares fixation times at the end of the pronoun sentence with fixation times at various midsentence points for four experiments across the various conditions of those experiments. It is clear that readers spend extra time fixating the end of the sentence, presumably to complete some of the processing that lagged behind while the eyes kept moving.

In summary: We believe that syntactic structure does influence fixation times, but that the influence generally takes place through global changes in processing load rather than through the control of specific fixation durations, at least as long as the syntactic analysis is going smoothly. (We will discuss cases of disruption below.) Finally, we believe that word-recognition processes are normally and regularly interrupted by syntactic and perhaps higher-level processing, but only at the boundaries of major constituents.

The Effects of Discourse-Integration Processes
After several carefully planned experiments that looked at physical and syntactic manipulations, we found no consistent effects that could be attributed to assigning the pronoun to the referent. In experiment 7, we cast off subtlety and investigated factors that our intuitions suggested must affect processing time. An example of the eight versions of one of our stimulus passages can be seen in table 15. Each subject read 64 such passages, eight from each of the eight conditions described below.

First, we feared that our short stimulus passages were failing to engage all of the discourse-processing machinery available to the language comprehender. Therefore, half of our passages were expanded to four sentences, surely stretching the limits of working memory; others were only two sentences long. These were called the Far and Near conditions, respectively, referring to the distance between the referent (always in the first sentence) and the pronoun (always in the last sentence).

Second, we introduced ambiguity to the process of finding the referent. There were either two possible same-gender referents or only one, with the other character of the opposite sex. These conditions are labeled Competing Referent and No Competing Referent, respectively.

Finally, we manipulated a factor that has received immense attention lately: the topic of the passage. We assigned the topic by the following criteria, most of which have met with some success in other language-processing experiments:

Table 14
Mean fixation durations for midsentence region and at end of
sentence for experiments 6 and 7 and two other studies, broken
down by experimental condition.

Condition	Midsentence	End of sentence
Experiment 6		
1	228	295
2	226	303
3	237	286
4	231	280
Experiment 7		
1	256	300
2	253	295
3	260	329
4	254	304
5	249	297
6	256	308
7	240	319
8	253	314
Experiment 8		
1	204	284
2	203	291
3	196	294
4	199	298
Experiment 9		
1	215	292
2	210	271
3	214	288
4	217	288

Note: Longer overall times for experiment 6 are largely attributable to use of smaller character set.

Table 15
Example sentence from experiment 10.

Topical referent / competing referent / near

The ballerina twirled to the center of the stage as Wendy watched from the balcony. When the music reached a climax, she leaped into the air and landed to the roaring sound of applause.

Topical referent / no competing referent / near

The ballerina twirled to the center of the stage as Roger watched from the balcony. When the music reached a climax, she leaped into the air and landed to the roaring sound of applause.

Topical referent / competing referent / far

The ballerina twirled to the center of the stage as Wendy watched from the balcony. The costume glittered under the stage lights. The precision and grace of the movements were breathtaking. When the music reached a climax, she leaped into the air and landed to the roaring sound of applause.

Topical referent / no competing referent / far

The ballerina twirled to the center of the stage as Roger watched from the balcony. The costume glittered under the stage lights. The precision and grace of the movements were breathtaking. When the music reached a climax, she leaped into the air and landed to the roaring sound of applause.

Nontopical referent / competing referent / near

Wendy watched the performance in awe from the balcony as the ballerina twirled on the stage. When the music reached a climax, she leaped into the air and landed to the roaring sound of applause.

Nontopical referent / no competing referent / near

Roger watched the performance in awe from the balcony as the ballerina twirled on the stage. When the music reached a climax, she leaped into the air and landed to the roaring sound of applause.

Non-topical referent / competing referent / far

Wendy watched the performance in awe from the balcony as the ballerina twirled on the stage. The costume glittered under the stage lights. The precision and grace of the movements were breathtaking. When the music reached a climax, she leaped into the air and landed to the roaring sound of applause.

Nontopical referent / no competing referent / far

Roger watched the performance in awe from the balcony as the ballerina twirled on the stage. The costume glittered under the stage lights. The precision and grace of the movements were breathtaking. When the music reached a climax, she leaped into the air and landed to the roaring sound of applause.

Table 16
Mean gaze duration in pronoun region from experiment 10.

	Competing referent	No competing referent
Topical		
Near	299	310
Far	296	291
Nontopical		
Near	299	300
Far	293	298

• The topic was always the first character mentioned in the passage.
• The topical character was always in the main clause, and the nontopical character in a subordinate clause.
• More descriptive information was given about the topical character than about the nontopical character.
• In the Far condition, the intervening sentences either were neutral with respect to the possible referents or they were changed to favor the topic.

The Nontopical condition is shown in the lower four passages in table 15. Particularly in sentences like the seventh one in the table—the Non-topical/Far condition with a Competing Referent—people report amusement and a mental double-take upon encountering the pronoun.

The predictions in this experiment again assumed that the characteristics of the discourse would influence the availability of the referent. When a character is the topic, it should be more accessible than when it is not. When there are two possible referents, pronoun processing time should be slower than when only one of the referents shares the gender feature of the pronoun. Finally, the referent should be more accessible when the text is shorter and the referent is in the immediately preceding sentence.

As table 16 shows, there were no consistent effects on the pronoun or immediately around it. This was also true for each of the three fixations following the pronoun and for cumulative gaze-duration measures out to nine characters to the right of the pronoun. In general, this measurement was consistent with the outcome of our other four experiments.

Table 17 gives several measures of processing in the region from the pronoun to the end of the sentence. Total reading time from the pronoun to the end of the sentence did show a significant effect of the distance between the pronoun and the referent. Reading time was longer in the Near condition than in the Far condition. Once again, this effect was in the opposite direction from what would be predicted for pronoun processing

Table 17
Summary data for reading region from pronoun to end of sentence in experiment 10.

		Total time	Number of fixations	Average fixation duration
Topical				
Competing referent	Near	2,655	11.1	245
	Far	2,322	9.5	248
No competing referent	Near	2,384	9.7	246
	Far	2,362	9.6	247
Nontopical				
Competing referent	Near	2,428	10.0	244
	Far	2,482	10.0	248
No competing referent	Near	2,638	10.7	248
	Far	2,469	10.0	249

time. In general, if there was no intervening sentence and, consequently, the passage was short and the referent nearby, processing took longer. An analysis of the number of fixations, shown in the second column, indicated that the longer reading times were due not to increased fixation durations, as can be seen in the third column, but to an increased number of fixations.

In short: This experiment, in accord with earlier studies, suggests that individual fixation durations are not greatly influenced by the coherence of the discourse.

Disruption Effects

Apparently, it should not simply be assumed, as it generally is, that reading is just a visual version of the speech-comprehension process. Whereas the speech processor apparently makes a direct contribution to the immediate structuring of a sentence, the visual processing system is genuinely an input conduit. It is not surprising that it is so much more difficult to learn to read than to comprehend speech. We believe that the individual fixation times in reading do not reflect all the processes that have been attributed to them. In fact, the strongest evidence seems to be that the normal automatic operation of the eye-movement system is under direct control of word-identification processes—generally ones that work in isolation from higher-order parts of the language processor.

Of course, reading is not an endlessly automatic process. Both introspection and eye-movement data indicate that the smooth flow of the automatic visual intake of information is occasionally interrupted, particularly by regressive eye movements. Regressions within words, by far the most common type of regression, could easily be controlled by the automatic word-recognition device. Other regressions, however, are certainly in response to other parts of the language-processing system encountering difficulty in the text.

These disruptions in eye-movement patterns are far from trivial. To the contrary, we think that it is precisely in them that the larger structure of the human language processor is revealed. For example, the immediate regressions in response to garden-path sentences (Frazier and Rayner 1982; Rayner, Carlson, and Frazier 1983) indicate the speed with which the syntactic processes can interrupt the normal flow of fixations.

We have been conducting several experiments to study the responses of readers to task demands. Though we are not yet prepared to report these studies, we will present a few bits of anecdotal evidence.

Experiment 11 is similar to one reported by Frazier and Rayner to offer a closer look at how readers respond to these disruptions. Figure 5 gives an example of one of the stumulus sentences from our study. The asterisks below each line of the sentence indicate the centers of the various fixations for this subject while he was reading the sentence. The pattern of fixations in this sentence makes it clear that the reader responds to the catastrophic breakdown in the syntactic structure of the sentence by regressing from the word *pupils* to a previous word. The two fixations on the word *cause* are 443 msec and 322 msec in duration. The average fixation duration in this sentence is 255 msec. Undoubtedly, there is considerable mental work taking place at this point. We believe that, somewhere in this sentence, the task changed from normal reading with specific syntactic and semantic decisions taking place in isolation from eye movements to a search-and-problem-solving process directly under the control of the language processor. Words and structures have become suspect, and normal processing has been suspended.

In Experiment 12, we asked subjects to memorize sentences verbatim. Relatively simple sentences were to be memorized one at a time. The task would appear to be a relatively trivial one, but it has led to some curious preliminary results. Figure 6 shows the pattern of fixations on one sentence as it was read by someone asked to understand the sentence but not to memorize it. This is a typical reading pattern. Nearly every word is fixated, but only once, and because the text is simple there are few regressions. Figure 6 also shows how the same sentence was read by someone with similar reading skills. Some people memorize without regressions, but a large proportion of our memorizers showed patterns like that in the example. Aside from noting that there are many regressions, notice the locations of the regressions. It appears that surface constituent structure

GARDEN-PATH EXPERIMENT

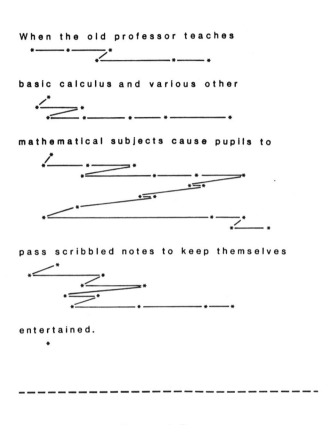

When the old professor teaches

basic calculus and various other

mathematical subjects cause pupils to

pass scribbled notes to keep themselves

entertained.

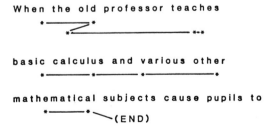

Second Pass

When the old professor teaches

basic calculus and various other

mathematical subjects cause pupils to

(END)

Figure 5
Fixation locations (indicated by asterisks) for a subject reading one of the sentences from experiment 11.

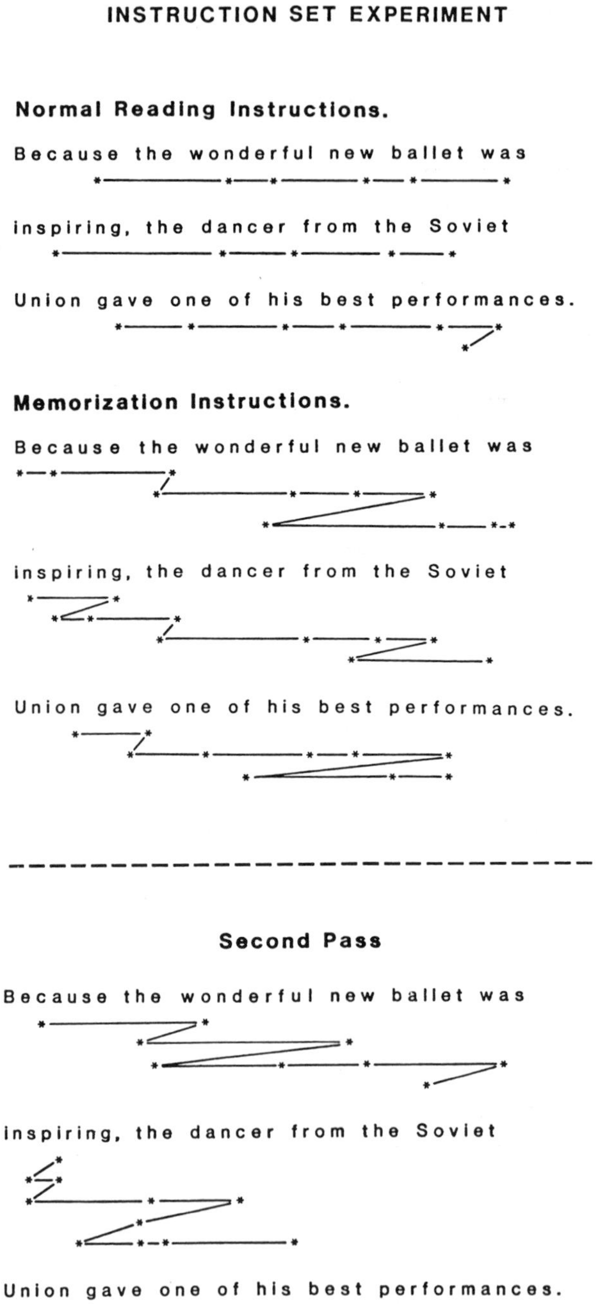

INSTRUCTION SET EXPERIMENT

Normal Reading Instructions.

Because the wonderful new ballet was

inspiring, the dancer from the Soviet

Union gave one of his best performances.

Memorization Instructions.

Because the wonderful new ballet was

inspiring, the dancer from the Soviet

Union gave one of his best performances.

- -

Second Pass

Because the wonderful new ballet was

inspiring, the dancer from the Soviet

Union gave one of his best performances.

Figure 6
Fixations locations (indicated by asterisks) for one subject under normal reading instructions and a different subject under memorization instructions in experiment 12.

exerts a strong influence on the memorizer's eye movements. The tendency to stay within the current noun phrase or prepositional phrase and not to regress across major constituent boundaries appears to be a typical memorization strategy. Function words, often ignored in normal reading, receive a great deal of attention, drawing a large percentage of the regressions. Fixation durations do appear to increase in general, but the primary change is in the pattern of fixations.

In summary: Our final evidence, a set of examples drawn somewhat selectively from a large corpus, demonstrates that the pattern of fixations, unlike the individual fixation durations, is highly responsive to the demands of language processing and to varying goals of the reader. We believe that this is a change in the state of the system from a reasonably automatic mode of processing to one initiated by an interrupt coming from the language processor and reflected in a greater amount of nonautomatic word-processing activity.

Conclusions

We have suggested that the auditory and visual pathways to the language processor serve different functions. In reading, the visual input system is distinct from the language processor. It is only at syntactically defined boundaries or at times when comprehension breaks down that the visual control system and the language processor interact directly. In contrast, the auditory input system makes a direct contribution to the structuring of sentences. The auditory pathway is well integrated with the levels of the language-processing system that analyze structure, leading to an initial representation of the input sentence containing both prosodic and syntactic information. However the language-processing module is ultimately defined, it will need to reconcile the differing contributions from the visual and auditory modalities.

Acknowledgment

We wish to thank Michael Guertin, Shari Speer, and Cheryl Wilson for their assistance in the preparation of the manuscript. Part of the research reported here was supported by NIH Grant 1 ROI NS21638-01 to Maria L. Slowiaczek.

Note

1. In this figure, the same-group trials look slower than the different-group trials for the long-short pattern. However, this is due to the unusually short response times to probe position 1, which has a long pause in the long-short pattern. When the data are analyzed with probe position as a factor, the same-group trials are faster than the different-group trials in all other probe positions.

12

Modularity and Interaction in Sentence Processing
Gerry Altmann

There has recently been much concern within the modularity debate over the relationship between syntax and semantics during the resolution of local syntactic ambiguity. At issue is whether such ambiguities are resolved on the basis of syntactic information alone, or whether they are ever resolved on the basis of "higher-level" semantic/pragmatic information. This is an empirical question: we must determine whether just the one kind of information is used during the resolution process, or whether different kinds of information (stemming from what might be considered different "domains") are brought together. It is to this issue that the present chapter is addressed.

A traditional starting point from which to consider local syntactic ambiguity has been the "garden path" phenomenon experienced with sentences such as the following:

The oil tycoon sold the off-shore oil tracts for a lot of money wanted to kill J.R.

Garden paths of this sort demonstrate that the human sentence-processing mechanism (HSPM) exhibits a preference for one analysis over another when faced with a local ambiguity. But why do these preferences exist? What information is the HSPM using when making its (incorrect) choice? One suggestion, originally proposed by Kimball (1973) and followed up more recently by Frazier (1979) and Rayner, Carlson, and Frazier (1983), is that the HSPM takes into account only the syntactic structure of these sentences. There are two possible structures that could be assigned to the ambiguous sentence fragment *The oil tycoon sold the off-shore oil tracts....* The Reduced Passive interpretation requires an extra NP node as compared with the Main Verb interpretation. Kimball (1975) and Frazier suggest that when more than one interpretation is possible, the HSPM pursues the interpretation that creates the structure with fewest nodes. This is what Frazier calls the Principle of Minimal Attachment.

This structural hypothesis proposes that an initial decision is made on grounds of syntactic structure alone. Only if it subsequently turns out to be the wrong decision (on grounds of "implausibility") is the alternative analysis then attempted. In support of this claim, Rayner et al. collected reading times and eye-movement data for sentences that (syntactically speaking) allow two attachment sites for a prepositional phrase; one attachment, to a noun phrase, requires an extra NP node as compared with the other attachment, which is to a verb phrase. The following examples, adapted from Rayner et al. 1983, are illustrative.

The burglar blew open the safe with the dynamite. (minimal attachment to VP)

The burglar blew open the safe with the diamonds. (nonminimal attachment to NP)

In the case of the nonminimally attached version, the correct attachment (to the NP) should have been attempted only after the minimal attachment to the VP had first been tried. As predicted by the structural hypothesis, reading times to the nonminimally attached versions were significantly longer than to the minimally attached versions.

An alternative to minimal attachment is proposed by Ford, Bresnan, and Kaplan (1982), who suggest that these preferences arise from the order in which lexical/syntactic rules in the grammar can be accessed (cf. Wanner's [1980] "implementation" of minimal attachment). The theory of lexical preference put forth by Ford et al. is more powerful than minimal attachment because this ordering can, in part, be determined by the actual lexical items that are involved. In other words, lexical information can effectively override the preferences that would otherwise be induced by minimal attachment.

Referential Success and Local Syntactic Ambiguity

Minimal attachment and lexical preference share a common concern for surface-structure parsing. Both proposals are based on structure. However, the construction of syntactic tree structures is not the primary aim of sentence processing. The listener/reader integrates the current sentence with information that has accumulated as a result of the preceding dialogue/text.

Working within this discourse-oriented framework, Crain (1980; see also Crain and Steedman 1985) noted that many of the garden-path sentences share the feature that, of the two possible analyses, one is functionally equivalent to a restrictive relative clause. Noun phrases are used by the speaker to refer to objects. The function of a restrictive relative is to give additional information as to who or what is being talked about. This additional information is necessary because without it there would not be sufficient evidence with which to determine who or what was being referred to. If one had just heard the expression *the oil tycoon* or *the safe*, one might not know just which candidate oil tycoon or which candidate safe was intended. But where do these different candidate oil tycoons and safes come from? Within a normal discourse, they will presumably have been already introduced and represented by the speaker and the hearer in some model of the discourse. In this sense, all the examples we have so far considered are unnatural because the sentences are presented in isolation. There are references to *the* oil tycoon and *the* off-shore oil tracts, but this is their first mention. The target sentences should be embedded in a context.

Crain and Steedman propose that the HSPM's choice of analysis is dependent on the context within which the locally ambiguous sentence is to be interpreted. They suggest that this choice is governed, where appropriate, by a principle of Referential Success: "If there is a reading which succeeds in referring to an entity already established in the hearer's mental model of the domain of discourse, then it is favored over one that does not."[1] (Crain and Steedman 1985) To test this principle, Crain—using a class of ambiguity different in form from the present examples but the same in principle—showed that garden-path effects could be overcome or induced depending on the referential nature of the context (i.e., depending on whether just one oil tycoon or more than one had been introduced in the preceding text). It follows from Crain's work, in which an incremental grammaticality-judgment task was used, that a suitable test of the generality of the results of Rayner et al. is to replicate their experiment using the same reading-time task but using contexts felicitous to one or the other of the two versions of their examples. This notion of felicity is illustrated by the following examples, which were devised for an experiment (Altmann 1986; Altmann and Steedman, forthcoming).

To induce attachment to NP:
A burglar carrying some dynamite broke into an heiress's house. Once inside he found two safes. One of them had some diamonds inside while the other had several priceless emeralds.

To induce attachment to VP:
A burglar carrying some dynamite broke into an heiress's house. Once inside he found *a safe and a jewelry box*. One of them had some diamonds inside while the other had several priceless emeralds.

Following these contexts, one of two continuations might be seen.

Minimal (VP) attachment:
The burglar blew open the safe with the dynamite.

Nonminimal (NP) attachment:
The burglar blew open the safe with the diamonds.

The contexts are identical except that one mentions two safes and the other a safe and a jewelry box. In theory, this difference affects only the cardinality of the set of safes in the reader's model of the text. The NP-inducing context should be felicitous with the nonminimally (NP) attached target, and the VP-inducing context with the minimally (VP) attached target.

Reading times were collected for each target sentence preceded by either one or the other context. Texts (i.e. context and target) were presented to a computer-controlled display one sentence at a time. The target sentences were distinguished from their preceding context only insofar as they constituted the last sentence of the text.

For the nonminimally (NP) attached targets, there was a strong effect of referential context on reading time (230 msec). Furthermore, reading times to nonminimal targets in both contexts were considerably shorter than reading times to the minimally (VP) attached versions. (There was a difference of 348 msec in the NP-inducing conditions, and 190 msec overall.[2]) This is the reverse of what would be expected on a minimal-attachment or a lexical-preference account, neither of which could account for this effect unless the experimental evidence that currently supports them were to be discounted.[3]

However, no effect of context on the minimally (VP) attached targets was found. (The difference in reading time across the two context conditions was only 78 msec.) This was surprising; the VP-inducing context should have been felicitous with this target, and the NP-inducing context infelicitous. On further consideration of the materials it becomes apparent, however, that neither of these contexts was in fact felicitous with VP-attachment.

The function of a PP attached to an NP, in these examples, is to provide additional and necessary information with which to identify a particular object in the discourse model. Thus, it must be providing information already given in the text (see Clark and Haviland 1977). The function of a PP attached to a verb, in these examples, is to provide new information about the action denoted by the verb: The burglar didn't simply blow open the safe, he blew it open with the dynamite. This, in turn, presupposes that the action denoted by the verb (*blow open*) is given. In the VP-inducing context, this was not the case; this presupposition was violated. The action denoted by the verb was not given. The fact that no effect of context was found for the VP-attached targets may have been due to this. Any facilitatory effect of context may have been masked by an increase in reading time brought about by this violation. A second experiment was therefore run in which the blowing open was known about by subjects in advance of the target sentence (i.e., it was given): this time, strong effects of context were found for both kinds of target (113 msec for NP-attached targets across the two conditions of context, 358 msec for the VP-attached targets). Once again, the nonminimally attached targets were significantly faster than the minimally attached targets (486 msec in the NP-inducing condition, 245 msec overall).

The internal syntactic form of a construction seems to be less important than the presuppositions implied by its use. If these presuppositions are satisfied, then that construction will be favored over a construction whose associated presuppositions have not been satisfied. If we want to think of the HSPM as consisting of a number of separable subprocessors, then such an approach requires that the operations of the syntactic subprocessor be closely interleaved with the operations of the other subprocessor(s) responsible for establishing and maintaining the discourse model. We would have to assume an interactive relationship between these subprocessors.

Inferencing and the Processing of Restrictive Relatives

In the above-mentioned experiments we found that reading times were affected by factors that were not necessarily syntactic in origin. It is clearly important, when considering reading time, to distinguish between effects that are due to syntactic (re)analyses and effects that are due to other kinds of nonsyntactic process. This notion is important because its application to another class of ambiguity phenomena suggests that other evidence, previously thought to favor lexical or structural accounts of the resolution process, does not bear on the issue of ambiguity resolution at all.

In the ambiguous sentence *The boy told the girl that he liked the story*, the complement-clause analysis of the *that*-clause is preferred to the relative-clause analysis (Wanner, Kaplan, and Shiner 1974). And even when the relative-clause analysis is initially chosen, these examples take longer to process (as measured by reading time) than when the complement-clause analysis is chosen (Wanner et al. 1974; Altmann 1986). In other words, the relative-clause analysis is not just less preferred; it is also more complex. The generally accepted explanation is that complex NP expansions require more processing time than simple NP expansions. In Wanner et al. 1974 and Wanner 1980, these effects are modeled using an ATN, and it is shown that they can be made to arise from peculiarities in the order in which arcs leave certain states. Frazier and Fodor (1978) cite these effects in support of minimal attachment; Ford et al. (1982) would predict them on the basis of their theory of lexical and syntactic preferences, in which the simple NP expansion rule is ordered before the complex NP expansion rule.

Crain's original demonstration of referential-context effects did in fact use examples that exhibited this same class of local ambiguity. However, the nature of Crain's task means that he did not address the issue of complexity.

If, as has been claimed, restrictive relatives provide given information, then the information contained within the relative clause must be matched against information that already exists in the hearer's model of the discourse/text. This matching process presumably requires a certain amount of inferencing, or "bridging" (Haviland and Clark 1974; Sanford and Garrod 1981). It might only be possible to infer that the information contained within the relative clause is intended to match to something already known to the hearer. Complement clauses require no such matching process and are therefore less complex. The inferencing process can be controlled for only if the materials under study are preceded by felicitous contexts. To assess the contribution of inferencing to processing time, an experiment was run (Altmann, forthcoming) using stimuli of the following sorts, which are similar to those used by Crain (1980).[4]

"Inferencing" context (relative-inducing):
A policeman was questioning two women. He was suspicious of one of them but not of the other.

"Minimal inferencing" context (relative-inducing):
A policeman was questioning two women. He had his doubts about one of them but not about the other.

Relative-clause target:
The policeman told the woman that he had his doubts about to tell the truth.

Complement-clause target:
The policeman told the woman that he had his doubts about her clever alibi.

The amount of inferencing required to process the relative target was manipulated by changing the wording in the preceding context from *was suspicious of* ("inferencing") to *had his doubts about* ("minimal inferencing"). Given the relative clause *that he had his doubts about*, it was assumed that a change in the preceding context from *He had his doubts about one of them* to *He was suspicious of one of them* would be accompanied by an increase in the amount of inferencing required during the processing of the relative. As in the case of the earlier experiments, each target sentence was preceded by each possible context.

Apart from finding strong effects of context (thereby replicating Crain's experiment but using a reading-time technique), we found no significant absolute difference between complement-clause targets and relative-clause targets once context and inferencing were controlled for (only 31 msec in the "minimal inferencing" condition, versus 385 msec in the "inferencing" condition).

This experiment demonstrates the effects on reading times of two separate kinds of processes: those whose effects reflect the inferencing processes that link the contents of a sentence to the contents of the discourse model and those whose effects reflect the context-sensitive parsing processes responsible for the resolution of this particular kind of local syntactic ambiguity.

All the data suggest, then, that syntactic decisions are not made in isolation from contextual, nonsyntactic information. It follows that different kinds of information interact during the resolution process.

Referential Failure and Local Syntactic Ambiguity

Crain and Steedman's Principle of Referential Success requires that the processor wait until it succeeds in identifying the intended referent before choosing between alternative analyses. This would require of the following text that the processor make its decision only at the end of the italicized segment:

In the restaurant were two oil tycoons. One of them had bought some off-shore oil tracts for a lot of money, while the other had bought some very cheaply. *The oil tycoon sold the off-shore oil tracts for a lot of money* wanted to kill J.R.

It seems more appropriate, however, to suppose that the choice of analysis is determined not on the basis of referential success but on the basis of referential failure.

Principle of Referential Failure: If a referring expression fails to refer to an entity already established in the hearer's mental model of the domain of discourse, then an analysis that treats subsequent material as a modifier for that referring expression (i.e., as providing information that may lead to successful reference), will be favored over one that does not.

Unlike the Principle of Referential Success, Referential Failure requires that the parser interpret noun phrases (i.e., attempt to establish their intended referents) as soon as they are encountered. Referential Failure thus relies on the ability to establish early on what is, and what is not, already known (given) to the hearer.

The account I have developed so far explains certain parsing preferences when a target sentence is embedded in a discourse. But can we also account for the preferences exhibited in isolated sentences (the "null context"—as in the original "oil tycoon" example)? In the absence of any preceding discourse, there can exist no discourse model within which to integrate the information contained in the isolated sentence. In such cases, nothing can be successfully interpreted as given information. It follows that all incoming material must be treated as if it provides new information. If the incoming material is ambiguous between a reading that promises new information (e.g. a complement clause) and one that promises given information (e.g. a relative clause), then in the null context the former interpretation must be chosen. In general, if there is a choice between a complex NP analysis, which implicates additional given information by which to identify the intended referent, and a simple NP analysis which carries no such implication, then in the null context the simple NP analysis must be chosen.[5]

Conclusions

Structure-based theories of local-syntactic-ambiguity resolution can account for the null-context data, but cannot account for the data concerning contextual effects on ambiguity resolution. The present account accommodates both sets of data.[6] Moreover, while minimal attachment, as applied to the treatment of simple/complex noun phrases, correctly describes the behavior of the HSPM in the null context, the present account *explains* this behavior.

It has been shown that the resolution of local syntactic ambiguity does not depend only on syntactic factors. Semantic/pragmatic information does influence the resolution process. Thus, sentence processing is an interactive process in which decisions at one notional level of representation are made in the light of information at another notional level.

But what are the implications of such a result for the modularity hypothesis? Is the hypothesis compromised by these results? The principle of referential failure requires that syntactic and semantic/pragmatic processing be closely interleaved. Crain and Steedman (1982), Steedman (this volume) and Altmann (1986) advocate a model of the HSPM in which the syntactic processor can independently propose alternative syntactic analyses, which the semantic processor can then choose between on a word-by-word basis (these are what Crain and Steedman call "radical" weak interactions). However, syntax and semantics can still each be "domain specific, innately specified, hardwired, autonomous, and not assembled" (Fodor 1983, p. 37). Modularity is therefore consistent with the model of the HSPM we have described, but it is not among its experimentally addressable predictions.

Acknowledgments

The work reported here was carried out at the University of Edinburgh while I was in the School of Epistemics on an S.E.R.C. postgraduate research studentship. My thanks to the Centre for Speech Technology Research and the Alvey Large Scale Demonstrator Project for providing additional financial support, and to my supervisors Ellen Gurman Bard and Mark Steedman for providing moral support.

This is an expanded version of a paper which appears in the proceedings of the second meeting of the Association of Computational Linguistics (European Chapter), March 28–29, 1985.

Notes

1. A similar principle was implemented in a program described by Winograd (1972). This consisted of a simulated robot (SHRDLU) which responded to commands such as "Put the blue pyramid on the block in the box." This command is of course ambiguous: The blue pyramid could already be on the block or the block could be in the box. Winograd's SHRDLU resolved the ambiguity as follows: On finding a definite noun phrase, SHRDLU would search the blocks world (and also a representation of the preceding discourse) for a referent to this referring expression. If a unique referent (or antecedent) could be found to the referring expression *the blue pyramid*, SHRDLU would look for "the block in the box." If no unique referent could be found for *the blue pyramid*, SHRDLU would then look for "the blue pyramid on the block."

2. All reported differences were significant on $MinF'$ (Clark 1973) at least at $P < 0.05$.

3. The experiment also contained a null-context condition (i.e., no prior text) in which reading times to the minimally attached sentences were faster than those to the non-minimally attached sentences (231 msec). Reading times in the null context were all slower than corresponding times in either of the two context conditions.

4. Though only the relative-inducing contexts are given here, complement-inducing contexts were also included in the experiment.

5. Although this explains the preference, in the null context, for complement clauses over relative clauses, it does not explain the increased complexity of relative clauses in the null context. This is explained as follows: The relative-clause interpretation violates more presuppositions (concerning the state of the hearer's discourse model) than the complement-clause interpretation. (See Crain and Steedman 1985 and Altmann and Steedman [in prep.] for discussion.) The experiments on prepositional phrases demonstrated that such violations lead to increased reading times. If it is assumed that increasing the number of violations leads to longer reading times, then one should expect relative clauses to induce longer reading times than complement clauses.

6. It is argued in Altmann 1986 and Altmann and Steedman (in prep.) that an account based on the distinction between what is and what is not already known to the hearer/reader (here defined as the distinction between the given and the new) may also generalize to the examples that have, on "structural" accounts, been explained by right association (Kimball 1973) and late closure (Frazier 1979).

13
Modularity in the Syntactic Parser
Amy Weinberg

Most of the chapters in this volume deal with the accessing of components of the grammar (for example, the lexicon or the syntactic component), grammatical information, or extragrammatical information during language processing. However, one may ask similar questions about how information within a given grammatical component is processed. In this chapter I will be dealing with the question whether all the information needed to construct a licit syntactic representation is treated uniformly by the syntactic processor. I will try to argue on the basis of considerations of processing efficiency and syntactic naturalness that the syntactic processor first creates a basic syntactic tree using phrase-structure, selectional, and subcategorization features together with information retrieved using a bounded amount of prior context. From the first-stage representation it constructs another structure, which it uses to establish binding relationships between categories. Given this two-stage model, I expect that constraints on syntactic binding are ignored at the first level of representation. I will review the independent arguments for this notion of efficiency presented in Berwick and Weinberg 1984 and the functional derivation that it provides for the important grammatical constraint of subjacency (Chomsky 1973). It will be seen that the predictions I make about the design of the two-stage model are borne out in the main by a set of recent experiments by Freedman and Forster (1985). More important, it will be seen that examining questions of grammatical naturalness and processing complexity allows us to make sense of the division of labor in syntactic processing that Freedman and Forster discovered. This suggests an area of fruitful interaction between linguistics, computational linguistics, and psycholinguistics.

I will also suggest ways of dealing with the Freedman-Forster data that superficially counterexemplify the theory of Berwick and Weinberg (1985, 1984, 1986). Along the way I will suggest how this picture bears on the choice of the underlying parsing algorithm and grammatical theory used by the language processor.

Representational Format

As every syntactician knows, sentences may be ungrammatical[1] for a variety of reasons. A sentence may violate the head-modifier-complement structure or a selectional or subcategorizational restriction imposed by one of the sentence's categories. Examples are given in (1).

(1)   *a.   The men a peach eat.
       *b.   The men eats a peach.
       *c.   The men hit.

The first example is ungrammatical because phrasal heads must occur to the left of their complements in English and VPs can select only a single NP subject. Thus, the structure NP NP V cannot be produced by the phrase-structure component of a grammar of English. The second example is out because the singular VP *eats a peach* selects a singular subject. The third example is out because *hit* obligatorily subcategorizes a nominal complement but there is no NP in the structure to satisfy this restriction. Earlier generative accounts capture the ordering restrictions between heads and complements and between phrases by means of phrase-structure rules of the following form[2]:

(2)   VP → V (NP) (PP)*

Subcategorization and selectional restrictions are stored as part of an item's lexical entry.

  Natural-language parsers must also construct licit phrase markers. All these restrictions are used in constructing phrase-structure trees on line (Wanner and Maratsos 1978; Fodor 1979). Particularly clear examples come from cases where the parser must expand the phrase-structure tree with an empty category. In a case like (3), it has been claimed, the parser uses the subcategorization information that *hit* is a verb that obligatorily subcategorizes an object and the information from X′ phrase-structure syntax that objects follow verb phrases to hypothesize that an empty category should be inserted after *hit* as in (4), signifying that the *wh-* word is linked to a category (i.e., interpreted) in this position.

(3)   Who did Mary hit?

(4)   Who$_i$ did Mary hit e$_i$

The integrated use of this information is not the only logical possibility, however. One could claim that the parser constructs a basic representation using only information from phrase structure (X′ syntax). This representation would be overgeneral; an unacceptable case like (1c) conforms to the principles of English phrase structure, as is shown by the need for PS rules like (5a) to generate sentences like (5b).

(5)   a. VP → V (NP) (PP) [3]
       b. The man ate (in the garden).

Cases like (1c) would be filtered out under this theory by having subcategorization and selectional restrictions apply to the representations's output by the phrase structure. Although this is a logically possible solution, we can see that it is unnatural and inefficient if we assume that the parser uses the independently justified representations of the linguist's grammar to encode this information. Chomsky (1965) argued that a lexical item's category type, and selectional and· subcategorization restrictions, should be stored as part of that item's lexical entry. Thus, the verb *hit* would be represented in the lexicon as in (6), which indicates that it is a verb that obligatorily subcategorizes an object that is concrete.[4]

(6)   HIT:
       VERB: _____ NP
             [+ concrete]

In order to apply the phrase-structure rules of a grammar (or the principles from which they derive) we have to know the category associated with items in the input stream. Input cannot even be grouped into phrases unless one knows the category of the elements it contains. However, given that all three types of information are stored together, the parser will, by looking up an item's lexical entry, have access to information about category type and about selectional and subcategorization restrictions. It would be extremely inefficient if the parser did not use such information to govern its construction of well-formed trees, because in this case the parser would have to construct a representation and then rescan it entirely using information that it possessed when it constructed the representation in the first place. This conclusion becomes inevitable for approaches such as the current Government and Binding (GB) framework, where phrase-structure rules are dispensed with completely and replaced by the direct use of lexical and X' information. In addition, both subcategorization and selectional restrictions can be checked in a bounded syntactic domain which has been termed the government domain.[5] Informally, government is a relationship that obtains between categories that are separated by no intervening maximal phrasal projections.[6] Sentences can be ungrammatical, however, even if the lexical restrictions discussed above are met. A subclass of relevant cases involve improper binding. By binding we mean either an operation linking a quasi-quantifier with a syntactic variable or a convention by which two noun phrases are interpreted as coreferential. These constructions are illustrated in (7).

(7)   *a. Who$_i$ did you see Leonardo's pictures of e$_i$.
      *b. Mary$_i$ saw the men's pictures of herself$_i$.
      *c. Mary$_i$ likes her$_i$.

All selectional, phrase-structure, and subcategorization restrictions are met in these examples, as can be seen by comparing these cases with the corresponding grammatical sentences in (8).

(8)   a. Mary saw Leonardo's pictures of the Mona Lisa.
      b. Mary$_i$ saw Leonardo's pictures of her$_i$.
      c. Mary$_i$ likes her$_j$.

Examples 7 violate conditions on proper binding. Example 7a violates the specificity condition proposed in Chomsky 1973 and in Fiengo and Higginbotham 1981. Examples 7b and 7c violate conditions A and B of the binding theory of Chomsky (1981). The question is whether the binding theory and specificity restrictions are used to constrain the parser's choice of possible phrase expansions. Before answering this question, it is wise to underscore that the above example of the use of lexical properties (categorization, subcategorization, and selection) was meant to show that questions about efficiency and naturalness can be judged only in the context of some theory of representation. Choosing to encode information in a way that is independently motivated by grammatical considerations motivates certain assumptions about the way to most efficiently process this information. In the next section, it will be shown that this argument works in the other direction as well. That is, by making certain assumptions about natural grammatical encoding in a parser, we constrain the choice of efficient processors, which in turn enforces a particular mechanism for encoding "unbounded dependencies" and a particular choice about the representations to which binding restrictions apply.

Efficiency and the Transparent Encoding of a Grammar

As many have noted before, one of the main conditions on an adequate theory of parsing is that it be able to model the fact that natural-language understanding is efficient, in the sense that we can understand a sentence basically as we hear it. Thus, it is incumbent on someone who claims that natural-language parsers use the kinds of grammars proposed by the Government and Binding theory (a version of transformational grammar; see Chomsky 1981) to show that these grammars can be used to construct efficient parsers. In Berwick and Weinberg 1984 we presented a model—based on Knuth's (1965) theory of deterministic parsing—that does so. As many have noted, the main problem confronting the natural-language parser is the ambiguity of natural language. Example 9 will illustrate the point.

(9)   a. John believes Mary is adorable.
        b. John believes Mary.

Even if the parser has appropriately structured all the material up to the NP *Mary*, it still cannot tell whether it is looking at a simple NP complement or the beginning of a sentential complement. Deterministic and nondeterministic parsers differ in the options open to them when confronted with the ambiguities of natural language. A nondeterministic parser can deal with ambiguous situations in one of two ways. It can proceed with all possible analyses of the sentence, deleting one path when it reaches a disambiguating context, or it can pursue one possible path arbitrarily and back up to correct its mistakes in case of an error. In the case of (9), this means that, on the first story, the parser will create two representations: one hypothesizing a following sentential and one a following nominal complement. When the parser reaches the disambiguating verbal complement, it deletes the analysis that postulated only a simple NP complement. The "backtracking" analysis might arbitrarily pursue the simple nominal analysis, thus postulating only a postverbal NP after *believe*. When it reached the verb, it would back up and insert an S between the verb and the NP, thus yielding structure like (10).

(10)   John believes $[_{S'} [_{NP}$ Mary] . . .

A deterministic solution, in contrast, must get the right answer on the first try. Any structure built must be part of the analysis of the sentence that the deterministic parser outputs, and no structure can be erased. To handle a case like (9), the parser must wait until it has evidence about the correct analysis of this phrase before incorporating it into the phrase-structure tree that it builds. It must be able to wait for a finite amount of time in order to check for following disambiguating material (in this case, if there is an infinitive or verbal element following the noun phrase.) As is well known, deterministic parsers can be made to run extraordinarily efficiently. For example, Knuth (1965) has proposed a deterministic parser that can run in linear time: an LR(k) parser. This means that if we can develop a parsing algorithm for our grammars that is LR(k) we will be able to successfully model the fact that we can comprehend speech in basically the time that it takes for us to hear it. Assume for the moment that people use an LR(k) system during the course of language comprehension.[7] For the moment, this assumption will be justified only by such a device's ability to model the efficiency of comprehension. It will be shown later that the properties of such a system are crucial to te functional explanations for subjacency that will be provided. The main properties that guarantee LR(k) parsing efficiency are the following:

• These parsers are deterministic. This means that the parser must be able to correctly expand a phrase-structure tree on the first try.[8]
• Previously analyzed material must be representable in the finite control table of the device.[9]

This means that decisions about the correct expansion of the phrase-structure tree that involve the use of previously analyzed material (left context) must be finitely representable. This didn't seem like much of a problem in the previously discussed cases of tree expansion, which involved the use of a minimal amount of left context (the government domain). Moreover, in the majority of cases, lexical properties of the verb suffice to tell us how to properly expand the tree, even in the case where we must expand it with an empty variable (gap). However, there are cases involving empty categories where the only way that we can resolve local parsing ambiguities is by reference to previously analyzed structure. These are cases involving verbs that can be either transitive or intransitive. Examples like (11) are illustrative.

(11) a. What$_i$ do you believe John ate e$_i$?
      b. Do you believe John ate?
      c. What do you think John read e$_i$
      d. Do you think John read today?

Since these verbs have two subcategorization frames, the parser cannot tell at the point where it detects the ambiguity, using information in the government domain alone, whether an empty category should be inserted in the postverbal position. This ambiguity can be resolved only by scanning the previously encountered portion of the sentence to see whether it contains an overt *wh-* element. Therefore, if we want to ensure that the parser can deterministically (without making a mistake) tell whether to insert a postverbal empty category in these cases, it must be able to access the previously encountered question word. The assumption of determinism is crucial here. For example, if we allowed our parser to pursue all possible analyses of a sentence at once, then we could simply provide two analyses for the structures in (11), subsequently discarding the incorrect analysis. There would be no reason to refer to any previously analyzed material in these cases.

The superficial problem that these structures create is that the empty position can be unboundedly far from the *wh-* element that unambiguously signals its presence. This is shown by example 12.

(12) What$_i$ do you believe that Mary said that Sue thought that John expected ... to eat e$_i$.

Thus, it looks as if the parser would have to store an unbounded number of nonterminal symbols from the left context in its finite control table. But a finite control table cannot store unbounded numbers of categories, by definition. Thus, we must find a finite representation for the left context even in these cases or we will incorrectly predict that they are unparseable.

Our decision to incorporate the grammar without the use of *ad hoc* nonterminal symbols constrains our method of finitely encoding the needed left context. LR(k) devices can finitely encode left context using either literal or generative methods. A generative method involves mimicking the use of an essential variable.[10] I will give two examples of what a generative encoding would look like and show why neither of these options is available.

A first type is like that discussed by Wanner and Maratsos (1978), who claim that the parser has a HOLD store where it can place copies of *wh-* elements as soon as it encounters them in a parse. This HOLD cell can be accessed at any time in the course of processing. In the context of a sentence like (12), this means that the parser could resolve the local ambiguity of the embedded clause by checking to see whether the HOLD cell contains a *wh-* element. If the HOLD cell contains a *wh-* element, the parser pursues the transitive reading; otherwise the intransitive option is taken and no empty category is incorporated into the phrase-structure tree.

One could also encode the presence of the *wh-* element by using complex nonterminals, as is done in the tradition of "generalized phrase-structure grammar" (a descendent of Harman's phrase-structure approach to natural language). In this approach, when one encounters a *wh-* element in the course of a parse, one annotates the phrase-structure rules with a notation that indicates that a gap will appear later in the structure and must be filled. This is done by annotating every node intervening between the quantifier and the gap position with this information. An example of the way this system proceeds is given in (13a); (13b) shows the phrase-structure representation of (12) at the point of ambiguity.

(13) a.   S → NP VP
           S/NP → NP VP/NP
      VP → V NP
      VP/NP → V NP/NP (interpreted as a gap)

b.

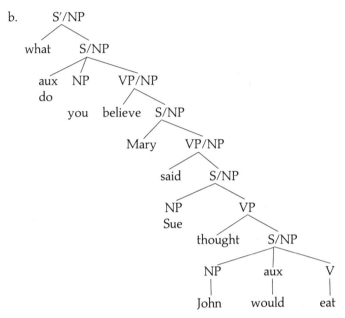

This solution also allows for the local encoding of left context, because at the point of ambiguity in a case like (12) the parser need only look back in the tree as far as its immediately dominating node (the government domain) to see whether this node is a "slashed category" ("VP/NP", indicating the presence of a previously encountered word) or a simple VP. If a complex nonterminal "slashed category" is encountered, the parser places an empty category in the postverbal position; otherwise the position is left unfilled.

Both of these solutions use devices that have no motivation in the GB framework, and thus they are not available to a parser that naturally implements a GB grammar in the sense described above. The GB framework does not use complex nonterminals, nor does it make any independent reference to a HOLD cell. Moreover, the choice of the complex-nonterminal encoding is motivated in generalized phrase-structure grammar by the ability of this notation to encode unbounded dependencies in a system with the weak generative capacity of a context-free grammar.

Even if reduction of weak generative power is a worthwhile aim for linguistic theory, a corresponding reduction in the weak generative capacity of a GB grammar would not be achieved by these means, because the representation of other constructions gives the system context-sensitive weak generative power. Thus, the use of this notation would be unmotivated in the GB framework. (For arguments against the standard interpretation of weak-generative-capacity arguments see Berwick and Weinberg

1981, 1984; Weinberg 1987.) Therefore, we must find a representation that can finitely encode left context using a literally finite representation.[11] An LR(k) parser using a literally finite encoding is called a *bounded-context* parser. We can use this kind of parser only if we adopt a grammar governed by the subjacency condition.

Consider the following contrasts:

(14) a. I believe the claim that Bill thought Mary would eat ice cream.
      b. *What$_i$ do you believe the claim that Bill thought that Mary would eat e$_i$.

(15) a. I wonder who John likes.
      b. *What$_i$ you wonder who John likes e$_i$.

Chomsky (1973) proposes to rule out these structures by the following condition:

No rule may relate X and Y in the configuration: Y .... [$_a$ .... [$_b$ .... X ...]$_b$ ...]$_a$ .. Y where a and b are the bounding nodes NP or S.

The question then becomes why the grammatical sentence 16 doesn't violate subjacency as well.

(16) Who$_i$ do you believe [$_S$ Bill thought [$_S$ Mary claimed [$_S$ Fred to be engaged to e$_i$]]].

Here there are, at least superficially, many bounding nodes intervening between the *wh-* element and the gap that it must bind. Chomsky (1973) deals with this problem by proposing the successive cyclic theory of movement, in which it is assumed that sentences are introduced by the rule.

S′ → COMP   S

Chomsky assumes that this complementizer can hold an empty category that will eventually be linked with the argument position of the variable. Thus the structure of (16) would be as in (17). The *wh-* element *who* moves from its thematic position by landing successively in the complementizer position of every intervening sentence, thus satisfying the subjacency restriction.

(17) [$_S$ who$_i$ [$_S$ do you believe $_S$[e$_i$ [Bill thought $_S$[e$_{is}$[Mary claimed $_S$[e$_{is}$[Fred to be engaged to e$_i$]]]

In parsing terms: We assume that the parser's expansion rule for empty categories allows it to check the adjacent complementizer slot to see whether the parser has previously inserted a trace into this position. If there is a trace, the parser expands a potential argument or complementizer position with a trace. Thus the subjacency condition governs the way the parser builds the tree and is accessed during this tree-building operation.

Successive cyclic movement will not save the derivations in (14b) and (15b), though. In (14b), even if it is assumed that the first move of the *wh*-phrase is to the complementizer of the relative clause, the next move will violate subjacency because this category must move out of a noun phrase, thus crossing over two bounding nodes and the S node of the clause that dominates the relative clause. Thus subjacency is violated and the sentence is ruled out. Similar remarks serve to rule out (15b). Assuming that we cannot allow two elements to fill the complementizer slot, the *what* phrase must cross the S bounding nodes of both the matrix and the embedded sentence. This constraint does not condition all binding relationships; for example, the binding of the reciprocal phrase *each other* or the reflexive *himself* takes place over a nonsubjacent domain in example 18.

(18)   The men$_i$ expect [[pictures of each other $_i$]] to be on sale.
        The men$_i$ expect $_S$[[pictures$_{NP}$ of themselves$_i$] to be on sale.

Similarly, pronominal binding is not constrained by subjacency; see example 19.

(19)   The men$_i$ believe that [John would sell [all$_{NP}$ the pictures $_S$[that they$_i$ painted]] for a cheap price.]]

Why does this constraint apply to the range of constructions that it does? Why doesn't it govern the binding of all constructions? Recall that we were forced to look at left context only when the parser was uncertain about how to proceed with phrase-structure-tree expansion. Rules involving the creation of empty categories are governed by bounding constraints because we needed to access left context in order to correctly expand the phrase-structure tree. With this in mind, contrast a case like (15) or (16) with (18). In (18) or (19) there is no ambiguity about the presence of the postverbal category. Its presence is signaled by the fact that it is phonologically realized. Its binding possibilities (the categories that it can be bound to) cannot be determined from local context, but now we have a principled distinction between those conditions that must be available to the parser in order to allow it to construct a syntactic tree and those conditions that tell the parser how to search that tree in order to determine licit binding relations. Overt reciprocals (*each other*), pronominals, and reflexives cause no problem for the phrase-structure-expansion stage of the parse. We can incorporate these categories correctly into the phrase-structure tree even if we do not know how or whether the category is bound. To repeat, however: In the case of empty categories, both the expansion of the phrase-structure tree (by the creation of an empty category) and the binding of the category are involved. Since expansion of the phrase-structure tree is a parsing decision, its efficiency can be made to depend on its respecting principles of determinism.

Our next step is to motivate the postulation of a distinct representation from which to compute binding relationships. If we can do this, then we can provide a principled reason for why a first-level representation that respected the subjacency condition but did not necessarily respect conditions on proper binding would be constructed by the parser.[12]

One could argue against this approach by claiming that one might expect a system that has to build two separate representations to be less efficient than a system that can simultaneously build a tree and bind categories contained in that tree. However, in Berwick and Weinberg 1984 we showed that the first-stage representation (without binding) can be computed by a bounded-context LR(k) device in linear time (more correctly, in time cn, where c is a constant depending on the output phrasal structure, the size of the grammar, and the length of the sentence). We showed in that book that, if we try to compute binding relationships from this representation as well, we will increase our analysis time in the worst case to kn^2, where n depends again on the length of the sentence and k on the size of the phrasal output. Thus, we move from guaranteed linear to exponential parse time. To see informally why this is so, recall that in a case like (19) the antecedent can be indefinitely far from the pronoun. In fact, some referential dependencies can even cut across sentences and can involve any object mentioned in a discourse, as is shown in (20).

(20)   John$_i$ walked into the room. Sheila$_j$ came in next. He$_i$ began talking to her$_j$ about the peach crop.

A search for an antecedent over a potentially unbounded distance is going to involve storing a potentially unbounded left context and allowing the parser to rescan complex tree shapes and many irrelevant structures. For example, when we are coindexing, we are interested only in noun-noun relationships, but we will have to scan over many other categories as well. This is what makes the process nonlinear.[13] Thus, if we want to guarantee our linear-time result we would do well to compute binding decisions from some other representation. We do not want the tree-building operation in a case like (20) to have to stop until it finds the antecedent for the pronoun in the third sentence; otherwise this algorithm as a whole will become exponential as well.

It was shown in Berwick and Weinberg 1984 that splitting up the procedure makes the search for the antecedents of referentially dependent items more efficient as well. Instead of running our procedure in time cn where c is large, we build a representation that is well suited to computing binding relationships, and thus we can run a binding algorithm in kn where k is small, consisting of a propositional list of NPs and predicates that extensionally represents c-command relations in given sentences.[14] We demonstrated that it is a simple matter to build a finite-state transducer that projects a representation including just the NPs from the first-level tree representation. It is because we have isolated these items (the only things an NP can be referentially dependent on) on a separate level that the search for referential dependents is made easier. In most cases there will be only a few NPs to look at.[15]

To review: I have argued that the computation of the basic tree structure should include a computation of binding dependencies only when computation of those dependencies is required to ensure a deterministic expansion of the phrase-structure tree. Binding relationships are computed from a second-level representation, and constraints on these relations are not accessed at the first level.

Experimental Support?

This division of labor is supported in the main by recent results of Freedman and Forster (1985) which show that a matching task is sensitive to whether or not one can create a basic phrase-structure tree. Freedman and Forster asked experimental subjects whether pairs of sentences were the same or Different. They had independently established in previous experiments that this task reflected on-line processes and that latencies were affected by whether a subject could compute a complete representation at the appropriate level. The logic of the experiment is that if rules at the appropriate level permit the encoding of a sound sequence as a unit, then comparing the sequence to a matching category involves comparison of two objects (e.g., two words *teacher teacher*). In a nonword case like *Deacher Deacher*, the parser cannot structure the items as single units and so must compare each part of the word (letter or syllable) separately. Since more pairs must be checked for matching in the latter condition, matching should take longer in this case. Freedman and Forster hypothesized that the same factors should influence the task at the level of syntactic representation. That is, matching would be speeded up to the extent that subjects could structure the sound stream into a well-formed syntactic tree. Their experiments suggest that sentences with violations of selectional, subcategorization, or phrase-structure restrictions prevented subjects from constructing syntactic trees.[16]

This experimentally confirms our view that these factors influence the creation of the first level of syntactic representation. That is, subcategorization, selectional, and category restrictions must be satisfied for a parser to construct a syntactic tree. If these restrictions are not satisfied, the parser stores the input as unintegrated phrasal chunks.

Freedman and Forster's experiments also confirm the view that constraints governing binding are not relevant to this level of representation. Matching times were not significantly longer for sentences violating the specificity condition of Chomsky (1973) and Fiengo and Higginbotham (1981). Put informally: The specificity condition prevents binding of a category to an element over an intervening NP with a specific determiner.[17] Unlike the subjacency condition, it applies to both empty and overt categories, as example 21 shows.

(21) a. *Which person$_i$ did you see $_{NP}$[Leonardo's picture of e$_i$]
      b. I saw $_{NP}$[Leonardo's picture of the Mona Lisa]
      c. *Someone saw [those pictures of everyone] (see footnote)
      d. Someone saw $_{NP}$[pictures of everyone]

(21a) is out because the trace inside the NP *Leonardo's pictures* is not bound inside the domain of that specific NP. Correspondingly, in (21c) *everyone* can only have narrow scope, whereas in (21d) it has both wide and narrow scope and is grammatical on both readings. Since this condition applies both to cases with empty categories and to overt categories where the question of how to expand the tree is not in doubt, we can predict that it does not govern the first stage of representation. This is exactly what Freedman and Forster found. Sentences like (22a), which respect subcategorization, selection, phrase-structure requirements, and subjacency take no longer to match than grammatical cases like (22b)–(22d).

(22) a. Who$_i$ did you see Leonardo's pictures of e$_i$.
      b. I saw Leonardo's picture of the Mona Lisa.
      c. Who$_i$ did you see a picture of e$_i$?
      d. I saw a picture of the Mona Lisa.

Thus our model has the value of providing an explanation, in terms of the representations used and the efficiency claims made, for why Freedman and Forster's results turned out the way they did. Information that is necessary for the deterministic expansion of a syntactic tree is made available at one stage of the parsing process. Thus, a category's position in a syntactic tree must be determined unambiguously on the line. The possible binding relationships that the category enters into are not determined, however, until later in the parsing process. There is one serious problem: Freedman and Forster found that sentences that they claim violate subjacency were matched as quickly as their grammatical counterparts. Given our previous interpretation of their results, this means that sentences violating sub-

(On the reading where *everyone* is interpreted as being outside the scope of pictures. That is, (21c) is grammatical only on the reading where someone saw group pictures with everyone in them. Crucially, the "wide scope" reading which can mean "Someone saw pictures of Mary, someone else saw pictures of Lenore, etc." is not available.)

jacency were still compiled into a phrase-structure tree in their experiments. Since we assume that a trace is not inserted into the phrase marker unless there is a *wh*- or a trace in an adjacent COMP, we expect a sentence like (23) to be unparseable because it would be represented as in (23b). Thus the sentence would violate the subcategorization restrictions of a verb like *take*, which is obligatorily transitive.

(23)   a.   Which job$_i$ did you decline $_{NP}$[an offer $_S$[to take e$_i$]]
        b.   Which job$_i$ did you decline an offer to take.

Construed in this way, Freedman and Forster's results suggest either that the parser does not look back for an antecedent and thus uses only local subcategorization information to decide whether to expand empty categories or that the parser can look infinitely far back in the string. Both of these strategies are directly contradictory to the assumptions we needed to functionally derive subjacency.

I would like to argue, however, that these results are misleading because examples like (23)—which make up about a third of Freedman and Forster's corpus of sentences that violate subjacency—are in fact grammatical because the trace in these cases is subjacent to its antecedent. This involves a slight, independently motivated redefinition of the subjacency condition. Compare (23) with a case like the ungrammatical (24).

(24) $_S$[Which book$_i$ $_S$[do you believe [the claim $_S$ [e$_i$ hat Mary read e$_i$]]]]
                                                                        NP

We can use various tests to show that these sentences in fact have different structures and that it is only the second structure that violates subjacency. Relative clauses can be structured either as (25a) or as (25b).

(25)   a.   b.

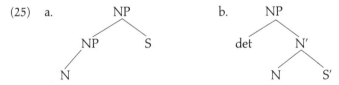

Stowell (1981) and Weinberg, Aoun, Hornstein, and Lightfoot (1987) argue that *that* complementizers can be deleted only if they are governed. The grammaticality of (26a) shows, then, that the complementizer (and the S') is governed by the head noun of the noun complement structure. The ungrammaticality of (26c) shows that there is no government relation between head and relative. (26c) and (26d) have the structure of (25a).

(26)   a.   I'll make you an offer you'll want to take.
        b.   I'll make you an offer that you'll want to take.
    *c.   I believe the claim Mary read that book.
        d.   I believe the claim that Mary read that book.

Chomsky (1986), Weinberg et al. (in press), and Weinberg (forthcoming) all argue that a category counts as a bounding node in structures like those in (26) only if it is not governed. Thus, in a case like (23) the trace is subjacent to the *wh-* element, whereas in (24) it is not.[18] The relevant structures are given in (27), with the relevant bounding nodes appropriately marked.

(27)   a. $_S$[which job$_i$ $_S$[did you decline [an[$_{NP}$[det
       b. $_S$[which book$_i$ $_S$[do you believe $_{NP}$[the claim]
            $_S$[e$_i$ $_S$[that many read e$_i$]]]]]

Evidence about the interpretation of PRO confirms our predictions.[19] Manzini (1983), Bouchard (1984) and Hornstein and Lightfoot (in press) argue that the null element PRO can only have an arbitrary interpretation if it is ungoverned. The PRO in the relative clause in (27) has both a controlled and an arbitrary reading, which shows that the relative clause can have either structure in (28) and correspond to the structure 25b.

(28)   I will reject any offer PRO to publish the journal.
       a.   I$_i$ will reject [[$_{NP}$ any$_{N'}$ [$_{S'}$ offer (for me)$_i$ to publish the journal.]$_{S'}$]$_N$]]
       b.   I will reject [$_{NP}$ [$_{NP}$ any offer] [for anyone to publish the journal.]$_S$]$_{NP}$

If we pull a *wh-* element out of the relative clause, we predict that subjacency must be obeyed. This in turn predicts that we will get the governed (controlled) interpretation for the relative clause in this case, because it is the only one compatible with the structure needed if movement obeys the subjacency condition. This prediction is borne out by (29).

(29)   Which journal$_j$ will you$_i$ reject any offer PRO$_i$ to publish e$_j$?

The incorporation of grammatical stimuli like (22) into Freedman and Forster's experiments as ungrammatical examples could lead them to find no difference between "grammatical" and "ungrammatical" stimuli. A full reanalysis of this experiment should be carried out, but hopefully we will be able to show that these experiments are fully compatible with our model.

General Conclusions

In this paper we attempted to do three things. First, we showed in general how linguistic theory can be used to constrain the design of natural-language parsers in the sense that the notion "most efficient parser" is a term that can be defined only with respect to a particular theory of representation. Different representations suggest different "most efficient solutions," and we can use linguistic theory to provide independently justified representations. The functional derivation of the subjacency constraint is of interest to people whose main focus is the construction of models of language use in that this derivation depends on a very particular view of what the parsing algorithm for natural languages looks like. The derivation does not go through on the assumption that the underlying processor is nondeterministic or on the assumption that it uses a generative method of encoding so-called unbounded dependencies. Arguments of this type thus allow us to eliminate whole classes of possible parsers and give us a sharper focus on the general features of the parsing algorithm for natural language. Second, we tried to show that the model was, for the most part, experimentally verified by the results of Freedman and Forster and, more important, could explain why the experimentally obtained results were natural. The linguistically justified view that category, selectional, and subcategorization restrictions are stored in the same representation (the lexical entry) explains why all this information would be accessed in the construction of the preliminary linguistic representation. The theory of representation coupled with general results from computational linguistics lead us to a small class of efficient parsers for this system. This view of efficiency gives us a reason for expecting decisions about binding relationships to be delayed until the parser computes a second level of representation. Experimental problems for this view were dealt with in the last section.

This chapter should be seen as a small exercise in showing how results from linguistics, the theory of computation, and psycholinguistics can mutually reinforce one another and guide us to a more adequate theory of language use.

Notes

1. By ungrammatical, I mean unacceptable because of a deviant syntactic representation.
2. Whether we actually employ explicit phrase-structure rules or employ restrictions directly to express the notion of "licit phrase markers" in terms of the X' convention (see Chomsky 1970; Jackendoff 1977) is irrelevant for our purposes.
3. The elimination of phrase-structure rules is proposed by Chomsky (1981), who replaces this component of the grammar with an explicit use of X', subcategorization, and selectional principles and a stipulation that lexical properties of a predicate must be respected at all levels of a derivation. The elimination of these rules does not bear directly on this point.
4. The restriction to concrete nouns rules out a sentence like *The man hit sincerity.*
5. This is slightly misleading, in that some selectional restrictions are not recoverable in a government domain (Barbara Partee, personal communication). We will see that the subclass of selectional restrictions relevant to the Freedman-Forster results are strictly local.

6. For a formal definition, see Aoun and Sportiche 1983 and Chomsky 1981. Given this definition, in a structure like

the verb governs the NP object but the verb does not govern the subject because the intervening VP that dominates it does not dominate the subject. The VP, however, does govern the subject.

7. The choice of Knuth's algorithm is not entirely the result of some arbitrary choice. A parser based on a GB grammar cannot use general-purpose efficiency algorithms based solely on the weak generative capacity of the system (like the Earley algorithm), because we cannot guarantee that a GB grammar will generate all and only languages of the appropriate weak generative capacity. See Berwick and Weinberg 1981 and Weinberg 1987 for arguments that weak-generative-capacity results are not in general relevant to the evaluation of possible human grammars.

8. As noted in Marcus 1980, we interpret this to mean that the parser will correctly expand sentences that people have no difficulty processing on the first try. The inability to deterministically parse a sentence correctly should correlate with the difficulty that listeners have in finding its appropriate interpretation.

9. See Berwick and Weinberg 1984 for a complete discussion of the conditions on the use of right context needed to ensure LR(k) parsing. These conditions are not relevant to the present discussion, and in Berwick and Weinberg 1984 it is shown that a parser based on a GB-style grammar meets these conditions in any case.

10. By definition, we cannot encode essential variables directly into the finite control table of an LR(k) device. That is, we cannot express the notion that we can link a *wh*- element to a variable in the environment *wh*-.....X.....e, where X refers to an unbounded stretch of material in the LR(k) device's finite control table. See Berwick and Weinberg 1984 and Knuth 1965 for details.

11. This follows given that all other methods of generative encoding involve supplementing the nonterminal vocabulary of the underlying grammar.

12. The following discussion is taken from Berwick and Weinberg 1986.

13. We note in Berwick and Weinberg 1986 that this argument, involving as it does worst cases, is not completely straightforward because we must also argue that these worst-case results can arise in the natural-language case. Consideration of cases like pronoun binding, where one can refer to an antecedent that is unboundedly far away in the discourse, gives at least informal support to the suspicion that this result is relevant in the natural-language case.

14. We must represent c-command in this list because this condition crucially governs relationships of proper binding.

15. This representation may also have some linguistic support if Hornstein (this volume) is correct.

16. Experiment 3 of Freedman and Forster shows the influence of phrase-structure information (called a word scramble). Word scrambles (like (a) below) took significantly longer to match than correspondingly grammatical sentences like (b) (1,610 msec for scrambles, 1,262 msec for grammatical sentences).

(a) Before sick called home Mike. (F&F 24)
(b) John looked tired after work. (F&F 23)

Experiment 4 of Freedman and Forster shows the influence of selectional restrictions, as cases like (a) (violating number agreement) again took significantly longer than their grammatical counterparts. (1,427 vs. 1,385 msec).

(a) Mary were writing a letter to her husband. (F&F 29)
(b) Mary was writing a letter to her husband.

Experiment 5 shows that violations of subcategorization restrictions are also associated with longer latencies. A case like (a), where subcategorization restrictions of the transitive verb *admit* are violated because there is no postverbal object, were significantly harder to match the corresponding grammatical cases.

(a) The spy admitted by the judge (F&F 41)
(b) The spy admitted that his plan failed. (F&F 39)

17. That is, they must be bound to internally in NPs that have a definite and specific reference.

18. The way to express the relevance of government to subjacency is a matter of some controversy. The following definition will suffice for our purpose: B is subjacent to α if they are separated by at most one bounding node, where a bounding node is defined as an ungoverned category. To derive successive cyclic movement, we say (roughly) that S always counts as a bounding node because, since it is only dominated by a complementizer or a *wh-* word, it is never lexically governed. For alternative (more precise) formulations, see Chomsky 1986 and Weinberg 1987.

19. PRO is the empty element that is interpreted as the subject of the embedded clause in a case like (28).

14

Modularity in Sentence Comprehension

Charles Clifton, Jr., and Fernanda Ferreira

Our goal in this chapter is to describe some work we have been doing on sentence comprehension with Lyn Frazier and our colleagues, most notably Keith Rayner. We have, for several years, been trying to identify autonomously functioning components that may exist in the language-comprehension system, and to determine the types of information each component deals with and the manner in which each works. We have various motivations for this endeavor. One is our interest in the question of why language takes the form it does. We would like to be able to trace some of the constraints one finds in languages back to constraints in the language-processing system. Another interest, coming from our training as information-processing psychologists, is somewhat different. We would like to trace the flow of information through the nooks and crannies of the mind. We have fixed on examining the system for processing linguistic information, in the belief that studying such a highly evolved system is apt to lead to the sharpest answers to the question of how people process information. It is in such systems, we suspect, that effective specialized functions have developed. We think that one would have a pretty decent understanding of a complex system if one had an understanding of each of these individually specialized functions and their interactions. Our interests, though varied, lead us to a common belief: There may well be specialized subcomponents in the language-processing system, and it is a good re-search strategy to search for them. We believe that we have made progress in documenting the existence of some such subcomponents, and in under-standing their operation.

We were delighted to see Jerry Fodor's much-acclaimed book *The Modularity of Mind* (1983), in which he raises these beliefs to the status of a general theory of mind. The structured subcomponents we are searching for can be identified as Fodorian modules, and our questions become questions such as: What is the grain of modularization in the language-processing system? What distinct modules exist? How do they work?

We take a fairly conventional view of what modularity is. A module is a distinct information-processing element, a tightly constrained system of a small number of elementary processes operating on representations phrased in a constrained and partly specialized vocabulary. Each module is domain-specific and informationally encapsulated, fast and dumb. These properties can be understood from one perspective in terms of evolutionary pressures toward specialization for important tasks, and from another perspective in terms of the distinct representational vocabulary and elementary processes that characterize each module. Each module operates in a largely autonomous fashion, but some limited intercommunication among the modules must exist if the language-processing system is to serve its function of transforming information about auditory waveforms or marks on printed pages into mental representations that can determine belief or action. The questions raised by this perspective include the following: What are the modules? What processes and vocabulary characterize each module? How do the modules interact with one another?

It is worth asking what alternatives to this perspective exist. One alternative taken by a good many cognitive psychologists (see Rumelhart 1977; van Dijk and Kintsch 1983) focuses on the properties of some particular theoretical device, rather than on the properties of language and the language-processing system. These psychologists ask such questions as: Can a production system or a system of excitatory and inhibitory connections among nodes be built that will account for the phenomena of language processing? A second alternative, often occuring in association with the first, is the belief that mind is best analyzed as a single, general-purpose information-processing system that uses all available information in an efficient way to guide each step of processing. Information of any type— phonological information, syntactic information, knowledge of the world or of one's conversational partner's beliefs, etc.—could in principle guide any decision about how to represent incoming language. The value of one piece of information in building a representation is affected by any other relevant information. Crain and Steedman (1985) term this position *strong interaction*. It appears to be the position espoused by some workers in artificial intelligence, including Roger Schank (see Reisbeck and Schank 1978). The early writings of Marslen-Wilson and Tyler (1980) also exemplify this position (without many of the excesses seen in the works of the AI school), and the processing-strategies approach that stemmed from Bever's work (1970) probably falls in this category. Many psychologists interested in text and discourse processing have explicitly adopted such a position. Crain and Steedman themselves do not adopt this strong interaction position in their 1985 paper. They propose yet another alternative (which they term *weak interaction*), together with "radical nonautonomy of representation." As best we can understand it, this amounts to a position of autonomously functioning modules, with the stipulation that the module that uses syntactic information constructs semantic representations directly, not syntactic representations. This module presents semantic interpretations in a word-by-word manner to a component that evaluates them with respect to discourse and world-knowledge information, and in turn discards representations that cannot easily be added to a mental model of the discourse. If this reading is correct, then Crain and Steedman's "weak interaction" position is a modular position, but one that makes a claim about what the representational vocabulary is (namely, some unspecified semantic, rather than syntactic, representation) and a claim about how modules communicate with one another (very rapid filtering of these semantic representations by a mechanism that has access to discourse and world knowledge).

The stand we and our colleagues take on these questions is different from that taken by Crain and Steedman. Our research has led us to believe that there is a grammatical-processing system with modular subcomponents, including a lexical-processing module (which processes both visual and auditory information), one or several distinct syntactic-processing modules, and some mechanism for interfacing between grammatical representations and general knowledge of discourse and the world. Frazier (see Rayner, Carlson, and Frazier 1983) has called this last mechanism a *thematic processor* and has suggested that it may operate in a vocabulary of thematic frames, shared by the grammatical system and by a general knowledge system. The best-understood of the modules in the grammatical-processing system is one that uses phrase-structure rules and case information to build phrase-structure representations of sentences. This phrase-structure module operates on the simple and reasonable basis of accepting the first analysis of an input that it can compute and making this single analysis available to other modules. These other modules may then check it for obedience to (for instance) binding theory, and may even check the plausibility of the thematic relations it expresses. Since the phrase-structure module operates on the first-available-analysis principle, it will sometimes make mistakes at points of temporary ambiguity. One class of mistakes follows from a particular version of the first-available-analysis principle: the Minimal Attachment principle, which Frazier has discussed in numerous places (e.g., Frazier 1979; Frazier and Rayner 1982). Minimal Attachment says that each new incoming item is added to the phrase-structure representation with the least possible number of new syntactic phrase nodes needed at the moment of its arrival. Such an attachment requires the smallest number of phrase-structure-rule applications, and will therefore be accomplished in the shortest time. What matters is the number of nodes that must be added at a point of ambiguity, as the parser works through the sentence in a left-to-right fashion. The minimal-attachment strategy is insensitive to the possibility that this initial choice may result in increased syntactic complexity later in the sentence.

The operation of the Minimal Attachment principle is illustrated in example 1.

(1)   a. MA: Sam loaded the boxes on the cart *before lunch.*
       b. NMA: Sam loaded the boxes on the cart *onto the van.*

In (1a), the prepositional phrase *on the cart* attaches to the verb phrase, as a sister to the noun phrase *the boxes.* In (1b), however, it is necessary at some point to introduce a second NP node, dominating both *the boxes* and the PP *on the cart.* This option is not taken until it is forced by the final PP *onto the van,* because it would require constructing a greater-than-minimal number of phrase-structure nodes. Taking it at this late point requires revising the initial attachment of *on the cart* to the VP.

Evidence for the Minimal Attachment principle has been obtained for a variety of sentence constructions by a variety of experimental techniques. For example, Frazier and Rayner (1982) have shown that the eye movements a reader makes while reading sentences that can be analyzed as being like those in example 1 are disrupted in the italicized (disambiguating) region of the nonminimal-attachment sentences. This indicates that the reader had first made the minimal-attachment assignment and then had to revise it when unambiguous syntactic information indicated that it was incorrect.

The research we present here asks whether the initial stages of comprehending sentences—stages that presumably reflect the operation of the phrase-structure module we have described—are sensitive to information outside the grammatical system. The question is: Does information about the world or the current discourse affect initial parsing decisions? A position of strong interaction would claim that such information should influence initial parsing decisions if it is made available early enough. The modular position advocated by Crain and Steedman (1985) makes the same claim, at least for information about the current discourse that determines the ease with which different interpretations of a word or phrase can be added to the reader's or listener's mental model. The modular position we have taken claims that world and discourse information, being outside the phrase-structure module, will not influence its operation, and will therefore not influence the initial parsing decisions. Any model, of course, must acknowledge that world and discourse knowledge is eventually consulted. It is a brute fact that we usually make sensible interpretations of ambiguous constructions, and how we do this is an absolutely crucial question. However, from the present perspective, the relevant question focuses on the initial—not the final—analysis assigned to a syntactically ambiguous stretch of text, and the only relevant evidence will be evidence about such initial analyses. Evidence about the time to read and interpret whole sentences or about the final interpretations made of sentences is generally beside the point.

The basic experimental paradigm we and our colleagues have used has the following abstract specification:

1. Engage a subject in a task that is demonstrably sensitive to one type of information, e.g. phrase-structure syntax. In most of our work, this amounts to showing a garden-path effect under some conditions.
2. Determine whether performance in this task is influenced by the presentation of a distinct type of information (e.g. pragmatic information) that in principle is sufficient to influence it. Typically, this amounts to seeing whether the second type of information blocks the garden path.
3. Conclude that distinct modules are involved in processing the two types of information if the second type of information fails to influence performance.

There are pitfalls to this paradigm, which we will enumerate and evaluate:

1. The subject may not be sensitive to the second type of information. Clearly, the experimenter must show, using another task (preferably one concurrent with the first), that the subject is sensitive to the information.
2. The experiment is structured so that accepting the null hypothesis will support the modular position, and a good way to get the results one wants in such a case is to do weak experiments. Clearly, the experimenter has the responsibility of doing powerful experiments and showing that the experiment is sensitive to information that is used.
3. The experiment has an escape hatch: If performance turns out to be sensitive to the second kind of information, then the experimenter can reinterpret the task as being sensitive to more than a single module. Crain and Fodor (1985) have pointed out that this option makes the modularity position, which superficially seems to be a highly constraining position, weak in its experimental predictions. We can only concede this point—while noting that contrasting positions always have exactly the opposite escape hatch, of arguing that some type of information failed to show its effect because some experimental task was too insensitive. We think that the only reasonable conclusion is that no one experiment will settle the issue, but we can hope that a good understanding of the system will develop from a network of compatible experimental results.

In a reference experiment, Rayner, Carlson, and Frazier (1983) presented sentences like those shown in example 2.

(2)   a. MA. The kids played all the albums *on the stereo* before they went to bed.
       b. NMA. The kids played all the albums *on the shelf* before they went to bed.

These sentences differ in that pragmatic factors indicate that the italicized PP should be attached minimally to the VP in (2a) but nonminimally to the NP in (2b). Normally, this difference in syntactic analysis is associated with a difference in processing ease: Nonminimal sentences like (2b) are harder. However, our knowledge of what kinds of devices albums can be played on could, in principle, be used to guide the syntactic analysis, blocking the attachment of *on the shelf* to the VP headed by *played*. If such world knowledge is used, the difficulty of (2b) should disappear. In the experiment of Rayner et al. it did not disappear; this indicated that world knowledge was not consulted by the module that assigns phrase-structure analyses. However, the world-knowledge information was available to the readers, and was eventually used—the overwhelming number of paraphrases of these sentences honored the pragmatic distinction between them.

These data convincingly tested the hypothesis they were designed to test: namely, the claim that pragmatic information determines the first analysis of sentences such as these. However, proponents of interactive positions have proposed alternative interpretations of these data. One concern is that the disambiguating pragmatic information simply arrives too late to be useful in guiding the parser, and in such cases the parser will fall back on syntactic principles. A second concern accepts the point that not all knowledge of the world guides syntactic analysis, but suggests that some world knowledge may be of enough systematic importance to be encoded in the grammatical-processing system, and such information will guide parsing. An example is information about potential thematic role, e.g., the fact that some verbs demand an animate agent and result in anomalous or metaphoric sentences when used with an inanimate subject.

We have completed an experiment that addresses both of these concerns. We measured eye movements while subjects read sentences like those shown in example 3.

(3)   a. The defendant examined *by the lawyer* turned out to be unreliable.
      b. The evidence examined *by the lawyer* turned out to be unreliable.
      c. The defendant that was examined by the lawyer turned out to be unreliable.
      d. The evidence that was examined by the lawyer turned out to be unreliable.

Sentences 3a and 3b are reduced relative clauses, with a temporary syntactic ambiguity that is in practice disambiguated by the *by*-phrase (and fully disambiguated by the following main verb). These are nonminimal-attachment sentences, in that the Minimal Attachment reading would take the first verb (*examined*) to be the main verb of the sentence. They have a well-documented source of processing difficulty, observable at the point

Table 1
Mean first-pass and second-pass reading times per character, in msec, for experiment 1.

Form	First pass Region			Second pass Region		
	1st verb	by-phrase	main verb	1st verb	by-phrase	main verb
Animate reduced	33.3	40.4	31.9	15.3	8.2	12.8
Inanimate reduced	37.7	38.4	32.6	12.6	14.9	16.9
Animate unreduced	31.9	30.7	33.1	6.9	3.6	8.0
Inanimate unreduced	30.1	30.3	28.6	0.0	0.0	2.5

of disambiguation, that is not shared by the syntactically unambiguous unreduced-relative-clause sentences 3c and 3d.

The new manipulation we introduced is seen in the contrast between (3a) and (3b). The first verb in these sentences requires an agent. The subject of (3a), *defendant*, is semantically a potential agent, but the subject of (3b), *evidence*, is not. If this semantic information can be used to guide the analysis of these sentences, because it arrives early enough or because it has systematic grammatical importance, the difficulty of (3b) should be reduced or eliminated. On the other hand, if the parser still initially constructs a Minimal Attachment analysis, even in the face of the semantic information, then the most the semantic information can do is hasten reanalysis, resulting perhaps in a less long-lasting disruption for (3b) than for (3a).

The data are given in table 1. They were gathered in Keith Rayner's laboratory, using a SRI dual-Purkinje image eyetracker, while subjects read the critical sentences as the first sentence of two-sentence paragraphs. The numbers are the first-pass and second-pass fixation times in the region of the first verb (the verb of the subordinate clause), the disambiguating by-phrase, and the main verb of the sentence, divided by the number of characters in the region. Both reduced relative sentences were subject to the normal difficulty in the region of the disambiguating by-phrase, presumably reflecting garden-pathing brought about by the Minimal Attachment preference for the ambiguous region. The presence of disambiguating syntactic information in the unreduced relative sentences eliminated this difficulty, indicating that the task is sensitive to the phrase-structure module's use of syntactic information. However, the difficulty of the reduced relative sentence during the disambiguating by-phrase persisted even when the Minimal Attachment analysis was blocked by the inanimacy of the subject NP of sentence, which made that NP unfit as the subject of the first verb. Readers thus did not use semantic-category information to guide their syntactic analysis. The crucial point, however, is that this information was demonstrably available to them at the point where the syntactic analysis was being done. Reading times for the verb *examined* were long when it followed the inanimate NP *evidence*, indicating that readers were sensitive to the fact that the preferred analysis resulted in an anomaly. However, readers apparently did not resolve this anomaly on a semantic basis, but instead waited for syntactic information.

This experiment demonstrates that the failure to use pragmatic information in the experiment of Rayner et al. (1983) cannot be attributed to the delayed availability of pragmatic information or its lack of systematic grammatical relevance. However, these are not the only bases upon which the conclusions made by Rayner et al. have been challenged. A common version of the suggestion that the pragmatic information was not available early enough in their study suggests that it would have been used if it had been made available in the left context of the critical sentence and not just in the sentence itself. A sophisticated version of this suggestion appears in Crain and Steedman 1985, where it is suggested that sentences of the kinds we have described as Nonminimal Attachment sentences are difficult not because of their syntactic structure but because only certain sorts of contexts satisfy the referential presuppositions they make. One can felicitously use a phrase like *the records on the shelf*, Crain and Steedman suggest, only if one has established the existence of several sets of records, one of which is on some specific shelf. One should use a phrase like *the evidence examined by the lawyer* only if one has established the existence of several sets of evidence, one of which was examined by a lawyer. In the absence of context, these presuppositions fail and the sentences are hard to process.

This position, which we have described all too briefly, is subject to some criticisms. It is simply not correct that a relative clause or a PP attached to an NP presupposes several sets of potential referents, from which it chooses a specific one. One can refer to the shirt on one's back with no sense of violating a presupposition that there must be other shirts around. Or again, it is very difficult to see how the position that appeals to satisfying presuppositions applies to other sorts of nonminimal-attachment sentences whose difficulty has been documented (e.g., *The wife will claim the inheritance belongs to her* as against the minimal-attachment sentence *The wife will claim the inheritance*). However, we will grant that one felicitous use of reduced relatives and PPs that modify NPs is to choose among alternative referents, and we will grant the possibility that the difficulty of so-called nonminimal-attachment sentences may stem from several distinct sources.

The obvious test of the Crain-Steedman position, as contrasted with the syntactically based garden-pathing position we have described, is to place minimal-attachment and nonminimal-attachment sentences in disambiguating contexts—contexts that satisfy the presuppositions stated by Crain and Steedman—and see whether the difficulty of the nonminimal-attachment sentences is reduced in comparison with when they are placed in contexts that fail to satisfy their presuppositions. The second author has done just this (Ferreira 1985; cf. Ferreira and Clifton 1986). She used sentences like those shown in (4), together with main-verb vs. reduced-relative sentences. The main verbs of the "double-argument" sentences obligatorily subcategorize for a locative prepositional phrase, and these sentences are syntactically disambiguated by the presence of one or two prepositional phrases. The main verbs of the "conjunction control" sentences do not require such a prepositional-phrase argument, so these sentences had to be disambiguated stylistically. This was done by following the ambiguous region with an unambiguous phrase that was parallel syntactically to one or the other of its readings. (This method of disambiguation proved to be somewhat confusing to the subjects, and therefore ineffective.)

(4)   a. MA (double argument): Sam loaded the boxes on the cart *after his coffee break.*
       b. NMA (double argument): Sam loaded the boxes on the cart onto the van.
       c. MA (conjunction control): Boris spilled the beer on the blanket, a glass of wine onto his girlfriend, and the soda onto the grass.
       d. NMA (conjunction control): Boris spilled the beer on the blanket, a glass of wine, and the soda.

Each sentence appeared in two different sentence paragraph-long contexts (only one of which was seen by any one subject). One context was designed to be neutral between the two readings, and to permit either one. In the case of the examples 4a and 4b, the neutral context referred to an indefinite number of boxes, but did not specify any one as being on a cart (although it mentioned a cart, and permitted the inference that it had boxes on it). The other contexts used for a sentence were designed to be biased toward the syntactically determined interpretation of the sentence. In the case of a nonminimal-attachment sentence, two sets of boxes were mentioned, and it was asserted that one set was placed on a cart. This context, unlike the neutral context, satisfies the presuppositions of the nonminimal-attachment phrase, in which the PP modifies the NP. For a minimal-attachment sentence, only one set of boxes was mentioned, and nothing was stated about its location.

Examples of some types of sentences to be discussed here can be seen in table 2. The predictions made from the position that the syntactic processor functions autonomously are that the initial stages of processing the minimal-attachment sentences should be easy in either context and that the initial stages of processing the nonminimal-attachment sentences should be hard. The positions that claim context is used very quickly, either to guide

Table 2
Examples of sentences used in experiment 2.

Sentence type		critical − 2	critical − 1	critical	critical + 1
		Region			
Active vs. reduced relative	NMA		The editor played the tape	agreed	the story was big.
	MA		The editor played the tape	and agreed	the story was big.
Prepositional phrase: double arguments	NMA	Sam loaded	the boxes on the cart	onto the van.	
	MA	Sam loaded	the boxes on the cart	before his coffee break.	

syntactic analysis or to immediately filter out pragmatically unlikely analyses as they are developing, make a different claim. Since the nonminimal context satisfies the presuppositions of a nonminimal-attachment sentence, while the neutral context fails to satisfy them directly, the Nonminimal Attachment interpretation (the NP-attachment reading) should be more favored in the nonminimal than in the neutral context, and therefore nonminimal-attachment sentences should be easier in the former than in the latter contexts. If, by any chance, our analysis of the contexts is in error, and the supposedly neutral context actually favors a nonminimal-attachment reading, then there might be no difference between nonminimal-attachment sentences in nonminimal vs. neutral contexts. However, in this case, minimal-attachment sentences would be harder to process in the biased-nonminimal "neutral" context than in a biased-minimal context.

The data, given in table 3, contradict the predictions of the interactive theories. These data are reading times per character. The top panel presents the reading times before any regressions occurred in the eye-movement record, while the bottom panel presents the reading times after a regression from the ambiguous or following regions had occurred. Region "critical − 1" is the ambiguous region, which can be taken (nonminimally) as a complex NP or (minimally) as the arguments of a VP or as a subject plus a main verb. Context had no effect on reading times for this region, for any construction. Region "critical" is the disambiguating region. Here, reading times were longer for the nonminimal-attachment sentences than for the minimal-attachment sentences (although in the case of the conjunction-

Table 3
Reading times per character, in msec, for experiment 2.

Form	Region		
	critical − 1	critical	critical + 1
First-pass reading times			
Relative clause			
Neutral-MA	25.3	24.4	25.0
MA-MA	24.2	26.8	23.7
Neutral-NMA	24.4	31.6	27.9
NMA-NMA	26.0	32.1	28.8
Prep. phrase, double argument			
Neutral-MA	22.7	24.0	
MA-MA	24.8	25.4	
Neutral-NMA	19.7	30.2	
NMA-NMA	20.6	34.9	
Prep. phrase, conjunction control			
Neutral-MA	21.9	27.6	24.7
MA-MA	26.1	28.0	24.8
Neutral-NMA	24.4	26.1	30.8
NMA-NMA	24.2	30.3	27.8
Second-pass reading times			
Relative clause			
Neutral-MA	4.7	4.6	6.9
MA-MA	2.6	3.9	2.7
Neutral-NMA	7.8	11.3	11.0
NMA-NMA	10.2	19.2	7.1
Prep. phrase, double argument			
Neutral-MA	6.2	8.9	
MA-MA	3.7	3.3	
Neutral-NMA	16.7	24.8	
NMA-NMA	5.9	13.3	
Prep. phrase, conjunction control			
Neutral-MA	6.8	6.2	3.2
MA-MA	4.0	3.6	2.4
Neutral-NMA	12.7	20.7	16.5
NMA-NMA	8.6	15.1	8.2

Table 4
Mean number of regressions per target sentence and percentage correct, experiment 2

Condition	Regressions	Percentage correct
NMA-NMA	0.675	73
MA-MA	0.240	88
Neutral-NMA	0.523	66
Neutral-MA	0.333	74

control PP-attachment sentences the difference was substantial only when post-regression fixations were considered). Crucially, the nonminimal-attachment sentences were not read faster in a biased nonminimal context than in a neutral context, nor were minimal-attachment sentences slower in the neutral than in the biased minimal context. The nonminimal versions of the double-argument prepositional-phrase sentences in fact showed a non-significant tendency toward slower reading times in the biasing than in the neutral context. There did appear to be a tendency toward shorter second-pass reading times for nonminimal-attachment PP sentences in biasing contexts than in neutral contexts, but this difference was statistically non-significant (see Ferreira and Clifton 1986).

Not only did the left context meet theoretical specifications for appropriateness, it was actually used by the readers eventually in understanding the texts. This was evident when subjects were asked a true-false question after each story. All questions focused on the critical sentence, and half were true under the minimal-attachment reading, while half were true under the nonminimal-attachment reading. As is shown in table 4, subjects were more accurate after reading minimal-attachment sentences than after reading nonminimal-attachment sentences and (crucially) were more accurate in biasing contexts than in neutral contexts. We believe that the reading-time data show quite convincingly that discourse context does not guide parsing decisions of the kind the Minimal Attachment strategy has been shown to control. However, several objections have been raised to this interpretation.

One objection is that a crucial comparison was omitted from the present experiment. We should have included cases in which a minimal-attachment sentence appears in a nonminimal context, and vice versa. All claims that we have considered would predict that a nonminimal-attachment sentence would be difficult in a minimal-biasing context, so this case is of no interest. The case of a minimal-attachment sentence in a nonminimal-biasing context is of more interest. A claim like that of Crain and Steedman, or the claim of strong interaction, would certainly predict that reading times in this case would be slow, reflecting processing difficulty. One might argue that an autonomously functioning syntactic processor would predict that reading times here would be fast. If this is so, then we have indeed overlooked an important source of evidence. But it is not necessarily so. Consider the case of a context in which it is asserted that some boxes had been stacked on a cart while some others had been left in a warehouse. The critical sentence asserts that Sam later loaded the boxes onto the cart. At some point, the reader must note the apparent incongruity between these two assertions, and must decide which of the distinct sets of boxes the critical sentence referred to (perhaps by deciding that Sam loaded the other boxes onto the cart). This point may come very early, given our belief that evaluations of meaning and thematic relations occur concurrently with the process of syntactic analysis. It would very likely come before the disambiguating region was completely read, and, since eye movements seem to reflect conceptual as well as syntactic confusion, fixations would be lengthened in the disambiguating region. Thus, in fact, all positions lead to the expectation of processing difficulty when syntax is inconsistent with context, so the condition in which a minimal-attachment sentence is presented in a nonminimal context is un-informative.

A second objection focuses on the comparison that can be made between the nonminimal-attachment and the minimal-attachment sentences rather than on the crucial comparison between sentences in the different contexts. This objection suggests that the difficulty of the nonminimal-attachment sentences is due not to the syntactic reanalysis they occasion but to the fact that extra work must be done during the evaluation of the ambiguous NP to establish its antecedent. To interpret *the boxes on the cart* as a noun phrase referring to some specific boxes on some specific cart, one must have a representation of those boxes in one's mental model. It may be necessary to infer their existence from some other information presented in the context, when faced with the possibility of a phrase that could refer to them. This inference time may be reflected in the long reading times for what we have called nonminimal-attachment sentences.

There are several difficulties with this second objection. First, although the sort of inference we have described might well be needed in the neutral-context conditions, where only a vague mention of several sets of boxes is made, no inference is needed in the context that biases toward the nonminimal-attachment reading. The context asserted that there was a pile of boxes on a cart and another pile of boxes on the floor. If some extra work is nonetheless required to find the referent of a nonminimal-attachment phrase, a second very telling difficulty is apparent: Any work of inference or referent-finding should be done during the reading of the ambiguous noun phrase according to a model like that of Crain and Steed-man, in which the semantic processor shadows the syntactic analysis very closely. There is no reason why the inference work would be delayed until after syntactically disambiguating information was presented, unless the inferencing follows the syntactically based resolution of syntactic-processing biases. However, as we indicated in the presentation of the data, no hint of long reading times was seen during the ambiguous noun phrases when they occurred in a neutral or nonminimal-biased context. The only effects appeared after unambiguous syntactic information had been presented.

Even after close examination, we think it must be concluded that the evidence we have presented points very strongly to the position that there is an autonomously functioning syntactic-processing module, sensitive at least to phase-structure information but not to information about pragmatic plausibility, semantic categories, or discourse context. Reaching this position is certainly only a small step toward understanding how we understand sentences. We must still learn whether there are actually several distinct syntactic-processing modules (as some data we have presented elsewhere seem to indicate) or whether there is only a single, homogeneously functioning syntactic-processing module (as Crain and Fodor [1985], among others, have argued). We must learn how the distinct modules intercommunicate if we are ever to understand how knowledge of discourse content and world facts affects the final comprehension of sentences, as it undeniably does. It clearly will not do to claim that early-operating modules generate multiple representations of a sentence, with late-operating modules sorting through these and discarding them (as may be the case in recognizing lexical entries). There is just too much evidence that the sentence processor makes an initial commitment to a single analysis in the case of syntactic ambiguity. A more attractive possibility is that the modules do interact, but only through the very limited portions of their representational vocabularies that they may share with one another. Some representational vocabulary—for instance, thematic roles—may even be shared between the modules of the grammatical system and the general-purpose system for representing knowledge and beliefs, permitting a very limited avenue whereby world knowledge could influence sentence comprehension.

The tasks are enormous. But we suggest that accepting the existence of a syntactic processor that functions in a basically autonomous fashion is a positive step toward accomplishing them.

Acknowledgments

The work described here was supported in part by grant HD-18708 to Lyn Frazier and Charles Clifton, by grant HD-17246 to Keith Rayner and Lyn Frazier, and by an NSERC (Canada) scholarship to Fernanda Ferreira.

15

Theories of Sentence Processing

Lyn Frazier

Current psycholinguistic theories of sentence processing vary along several dimensions. In terms of the architecture of the system, proposals range from those entailing a highly articulated and structured system subsuming several subsystems (each with its own peculiar properties and information sources) to monolithic, fully interactive systems claiming efficient and undifferentiated use of all grammatical and nongrammatical information sources. Most models implicitly or explicitly assume that there are processing principles involving pragmatic notions concerning the communicative function of natural-language expressions. In less differentiated or less modular systems, such principles govern virtually all aspects of language processing; in systems with a more highly articulated structure, such principles are implicitly assumed but are thought to operate only in relatively late stages of language processing. Thus, earlier stages of processing are governed by nonpragmatic principles (perhaps structure-based) or by frequency-based strategies. What principles are incorporated into a model depends in part on the mode of operation of the processor, i.e., whether it simultaneously considers all possible analyses of an input in parallel or whether it has some principle or selection procedure that results in initial consideration of only a single analysis of the input.

In at least one area of psycholinguistic investigation there seems to be something like a consensus emerging—namely, with respect to the lexicon. Most theories seem to assume that the language-comprehension system contains a subsystem concerned with the recognition of lexical items, and there is now a fairly extensive literature suggesting that this system operates in a parallel fashion, recognizing all possible lexical analyses of an input. However, there is less agreement with respect to syntactic aspects of processing. What I wish to do here is examine the dominant approaches to syntactic recognition routines and discuss the major challenge for each approach.

Throughout the chapter I will assume that one central goal of psycholinguistics is to construct a detailed explanatory theory of human language processing. The theory is detailed in that it provides an explicit account of precisely what information and operations are available to the processor,

and it is explanatory in that it offers insight into why the language processor has the structure it does, why certain principles govern its operation
rather than conceivable alternatives, and so forth. Of course the model
must be empirically motivated, since the goal is to discover how people
actually process language and not how they (or computers) might efficiently process a natural language. Finally, I assume that a theory of human
language processing must be capable of accounting for the processing of
any natural language, whether it be Walpiri, Swahili, Japanese, or English.

I will begin by discussing three general approaches to sentence processing: an autonomy model of the sort envisioned by Forster, a discourse-
based approach in which early structuring of an input (including syntactic
analysis) is claimed to be governed by preference strategies concerned with
the communicative function of language, and "first analysis" models (which
claim that humans consistently initially prefer one particular constituent-
structure analysis of a given lexical string).

The Autonomy Model

In the autonomy model of Forster (1979) the language-processing system
proper consists of phonological, syntactic, and message-level processors.
Each operates independently, with access only to its own information
source and the output of the next lower processor. Its output is made
available to a "general problem solver," which has access to real-world
knowledge. Within this system the only natural way to deal with ambiguity is for the processor to compute all well-formed analyses at each level of
structure. Analyses that turn out to be ill formed or inappropriate at some
later level of analysis may simply be discarded at that level; for example, a
phonological representation that happens to be syntactically ill formed
may be discarded by the syntactic processor.

This model enjoys all sorts of explanatory advantages. Because of the
limited task and information sources of each component subsystem, the
model readily explains the evidence suggesting that the component processes (e.g., lexical access) are fast, dumb, and automatic, as well as the
evidence suggesting independence in the use of theoretically distinct information types. The major challenge for the model is empirical: It is
unclear how the model can account for the experimental evidence showing
that the processor initially computes just a single syntactic analysis of the
input.

Discourse-Based Approaches

In several recent papers it has been proposed that sentence processing is
best understood in terms of the construction of a model or a representation

of discourse (e.g., Crain and Steedman 1985; Altman 1985). On this approach, it is the complexity of constructing or adding to the discourse model that governs the operations of the sentence processor and thus predicts the relative complexity of different sentence structures and the particular analysis assigned to ambiguous inputs. For example, Crain and Steedman suggest that the reason why a main-clause analysis is favored in such classic garden-path sentences as *The horse raced past the barn fell* (compare *The horse ridden past ...*) is that the alternative (correct) reduced relative analysis presupposes a set of contextually relevant horses; the relative clause is used to identify a unique member of this set. If preceding context has not already resulted in a discourse model containing a representation of this multiple set, constructing the relevant model for the reduced relative will be more complex than constructing the model appropriate for the simple main-clause analysis. Within this approach, the strategies governing sentence analysis make crucial use of such notions as informativeness, given/new information, and strategies of referential failure and referential success. These notions are fundamentally pragmatic in nature; they concern the communicative function of structures and the way language is used to convey meaning.

Experimental evidence involving end-of-sentence measures of complexity or reading times for entire sentences has supported the operation of such strategies. However, recent on-line investigations (Ferreira and Clifton 1984; Ferreira and Clifton 1985) have used eye-movement recording. These investigations have shown that, even in contexts biased toward the reduced relative analysis or in neutral contexts satisfying the presuppositions of both syntactic analyses of a sentence, there is evidence that subjects initially construct the syntactically simpler main-clause analyses of such sentences. Thus, readers exhibit longer reading times in the disambiguating region of reduced-relative sentences, such as (1a), and in complex NP sentences, such as (2a), even in contexts where there are two editors (one of whom has been played a tape) or two sets of boxes (and it was asserted that one set had been placed on a cart).

(1)   a. The editor played the tape *agreed the story was big.* (nonminimal–reduced relative)
      b. The editor played the tape *and agreed the story was big.* (minimal–main clause)

(2)   a. Sam loaded the boxes on the cart *onto the van.* (nonminimal–complex NP)
      b. Sam loaded the boxes on the cart *after has coffee break.* (minimal–simple NP)

The general "discourse model"-oriented approach to sentence processing may be fleshed out in either a modular or a nonmodular model of comprehension. In the modular instantiation, all syntactic analyses of an input are computed and pragmatic strategies are used to select the pre-suppositionally simpler or referentially more successful analysis. This view, of course, will encounter the same empirical difficulties as the autonomous model discussed above, i.e, handling the evidence that certain syntactic structures are initially favored.[1] On the nonmodular view, pragmatic strategies govern which analysis is constructed initially, presumably by some ongoing process of matching each syntactic phrase against the model of discourse. On this view, the language processor is fundamentally non-modular; there is no principled distinction between syntactic and semantic processing, on the one hand, and semantic and pragmatic processing on the other. Further, if pragmatic principles cannot successfully operate without the benefit of nonlinguistic real-world knowledge, there is also no prin-cipled distinction in the grammatical and nongrammatical aspects of (post-lexical) comprehension processes.

There are many challenges for this nonmodular conception, primarily concerning the lack of explanation for various kinds of generalizations. I'll briefly illustrate the kinds of problems this approach must face. First, within a language like English, it has been argued that there is a natural class of processing preferences which may be subsumed by a strategy of attaching new input items to the current phrase or using a principle of the fewest possible syntactic nodes (henceforth "Minimal Attachment"). The prefer-ence for a main-clause analysis rather than a reduced-relative analysis has been analyzed as having the same source as a preference for a simple-direct-object (rather than a sentential-complement) analysis of the am-biguous phrase in (3), or a preference for NP (rather than sentential) con-junction of the ambiguous phrase in (4), or a preference for low attachment of the adverb in (5), to give only a few examples.

(3)   Mary knew *the answer*. . . . (Frazier and Rayner 1982)
       a. Mary knew [the answer] by heart.
       b. Mary knew [[the answer] was incorrect.]

(4)   John kissed Mary *and her sister*. . . . (Frazier 1979, 1985a)
       a. John kissed [Mary and her sister] too.
       b. [John kissed Mary] and [her sister langhed]

(5)   Ken said Dave left *yesterday*. (Kimball 1973)
       a. [Ken said [Dave left yesterday]]
       b. [Ken said [Dave left] yesterday]

It is unclear how pragmatic notions can account for such preferences. But then, if one must appeal to a principle of avoiding unnecessary nodes in general, how could we keep it from applying in examples like (1) and (2), resulting in the preference for a simple main-clause analysis in (1) and a simple NP analysis in (2)?

The second sort of problem concerns the cross-language predictions of the discourse-based approach to syntactic processing. There is at present very little evidence about the syntactic processing of languages other than English. What little evidence is available, however, suggests that the strategy of minimally attaching new items to the current phrase or clause is not specific to English but operates in other languages as well. Ueda (1984) presents intuitive evidence for the operation of minimal attachment in Japanese, a consistently head-final or left-branching language. Frazier (1985b) presents initial experimental evidence that the attachment strategies of English also operate in Dutch. Dutch is very similar to English in many respects, but it contains certain head-final structures—specifically, the verb must occur at the end of the verb phrase except in root clauses (owing to the presence of a verb-second constraint).

At first it might appear that the challenge posed by the cross-language data reduces to the problem noted above. That is, given an adequate explanation of the full set of parsing preferences within a language, the discourse-based strategies might apply equally well to other languages. But there is reason to suppose this is not the case, particularly when it comes to head-final structures. The reason is simple. A presuppositional account claims that the referential success or failure of a particular analysis of an ambiguous phrase determines which analysis is originally computed for the phrase. This strategy could not operate until the potentially referential head of a phrase (e.g., a relative clause) had been encountered. In consistently head-final languages, this entails long delays of analysis. Consider the English sentence in (6), which is ambiguous. Minimal Attachment predicts that *the girl* will be attached directly to the VP node, resulting in a sentential-complement analysis of the string *that Bill liked the story*. The alternative (relative-clause) analysis would require an NP to be inserted between the NP node dominating *the girl* and the VP node, as indicated by the left brackets in (6b).

(6) John told the girl that Bill liked the story.
 a. John told the girl [$_s$ that Bill liked the story]. (complement clause)
 b. John told [[the girl [that Bill liked]] the story. (relative clause)

(7) [[Bill __ liked] girl]]

In a language where the head of the relative clause (*the girl*) followed the relative, as in (7), it would not be possible to determine whether *girl* picked out a unique member of a set of girls that had already been introduced into discourse until the head noun delimiting the relevant set was encountered. In other words, the operation of referential strategies would necessarily impose delays of processing in head-final languages. At present we do not have evidence on the processing of these particular structures, but it would certainly be surprising if these predictions were to be confirmed.

In short: Discourse-based strategies, those based on the communicative function of phrases, must either appeal to different strategies in different languages or predict the existence of long delays in syntactic analysis in some languages. By contrast, a syntactic approach seems to enjoy a clear advantage: The grammar of a particular language will determine precisely where ambiguities of analysis will arise, but there is no reason at present to believe that the strategies governing the selection of an initial analysis must differ. A minimal-nodes principle may apply equally well in various types of languages and does not impose delays in syntactic analysis of phrases with head-final word order.

The apparent fact that humans are specialized for language may also pose a challenge for nonmodular discourse-oriented approach to sentence processing. It appears that the successful operation of pragmatic principles requires the full inferential machinery of the general cognitive system. Consider, for example, the processing required to determine the referent in a sequence like *A Datsun . . . The vehicle . . .* or *The cowboy in the White House,* not to mention the assessment of the speaker's current state and intentions required to interpret an utterance like *The window is open* as a request. If (as implied by nonmodular discourse approaches) all postlexical comprehension processes are governed by pragmatic principles, then it becomes quite unclear what is is humans are specialized for. Let me illustrate the problem with a study conducted by Josef Bayer.

Bayer exploited the fact that in German focus particles (*even, only, just*) are ambiguous between a semantic interpretation (where they contribute to the truth conditions of an utterance) and a pragmatic interpretation (where they contribute only to the pragmatic force of an utterance, or to the speech act performed). By the construction of different paragraph contexts, the crucial sentence containing the particle was disambiguated toward either the semantic or the pragmatic interpretation. After subjects received the context material, the target particle was presented tachistoscopically, permitting presentation to either the left or the right hemisphere. Native German speakers exhibited a clear left-hemisphere superiority in their response times for detecting semantic ill-formedness. No comparable hemispheric differences were observed for violations of pragmatic well-formedness. Ideally we would like a large set of consistent findings supporting this contrast, not just a few isolated studies. What I wish to emphasize here, however, is the problem or challenge this type of finding poses. Clearly, we cannot assume that the left (or language-dominant) hemisphere is specialized for all aspects of language processing. But then what, beyond phonetic processing, is it specialized for? With a modular approach to sentence processing, a plausible answer suggests itself: that humans are biologically specialized for the grammatical aspects of sentence processing. But in a nonmodular discourse-oriented approach, it is not at all clear how we can draw this distinction if the general cognitive machinery is part and parcel of all postlexical comprehension processes.

A related problem concerns standard effects of automaticity. For example, in naming, lexical-decision, and matching tasks one finds syntactic effects, even though they are irrelevant to the task at hand. Further, in eye-movement studies, Flores D'Aracais (1982) has found that syntactic violations result in longer reading times even when subjects do not detect the violation and are not consciously aware of it. In a Fodorian kind of view, where the language subsystems have the properties expected of an input system (fast, dumb, and automatic), these sorts of effects are expected; a syntactic module automatically operates on any input with the appropriate characteristics. But if the syntactic structuring of an input string is governed by pragmatic principles, this account does not seem to be open. Unconstrained reasoning is not automatic. Thus, we must find some other distinction between automatic (mandatory) and nonautomatic processes.

To summarize: A model of semantic processing based on pragmatic notions of presuppositional and referential success (or failure), relevance, informativeness, and so forth faces several challenges. One, derived from the empirical findings of Ferreira and Clifton (1984, 1986), suggests that principles involving referential success are operative only after an initial syntactic analysis has already been partially constructed, as indicated by the existence of garden-path effects even in biased contexts. There is also a substantial and quite consistent literature showing that subjects are faster and more accurate at evaluating explicitly asserted information than at evaluating presupposed information and detecting a mismatch or conflict between the presuppositions of a sentence and content established by preceding material (Hornby 1974; Holmes 1979; Cutler and Foss 1977; Cutler and Fodor 1979). If pragmatic notions involving presuppositions and referential success operated early in sentence processing to govern the syntactic analysis of an input, we might have expected just the reverse.

The discourse-based model must also face several explanatory challenges. Within a language, it must account for the parsing preferences in a large range of constructions and provide some explanation for how and why the principles governing the analysis of these constructions are prevented from applying in examples where referential and presuppositional factors ultimately prove to be important. It must also say something about the processing of ambiguous head-final constructions where a referential phrase follows its modifier or complement. Explaining evidence about biological specialization for language and automaticity effects is also problematic, at least for nonmodular versions of the discourse-based approach.

First-Analysis Models

We turn now to one final class of models. Though the models differ in important ways, they all claim that the processor initially computes just a single syntactic analysis of an input. For the moment, it is not important whether the preferred syntactic analysis is identified with reference to the "strongest lexical form" of heads of phrases (Ford, Bresnan, and Kaplan 1982) or by purely structural principles, or whether purely structural principles operate with the benefit of all syntactic-well-formedness conditions (Crain and Fodor 1985) or with only a subset of them (Frazier, Clifton, and Randall 1983; Frazier 1985a). Many of the linguistically oriented computational models also fall into this class, including the depth-first ATNS (Wanner and Maratsos 1978) and even the deterministic models of Marcus (1980) and Berwick and Weinberg (1984) (since, in addition to conscious garden paths, the models have default priorities invoked in the analysis of short ambiguous sentences, sentences with optional parasitic gaps, etc.). The entire class of models predicts that the processor initially computes only a single syntactic analysis of a sentence, though the precise circumstances and principles differ from model to model.

Before turning to general problems with this approach, let me briefly emphasize why I believe empirical evidence supports a first-analysis or garden-path model and why this evidence is difficult to handle without appealing to general structural-preference principles. I'll use two sets of findings to illustrate this. First, the eye-movement data of Frazier and Rayner (1982) show increases in fixation durations and reading time in the disambiguating region of nonminimal-attachment sentences like (8b).

(8)   a. John knew the answer to the physics problem by heart.
       b. John knew the answer to the physics problem was easy.

On their account, the postverbal NP is minimally attached into the matrix VP as a simple direct object of the verb *know*, because this requires the postulation of fewer nodes than the alternative analysis where this NP is the subject of a sentential complement to *know*. Hence, when subjects encounter the disambiguating region in (8b) they must revise this initial analysis; that accounts for the longer fixations in this region of the sentence and the longer average reading times in (8b) vs. (8a), as well as for an increase in regressive eye movements.

For a model in which all syntactic analyses of a string are constructed in parallel, this finding is difficult to accommodate. A parallel-analysis or a multiple-analysis hypothesis predicts that ambiguous strings should take longer than unambiguous ones, but in a temporarily ambiguous sentence it should make no difference whether items following the ambiguous portion of the sentence happen to be consistent with one analysis (e.g. the direct object) or the other (e.g. sentential complement analysis). In either type of sentence, the perceiver should construct both analyses and then, when disambiguating information arrives, simply choose the correct analysis. Similarly, the data pose difficulties for a discourse-based approach, since the postverbal string *the answer to the difficult physics problem* must be analyzed as a definite referential NP on either syntactic analysis. Thus, presuppositional and referential factors provide no apparent reason for favoring one particular structure. And for a deterministic model that delays (within its given memory limits) syntactic decisions until disambiguating information determines the correct analysis, there is again no reason to expect the disambiguating region of the b form to be associated with any extreme processing complexity.[2] Of course, in this framework one might try to appeal merely to the greater number of syntactic nodes *per se* in the correct analysis of the b form, rather than to an initial erroneous analysis. But this account seems inferior to a garden-path account. Although it might account for a slight increase in fixation durations, it does not really explain the increase in regressive eye movements. Further, the account is disconfirmed in other structures where the ambiguous nonminimal-attachment sentence was compared with an unambiguous counterpart that required the same number of nodes to be postulated (see experiment 1 of Rayner et al. 1983).

One final alternative to the structurally based parsing strategy approach is to assume there is indeed a garden path or incorrect analysis constructed in (8b), but that the reason for the garden path has nothing to do with the number of syntactic nodes required for the two analyses of the sentence. Rather, one may assume that *know* (and the other verbs that permit either an NP or an S in their complement) occur more frequently with a single NP object, as in the model of Ford, Bresnan, and Kaplan. But again, I think, several considerations militate against this explanation. First, one would like independent evidence that verbs like *know* really do occur more often with simple NP objects. Also, the generality of parsing preferences is again relevant: How and why would perceivers apply different strategies in different constructions within a language? Under a minimal-attachment characterization of the preferences, they may all be plausibly argued to result from the time pressures involved in comprehension—the parser simply adopts the first available analysis of all items that must be attached to the current phrase marker (Frazier and Fodor 1978). Further, the same strategies used in English may apply in languages with head-final constructions, where lexical restrictions are then used to confirm, disconfirm, or filter out inappropriate syntactic analyses whenever these lexical restrictions become available. In contrast, if the syntactic analysis of the complement of a verb is dictated by the lexical restrictions of the verb, then in verb-final verb phrases this would sometimes entail very long delays of analysis. There is little experimental evidence available at present on this point; however, as noted above, it would be surprising if it turned out that the analysis of complements was delayed until the head was received.

There is indirectly relevant evidence about the processing of head-final constructions, derived from a study I conducted in Dutch using self-paced frame-by-frame reading time as a measure of complexity. Because the verb occurs at the end of a Dutch VP (except in root clauses), Dutch relative clauses are temporarily ambiguous when the perceiver has encountered the head NP, a relative pronoun, and another NP. Either the subject or the object of the clause may have been relativized. If the two NPs are both singular or both plural, the relative clause may remain ambiguous even when the verb is encountered, as in (9). However, if the two NPs differ in number, then the number feature of the verb will disambiguate the relations of the NPs, owing to subject-verb number agreement. In my study, subjects' answers to questions about ambiguous relatives indicated a clear preference for subject relatives; two-thirds of the answers indicated that subjects had computed the subject-relative analysis, and the predominance of subject-relative responses held for every fully ambiguous relative-clause sentence. With respect to the unambiguous relatives, as in (10), reading times were longer for unambiguous object relatives than for unambiguous subject relatives.

(9)   Jan houd niet van [$_{NP}$ de Amerikaanse die de Nederlander will uitnodigen].
John likes not (from) the American who the Dutch person wants to invite.
a. John doesn't like the American who wanted to invite the Dutch person.
b. John doesn't like the American who the Dutch person wanted to invite.

(10)   a. Wij kennen/[de meisjes die de jongen zoeken].
We know the girls who were looking for (pl.) the boy. (subject relative)
b. Wij kennen/[de meisjes die de jongen zoekt].
We know the girls who the boy was looking for (sg.) ... (object relative)

Further, on roughly one-third of the trails where unambiguous relatives were questions, readers responsed incorrectly to questions, indicating that they had incorrectly constructed a subject-relative analysis of the unambiguous object relatives. This finding is expected on a garden-path account (assuming, roughly, a principle specifying that a HOLD mechanism is emptied as soon as possible). Readers always initially construct a subject-relative analysis, and they tend to revise this only when clear disambiguating information arrives. On the assumption that once perceivers have some analysis of the sentence they pay somewhat less attention to the input, it is not too surprising that our readers sometimes overlooked the one-character difference between the singular and plural verbs and thus failed to revise this initial analysis of unambiguous object relatives.[3]

However, if the readers had computed both subject-relative and object-relative analyses of these sentences, or if they had delayed analysis until disambiguating information had arrived, it is very surprising that they then ignored the disambiguating information when it did arrive in one-third of the unambiguous object-relative sentences. According to a delay hypothesis, if anything, one would have expected them to pay more attention to the end of the sentence (the verb), since by hypothesis they are on the lookout for disambiguating information. Thus, again, I want to suggest that a structure-based garden-path approach provides the best account of the data. The empirical results make perfect sense on this account without the additional often *post hoc* and *ad hoc* assumptions required for each new experiment.

Let us now return to the general problem confronting any model in which it is claimed that the sentence processor initially constructs just a single syntactic analysis of an input string. As a result of this basic characteristic, such models face a common challenge: specifying how the processor identifies a semantically or pragmatically more appropriate analysis of a sentence when its initial analysis is completely well formed and coherent.

The hypothesis proposed by Rayner, Carlson, and Frazier (1983) is the only attempt to solve this problem that I am aware of. They make the fairly standard assumption that verbs (and other heads of phrases) have associated thematic frames listed in their lexical entries. For example, one thematic frame for a verb like *see* contains a Theme and an Instrument as internal arguments of *see*; another frame includes only a Theme as an internal argument of *see*, as illustrated in (11).

(11)   *see* verb
      a. [(Experiencer) __ Theme-Instrument]
           NP   NP   PP
      (e.g., The spy saw [NP the cop] [PP with binoculars])
      b. [(Experiencer)__Theme]
           NP   NP
      (e.g., The spy saw [NP [NP the cop] [PP with a revolver])]

Rayner et al. suggest that a "Thematic Processor" is responsible for choosing the pragmatically most plausible thematic frame for each head of a phrase, with the benefit of discourse and real-world knowledge. If the thematic frame selected by the Thematic Processor is consistent with the initial constituent-structure analysis assigned by the syntactic processor, the sentence should be relatively easy to process. However, if the chosen thematic frame is inconsistent with the initially assigned constituent structure, this will serve as an error signal alerting the syntactic processor to the presence of a locally more plausible analysis of the input.

For example, Minimal Attachment predicts that the syntactic processor will initially analyze the string "VP NP PP" as a VP with an NP and PP complement, since this requires the postulation of fewer syntactic nodes than the alternative complex analysis (which requires an additional NP node, dominating the NP and the PP). In a sentence like (11a), the post-verbal string is semantically biased toward this analysis. Since binoculars make a very good instrument for an act of seeing, the Thematic Processor should choose the thematic frame that contains both a Theme and an Instrument in the complement to *see*. This frame will prove to be consistent with the minimal-attachment syntactic analysis, where *see* does in fact contain two sisters: an NP and a PP. In contrast, (11b) is biased toward the complex-NP interpretation, since revolvers do not make very good instruments for an act of seeing. Hence, the chosen thematic frame should conflict with the initial syntactic analysis of the sentence. Hence, the chosen thematic frame can alert the syntactic processor to the presence of a potentially more plausible analysis where *see* contains only an NP sister. This hypothesis thus predicts that perceivers should eventually arrive at the semantically and pragmatically most plausible analysis of a sentence, but it should take them longer to do so in cases like (11b), where a revision of the initial syntactic analysis is required. Using eye-movement recording, Rayner et al. confirmed this prediction for sentences like those above.

There are two aspects of this proposal that should be emphasized. First, it provides at least the outlines of a general solution to the problem of how the syntactic processor can discover the existence of an overlooked analysis of a sentence, even when its initial analysis does not break down. In addition, it addresses the question of how real-world knowledge can have any effect in the ongoing grammatical analysis of a sentence. The problem here is a central one. How can any factual knowledge a perceiver happens to have about the real-world properties of entities and the likely situations and relations they enter into influence decisions such as how to attach an NP into a phrase marker or whether to postulate an NP node?

The answer provided by the Thematic Processor hypothesis is obvious: The vocabulary of thematic relations—e.g., Agent, Patient, Experiencer, Goal, Theme, Source, Location—is shared by the linguistic and nonlinguistic systems. Because this vocabulary has extralinguistic dimensions, real-world knowledge can be used to assess the relative likelihood of different relations; because thematic relations have a grammatical dimension (due to the connection between thematic roles and syntactic categories established by the thematic frames stored in lexical entries), this knowledge may have consequences for the ongoing grammatical analysis of sentences.

In addition to the evidence presented by Rayner et al., there is an independent source of evidence favoring the Thematic Processor hypothesis: the early psycholinguistic literature on ambiguity resolution. It is now well known that this literature is filled with apparently contradictory conclusions. Some of the studies suggest that ambiguity increases processing complexity, and some that it does not. This was due in part to an incomplete understanding of the experimental techniques employed and in part to the fact that it was common to include several distinct types of ambiguity in a single study. However, when this literature is reviewed with the benefit of hindsight, an interesting generalization seems to emerge. Those syntactic ambiguities that supported the view that ambiguity increases complexity and have not been dismissed as experimental artifacts were found almost invariably in one of two types of constructions: those that were eventually disambiguated toward the unpreferred structure of a constituent-structure ambiguity and those that used to be characterized as "deep-structure" ambiguities (today these might better be characterized as thematic ambiguities). The former constructions receive a straightforward account in the models we have been considering: An initial structural analysis of the sentence must be revised, resulting in an increase in complexity. I want to focus here on constructions of the latter type—those that suggest that more than one analysis of the ambiguity is computed— since ambiguity *per se* increases complexity regardless of which structural analysis is ultimately appropriate.

Take for example the classic finding of Lackner and Garrett (1972) that presenting biasing sentences in the unattended channel in a dichotic listening task biased subjects' reports of the meanings of ambiguous sentences. These effects were significant for lexical ambiguities and for "deep-structure" ambiguities (e.g., *The police were told to stop drinking*) but not for surface-structure (bracketing) ambiguities.[4] In sentence-completion studies, Fodor, Bever, and Garrett (1974, p. 367) noted that significant effects of syntactic ambiguities were found only for deep-structure ambiguities (Bever, Garrett, and Hurtig 1973), or, though there may be some effects of surface ambiguities, the largest effects were found for these (as in MacKay 1966). Holmes (1979) examined the processing of several types of ambiguities and concluded (p. 238) that "it seems ... that deep-structure ambiguities are not consistently interpreted according to a given structure." The "deep-structure" ambiguities examined were of the *shooting of the hunters* variety—again involving an ambiguity in the assignment of thematic relations rather than in constituent structure. Thus, we seem to derive the correct distinction between structures were ambiguity complicates sentence analysis only when the unpreferred structure proves ultimately to be appropriate and structures where ambiguity apparently always (even initially) induces a comparison of alternative structures with no syntactic default. It follows as an automatic consequence of the assumption that the Constituent Structure Processor follows a first-analysis strategy whereas the Thematic Processor considers alternative possible thematic frames and thematic assignments.

Conclusions

In evaluating the different approaches to sentence processing, I have presented arguments and empirical evidence for believing that the human sentence processor has the following characteristics:

• Constituent-structure analysis of an input is accomplished by initially assigning just one analysis, presumably on the basis of general structural principles,
• Semantic and pragmatic factors operate and typically determine the ultimate analysis assigned to a structurally ambiguous input, perhaps by a mechanism responsible for evaluating the alternative thematic frames stored in the lexical entry for heads of phrases.
• The sentence processor has a modular structure, even if we cannot at present establish conclusively the subsystems involved—e.g., whether there is a single syntactic subsystem, as argued by Crain and Fodor, or two such subsystems, as argued by Frazier, Clifton, and Randall (1983) and by Freedman and Forster (1985), or whether the speech-perception subsystem operates with the benefit of lexical information (Samuel 1981; Ganong 1980; Connine and Clifton 1984) or on the basis of purely acoustic and phonetic information (Frauenfelder and Marcus 1984).

There is another set of findings about sentence processing which have not yet been discussed, many of them due to Marslen-Wilson and his colleagues. The findings are well known, so I will not review them here. What they seem to show is that all types of information are exploited very rapidly during the comprehension of language. These findings have often been interpreted as evidence against autonomous and modular theories of sentence processing. I want to suggest here that these findings are not inconsistent with a modular account of the processor; indeed, these findings are incompatible with a highly structured autonomous or modular system only if one assumes the existence of some basic unit of sentence processing (e.g. the clause) and of a linearly or sequentially ordered output-input relation holding between subsystems. I think this was a very common interpretation—or misinterpretation—of Forster's (1979) model.

A language-processing system with a highly articulated modular structure is completely compatible with the rapid use of various theoretically distinct types of information if one drops these assumptions. For purposes of illustration, consider a model in which phonological, syntactic, and semantic subsystems each operate in a strictly autonomous fashion exploiting only a highly restricted type of information (e.g., only phonological information for the phonological processor). Further, assume that each of these modules or processing subsystems operates on a single (shared) representation of the input, supplementing the current analysis of the input by adding to this representation whatever inferences the module may draw. We might illustrate this as follows.[5]

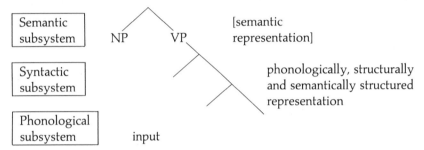

This is an entirely modular system; the fact that (say) the syntactic processor is operating on a representation that happens to contain phonological, semantic, or even real-world information will be absolutely irrelevant to the operation of the syntactic processor, on the assumption that its only information source (other than the representation of the input) is syntactic information. The fact that some input item may have some particular phonological characteristic (e.g., begin with a labial) or may refer to some particular semantic class will be absolutely irrelevant to the syntactic processor, on the assumption that such information is not stated in a syntactic vocabulary.

To see this, imagine a monolingual English module operating on a representation of an English sentence. A Chinese or Arabic translation of the sentence is added to the representation the English module is operating on. Including the translation will make no difference whatsoever for the operation of our monolingual English module, since by definition it is not equipped to draw any consequences from Chinese or Arabic. The point, of course, is that we may easily conceive of language modules with limited information sources which operate independent of each other and still rapidly exploit information stated within their own vocabulary. Hence, there is in principle no conflict or incompatibility between a highly structured or modular processing system and the empirical findings establishing rapid use of information.

On this view, informationally encapsulated language subsystems operating strictly in terms of restricted information types might even be influenced by real-world knowledge, provided that this knowledge is not processed by the grammatical subsystem *per se* (i.e., the real-world knowledge is not accessed by a grammatical subsystem and no nongrammatical inferences are drawn by the grammatical subsystems). This could happen only in cases where there is an overlap in the vocabulary of the grammatical subsystems and some nongrammatical one. The Thematic Processor sketched above provides one example of how this situation might arise. The speech-perception system may provide another. A linguistic subsystem exploiting articulatory features and concerned with phonetic identification may utilize articulatory information from a visual processing system, provided the output is represented in terms of the vocabulary of articulatory features.

Acknowledgment

This work was supported by NIH grant HD 18708.

Notes

1. I am assuming here that identifying the most plausible analysis of a string will involve a comparison of alternative possibilities. Hence, it would be necessary to construct all syntactic analyses of an input. However, as Chuck Clifton pointed out to me, one might consider a modular system in which lexical and pragmatic information are used to identify tempting analyses which are later checked or filtered using syntactic well-formedness conditions. The difficulties with this approach have been discussed extensively elsewhere (e.g., in chapter 2 of Frazier 1979), so I will not discuss them in detail here. One serious problem may be illustrated briefly. Consider the simple case in which a pragmatic processing module succeeds in identifying a single plausible "meaning" on the basis of lexical and pragmatic information. How could the language-processing system then determine whether this "meaning" is a grammatically permissible meaning for the input sentence? The system must either go into "analysis-by-synthesis" mode and use the meaning to begin generating sentences, in hope that one of the sentences it generates matches the input, or it must now construct one or more syntactic structures for the input to determine whether any of the structures may have the hypothetical meaning. In either case, the initial step of identifying a potential meaning on purely lexical and pragmatic grounds would seem to complicate sentence analysis, unless it can be shown how hypothesized meanings could efficiently guide syntactic analysis.

2. Berwick and Weinberg (1984) propose that a deterministic system may make decisions that underdetermine the eventual analysis of a sentence, e.g., by assuming that NP and S complements share some grammatical feature which may be assigned as soon as the postverbal NP is encountered. This "partial analysis" approach is extremely interesting. However, it is unclear how it could account for the inferiority of the sentential-complement analysis. The partial analysis constructed should be consistent with either continuation of a temporarily ambiguous sentence, and thus no garden path should arise.

3. If it is assumed that the Thematic Processor identifies the most likely antecedent or referent for thematic roles occurring as external arguments (e.g., the subject NP is the external argument of the verb), it will identify the most plausible interpretation for pragmatically controlled null pronominals, in addition to selecting the most plausible thematic frame. The operations required to perform the latter task will often require information about the referent for the external argument; e.g., determining whether someone shot "some man with a gun" or shot some man (by) using a gun will often depend on information known about the agent of *shoot*. Consider *The policeman stopped the tall burglar, shooting the man with a gun*. Here, determining the most plausible thematic frame for *shoot* might well depend on knowing who is the agent of *shoot* and whether the individual has a gun.

4. The substantial reading-time difference between unambiguous subject vs. object relatives approached but did not quite reach significance. Presumably this was due to the fact that readers often did not revise their initial incorrect analysis of the subject relatives, as indicated by their answers to questions. See Frazier 1985b.

5. This sort of model is similar to the "blackboard" models proposed by Tanenhaus, Carlson, and Seidenberg (1985). However, the commitment (in the present model) to the construction of a single globally structured syntactic analysis avoids many of the difficulties that confront "blackboard" models, since the syntactic phrase marker serves to coordinate hypotheses, maintaining consistency between locally possible analyses. Without this feature of the model, it appears that extensive "bookkeeping" or "control" operations would be required to determine the consequences of any local hypothesis for the overall well-formedness of the processor's analysis of a sentence.

16

Mandatory Processing in Speech Perception: A Case Study

Joanne L. Miller

Current models of the processing of spoken language differ widely in a number of respects, as is clear from the chapters in this volume. Nonetheless, virtually all models share the assumption that there is an early stage of processing during which the acoustic signal is analyzed in terms of those physical properties that specify the discrete linguistic units, which, in turn, define the individual items in the mental lexicon. My discussion focuses on these initial analytic processes.[1]

With this focus, the fundamental question is how the listener takes as input the continuously varying acoustic signal and derives the phonetic structure of the utterance. If we follow the lead of Jerry Fodor (1983) and Alvin Liberman (see, e.g., Liberman and Mattingly 1985), one possibility to consider is that the system that performs this computation is itself a self-contained "module" within the language-processing system. In *The Modularity of Mind* (1983), Fodor discusses a number of properties that together define a system as modular, one being that the operation of a module is mandatory. In this chapter I address the question of the modularity of the phonetic processing system, and I do so by examining one particular aspect of phonetic processing and determining whether it is mandatory.

The aspect of phonetic processing that provides our case study, as it were, is the following. When speakers talk, they do not maintain a constant rate of speech. Rather, they frequently speed up and slow down. The variation in rate that occurs during conversational speech can be quite substantial; the average duration of a syllable, for example, can change during conversation by hundreds of milliseconds (Miller, Grosjean, and Lomanto 1984). The problem this causes for deriving the phonetic structure of an utterance is that many of the acoustic properties that specify the identity of the phonetic segments are themselves temporal in nature and change with a change in speaking rate.

Given this acoustic variation, if listeners are to most effectively use these temporal acoustic properties to identify phonetic structure, they must somehow take into account the rate at which the speech was produced— that is, listeners must process speech in a rate-dependent manner. And, indeed, there is considerable evidence that listeners do just this; for a review, see Miller 1981. The question I want to consider is whether this adjustment for speaking rate is a mandatory aspect of phonetic perception; that is to say, whether listeners cannot process speech without taking account of the rate of articulation.

The plan of the paper is as follows. First, I describe more fully the phenomenon of rate-dependent phonetic perception, considering the kind of experimental data that allow us to infer that a listener has taken account of speaking rate when computing the phonetic structure of an utterance. Second, I present some recent data that are consistent with the view that adjusting for speaking rate is, indeed, a mandatory part of phonetic perception. Finally, I consider the nature of the perceptual mechanism that might underlie this form of rate-dependent processing.

The Phenomenon of Rate-Dependent Speech Processing

Let us begin with the phenomenon of rate-dependent processing, per se. The phonetic contrast that will serve as our example is that between voiced and voiceless stop consonants in syllable-initial position—specifically, the contrast between /b/ and /p/, as in bath-path, bill-pill, or bike-pike. A major property distinguishing /b/ and /p/ is the timing between the release of the consonant and the onset of vocal-fold vibration, or voicing. The time interval between these two events, labeled voice-onset time (VOT) by Lisker and Abramson (1964), is typically shorter for /b/ than for /p/, and is seen in acoustic terms as the delay between the abrupt increase in energy at consonantal release and the onset of quasi-periodic energy corresponding to voicing onset.

That listeners use this difference to classify the initial consonant of a word as /b/ or /p/ has been shown experimentally in the following way (Lisker and Abramson 1970): Through the use of either computer-editing techniques or speech synthesis, a series of speech items is created. These items vary systematically in VOT from a value appropriate for /b/ to one appropriate for /p/—for example, a series that ranges from bath to path. Many tokens of each item are then randomized and presented to listeners for identification. The classic finding in such an experiment is an identification function with the following characteristics: The word with the shortest VOT value is consistently identified as bath, that with the longest VOT value is consistently identified as path, and the crossover between predominantly bath and predominantly path responses (which is located at some given VOT value between the two extremes) is typically quite abrupt.

So far, the story of /b/ and /p/ is relatively simple: The phonetic segments are distinguished primarily by VOT, and listeners use this property to classify words as beginning with /b/ or /p/. But the situation is considerably more complex and more interesting. The specific complication that is of concern in this chapter is that the VOT values for /b/ and /p/, as in the word pair *bath-path*, are not constant, but rather change systematically with a change in speaking rate. As speech is speeded up and the word becomes shorter, the VOT interval (especially that of the voiceless /p/) becomes shorter. Conversely, as speech is slowed and the word becomes longer, the VOT interval (especially that of /p/) becomes longer (Miller, Green, and Reeves 1986; Summerfield 1975). What this means is that the VOT value that optimally separates the /b/ and /p/ VOT distributions is not constant but changes as a function of speaking rate; as speech varies from fast to slow, that criterion VOT value becomes increasingly longer.

Because of this pattern of acoustic change in speech production, the most effective strategy by which a listener can correctly identify /b/ and /p/, regardless of rate, is not to use a single perceptual criterion of VOT to categorize these phonetic segments but to have a relative criterion value. As speaking rate changes from fast to slow and the individual words become longer, the criterion VOT value that perceptually differentiates /b/ and /p/ should also become longer. This prediction can be tested experimentally by performing two operations on words from the *bath-path* series spoken at a moderate rate. First, we shorten each word in the series, thus creating a *bath-path* series with fast words. Second, we lengthen each word, thereby creating a series with slow words. We then present randomizations of the words at all three rates to listeners for identification. If there is no perceptual adjustment for speaking rate (that is, if listeners base their decision on the absolute VOT value), then all three identification functions— those for the fast, moderate, and slow words—should be the same. If, however, listeners do identify /b/ and /p/ on the basis of VOT value in relation to rate (specified in this case by word duration), then, in comparison with the moderate-rate identification function, the function for the fast words should be shifted toward shorter VOT values and the function for the slow words should be shifted toward longer VOT values. This is precisely what happens in such an experiment: The location of the phonetic-category boundary changes systematically with a change in rate. It is this pattern of change in phonetic-boundary location that is the basic phenomenon of rate-dependent processing. Although I have described the phenomenon in terms of a single example, such processing has been found to be pervasive in speech (Miller 1981).

Is Rate-Dependent Speech Processing Mandatory?

We turn now to the primary issue of the chapter: Does the phonetic processor operate so as to necessarily accommodate changes in speaking rate? Two recent investigations in our laboratory bear on this issue, one focusing on word-external rate information and the other on word-internal rate information.

Word-External Rate Information
The first investigation, which was concerned with word-external rate information (Miller, Green, and Schermer 1984), focused on the contrast between *bath* and *path*. The stimuli are shown in figure 1. The target series, shown on the right, ranged from *the bath* to *the path*; the /b/-/p/ contrast was specified by a change in VOT value from 7 to 73 msec in steps of about 4 msec. These items were computer-edited versions of natural speech spoken at a medium rate. Each of the target words was embedded in three different sentence frames, which are shown on the left. The sentence was *She is not thinking of . . .*, spoken at three different rates: fast, medium, and slow. With this design, the rate of the target words themselves is kept constant, but the rate of the precursor sentence changes. It has been shown that although the rate of the word itself is the primary rate information to which a listener adjusts, the rate of the sentence in which the word occurs also plays a role (Port and Dalby 1982; Summerfield 1981). We can thus expect the following pattern of results: When the target items are presented in the context of the slow sentence frame, listeners should require a relatively long VOT value to perceive *path* rather than *bath*. This will produce a shift in the identification function for the slow-sentence context toward longer VOT values, in comparison with that for the medium-sentence context. The converse is expected for the fast precursor sentence; the identification function for the fast-sentence context will be shifted toward shorter VOT values.

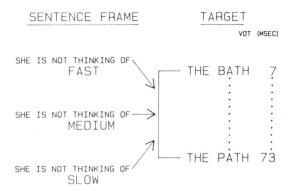

Figure 1
Stimulus design for studies investigating the influence of sentence rate on the identification of words from a *bath-path* series. Based on Miller, Green, and Schermer 1984.

The purpose of the first study in the series was to establish this basic effect with our stimuli. We presented the sentences in random order to listeners, who were asked to perform two tasks. First, they were to identify the word as *bath* or *path*. Second, they were to identify the rate of the sentence frame as fast, medium, or slow. The second task—which, as expected, was performed with very high accuracy—was included to ensure that the subjects did attend to the rate of the precursor sentence. The results from the first task are plotted in figure 2, which shows a small but highly reliable effect of the rate of the precursor sentence on identification.[2]

In the next study of the series, we asked whether this effect would still be obtained if on each trial the listener were required only to identify the word as *bath* or *path*, and not also to overtly identify the rate of the sentence frame. The same stimuli were presented to a new group of subjects, and the results mirrored those of the first study. Thus, even when not required explicitly to attend to the rate of the sentence frame, listeners adjust for that rate during phonetic perception.

Finally, we directly attempted to focus the listener's attention on the target word, at the expense of the sentence frame, by requiring each subject to identify the target word as quickly as possible. Even under these conditions, however, we obtained the effect. Moreover, the magnitude of the effect was the same as in the first two studies. Taken together, the three studies clearly reveal that it is not easy to eliminate the rate effect; thus, they provide at least preliminary support for the claim that the adjustment for speaking rate is a mandatory aspect of phonetic processing.

These experiments take on even more significance when compared with a parallel set of studies we were conducting at the same time (Miller, Green, and Schermer 1984). In these studies we used the same target series (*the bath–the path*) as in the experiments just described, but we investigated how

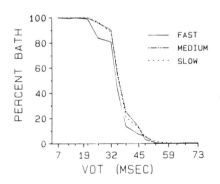

Figure 2
Mean percentage of *bath* responses as a function of VOT value for a *bath-path* series in fast, medium, and slow sentence contexts. From Miller, Green, and Schermer 1984.

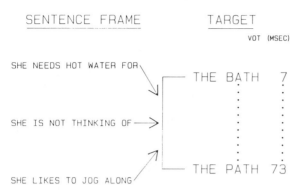

Figure 3
Stimulus design for studies investigating the influence of semantic context on the identification of words from a *bath-path* series. Based on Miller, Green, and Schermer 1984.

the identification of the words was affected not by the rate of the sentence frame in which they occurred but by the semantic value of the sentence. It had been shown previously (see, e.g., Garnes and Bond 1976) that listeners tend to identify acoustically ambiguous words such that they are semantically congruent with the sentence frame in which they occur. We studied this phenomenon by placing each item from the target series in each of three sentence frames that were spoken at a medium rate, as shown in figure 3. The top sentence (*she needs hot water for ...*) favors *bath* responses, the middle sentence (*she is not thinking of ...*) is neutral with respect to *bath* and *path*, and the bottom sentence (*she likes to jog along ...*) favors *path* responses.

We expected that, in comparison with the neutral *is not thinking* context, the *hot water* context would yield more *bath* responses and, consequently, the identification function would be shifted toward longer VOT values. Conversely, we expected that the *likes to jog* context would yield more *path* responses and thus shift the function toward lower VOT values. In all, we conducted three studies, which were analogous to the three speaking-rate studies described above. The purpose of the first study was to establish the effect. We gave subjects randomized sequences of the sentences and asked them to perform two tasks: to identify each word as *bath* or *path* and to identify each sentence frame. The latter ensured that the subjects would attend to the sentence context, at least to the extent required to perform the task; as expected, performance on this task was virtually perfect. The results of the first task, plotted in figure 4, were as predicted. The identification of the target words depended jointly on their VOT value and on the sentence frame in which they occurred.[3] The second study of the series, conducted on a new group of listeners, was identical to the first except that

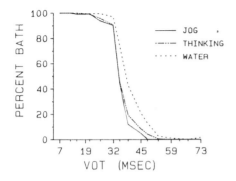

Figure 4
Mean percentage of *bath* responses as a function of VOT value for a *bath-path* series in three semantic contexts. From Miller, Green, and Schermer 1984.

only word-identification responses were required. In the analogous rate experiment we still obtained the rate effect; in this case, however, the semantic effect disappeared. And in the final study of the series, in which we asked listeners to respond to the target word as quickly as possible, we also obtained no effect of semantic context.

In summary: Although it was easy to eliminate the effect of semantic context on the identification of words beginning with /b/ and /p/, under precisely the same experimental conditions the effect of speaking rate remained. This is consistent with the claim that the adjustment for rate (but not for semantic congruence) is a mandatory part of those processes that derive the phonetic structure of the utterance.

Word-Internal Rate Information
In the second investigation (Miller, Dexter, and Pickard 1984), we focused not on the rate of the sentence in which the target word occurred but on the rate of the target word itself. As I indicated earlier, it is this word-internal rate information to which the listener primarily adjusts during phonetic perception. Our basic question, again, was whether this rate information plays a mandatory role in speech processing. In light of the distinction between the rate and semantic effects found in the previous experiments, we specifically designed the word-internal rate studies to be able to compare the rate effect with an effect we assumed was not mandatory: the effect of lexical status on identification (Ganong 1980).

Four series of stimuli were created for the experiment. The items in each varied in initial consonant from /b/ to /p/, specified by a change in VOT from 9 to 61 msec. Figure 5 displays the endpoint stimuli of the four series. The top two series ranged from *beace* (a nonsense word) to *peace* (a real word); the stimuli in one of these series were 210 msec in duration, whereas

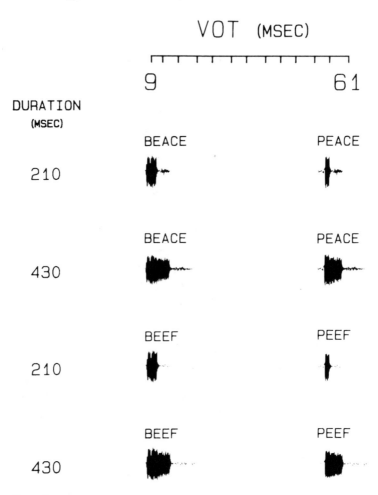

Figure 5
Stimulus design for studies investigating the influence of speaking rate and lexical status on identification of a 210- and 430-msec *beef-peef* series and a 210- and 430-msec *beace-peace* series. Based on Miller, Dexter, and Pickard 1984.

those in the other were 430 msec. The bottom two series ranged from *beef* (a real word) to *peef* (a nonsense word). Again, the stimuli in one of these series were 210 msec long, and those in the other were 430 msec long. With this stimulus set we were able to assess the influence of both speaking rate and lexical status, as follows.

With respect to the rate effect, we expected that for both the top two series (ranging from *beace* to *peace*) and the bottom two series (ranging from *beef* to *peef*) the /b/-/p/ boundary would be at a longer VOT value for the 430-msec stimuli than for the 210-msec stimuli. As for the lexical effect, we expected that for both the short (210 msec) and the long (430 msec) series we would obtain more *peace* responses on the *beace-peace* series and more *beef* responses on the *beef-peef* series. This would be seen as a shift in category boundary toward longer VOT values for the *beef-peef* series than for the *beace-peace* series.

The purpose of the first experiment in the series was to establish both effects. The entire set of stimuli were presented in random order to subjects, who were asked to identify each item as *beace, peace, beef,* or *peef.* This task ensured that the listeners would process the entire word and not just the VOT portion. The results are plotted in figure 6. The top graph shows the predicted rate effect for the two *beace-peace* series, and the bottom graph shows the predicted rate effect for the two *beef-peef* series. In both cases, as the stimuli became longer the category boundary shifted toward longer VOT values. The lexical effect is seen as a shift in the bottom two functions relative to the top two functions. This shift is made clearer in figure 7, where the same data are replotted with the graphs grouped by rate. It is clear that for both the fast syllables (top graph) and the slow syllables (bottom graph) we obtained the expected effect of lexical status on identification.

Having established these two effects with our stimuli, we then asked whether they could be eliminated. In a first attempt to do so, we presented the stimuli to a new group of listeners and changed the task. The new subjects were asked specifically to attend just to the beginnings of the items and to indicate whether each began with /b/ or /p/. If the subjects were just required to attend to word-initial information, would the later-occurring rate information still influence perception, with the lexical status of the item having no effect? The results were clear-cut. In line with our earlier studies on word-external information, we still obtained the rate effect under these task conditions. However, to our surprise, we also obtained the lexical effect. We pursued this finding in a third study, in which we tested a new group of listeners on the same stimuli with yet another modification in the task. Again we asked the listeners to attend just to the beginnings of the items, and to indicate whether each began with /b/ or /p/. In this case,

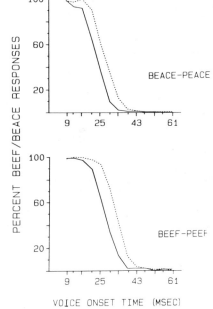

Figure 6
Mean percentage of *beef/beace* responses as a function of VOT value for a 210- and 430-msec *beef-peef* series and a 210- and 430-msec *beace-peace* series. Based on Miller, Dexter, and Pickard 1984.

however, we attempted to ensure that the subjects would ignore the endings of the items by asking them to make the /b/-/p/ judgment as quickly as they could. The data were as before. We obtained the rate effect and, again to our surprise, we also obtained the lexical effect.

One possible reason that the lexical effect was obtained under all conditions is that the influence of lexical information, like that of rate information, is mandatory. However, there is another possibility. Perhaps, as I am proposing, listeners manditorily process the endings of items in order to obtain the critical information about speaking rate. However, in the processing of the endings of the words, the lexical-status information becomes available and, once available, is used in the final /b/-/p/ decision. On this explanation, lexical status played a role because the use of the later-occurring rate information was mandatory for phonetic processing, and not because the use of the lexical information itself was mandatory.

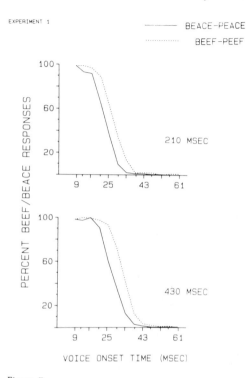

EXPERIMENT 1

———— BEACE-PEACE

·············· BEEF-PEEF

Figure 7

Mean percentage of *beef/beace* responses as a function of VOT value for 210-msec *beef-peef* and *beace-peace* series and for 430-msec beef-*peef* and *beace-peace* series. Based on Miller, Dexter, and Pickard 1984.

The Mechanism Underlying Rate-Dependent Speech Processing

In this final section, I turn to the nature of the perceptual mechanism that might underlie the type of rate-dependent processing I have been considering. One possibility that immediately comes to mind is that the rate effect derives from the operation of the auditory system itself. We know from the psychoacoustic literature that onsets of nonspeech stimuli are perceived in relation to their duration (Pastore 1981; Pisoni, Carrell, and Gans 1983). Perhaps it is an effect of this type that underlies the rate effect; for example, perhaps the effect arises at a very early auditory stage of processing, during which the VOT information is itself analyzed by the auditory system. If this is the case, then although the adjustment for rate clearly plays an important role in language processing, it does not derive from operations within the phonetic processing system itself.

A recent investigation in our laboratory (Green 1984; Green and Miller 1985) calls this account into question. The investigation was based on a

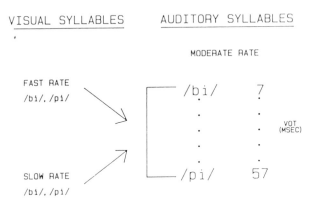

Figure 8
Stimulus design for studies investigating the use of visual and auditory rate information in the perception of a /bi/-/pi/ contrast. Based on Green and Miller 1985.

phenomenon known as the McGurk effect (McGurk and MacDonald 1976). One standard way of demonstrating this effect is to create a videotape of a person uttering a sequence of syllables. Then a second set of syllables is dubbed onto the audio track of the tape in synchrony with the first set of syllables on the video track. This procedure yields, for any given audio-visual pairing, a discrepancy in the auditory and visual information. Under certain conditions, however, what is perceived upon presentation of such a hybrid syllable is a single, unitary syllable, whose identity is jointly determined by the information from the two modalities. This phenomenon suggests that the phonetic processing system operates so as to combine the relevant auditory and visual information in deriving the phonetic percept.

We capitalized on this effect in designing the study schematized in figure 8. The first step in preparing the stimuli was to generate a series of auditory syllables. These varied from /bi/ to /pi/, with the voicing distinction specified by a change in VOT from 7 to 57 msec, and were produced at a moderate rate. In a preliminary study we established that when these stimuli were physically shortened the VOT boundary shifted toward shorter durations and, conversely, when they were lengthened the boundary shifted toward longer durations; that is, we produced the standard rate effect. The next step was to make a videotape of a speaker articulating /bi/ and /pi/ at two rates, fast and slow. Another preliminary study, involving just the video track of this tape, established that it was easy to discern the rate of articulation. However, the visual information alone was not sufficient to distinguish /b/ from /p/. Thus, the visual syllables alone provided rate information but not voicing information. The final step was to create a bimodal test tape by dubbing each auditory syllable from the /bi/-/pi/

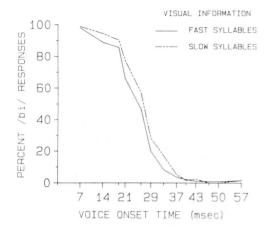

Figure 9
Mean percentage of /bi/ responses as a function of VOT value for a 210-msec auditory /bi/-/pi/ series when paired with fast and slow visual syllables. From Green and Miller 1985.

series onto each of the fast and slow visual syllables. The phenomenal experience upon attending to the dubbed videotape is striking. If you close your eyes, you perceive a random sequence of /bi/'s and /pi/'s, all at a moderate rate. If you open your eyes, you again perceive a random sequence of /bi/'s and /pi/'s, but now some are fast and some are slow. Moreover, you are unaware that the rate information in the two modalities is discrepant—on each trial you perceive a unitary syllable.

The critical question is whether the visual rate information influences not only the perceived rate of the audiovisual syllables as fast or slow but also the perception of the syllables as /bi/ versus /pi/. We tested this by asking subjects to identify each syllable on the final test tape as /bi/ or /pi/. We then compared the identification function obtained when the auditory syllables were paired with the fast visual syllables against the one obtained when they were paired with the slow visual syllables. If the basic rate effect is due to psychoacoustic processing, the two identification functions should be identical, since the auditory information remained constant. If, however, the rate effect arises at a stage of processing at which visual and auditory rate information are both available, then we would expect the two func-tions to be different; when paired with fast visual syllables, the identifi-cation function should be shifted toward shorter VOT values, and con-versely for the pairings with the slow visual syllables. As figure 9 shows, this is precisely what happened. This result indicates that visual rate in-formation from the face, as well as auditory rate information, is relevant for phonetic perception. It appears, then, that rate adjustment is not solely an auditory phenomenon.

Concluding Remarks

When listeners derive the phonetic structure of an utterance, they do not treat the phonetically relevant acoustic properties in terms of absolute values; instead, they treat them in relation to the rate at which the speech was produced—phonetic perception is rate-dependent. Moreover, across a variety of tasks, with different sets of stimuli, it has not been possible to eliminate this influence of rate. This finding is consistent with the claim that at least one aspect of phonetic processing—the adjustment for speaking rate—is indeed mandatory. Recent data suggest that this mandatory effect arises not within the auditory system itself, but at some later stage of processing at which visual and auditory rate information are integrated.

It will be of considerable interest to determine what other aspects of phonetic processing are mandatory and, more generally, to define the scope and the functional characteristics of the presumed phonetic module. At this point, we can only speculate that it is this phonetic module, operating in a rapid, mandatory manner during the earliest stages of language processing, that in part makes language comprehension as a whole as efficient and effortless as it appears to be.

Acknowledgments

The research was supported by NIH grants NS 14394, RCDA NS 00661, and BRSG RR 07143. I thank Peter D. Eimas for helpful comments on an earlier version of the manuscript.

The research reported here and related work are reviewed more extensively in my "Rate-Dependent Processing in Speech Perception," in *Progress in the Psychology of Language*, volume 3, ed. A. Ellis (Hillsdale, N.J.: Erlbaum).

Notes

1. The precise nature of these representational units has long been a matter of debate in the speech-perception literature. For the present purposes, I will assume that these units are the phonetic segments of the language. Arguments supporting the role of phonetic structure in natural-language processing can be found in Pisoni 1981.

2. As is apparent from figure 2, the effect was obtained between the fast and medium rates, but not between the medium and slow rates. For a discussion of this pattern of results, see note 7 of Miller, Green, and Schermer 1984.

3. Although the difference between the *is not thinking* and the *hot water* contexts was reliable, that between the *is not thinking* and the *likes to jog* contexts was not. The reason for this asymmetry, which was also found in a replication experiment, is not known.

IV
The Visual Module

Introduction

Neil Stillings

Any comprehensive treatment of modular organization in the mind and brain must consider the visual system. Since recent computationally oriented research on vision has focused on the overall structure of visual systems, it brings out issues of modularity clearly. Therefore, this part of the book is organized around computational theories.

David Marr's (1982) theory of vision constitutes the most ambitious and explicit set of claims for a highly modular structure to the visual system. In chapter 19 I discuss the issues raised by Marr's approach as well as several general issues in visual perception and cognition. Arbib, in chapter 17, critically examines claims about visual modularity and develops a theoretical and empirical argument for a high degree of cooperative computation among small modules. Burge's chapter (18) is a philosophical explication of Marr's naturalistic claim that the visual system embodies numerous assumptions about the physical nature of the visible world.

Varieties of Modularity

It is a commonplace belief in cognitive science that complex computational systems are at least weakly decomposable into components. That is, it is assumed that there exists a decomposition of the system such that the computational interactions within components are much more complex than those between components. This constitutes a very general notion of modularity that can be developed in a variety of ways, which can be difficult to distinguish both theoretically and empirically.

Fodor (1983) develops a notion of strong modularity. First, he has a theory of which cognitive systems are highly modular and which are not. Input systems are argued to be modular, and central systems are argued to be nonmodular. He argues that the visual system as a whole is a computational module that takes retinal inputs and delivers basic object identification as its output. He also discusses the submodules of the visual system proposed by Marr. Second, at the computational level of analysis he argues that modules are strongly encapsulated. Other processes cannot affect the internal workings of a module, and the information flow from input modules to central processes is largely—possibly exclusively—bottom-up. In the visual system, it is argued, high-level expectations about the content of a scene can have no, or only very small, effects on the processing of low-level visual information. Third, at the neurophysiological level of analysis Fodor argues that the computational modules are directly implemented in fixed neuronal structures that show highly characteristic ontogenetic development, probably with a high degree of genetic determination. There is considerable psychological and neurophysiological evidence that the structure and function of the primate visual system is highly predetermined and well developed in early infancy, given a normal visual environment.

Strong modularity is theoretically interesting only if the modules perform rather complex computations. If the largest modules in the visual system are small components, such as local feature detectors or schemas for individual objects, then strong modularity, even if correct, is not very interesting. Arbib's critique of strong modularity in chapter 17 can be seen as a claim that the modules in the visual system are indeed quite small and that the cooperative interaction among them is rich and important.

The theoretical character of strong modularity also depends on the claim that modular structure is fixed rather than modifiable. There are various forms of weak modularity that are hard to distinguish empirically from strong modularity. One possible form of weak modularity arises from the considerable developmental plasticity of input systems. The brain does have capacities to reorganize itself in response to early injuries or to gross distortions of the normal environment. It is possible that some forms of plasticity violate strong modularity, or at least particular formulations of it. For example, some computational function might be taken over by an unexpected chunk of neural tissue, or two computational modules might begin interacting to compensate for a deficit caused by injury or by a shift in the available environmental information. It is also, of course, possible that the reorganizations would prove to be precisely restricted by a hypothesized modular decomposition. In this case reorganization would always be a matter of setting various restricted parameters on the computations within modules and the communication between them. To date, the existing literature on developmental plasticity in the visual system has not been carefully reviewed in terms of the strong-modularity thesis.

More generally, we might say that weakly modular systems become modularized in a particular way because of contingencies in the task environment or the information-processing system but are potentially nonmodular, or modularizable in a different way, given other contingencies. One form of system contingency is time-course modularity. It may be that the computation of a certain piece of potentially useful information takes too long for it to contribute to some visual process or task. The point here is that there may be no other barrier to the use of the information. If the temporal demands of the task were slowed down, or if the slow computation were speeded up via diet or intensive practice, then a computational, and neural, interaction might appear. An example of contingency in the task environment might be called modularity by cue validity. A system that is potentially sensitive to a wide range of information sources might become tuned to those that are most valid and might cease to show effects of the others.

There is, in fact, a tremendous amount of weak modularity in human visual cognition that arises from the general characteristics of skill acquisition. Well-practiced skills become highly modularized, and it is arguable that they can meet all the criteria for strong modularity except the unmodifiability criterion. They are extremely fast relative to general problem-solving activity, and they make minimal demands on attention. They are mandatory in the sense that they are automatically triggered by their stimulus conditions without conscious intent or control. (The Stroop phenomenon is the classic demonstration here.) They are informationally encapsulated in the sense that clusters or sequences of computation that consistently recur are chunked or compiled so that they run autonomously. During acquisition they pass through a series of typical and well-defined stages. There is even some evidence that they can be implemented in identifiable parts of the brain. Visual letter and word recognition, which are visual skills in the above sense, can be selectively impaired by brain damage in the pure alexias (Hécaen and Albert 1978). Hart, Berndt, and Caramazza (1985) recently reported a patient who had selectively lost the ability to name fruits and vegetables.

A final form of weak modularity arises from what might be called failure of reduction. The strong-modularity thesis apparently includes the claim that modules identified by information-processing criteria will map neatly onto modules identified by physiological criteria. It is a commonplace that neat mappings from the cognitive to the physical level do not necessarily hold in complex systems. In fact, they do not hold for most computer programs in high-level languages runnings on general-purpose computers. Failure of reduction could occur in human cognition in a number of ways. To take one example, suppose that the uniform cognitive architecture proposed by Anderson (1983) turned out to be the best description of the human mind at the information-processing level. Thus, the same principles of learning in production systems turn out to explain first-language learning, high school geometry learning, motor-skill learning, and so on. Nevertheless, it also turns out that a different combination of cortical areas is involved in each of these tasks. It also turns out that there are some constraints on the ways in which the cortical areas can influence each other, which have anatomical and physiological explanations. In this case, strong modularity at the physiological level would have a minimal role in computational theory. At the computational level, the constraints on interaction would have no theoretical explanation and would simply appear as arbitrary limitations. The overwhelming theoretical generalization would be that the same data structures and algorithms occur everywhere, and that cooperative influences are never blocked by computational considerations. In such a world, psychological evidence that reflected neurophysiological modularity could easily masquerade as evidence for computational modularity. More generally, failures of reduction could occur between two levels of abstraction in computational analysis, with modularity at a lower level and powerful uniform principles at a higher level.

The pervasiveness of weak modularity and its ability to mimic strong modularity require an extensive network of converging evidence to evaluate claims of strong modularity. Research on vision provides one of the best testing grounds for evaluating strong modularity in input systems. Marr (1982) developed a compelling theoretical framework for exploring the nature of modularity in the visual system.

Modularity in Marr's Theory of Vision

Marr's theory of vision, presented in detail in Marr 1982 and summarized and explained quite effectively in Mayhew and Frisby 1984 and Bruce and Green 1985, contains two distinct claims about modularity. The first claim is that low-level or early visual processes constitute a module in Fodor's strong sense. The second claim is that there are submodules within the low-level vision system.

To begin with the first claim: It is hypothesized that the visual system computes a representation called the $2\frac{1}{2}$-D sketch from retinal input without top-down influences from expectations about the content of the current scene or partial analyses of the content. The retinal input is idealized to be a stereoscopic 2-dimensional image varying in time, delivered to stationary and computationally homogeneous retinas. No attempt is made to model eye movements or the dual organization of biological retinas into central and peripheral areas that perform different computations. The $2\frac{1}{2}$-D sketch closely resembles Gibson's (1966) classical notion of the layout of surfaces in the visual world. Formally, the $2\frac{1}{2}$-D sketch explicitly represents two pieces of information about each point or small patch in the input image: the approximate distance of the point from the observer, and the local orientation of the surface containing the point. In addition, the contours created by discontinuities in surface orientation or depth are explicitly represented. Discontinuities in surface orientation are created when two surfaces of an object meet in a sharp crease, e.g. the edge between two visible faces of a cube. Discontinuities in depth occur at the visible boundaries of an object, which separate it from a background surface that is farther away. The $2\frac{1}{2}$-D sketch does not contain explicit representations of the shapes of surfaces or objects, nor does it contain descriptions or identifications of objects.

The hypothesis that the $2\frac{1}{2}$-D sketch can be and is computed from retinal input without top-down influence has been disputed both in computer vision research and in classical perceptual theory. In chapter 17, Arbib argues that vision involves substantial cooperative interaction between high-level and low-level visual processes. Perceptual psychologists who are roughly in the Helmholtzian tradition typically argue that higher-level knowledge is necessary for the determination of the depths and orientations of surfaces, or at least that it does in fact substantially influence these determinations.

Given the assumption that low-level vision is a module, the hypothesis that the $2\frac{1}{2}$-D sketch represents the interface between high-level and low-level vision is also a significant empirical claim. Fodor (1983) argues that the visual module ought to make a basic description or identification of visual objects available.

The second claim about modularity is that low-level vision is a two-stage process and that each of the stages can be seen as a module that is further broken down into submodules. In the first stage the input image is converted into a representation called the primal sketch; in the second stage the primal sketch is converted into the $2\frac{1}{2}$-D sketch. There is no cooperative computation between the two stages, and the primal sketch is the main interface between them, although in some cases the second stage works on information that precedes the primal sketch.

The primal sketch explicitly represents the locations in the image at which there is a significant intensity change. Intensity changes that line up in a small local region are explicitly represented as an edge segment with a particular length, orientation, and contrast. The sketch also represents bars (formed by nearby, parallel segments) and blobs (formed by segments that enclose small areas). The primal sketch is computed in two stages. First the image is filtered at several spatial scales to find intensity changes, which are then locally grouped to form the raw primal sketch, containing the edges, bars, and blobs. Physiologically, the spatial filters are identified with the retinal-ganglion and lateral-geniculate-nucleus cells that have circular on-center or off-center receptive fields. The raw primal sketch is associated with the cortical simple cells discovered by Hubel and Wiesel. Marr marshals considerable psychophysical and physiological evidence that his computational scheme is a good model of biological visual systems at this level.

The full primal sketch is computed from the raw primal sketch by various grouping operations that explicitly represent the larger-scale organization of the tokens in the raw sketch. The grouping operations can cluster tokens into regions defined by (for example) average local intensity, size, and orientation. They can detect continuous contours formed by local edge segments that line up over larger parts of the image. They can also form virtual lines, for example, when the terminations of a group of segments are geometrically aligned. The hypothesized grouping operations are reasonably well supported by psychophysical studies of texture perception and Glass-pattern perception. The physiological locus of the grouping operations is not identified. They are not hypothesized to feed back to the spatial filters or to the operators that form local edges, bars, and blobs. Thus, the computation of the primal sketch has a highly structured and modular character.

In the second stage of low-level vision, the primal sketch is converted into the $2\frac{1}{2}$-D sketch. This computation is again broken down into several modular subcomponents, which work independently and in parallel on various kinds of information developed during primal-sketch computation. For example, a stereopsis module works on retinal-disparity values to develop local depth information for the $2\frac{1}{2}$-D sketch. Julesz's (1971) experiments with random-dot stereograms provide evidence for the modular nature of stereopsis. In these experiments, observers were able to perceive depth in displays that contained disparity information but were random otherwise. Richards (1971) used random-dot stereograms to demonstrate that some people show specific patterns of anomalous stereo vision that accord well with the types of disparity-sensitive cells that have been observed in monkey cortex. Marr and his associates ended up not using the primal sketch as the input to the stereopsis module. The empirical evidence and various aspects of the computational problem led them to use the output of the spatial filtering process prior to the primal sketch. This is an example of fine-grained modular structure, emphasized by Arbib in chapter 17, in which multiple representations of the input image are computed and fed to other processes. Other examples of modules contributing to the $2\frac{1}{2}$-D sketch are a visual-motion module that provides local depth information and a shape-from-shading module that extracts local surface orientation from shading information.

Computations are also hypothesized to occur within the $2\frac{1}{2}$-D sketch. The various modules contributing information to it (stereopsis, motion, etc.) will deliver more or less complete and mutually inconsistent information. Some sort of cooperative computation, which Marr did not describe in detail, is needed to extract a single, optimal, and consistent representation. In addition, the input modules may supply no information at some points or local patches in the image. These areas may be filled in by interpolation computations, which were studied computationally by Grimson (1981). The work on interpolation was inspired by evidence from very sparse random-dot stereograms. For stereograms with two disparity values, subjects perceive continuous planar surfaces in depth rather than isolated dots in depth even when the dot density is 2–3%. Grimson's attempt to get additional psychophysical evidence concerning the interpolation of curved surfaces showed evidence of more complex interpolation as well, although subjects had trouble localizing the perceived surface precisely relative to a probe dot.

It appears that Marr's avoidance of cooperative influences across the modules that contribute to the $2\frac{1}{2}$-D sketch during computation had empirical, theoretical, and heuristic motivations. There are psychophysical studies that lend empirical support to the independence of some of the hypothesized modules. In these experiments a visual display that is random except for one source of information leads to the perception of surfaces in depth. Julesz's random-dot stereograms, mentioned above, are the classic case. Similarly, displays that are random except for well-behaved visual motion can deliver depth perception (Braunstein 1976; Ullman 1979). Theoretically, Marr argued that each source of information represented an independent physical process in the world and that therefore it was possible and efficient to design computations independently. Heuristically, he argued that it was good research strategy to see how much information could be recovered from each source before leaning on the crutch of interaction with other sources.

The computation of the $2\frac{1}{2}$-D sketch is a good example of the subtlety of claims about strong modularity, which are also illustrated in detail in Fodor's (1983) discussion of the computation of grammatical form. On the one hand, the immediate input processes to the $2\frac{1}{2}$-D sketch are hypothesized to be completely independent, parallel, and data driven. On the other hand, the outputs of these processes are subjected to cooperative computation. Since the cooperative computation is completely restricted to one representational level within the visual domain, it is consistent with Fodor's hypothesis. On the other hand, other computer vision systems show complex mixtures of modularity and cooperation. The heuristic value and the empirical substance of the modularity thesis, at least insofar as it concerns information flow, are in danger of collapsing. If every theory has some modules and some highly interactive computation, then perhaps the only question is: Which theory is correct in detail? In chapter 17 Arbib devotes a good deal of argument to just this point. On this view, the only residual issue concerning the structure of computation might be the degree and the downward extent of top-down information flow.

Naturalism and Strong Modularity

The thesis of strong modularity is quite closely related to the prospects of naturalism in theories of cognition. Information processes are both purely formal and representational. Most cognitive scientists probably assume that cognitive theories should account for both the formal and the representational aspects of cognition. Fodor (1981) argued that purely formal accounts of information-processing systems were in principle possible, and in addition that they were the only kind of account likely to be forthcoming. He called the research strategy of sticking with purely formal accounts "methodological solipsism." A theory of the representational aspect of a cognitive system is a theory of the relation between the system and the world that accounts for the system's adaptive, or semantic, success. Representational theories, therefore, seem to require a theory, or at least a comprehensive description, of the world as well as of the internal computational workings of a system. Fodor was not enthusiastic about taking on the world as well as the mind.

One motive for an interest in cognitive modules is the hope that organism-environment relations can be rigorously characterized for the limited domain of a module. The particular attraction of Fodor's (1983) strong-modularity position is that he confines solipsistic pessimism to central mental processes. It seems plausible that the input systems do have well-defined domains and that the range of representational relations is fixed by biology.

In chapter 18 Burge addresses an important philosophical question about purely formal accounts of the mind. Such accounts are individualistic in the sense that they explain and predict the individual's behavior without reference to the world. Burge uses Marr's theory to argue that, under the naturalistic assumptions of Marr's theory, any individualistic account of visual perception will fail.

In chapter 19, I explore several issues in the modularity of vision further. The links between modularity and naturalism in Marr's theory are compared with those posited in classical perceptual theories. Three challenges to hypothesized modularity in the visual system are then discussed: cooperative computation, the problem of object recognition, and interactions between vision and language.

17

Modularity and Interaction of Brain Regions Underlying Visuomotor Coordination

Michael A. Arbib

Modules in the Brain

It is a standard notion that one can analyze a complex system by decomposing it into a set of interacting subsystems. Such a decomposition succeeds insofar as one can understand the relation between the inputs and the outputs of each individual subsystems and insofar as interactions between the subsystems can be explained via suitable connections between various of their inputs and outputs without further analysis of variables internal to the subsystems. Such a decomposition is structural to the extent that the subsystems can be mapped onto physical substructures of a physical structure embodying the overall system. In this section I show that neuroscientists have long sought structural decompositions of the brain and have in some cases referred to the physical substructures as *modules*. Recently, Fodor has popularized the use of the term *module* to denote a unit in a functional decomposition of a cognitive system. (Though modular subsystems in Fodor's sense must meet constraints beyond those specified above.) I shall argue that Fodor's analysis of cognitive systems is flawed and that the restrictions he introduces are not useful. Consequently, I shall use the term *module* as a synonym for the term *subsystem* as used above.

The work of the nineteenth-century neurologists led us to think of the brain in terms of large interacting regions, each with a more or less specified function. This localization was reinforced by the work of the anatomists who at the turn of the century subdivided the cerebral cortex on the basis of cell characteristics (cytoarchitectonics). It was at this same time that the discoveries of the neuroanatomist Ramon y Cajal and the neurophysiologist Sherrington helped establish the neuron doctrine, leading us to view the function of the brain in terms of the interaction of discrete units: the neurons. The issue for the brain theorist, then, is to map complex functions, behaviors, and patterns of thought upon the interactions of these rather large entities, the anatomically defined brain regions, or these very small and numerous components, the neurons. This has led many neuroscientists to look for structures intermediate in size and complexity between brain regions and neurons to provide stepping stones in an analysis of how neural structures subserve various functions. One early example was the Scheibels' (1958) suggestion that the reticular formation could be approximated by a stack of "poker chips" each incorporating a large number of neurons receiving roughly the same input and providing roughly the same output to their environments. This modular decomposition of the reticular formation provided the basis for the RETIC model (Kilmer, McCulloch, and Blum 1969). In another direction, the theoretical ideas of Pitts and McCulloch (1947) and the empirical observations of Lettvin, Maturana, McCulloch, and Pitts (1959) on the frog visual system suggested that one might think of important portions of the brain in terms of interacting layers of neurons, with each layer being retinotopic in that the position of neurons in the layer was correlated with position on the retina, and thus in the visual field. The work of Powell and Mountcastle (1959) in somatosensory cortex and that of Hubel and Wiesel (1974) in visual cortex established the notion of the column as a "vertical" aggregate of cells in visual cortex, again working on a common set of inputs to provide a well-defined set of outputs. With all these considerations, the notion of the brain as an interconnected set of modules—intermediate in complexity between neurons and brain regions—was well established. Consider, for example, the following passage from Szentagothai and Arbib 1974:

> The concept of a modular structure or arrangement of the neuropil has two basic sources:
>
> (1) a more indirect one from the notion that neuronal networks ought to be subdivided into distinct functional units; and
>
> (2) a direct one from observation of the neuropil.... Recent anatomical data on the cerebral cortex suggest the existence of both a fine grain and coarse grain of modular organization.

Subsequently, Mountcastle (1978) wrote:

> The large entities of the brain we know as areas (or nuclei) ... are themselves composed of replicated ... modules.... Each module processes information from its input to its output and in that processing imposes transforms determined by the general properties of the entity and its extrinsic connections.... Closely linked ... subsets of modules ... form precisely connected but distributed systems.... A single module of an entity may be a member of several (but not many) such systems.

With this, it is clear that the concept of a module is well established within neuroscience as a structural entity. However, the task of this paper is to confront it with the notion of a module as a functional entity, as developed in the elegant monograph *The Modularity of Mind* by Jerry Fodor (1983).

To see this, it will help to distinguish what has been called top-down brain theory from bottom-up theory, and to see how they are brought together in what might be called "middle-out" brain theory. Top-down theory is essentially functional in nature, in that it starts with the isolation of some overall function, such as some pattern of behavior or linguistic performance or type of perception, and seeks to explain it by decomposing it into the interaction of a number of subsystems. What makes this exercise brain theory as distinct from cognitive psychology is that the choice of subsystems is biased in part by what we know about the function of different parts of the brain, as obtained (for example) by analysis of the effects of brain lesions, so that there is some attempt to map the subsystems onto anatomical regions.

In bottom-up brain theory, the emphasis tends to be on neural circuits. Given a specific set of neurons, the attempt is made to use them to implement a given function, or to analyze given circuitry to determine what functions it can perform. Clearly, the primary sources of data for such bottom-up brain theory come from both neuroanatomy (in looking at the detailed interconnections of neurons) and neurophysiology (in studying the behavior of the network under varying conditions).

In its full development, brain theory incorporates a cycle of both top-down and bottom-up modeling. An attempt is made to map functional units onto brain regions, constrained for example by lesion studies. But this map is not one to one, and a further constraint is to try to implement regional functions via neural networks meeting anatomical and physiological constraints. Not only may new information yield different suggestions as to how circuitry may subserve a given function; it also may lead to changes in our ideas about how functions are distributed around the regions of the brain. In particular, we shall see that there is a continual tension between functional decomposition and structural decomposition, that in general a given "functional module" may be subserved by the interaction of several "brain modules," and that a given "brain module" may be involved in subserving a number of different functions—as was indeed suggested by the quote from Mountcastle above.

Fodor's Taxonomy of the Mind

For Fodor, a computational theory of cognitive science seeks a set of mechanisms each of which provides a characteristic pattern of transformations of mental represntations [F13].* For him, a computational process is by definition syntactic [F40]. Motivated by Gall's view of faculties, Fodor

---

*[F13] refers to page 13 of Fodor 1983. [FIII.5] refers to section III.5 of that volume.

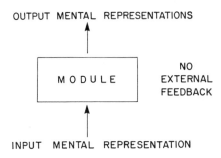

OUTPUT MENTAL REPRESENTATIONS

MODULE

NO
EXTERNAL
FEEDBACK

INPUT   MENTAL   REPRESENTATION

Figure 1
A key property of a module is that it be computationally autonomous and informationally encapsulated. Moreover, its input cannot depend upon its output via paths internal to the cognitive system in which it is embedded.

seeks cognitive mechanisms that form modules in the sense that they are [F21, F37]

(i)   domain-specific,
(ii)   innately specified,
(iii) associated with distinct neural structures, and
(iv)   computationally autonomous.

I shall not address claims (ii) and (iii), but shall restrict myself to setting forth my argument that cognitive science will not be served by an emphasis on domain-specific and computationally autonomous modules.

The term *domain-specific* seems to refer to gross modalities like "vision" or "language" rather than to Gall's faculties or the "domains" or "microworlds" of current research in artificial intelligence. The key concept is that of *computational autonomy*: Modules "do not share, and hence do not compete for, such horizontal resources as memory, attention, judgment, intelligence, etc." [F21]. More generally, the modules considered by Fodor are *informationally encapsulated* [FIII.5], which means that, while there may be internal feedback between the representations within the module, these internal representations are not involved in paths to or from external modules. Moreover, Fodor argues that there is no external feedback path whereby the output of the module can affect its input (figure 1).

Fodor argues for an exclusive but not exhaustive functional taxonomy of the mind as divided into transducers, input systems, and central processors [F41]. He views the input systems as delivering representations that are most naturally interpreted as characterizing the arrangement of things in the world [F42]. He then lumps perceptual systems with language as constituting the input systems, with the note [F45] that the correspondence between (say) visual stimuli and distal layouts is underwritten by (roughly)

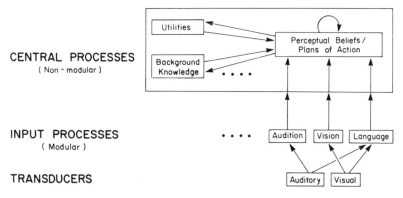

Figure 2
Fodor's taxonomy of the mind. The arrows linking the central processes have no significance other than to indicate the promiscuity of data flow, which renders the central processes nonmodular. In contrast, the lack of feedback paths around each input process is crucial to Fodor's theory.

the laws of light reflectance, whereas the correspondence between token utterances and distal layouts is underwritten by (roughly) a convention of truth-telling that makes it possible to infer from what one hears to the way the world is.

Fodor's central hypothesis about the mind is that the input systems (perceptual systems and language) are precisely the modules of the mind— "domain-specific computational systems characterized by informational encapsulation, high speed, restricted access, and neural specificity" [F101]. "The input systems being informationally encapsulated compute representations of the distal layout on the basis of less information about the distant layout than the organism has available. Such representations want correction in the light of background knowledge and of the simultaneous results of analysis in other domains. Call the process of arriving at such corrected representations 'the fixation of perceptual belief.'" [F102]

Fodor then argues [F103] that an interface between perception and utilities must take place somewhere if we are to use the information that input systems deliver to determine how we ought to act. Then he argues that these central processes for thought and problem solving are unencapsulated and so are not plausibly viewed as modular [F103]. Although Fodor gives no diagrams in his book, his theory of the mind is, I think fairly, captured in my figure 2.

Some comments are in order. First, I reiterate that Fodor's use of "domain" seems to refer to "language or a sensory modality." Second, Fodor gives no analysis of action and motor control, so it is open as to whether or not he would regard these as modular, e.g., with modules for locomotion,

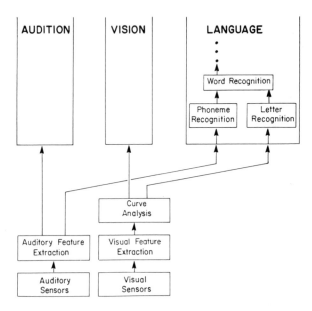

Figure 3
A hypothetical refinement of the transducers and input processes of figure 2.

manipulation, and speech. But third—and this provides the starting point for my critique—Fodor is silent about which transducers feed the language module. Ignoring braille, I have arbitrarily shown auditory and visual transducers providing this input. But once one insists that, e.g., the visual transducers deliver input to vision, audition, and language without cross-talk between these modules (for such cross-talk would break the posited informational encapsulation), the transducers no longer "merely" transduce sensory signals, but carry out some moderately sophisticated transformations of their own, as sketched in figure 3. For example, since the visual recognition of curves is helpful both in seeing objects and in recognizing letters, we must make this curve analysis part of the visual transducer or else we must see it as constituting an input module that is not domain specific. In either case, the distinction between transducers and input processes now seems less comfortable, and it will become even less comfortable if we try to refine the language, vision, and touch modules in a way that will accommodate the learning of Braille and sign language, for then the intermixing of language with touch and motor control will make claims for the informational encapsulation of the modules of figure 2 well nigh untenable.

However, my fundamental point is that Fodor's modules are too large. It is clear from figure 3 that a computational theory of cognition must use a far finer grain of analysis than that offered by Fodor (figure 2). Fodor offers big modules, argues vociferously that they are computationally autonomous, and despairs at the problem of explaining the central processes, since they are not informationally encapsulated. My approach, in contrast, is to analyze the brain in terms of smaller components. Since the interactions between these components play a vital role in my models, the case for the autonomy of large modules becomes less plausible—a useful measure of parsimony, rather than a fundamental principle.

In the next three sections I shall try to exemplify this approach to the study of modularity and interaction of brain regions by looking at a number of models of visual perception and of visuomotor coordination. In the first two and one-half of these sections, I will be guided by the slogan I set forth in *The Metaphorical Brain* (Arbib 1972) that "the brain should be modeled in terms of distributed action-oriented computation in layered somatotopically organized machines." The term *distributed* emphasizes the notion that the brain is made up of many different systems which are simultaneously active and so is not to be modeled in terms of serial computation, in which one localized operation is conducted at a time. In addition, the notion that the brain is "action oriented" emphasizes that we should not think of vision (e.g.) purely in terms of rendering some sort of objective representation of the visual world within the brain, but that rather we should ask how that visual representation can provide information that is relevant to the activity of that particular organism. For example, we shall see that the visual system of a frog is quite different from the visual system of a human, even though we shall at the same time strive to find general principles that will help us understand what is involved in the structure of these systems. Finally, the slogan that the brain is "a layered somatotopically organized machine" will correspond to the claim, made above, that many parts of the brain can be analyzed in terms of the interaction of layers of similar components. However, I will point out that there are processes that do not seem to be naturally thought of in terms of somatotopic or retinotopic computation in a layered structure. This will serve to introduce the notion of *schema* as a fine-grained functional module, corresponding to (e.g.) the knowledge required to recognize a house or grasp a mug. I shall offer no data on the extent to which schemas may be considered psychologically or neurophysiologically verifiable, but shall simply show their computational role in a model of high-level vision. In other writings, I have presented the notion in the context of general visuomotor coordination (Arbib 1981), developed its use for explaining skilled manual behavior (Arbib and House 1987), and explored with my colleagues the use of schemas in developing various models of language (Arbib, Conklin, and Hill 1986).

Depth Perception

A chapter in brain theory usually starts by trying to characterize some overall function which one thinks might constitute a "brain module" in that one might hope to find specific brain circuitry devoted to its implementation. For example, it seems reasonable to think that "solving differential equations" would not be a suitable module for such a study, and that our eventual understanding of its brain implementation will come by seeing how cerebral circuitry capable of implementing many different human skills can be tuned by experience and instruction to subserve this particular mathematical ability. In contrast, we have every reason to think of vision as having special circuitry, from the retina of the eye to the tectum of the midbrain and the lateral geniculate nucleus of the thalamus up to a number of regions designated as visual cortex. In fact, the work of the last twenty years has taken us beyond this conception; we now talk of the "many visual systems," having found that there are tens of anatomically distinct brain regions each subserving distinctive functions of vision. Within this context, then, we may seek to find natural functional modules that subserve part of the task of vision, thus focusing our attention on a more restricted system of neural circuitry. One such natural candidate is depth perception, which enables us to determine the world in terms of objects located at various distances from us. This is clearly very important from an action-oriented perspective, since the way in which we will interact with objects will depend crucially on how near or far they may be.

It is a familiar experience from using stereo viewers that the view of a three-dimensional scene presented at the left eye differs from that presented to the right eye, and that the disparity or displacement between these two images provides the crucial cue to the distance in space from which they come. A key concern of the nineteenth century was whether depth perception comes before or after pattern recognition. Is it that the brain takes the image from each eye separately to recognize (e.g.) a house, and then uses the disparity between the two house images to recognize the depth of the house in space; or is it that our visual system matches local stimuli presented to both eyes, thus building up a depth map of surfaces and small objects in space which provides the input for perceptual recognition? It was the great achievement of Bela Julesz to invent the method of random-dot stereograms. These are stimulus pairs each of which contains only visual noise. They are, however, so designed that when presented in stereo, one to each eye, they yield visual information. Patches of random light and dark presented to one retina were identical to, but at varying disparities from, patches of light and dark presented to the other retina. Julesz found that human subjects were in fact able to carry out the appropriate matching to see surfaces stippled with random patterning at varying depths in space. In other words, without precluding that some depth perception could follow pattern recognition, he established that the forming of a depth map of space could precede the recognition of pattern. He offered a model of this process in terms of cooperative computation involving an array of magnetic dipoles connected by springs.

For the brain theorist, the following issue was thus raised: Could the depth map be computed by a cooperative process involving realistic neurons? The data on what constituted realistic neurons were provided by Barlow and various co-workers. One of the first papers to address this issue was that by Arbib, Boylls, and Dev (1974), who built a neural-net cooperative-computation model for building the depth map "guided by the plausible hypothesis that our visual world is made up of relatively few connected regions." The neural manifold of this model had cells whose firing level represented a degree of confidence that a point was located at a corresponding position in three-dimensional space. The neurons were so connected via inhibitory interneurons as to embody the principle that cells that coded for nearby direction in space and similar depth should excite one another whereas cells that corresponded to nearby direction in space and dissimilar depth should inhibit one another. It was shown by computer simulation (Dev 1975) and later established by mathematical analysis (Amari and Arbib 1977) that this system did indeed yield a segregation of the visual input into connected regions. Later, a variant of this model was published by Marr and Poggio (1976), and in subsequent writings Marr took the "plausible hypothesis that our visual world is made up of relatively few connected regions" and showed how it could be developed into an elegant mathematical theorem relating the structure of a depth perception algorithm to the nature of surfaces in the physical world.

With this work, then, it was established that the perception of depth maps could be constructed by a method of computation that was guided by the hypothesis that the world was made up of surfaces, and that the algorithm could involve some form of cooperative computation. However, the cooperative-computation algorithms discussed above exhibited false minima. Consider, for example, a picket fence. Suppose by pure randomness that the system starts by matching a number of fence posts presented to one eye with the images of their neighbors one to the left presented to the other eye. In the cooperative-computation model, this initial mismatch could co-opt the possible choices of neighbors and lead to a high-confidence estimate that the fence was at a different depth from that at which it actually occurred. This provides a local "energy minimum" for the algorithm. The question then arises of how one could come up with an alogirthm that would avoid at least some of these false minima. The answer provided by Marr and Poggio (1979) can be seen as rooted in two contributions, one from machine vision and one from psychophysics. Within the machine-vision community, such workers as Rosenfeld and Hanson and Riseman had put forward the idea of pyramids or processing cones—the notion that one could look at a visual image at different scales of resolution, and that for some problems a blurred image would allow one to quickly extract a first approximation to needed information about the image (information that would in fact be costly and time consuming to extract when working at the full detail of the original image). Meanwhile, the Cambridge school of psychophysicists headed by Fergus Campbell had discovered that the brain itself appeared to employ a form of multiple levels of resolution—that there were cells tuned to different spatial frequencies, and that these spatial frequencies tended to fall into four or perhaps five different channels. This led Marr and Poggio to develop a system in which, with hardly any cooperative computation, a fairly confident rough depth estimate for different surfaces could be made using the low-spatial-frequency channels, and then a more detailed spatial map could be sculpted on the first approximation through the more detailed disparity information provided via channels of higher spatial frequency. Subsequent psychophysical studies by Frisby and Mayhew have shown that there is much to be said for this model as a model of human depth perception. They have, however, also provided data which have led to refinements in the model, and which suggest that some measure of cooperativity is required. Prazdny has come up with further material for modifying and changing the model.)

However, the fact that a brain mechanism is employed to implement a particular functional module by the brain of one animal does not imply that this is the mechanism used by a distinct species. It is known that frogs and toads can snap with moderate accuracy at prey located in the monocular visual field, and this led Ingle et al. (1982) to hypothesize that for the frog it was accomodation, focal-length information for the lens, that subserved depth perception. More detailed experiments by Collett (1982), involving placing on the nose of the toad spectacles holding either prisms or lenses, showed that the story was more complex. Collett was able to show that the monocular animal did indeed use accommodation as the depth cue, but that in an animal with prey in the binocular field the major depth cue was disparity, with accommodation cues exerting perhaps a 6 percent bias on the depth judgment based on disparity. This led House (1982) to suggest that another route to solving the problem of false minima was to use accommodation cues to bias disparity. This is exemplified by figure 4, which shows two depth maps corresponding to two "worms" presented as visual targets to the simulated toad. In the accommodation map, the level of activity at a particular position and depth corresponds to how sharp an image was obtained at that position when the lens was focused at the given depth. Thus, the activity has one peak for each worm, but the peak is rather broad, giving poor localization information. In contrast, although the dis-

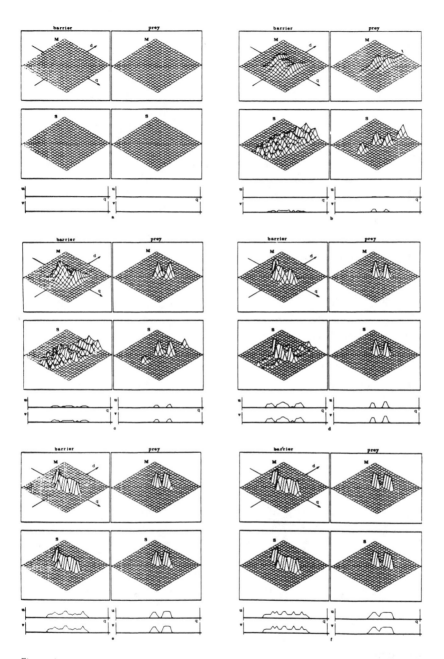

Figure 4
Time course of the model—base case. The time course of the depth model from its initially inert state (a) to a satisfactory depth segmentation (f) is shown here. The full monocular/ binocular model was used with two input planes: one for accommodation and one for disparity. All figures are in the retinal angle vs. disparity coordinate system. Successive figures are temporally spaced $1\frac{1}{3}$ field time constants apart. Thus, the elapsed simulation time represented is nearly seven time constants. The two-dimensional grids show the level of excitation of the various fields, and the line graphs under the grids indicate the intensity and localization along the retinal angle axis of excitation in the inhibitory pools. Source: House 1982.

parity map of depth gained by pairing stimuli on the two eyes gives precise localization of the two worms, it also gives precise localization of the "ghost worms" obtained by matching a stimulus on one eye with the wrong stimulus on the other eye. The key observation here is that the two sources of depth information provide conplementary information. House's model uses a variant of Dev's model to refine the depth estimates within each depth field, but adds mutual coupling between the models so that activity localized within one map helps increase activity at the corresponding locus on the other map. Simply looking at the figure, without knowing any further details, makes it clear that this interaction can yield both a sharpening of the peaks in the accommodation map and a suppression of the "ghost peaks" in the disparity map, so that the process finally converges on a state in which the two maps agree and present a sharp, accurate localization of the targets.

Thus, there is no unique algorithm for solving a given problem, in part because many different sources of information can be employed. Furthermore, any one source of information will be incomplete, and it will often take the skillful deployment of several sources of information—whether it be disparity information at several levels of resolution, or disparity and accommodation information in conjunction—to yield a far better estimate than could be gained by using one source alone. As has been shown, these considerations lead us to a far finer modular decomposition than that offered by Fodor.

Visuomotor Coordination in the Frog and the Toad

In this section, we will return to the action-oriented view of visual perception by looking at something of the behavioral repertoire of frog and toad and asking what type of visual system could make the appropriate information available. That is to say, we seek to determine—in the words of Lettvin et al. (1959)—"what the frog's eye tells the frog's brain." The key to the work of Lettvin et al. was the use of naturalistic stimuli, such as small moving objects similar to the frog's prey of flies and worms. Indeed, Lettvin et al., extending the results of Barlow (1953), found that there were cells in the retina that seemed to serve as "bug detectors," sending information back retinotopically to the tectum (the visual midbrain). They found that the retina not only sent back a map of where the bugs might be but also sent back other maps in spatial register, including a map of where there were large dark moving objects in the visual field. It was also known that an animal without a tectum would not engage in prey-acquisition behavior. This led to the first model of prey acquisition, which involved two modules: the retina (the prey-recognition module) and the tectum (the module subserving motor control for prey acquisition).

A number of experiments by Ewert led to a somewhat more subtle view of the situation. First, he observed that removing the pretectum, a small brain region just in front of the brain tectum, yielded a toad that would snap even at large moving objects. This immediately leads to a different functional decomposition of the brain into modules. Where before we had a module for recognizing prey, now it would seem that we have two distinct modules: one for recognizing moving objects and one for recognizing large moving objects. It is inhibition of prey acquisition by the latter that yields the appearance of a module for the detection of small moving objects *per se*. Further work reviewed by Ewert (1976) replaced the use of naturalistic stimuli with precise patterns to quantify the animal's response. He found that whereas rectangles elongated in their direction of movement (worms) were stimuli of increasing effectiveness with increasing length, an antiworm (a rectangle moving in a direction orthogonal to its long axis) quickly became an ineffective stimulus as it was elongated; a square had an intermediate effect, with bigger squares being more effective stimuli until a certain critical size after which they became less effective. On the basis of this, Ewert and von Seelen came up with the model illustrated here in figure 5, in which the retina was seen as preprocessor of visual stimuli; the pretectum as a module for antiworm recognition, supplying inhibition to the motor output system; and the tectum as comprising two modules, one for worm recognition and one for motor control for prey acquisition. This motor-control module was excited by the worm-recognition module and inhibited by the antiworm-recognition module.

Cervantes, Lara, and Arbib (1985) carried this work further by going from the modules defined purely by an overall linear response function to modules defined by the detailed interaction of neurons. Lara, Arbib, and Cromarty (1982) had built on the neuroanatomical observations of Szekely and Lazar (1976) to define the "tectal column" as a basic cluster of cells working together at one locus in the tectual layers. Cervantes et al. then modeled the tectum (as shown here in figure 6) as an array of such columns interfaced with an array of pretectal "antiworm-detector" neurons, all driven by suitable classes of retinal input, and then showed that this model could explain the spatial and temporal properties of prey-predator discrimination in terms of neural interactions.

In this last model, the process of prey acquisition is subserved by three anatomically defined modules—the retina, the tectum, and the pretectum —but is composed of four different functional modules, at least. The tectum is not separable into distinct anatomical subsystems for its two functions of "worm filtering" and "motor control," although we can certainly discriminate the contributions that different cells make to both these functions. Moreover, the interaction among these three regions is retinotopic, and is mediated by different cellular pathways, so that the tectum

346   Arbib

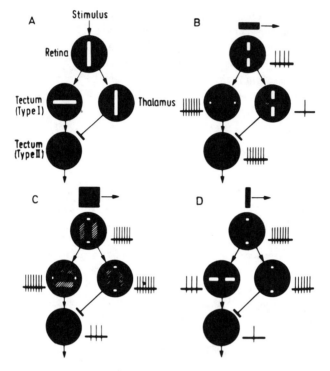

Figure 5
A lumped model of prey-predator discrimination. A worm filter provides excitatory input to an output cell, which also receives inhibitory input from an antiworm cell. The result is that (B) a worm provides a potent response, (C) a square provides an intermediate response, while (D) an antiworm yields little or no response. Source: Ewert and von Seelen 1974.

(e.g.) receives three classes of retinal input as well as a class of tectal input, and these inputs are not all provided to one common input layer for the tectum, but are in fact systematically distributed in layers of termination segregated at different depths and thus making contact with different cell types within the tectum.

Now let us try to embed this set of modules in a functional account of a more complex behavior. Collett has shown that there is a sense in which the toad builds a spatial map of its world. If the toad is confronted by a fence through which it can see a worm, then under some circumstances it will advance directly to snap at the worm, but in many other cases it will sidestep. When it sidesteps around the fence, the direction in which it turns after sidestepping will be correlated closely with the position of the worm, even if the experimentalist has taken care to ensure that the worm is no longer visible at this time. Thus, the animal must make a depth map

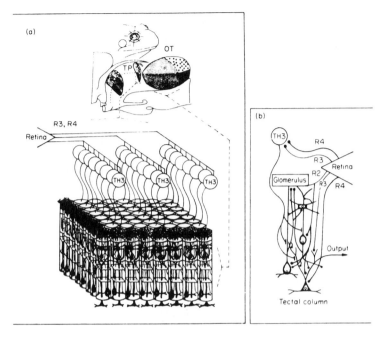

Figure 6
Interactions among retina, optic tectum, and pretectum. The retina sends fibers in a retinotopic fashion to both optic tectum (classes R2, R3, and R4) and pretectum (classes R3 and
R4). (a) TH3 neurons also project retinotopically to the optic tectum. For simplicity, only the
projections of three rows of TH3 cells upon the tectal columns are shown. (b) A closer look
at the interactions among retinal, tectal, and pretectal cells. The TH3 cell of the pretectal
column inhibits LP, SP, and PY of the tectal column, corresponding to its retinotopic
projection. Source: Cervantes-Perez et al. 1985.

including the position of the worm and the position of the fence, and it
must use this map to control a variety of motor behaviors, including
sidestepping, orienting, and snapping. Moreover, Ingle has provided data
showing that snapping and orienting can be dissociated by suitable lesions;
thus, processes to control these behaviors must be localized in different
parts of the brain.

Building on these and other observations, we (Arbib and House 1983)
have advanced a model of the interactions in the brain that subserve this,
and House (1984) has further refined the models of the depth-perception
mechanisms that are involved. The overall structure of the model is shown
in figure 7, and I will not go into any detailed exposition of it here. What I
do want to stress is that there are two distinct modules for depth perception. One provides a map of the position and depth of the barriers in front
of the frog. It is my hypothesis that this depth map is based on the above-

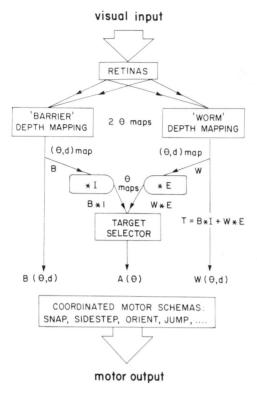

Figure 7
Conceptual schematic of visual/motor pathway. Assumptions made in this diagram are that separate depth maps are maintained for prey and barrier stimuli, that direction for an orientation turn is obtained by combining information from these two depth maps, and that information on preferred orientation and depth of prey and barriers is available simultaneously to motor schemas. These schemas are capable of integrating this information to produce a coordinated motor output. Source: Arbib and House 1987.

discussed constraint that if the world is made up of surfaces, the depth-mapping algorithm can exploit this within its structure. However, when it comes to locating the position of small moving objects in space, this surface constraint is no longer viable; in fact, lesion studies have led House (1984) to come up with a very different model for prey localization, which essentially has each side of the brain select a prey target and then use triangulation to fix its position in space. Pathways linking the two sides of the brain and involving the control of the accommodation of the eyes provide the measure of coherence that will, in most circumstances, ensure that each half of the brain picks the same target. What we have established here is that the output from the two eyes is incorporated not in one low-level visual representation but in two. When we consider how intimately these two are linked with the particular problems of depth and detour behavior, there is no reason to exclude the discovery of yet other visual maps driving the computation of appropriate behavior for the animals. One other comment: Figure 7 decomposes into two quite distinct parts. The retina, the depth-perception maps, and the target selector all function as layered retinotopically organized stuctures. However, the motor schemas for sidestepping, orienting, snapping, and so on are no longer to be thought of as retinotopically coded. Yes, at some point the target of those movements is encoded retinotopically, but the brain stem and the spinal cord must then translate that retinotopic-coordinate specification into parameters of motor-neuron firing. In some sense, the motor schema is then embedded in a neural circuit, which must use patterns of firing to represent parameters in a way quite distinct from the use of location of firing to specify a parameter in a retinotopic or somatopically structured layer.

This section has established not only that cognitive science needs a modular decomposition finer than Fodor's, but also that the choice of modules can be constrained by the data of neuroscience. Since my examples are taken from visuomotor coordination, they are specific to the domain of vision, but they do violate Fodor's argument that modules have no external feedback path whereby the output of the module can affect its input.

The Structure of Visual Systems

In the field of machine vision, it has become commonplace to distinguish "low-level" and "high-level" vision. Basically, *low-level vision* takes the retinal input and codes it into a form suitable for interpretation of, or interaction with, the world, but does not depend upon knowledge of what particular objects are in the world (though it may well depend on general properties of the world, such as the hypothesis that the world is "made up of relatively few connected regions"). *High-level vision* is the process whereby this intermediate representation is used to guide the actual interpretation of the world in terms of objects, or to determine patterns of interaction with, or navigation through, the world.

In the preceding two sections I have given some sense of what can be done in the way of layered computation in the early stages of visual processing. In this section, I will expand the analysis of modular decomposition by showing how the module for low-level vision may be decomposed into a small number of layered submodules, whereas high-level vision is decomposed into the interaction of a vast number of small modules called *schemas*. Such schema networks embody (though I shall not argue this explicitly here) many of the Quineian and isotropic properties that, Fodor holds, characterize central processes and distinguishes them from input modules.

It was J. J. Gibson who, perhaps more than anyone else, drew attention to the immense amount of information about the structure of the world that could be inferred from the properties of surfaces and the way in which they reflected and transformed environmental energy as it passed to the receptors. However, the full impact of this work was delayed because the Gibsonians talked of "direct perception," without addressing what to most of us would seem the self-evident fact that some mechanisms within the brain must be required to carry out the inference back from those environmental energies to the distal objects that transformed them. The sort of work reviewed in the above section on depth perception marked the beginning of the use of Gibson's insights, but in the computational framework that Gibson himself rejected. Marr, as already mentioned, has been in the vanguard of those who would create a computational Gibsonianism; however, his school has paid perhaps too little attention to the lessons that Gibson taught. For example, Shimon Ullman, whose work on motion detection can be seen as giving computational expression to Gibsonian principles, wrote a well-known article ("Against Direct Perception") which, perhaps, let the debates against Gibson's anti-computationalism obscure the debt to him.

In this section, I want to look briefly at the issue of what representations the low-level vision can deliver, and what methods are available for interpreting it. One example was given in the preceding section's discussion of how low-level vision, in the form of barrier-depth mapping and prey-depth mapping, could deliver suitable information to the processes involved in detour behavior and prey acquisition. In this section, I want to turn to two approaches which represent rather the sort of processing that a human brain might go through in coming up with the recognition of the specific object within a visual scene. I shall contrast two overall specifications, one due to Marr and one due to Hanson and Riseman.

As the upper diagram in figure 8 shows, Marr postulates a one-way flow

MARR

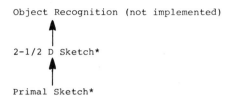

HANSON and RISEMAN

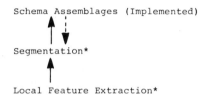

*Layered Computations

Figure 8

from the primal sketch (a fancy name for the sort of feature map that we have come to see as the result of the earlier stages of visual processing, as in the bug detectors in the retina discussed by Lettvin et al. or the edge detectors in the cortex discussed by Hubel and Wiesel). Marr then sees the interface between low-level vision and high-level vision given by the $2\frac{1}{2}$-D sketch, which specifies for each portion of the visual field the depth of the corresponding distal object, and the local orientation of the surface at that point. This then provides the input to the object-recognition process. Marr and Nishihara (in a suggestion that was not implemented on the computer) have suggested that many objects can be represented in terms of the connection of a variety of generalized cylinders, and have suggested how the $2\frac{1}{2}$-D sketch might be processed to find such cylinders, whose description could be used to key a database of known objects.

Whereas Marr's theory is offered as a theory of the way the human visual system must work, Hanson and Riseman's work is offered as a useful way to build a machine-vision system. However, I will draw lessons from both approaches for our understanding of the human mind. First, their system has a process for extracting local features, akin to the primal sketch; but since they are working with the recognition of images provided by

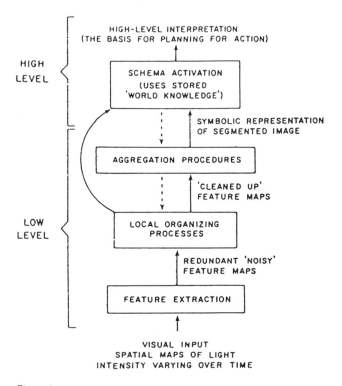

Figure 9

single color photographs, their next level is not a depth map but rather a segmentation of the scene into regions demarcated from one another by such cues as color and texture. The resultant description of the image in terms of regions of various shapes and colors and textures then provides the input for high-level vision, which through a process of cooperative excitation of various schemas leads to the final interpretation of the image, through processes which I will outline later in this section. As will I think be clear from the discussion in the preceding section, it is not my intention to argue that Marr and Hanson are exclusively right in what they offer as the output map from low-level vision to high-level vision. In fact, the colleagues of each have also worked on ways of using the Gibsonian notion of optic flow to map the world in terms of its patterns of movement relative to the observer, and such a movement map enriches the descriptions to be offered by segmentation and depth maps. Thus, I think the correct picture is that low-level vision provides not one but several maps, which can be used (perhaps to different ends) by processes involved in understanding images or determining behavior. I suggest this in figure 9 by

a   b

Figure 10
(a) A house image. (b) The image segmented using low-level segmentation techniques.

showing that local organizing processes and aggregation procedures can provide a symbolic representation of the segmented image without a commitment as to what that representation might be. As I have said, I think that in fact it comprises several representations, and this certainly is borne out by the increasing discovery of the division of the brain into "many visual systems." In the remainder of this section, I simply want to outline the approach that Hanson and Riseman have offered for high-level vision in terms of the interaction of schemas, since this approach embodies some of my own views about the sort of fine-grain functional decomposition of the brain's activity that we are not yet able to follow through to detailed implementation in terms of neural networks (Arbib 1981). I see the reconciliation of the view of functional activity in terms of schema interaction with our growing but still limited knowledge of detailed neurophysiology as the major challenge for brain theory in the next fifteen years.

To complement the above general observations, I shall now present a more concrete discussion of how Hanson and Riseman orchestrate schemas in successful visual perception. Figure 10b shows the result of running segmentation algorithms on the image of figure 10a. The top and bottom of the roof are fairly well delineated, but the left edge is occluded and the right edge "bleeds" into the sky and foliage. This figure also illustrates that highlighting or variation in texture may lead the algorithm to subdivide a natural region into several segments, as it does here for several of the shutters. The problem, then, is to design algorithms that can split a region into parts giving information about different objects, and on the other hand, will aggregate regions that together characterize some distinctive

Figure 11
What is it? See the small box in figure 10a.

portion of the image. The process of *image interpretation* calls on "high-level" information about possible objects in the scene. For example, information about houses would, among other things, initiate a search for a near-parallelogram as a candidate for the roof image. However, the program would not fail if there were no parallelogram in the image; it might then pursue more subtle possibilities, such as "If you find two approximately parallel lines at top and bottom and portions of approximately parallel lines on the left and right, join up the lines, and explore the hypothesis that the resultant parallelogram is a roof." Given a confident roof hypothesis, the system can hypothesize that below the roof the image will contain shutters or windows. Thus, if regions there can be aggregated into a rectangle, the program can indeed follow the hypothesis that there is a rectangle.

Consider figure 11. It is not at all clear from inspection what it is, until one recognizes that it is an enlargement of the portion outlined by the small white box in figure 10a. It is then clear that it is a bush—easy to recognize in context, but hard to recognize out of context. This suggests that in designing a machine vision system, or in understanding the human visual system, we must understand the representation of knowledge—the interactions between schemas—that make this use of context possible.

Figure 12a shows a house set among trees, and figure 12b shows the initial segmentation offered by the low-level vision system. A number of different schemas then work on the image to try to find regions that can be assimilated to their corresponding objects. For example, the sky schema will look for regions that are high in the image and that have a color in the appropriate blue-to-gray range. In this case, the system comes up with a

a

b

c

Figure 12
(a) A second house scene. (b) Its segmentation. (c) The image interpreted as a result of schema interaction.

very confident assessment that what is in fact the sky region is sky and a lower confidence value that the roof (which is in the upper half of the image and which has somewhat sky-like color) could be an instance of sky. The roof schema is able to come up with a much more confident estimate that the roof region is indeed roof; it has the contextual information that the roof region is just beneath a region that has been confidently estimated to be sky, and it also has geometric information which tells it that the roof does indeed have the right shape (a partially occluded parallelogram).

The logic is inherently parallel. Each schema can have a separate instantiation, corresponding to each region for which there is a nontrivial confidence level for the object that the schema represents. All the active schema instantiations can then communicate with one another. In the fashion that we have seen before, the activity of a schema in one region may lead to the instantiation of a schema in another region to check context. If the newly activated schema does indeed find the expected context, then the confidence level of the original schema can be raised. Although research on the implementing of schemas on computer networks is underway, most work is currently done by simulating the interaction of schemas on a serial computer. Thus, a number of scheduling strategies may be imposed upon the logical parallelism of the schemas. However, in what follows I will not discuss these present implementation details; rather, I will stress a number of the properties of schema-based interpretation.

In the present example, the high confidence level of the roof schema activates the house schema and then searches for walls (which, in both senses of the word, support the roof). The confidence level for the wall schema can be increased for a region that not only is beneath the roof but also contains rectangular "cutouts," which could correspond to shutters, doors, or windows.

The foliage schema is activated by finding regions that meet certain color conditions, as is the grass schema. The final interpretation, shown in figure 12c, gives a fairly accurate interpretation of the sky, the foliage, the roof, the wall, some of the shutters, and the grass in the original scene. The system has no information about the roadway, and so this region is left uncharacterized. A number of other regions are also missed by the system.

It may be instructive in trying to understand the use of cooperative computation in an expert system (in this case for schema interpretation) to see what sort of knowledge one would have to add to the system to make it more successful. Let us focus on two aspects of the image in figure 12a that went unnoticed when it was analyzed by the system. The first is the mailbox—the small white rectangle atop a black post on the left side of the image, about halfway up. (The mailbox is in fact a good example of how much specific knowledge must be given to a successful interpretation system. America is one of the few countries in which it is common for mailboxes to be set out near the road on a post in this fashion. Thus, the schema that many non-Americans have for a mailbox will not include objects of this kind.) Even if the knowledge base were augmented to include a mailbox schema, this mailbox would not have been "seen" by the system as currently constituted. This is because a small region is in danger of getting "lost." This could be corrected for by the use of a measure of region salience, which would score the strength of the contrast between a region—even a small one—and the surrounding region. Thus, the distinctive white of the region would focus processing on it to find a schema that matches, rather than allow it to be subsumed as part of the grass.

Perhaps even more interesting is that one of the uninterpreted regions corresponds to a wall of the house peeking through the trees, separated from what has been interpreted as the house. Again, this region can be lost unless a measure of salience focuses more schema activity upon it. What extra knowledge would have to be included in the system for successful processing? First, it would have to be recognized that the color of this region matches the color of the house wall, thus causing the activation of an instantiation of the wall schema to cover that region. This would then cause the activation of shutter schemas to look for rectangular regions of the same color as the shutters already found in the other wall. In the present image, the color of the shutters matches so well the color of the foliage that the shutters are segmented as part of the foliage. However, if a schema were looking for rectangular shape, it would be able to pull out the shutters from the foliage and to come up with a more subtle interpretation of the scene.

The second scene that we shall analyze is the one shown in figure 10a, whose segmentation (figure 10b) lacks a crucial edge: the edge separating the left wall from the sky. In this case the sky schema, looking for a region that is of the right color and is at the top of the image, assigns a high confidence level to the region including the sky and that region of the wall, and the wall schema (assuming that the roof schema has already recognized the roof with high confidence) assigns a high confidence level to regions that extend beneath the roof and have rectangular cutouts—thus assigning the wall hypothesis not only to the front wall but also to the region embracing the side wall and the sky. Our schemas are so designed that when two different schemas assign a very high confidence level to the same region, they then call for low-level processes to resegment that region. The region of contention (figure 13a) is very large, and resegmenting at a greater level of detail in the attempt to find the missing edge is a very expensive process. Here, if the schemas had more knowledge, they would be able to economize. Recognizing that the contention is between wall and sky, they would "know" that if there is a missing edge it should be near the roofline, and they would thus be able to concentrate the finer

a   b

c

Figure 13
Because the segmentation of figure 10b omitted a crucial edge, the large region of (a) is
initially treated as a unit and yields strong activation of both the sky schema and the wall
schema. This conflict triggers a finer segmentation of the region, with the result shown in
(b). On this basis, the system proceeds to yield the final interpretation shown in (c).

segmentation on a small region of the image—in much the way that humans achieve with their eye movements. However, lacking this measure of "intelligence," the present implementation of the system calls for the expensive segmentation of the whole region. Subsequently, all the new subregions (figure 13b) contained in what was earlier one large region will be processed by the sky schema and the wall schema. This time there is no problem; those regions that are at the top of the image and of the right color become sky, while those regions that are below the roofline and abut the rectangles are interpreted as wall. The system then proceeds to the segmentation shown in figure 13c.

This last example makes clear two important principles;

• Cooperative computation is not a one-way process. Although some low-level processing may be required to initiate high-level schema activity, once this schema activity is underway it may call for the low-level processing as appropriate. In fact, in some cases, schema activity may precede low-level processing—as when one scans a room for some object that one needs.

• Intelligence can save a lot of work. In our specific example, we saw that adding a rather small number of high-level rules would allow us to avoid a great deal of expansive, highly parallel, low-level processing.

High-level vision, then, involves the interleaving of multiple processes—a cooperative computation in which each is invoked where appropriate, possibly many times, and hypotheses are generated and discarded until the system converges on as good an interpretation as it is able to give with the facilities available to it. This style is claimed to characterize the perceptual mechanisms of brains, but it also is a useful model for "central" processes.

The Prospect for Modeling Central Processes

I agree with the notion of a module within a cognitive system as a subsystem having a well-defined set of inputs, a well-defined set of outputs, and a well-defined relation between inputs and outputs. This relation may involve the mediation of state variables internal to the module, but the values of these state variables will affect other modules only to the extent that they determine the outputs of the modules. However, in the preceding sections I have sought to establish the following:

• Fodor's modules are only a subclass of modules in this sense, and his defining conditions may even be inconsistent.

• Fodor's modules are too big, in that he would view the visual system as a single module, whereas cognitive science must offer an analysis in which the grain of the modules is at least as fine as that of the rectangle of figure 3, 7, or 9.

• In the light of the preceding point, I reject Fodor's claim that there is no external feedback path whereby the output of the module can affect its input.

• The concept of module is not a new one initiated by Fodor, but has a long history in the functional analysis of cognitive systems and in the structural analysis of brain mechanisms of cognitive functions. The give-and-take between functional and structural (neural) decompositions of cognitive systems provides an important tool for cognitive science.

In this last section, I turn to Fodor's views on central processes. I could argue that the schema interactions posited for high-level vision in the preceding section constitute a viable model for the analysis of central processes, but I shall restrict myself to a critique of three dichotomies offered by Fodor as a grounding for his distinction between input processes and central processes. Rather disarmingly, Fodor admits that "there is practically no direct evidence, pro or con, on the question whether central systems are modular.... When you run out of direct evidence, you might just as well try arguing from analogies, and that is what I propose to do." [F104] He assumes that "the typical function of central systems is the fixation of belief (perceptual or otherwise) by nondemonstrative inference. Central systems look at what the input systems deliver, and they look at what is in memory, and they use this information to constrain the computation of 'best hypotheses' about what the world is like." [F104] This leads Fodor to use scientific confirmation as the analogy to structure his model of central processes. The key to his argument is that scientific confirmation is isotropic (i.e., that facts relevant to the confirmation of scientific hypotheses may be drawn from anywhere in the field of previously established truths) and that it is Quineian (i.e., that "the degree of confirmation assigned to any given hypothesis is sensitive to properties of the entire belief system" [F107]—that the degree of confirmation is based on, for example, a measure of simplicity, plausibility, or conservation that is a metric over global properties of belief system.

Having accepted the force of his analogy, Fodor concludes that "even if the flow of data is unconstrained *within* a module, encapsulation implies constraints upon the access of intramodular processes to extramodular information sources ... [, whereas if] isotropic and Quineian considerations are especially pressing in determining the course of the computations that central systems perform, it should follow that these systems differ in their computational character from the [modules]." [F110–111] On this basis, Fodor claims that the following three taxonomies are coextensive: *functional taxonomy* ("input analysis versus fixation of belief"), *taxonomy by subject matter* ("domain specific versus domain neutral"), and *taxonomy by computational character* ("encapsulated versus Quineian/isotropic") [F112].

He remarks that this coextension, if it holds, is a deep fact about the structure of the mind. I shall argue not only that it does not hold, but that the individual taxonomies are not themselves useful.

Input Analysis vs. Fixation of Belief
Fodor rejects Marr's primal, $2\frac{1}{2}$-D, and 3-D sketches as defining the outputs of the visual processor, since then the visual input module would not provide for the recognition of objects and events. He argues [F94–95] that basic perceptual categories constitute the output of the vision module—these are the "middle levels" in implicational hierarchies, e.g. "dog" rather than "poodle" or "thing". In other words, it follows from Fodor's own account that the visual input module can, with appropriate visual stimulation, deliver to central processes a confident report that the distal stimulus is a dog. But in this case, no further central processing is required to fix the belief "I see a dog". Though it is incontestable that there are many beliefs whose fixation cannot be achieved by input analysis alone, Fodor's own view of the vision module denies that input analysis vs. fixation of belief constitutes a clear dichotomy.

Domain Specific vs. Domain Neutral
This has been a useful taxonomy in artificial intelligence, but Fodor's use of "domain" is different. "Vision" and "language" are domains for him, but "bacterial diagnosis" and "the blocks world" apparently serve only as objects of ridicule. Fodor asserts that early AI tried to "treat central processes as though they were modular. Intellectual capacities were divided into ... arbitrary subdepartments ... and the attempted simulations proceeded by supplying machines with very large amounts of more or less disorganized, highly topic-specific facts and heuristics.... What emerged was a picture of the mind that looked embarassingly like a Sears catalogue.... I take it that the bankruptcy of this sort of AI is self-evident and constitutes a strong prima facie argument that the organization of central processes is, in fact, not modular." [F127; F139, note 43]

However, it not self-evident to me that this approach is bankrupt. I think that many cognitive scientists would agree that it is only by using a "microworld" to reduce problems of ambiguity and to limit the amount of information to be represented in a model that we can make the progress in analyzing process and representation that can provide the inductive base for the inference of more general mechanisms. However, a more telling point in the context of Fodor's argument is that scientific confirmation, his key analogue for central processes, itself looks "like a Sears catalogue." There are scientific societies for the study of physics, biology, chemistry, etc., and the volume of scientific research has grown to such an extent that the work of most scientists is confined to narrow subdisciplines with little communication between them. Within cognitive science, work in linguistics is little affected by work in vision; within linguistics, a researcher in language acquisition may pay little heed to studies of historical phonology. We may decry this specialization, but it is neither "embarassing" nor "self-evidence of bankruptcy." If we accept AI usage, then the dichotomy between domain specificity and domain neutrality does not match Fodor's other dichotomies. An AI model of a central process will often span the dichotomy, using a domain-neutral "inference engine" to process facts from a "domain-specific" database. Many of us would find even this dichotomy mistaken, arguing that knowledge and processes are often intertwined. If we insist on Fodor's usage of *domain*, we find that it is not defined but is given by a list ("vision, language,...") whose continuation is unclear. Is "reading" a domain; or is it to be regarded as "sort of domain specific," involving language and vision but not certain other domains; or is it "domain neutral," since neurological studies show it to involve many interacting submodules, including ones linked to vision, language, and hearing? In any case, the dichotomy has become a trichotomy. But the situation is even worse than this. Lacking any clear definition of domain other than "like an input module," Fodor's use of his dichotomy is vacuous, and any claim that it is a deep fact that "domain specific vs. domain neutral" might match "input module vs. central process" is reduced to empty tautology.

Encapsulated vs. Quineian/Isotropic
Now that we have confronted the issue of scientific specialization, we see that this dichotomy does not usefully describe scientific confirmation. We may regard science as organized into modules with relatively restricted flows of data between them. To a first approximation, each specialty is encapsulated. However, work within the discipline is certainly Quineian and isotropic with respect to the facts and theories of the discipline itself, and only secondarily and with much longer time constants with respect to science as a whole. Since two can play at the analogies game, I might suggest that input modules correspond to scientific specialities whereas central processes correspond to the integrative aspects of science. If this analogy is accepted, encapsulation of the input processes is at best a first approximation; rejecting it suggests that modulatiry provides a good first approximation to the structure of the central processes. In either case, the claim that the dichotomy between encapsulated and Quineian/isotropic is coextensive with that between input processes and modular processes. Moreover, it becomes possible to counter the profound pessimism with which Fodor concludes his book when he argues that "if central processes have the sort of properties that I have ascribed to them, then they are bad candidates for study" [F127]. He ascribes what progress there has been in

cognitive science to the fact that we have been able to study modular input systems. But if, as I argue, input processes are less encapsulated and some central processes are more encapsulated than Fodor believes, then there is no reason to accept the input process/central process taxonomy as setting a dispiriting limit to the success of cognitive science.

Acknowledgment

Preparation of this chapter was supported in part by NIH grant NS14971.

18

Marr's Theory of Vision

Tyler Burge

In recent years I have given several arguments against a common doctrine in the philosophy of psychology called *individualism*. Individualism is the view that if one fixes a person's (or an animal's) physical history in non-intentional terms and in such a way that one makes no assumptions about the nature of the subject's environment beyond the subject's surfaces, then it is impossible for the subject's intentional states or events to have been different from what they are. The strategy of my arguments against this view has been to show that a subject's concepts or mental states are individuated in ways that lean on assumptions about the environment. For example, a person's concept of aluminum is typically what it is partly because the person has interacted (perhaps indirectly, through other people) with instances of aluminum in the world. One can coherently imagine varying the environment, without relevantly affecting an individual's physical makeup, in such a way as to vary the person's concepts and mental states.[1] Most of the arguments that I have given to this end rely on higher cognitive faculties. It would be interesting to apply the strategy of the argument to relatively primitive and thoroughly modular cognitive faculties. That is what I propose to do here.

Not all aspects of psychology involve the ascription of intentional states and events. I do not care to argue over whether these aspects are individualistic. I shall focus purely on aspects of psychological theory that are intentional. The general picture of these aspects of psychological explanation is as follows.

Ascription of intentional states and events in psychology constitutes a type of individuation and explanation that carries presuppositions about the specific nature of the person's environment. Moreover, states and events are individuated so as to set the terms for specific evaluations of them for truth or other types of success. We can judge directly whether conative states are practically successful and cognitive states are veridical. For example, by characterizing a subject as visually representing an X and specifying whether the visual state appropriately derives from an X in the particular case, we can judge whether the subject's state is veridical. Theories of vision, belief formation, memory, learning, decision-making, categorization, and perhaps even reasoning all attribute states that are subject to practical and semantical evaluation by reference to standards partly set by a wider environment.

Psychological theories are not themselves evaluative theories. But they often individuate phenomena so as to make evaluation readily accessible because they are partly motivated by such judgments. Thus, we judge that in certain delimitable contexts people get what they want, know what is the case, and perceive what is there. And we try to frame explanations that account for these successes, and the correlative failures, in such a way as to illumine as specifically as possible the mechanisms that underlie and make true our evaluations.

I want to illustrate and develop these points by considering at some length David Marr's theory of vision. I choose this example primarily because it is a very advanced and impressive theory, and because it admits of being treated in some depth. Its information-processing approach is congenial with mainstream work in cognitive psychology. Some of its intentional aspects are well understood—indeed, some of them are conceptually and mathematically far ahead of its formal (or syntactical) and · physiological aspects. Thus, the theory provides an example of a mentalistic theory with solid achievements to its credit.

The theory of vision maintains a pivotal position in psychology. Since perceptual processes provide the input for many higher cognitive processes, it is reasonable to think that if the theory of vision treats intentional states nonindividualistically, other central parts of cognitive psychology will do likewise. Information processed by more central capacities depends, to a large extent, on visual information.

Certain special aspects of the vision example must be noted at the outset. As I remarked, the arguments that I have previously published against individualism (see note 1) have centered on "higher" mental capacities, some of which essentially involve the use of language. This focus was motivated by an interest in the relation between thought and linguistic meaning and in certain sorts of intellectual responsibility. Early human vision makes use of a limited range of representations—representations of shape, texture, depth and other spatial relations, motion, color, and so forth. These representations (percepts) are formed by processes that are relatively immune to correction from other sources of information; and the representations of early vision appear to be fully independent of language. So the thought experiments that I have previously elaborated will not carry over simply to early human vision. (One would expect those thought experiments to be more relevant to social and developmental psychology, to concept learning, and to parts of "higher" cognitive psychology.) But the case against individualism need not center on higher cognitive capacities or on the relation between thought and language. The anti-individualistic conclusions of the previously published arguments can be shown to apply to early human vision. The abstract schema articulated by those thought experiments also applies.

The schema rests on three general facts. The first is that the entities in the objective world one normally intentionally interacts with, in the employment of many representational (intentional) types, affects the semantical properties of those representational types, what they are, and how one individuates them.[2] A near consequence of this first fact is that there can be slack between the way a subject's representational types apply to the world and what that person knows about (and how he or she can react to) the way they apply. It is possible for representational types to apply differently without the person's physical reactions or discriminative powers being different. These facts, together with the fact that many fundamental mental states and events are individuated in terms of the relevant representational types, suffice to generate the conclusion that many paradigmatic mental states and events are not individualistically individuated but may vary while a person's body and discriminative powers are conceived as constant. By the second fact one can conceive of the way a person's representational types apply to the objective world as varying while that person's history, nonintentionally and individualistically specified, is held constant. By the first fact such variation may vary the individuation of the person's representational types. By the third fact such variation may affect the individuation of the person's mental states and events. I shall illustrate how instances of this schema are supported by Marr's theory of vision.[3]

Marr's theory subsumes three explanatory enterprises: a theory of the computation of the information, an account of the representations used and of the algorithms by which they are manipulated, and a theory of the underlying physiology. Our primary interest is in the first level and in that part of the second that deals with the individuation of representations. These latter parts of the theory are fundamentally intentional.

The theory of the computation of information encompasses an account of what information is extracted from what antecedent resources and an account of the reference-preserving "logic" of the extraction. These accounts proceed against a set of biological background assumptions. It is assumed that visual systems have evolved to solve certain problems forced on them by the environment. Different species are set different problems and solve them differently. The theory of human vision specifies a general information-processing problem: that of generating reliable representations of certain objective, distal properties of the surrounding world on the basis of proximal stimulations.

The human visual system computes complex representations of certain visible properties on the basis of the values of light intensities in retinal images. The primary visible properties that Marr's theory treats are the shapes and locations of things in the world, but various other properties—motion, texture, color, lightness, shading—are also dealt with in some detail. The overall computation is broken down into stages of increasing complexity, each containing modules that solve various subproblems.

The theory of computation of information clearly treats the visual system as going through a series of intentional or representational states. At an early stage, the visual system is counted as representing objective features of the physical world.[4] There is no other way to treat the visual system as solving the problem that the theory sees it as solving than by attributing intentional states that represent objective, physical properties.

More than half of Marr's book is concerned with developing the theory of the computation of information and with individuating representational primitives. These parts of the theory are more deeply developed, both conceptually and mathematically, than the account of the algorithms. This point serves to correct the impression, often conveyed in recent philosophy of psychology, that intentional theories are regressive and all the development of genuine theory in psychology has been proceeding at the level of purely formal, "syntactical" transformations (algorithms) that are used in cognitive systems.

I now want, by a series of examples, to give a fairly concrete sense of how the theory treats the relation between the visual system and the physical environment. Understanding this relation will form essential background for understanding the nonindividualistic character of the theory. The reader may skip the detail and still follow the philosophical argument, but the detail is there to support the argument and to render the conception of explanation that the argument yields both concrete and vivid.

Initially, I will illustrate two broad points. The first is that the theory makes essential reference to the subject's distal stimuli and makes essential assumptions about contingent facts regarding the subject's physical environment. Not only do the basic questions of the theory refer to what one sees under normal conditions, but the computational theory and its theorems are derived from numerous explicit assumptions about the physical world. The second point is that the theory is set up to explain the reliability of a great variety of processes and subprocesses for acquiring information, at least to the extent that they are reliable. Reliability is presupposed in the formulations of the theory's basic questions. It is also explained through a detailed account of how, in certain specified, standard conditions, veridical information is derived from limited means. The theory explains not merely the reliability of the system as a whole, but the reliability of various stages in the visual process. It begins by assuming that we see certain objective properties and proceeds to explain particular successes by framing conditions under which success would be expected (where the conditions are in fact typical). Failures are explained primarily by reference to a failure of these conditions to obtain. To use a phrase of Bernie Kobes, the theory is not success-neutral. The explanations and the kinds of the theory presuppose that perception and numerous subroutines of perception are veridical in normal circumstances.

Example 1

In an early stage of the construction of visual representation, the outputs of channels or filters that are sensitive to spatial distributions of light intensities are combined to produce representations of local contours, edges, shadows, and so forth. The filters fall into groups of different sizes, in the sense that different groups are sensitive to different bands of spatial frequencies. The channels are primarily sensitive to sudden intensity changes, called *zero crossings*, at their scales (within their frequency bands). The theoretical question arises: How do we combine the results of the different-size channels to construct representations with physical meaning—representations that indicate edge segments or local contours in the external physical world? There is no *a priori* reason why zero crossings obtained from different-size filters should be related to one physical phenomenon in the environment. There is, however, a physical basis for their being thus related. This basis is identified by *the constraint of spatial localization*. Things in the world that give rise to intensity changes in the image, such as changes of illumination (caused by shadows, light sources) or changes in surface reflectance (caused by contours, creases, and surface boundaries), are spatially localized, not scattered, and not made up of waves. Because of this fact, if a zero crossing is present in a channel centered on a given frequency band, there should be a corresponding zero crossing at the same spatial location in larger-scale channels. If this ceases to be so at larger scales, it is because two or more local intensity changes are being averaged together in the larger channel (e.g., the edges of a thin bar may register radical frequency changes in small channels but go undetected in larger ones) or because two independent physical phenomena are producing intensity changes in the same area but at different scales (e.g. a shadow superimposed on a sudden reflectance change; if the shadow is located in a certain way, the positions of the zero crossings may not make possible a separation of the two physical phenomena). Some of these exceptions are sufficiently rare that the visual system need not and does not account for them, thus allowing for possible illusions; others are reflected in complications of the basic assumption that follows. The spatial-coincidence constraint yields the *spatial-coincidence assumption*: If a zero-crossing segment is present in a set of independent channels over a contiguous range of sizes, and the segment has the same position and orientation in each channel, then the set of such zero-crossing segments indicates the presence of an intensity change in the image that is due to a single physical phenomenon (a change in reflectance, illumination, depth, or surface orientation). Thus, the theory starts with the observation that physical edges produce roughly coincident zero crossings in channels of neighboring sizes. The spatial-coincidence assumption asserts that the coincidence of zero crossings of neighboring sizes is normally sufficient evidence of a real physical edge. Under such circumstances, according to the theory, a representation of an edge is formed.[5]

Example 2

Because of the laws of light and the way our eyes are made, positioned, and controlled, our brains typically receive similar image signals originating from two points that are fairly similarly located in the respective eyes or images, at the same horizontal level. If two objects are separated in depth from the viewer, the relative positions of their image signals will differ in the two eyes. The visual system determines the distance of physical surfaces by measuring the angular discrepancy in position (disparity) of the image of an object in the two eyes. This process is called stereopsis. To solve the problem of determining distance, the visual system must select a location on a surface as represented by one image, identify the same location in the other image, and measure the disparity between the corresponding image points. There is, of course no *a priori* means of matching points from the two images. The theory indicates how correct matches are produced by appealing to three physical constraints (the first of which is not made explicit but is relied upon): that the two eyes produce similar representations of the same external items, that a given point on a physical surface has a unique position in space at any given time, and that matter is cohesive (i.e., it is separated into objects, the surfaces of which are usually smooth in the sense that surface variation is small in comparison with the overall distance from the observer). These three physical constraints are rewritten as three corresponding constraints on matching: that two representational elements can match if and only if they normally could have arisen from the same physical item (e.g., in stereograms, dots match dots rather than bars), that nearly always each representational element can match only one element from the other image (except when two markings lie along the line of sight of one eye but are separately visible by the other eye, causing illusions), and that disparity varies smoothly almost everywhere (this derives from the third of the physical constraints, which implies that the distance to the visible surface varies approximately continuously except at object boundaries, which occupy a small fraction of the area of an image). Given suitable precisifications, these matching constraints can be used to prove the fundamental theory of stereopsis: If a correspondence is established between physically meaningful representational primitives extracted from the left and right images of a scene that contains a sufficient amount of detail (roughly 2 percent density for dot stereograms), and if the correspondence satisfies the three matching constraints, then that correspondence is physically correct and hence unique. The method is, again, to identify general physical conditions that give rise to a visual process, and then to use those conditions to motivate constraints on the form of the process that, when satisfied, will allow the process to be interpreted as providing reliable representations of the physical environment.[6]

These examples illustrate theories of the computation of information. The critical move is the formulation of general physical facts that limit the interpretation of a visual problem enough to allow one to interpret the machinations of the visual system as providing a unique and veridical solution, at least in typical cases. The primary aim of referring to contingent physical facts and properties is to enable the theory to explain the visual system's reliable acquisition of information about the physical world— that is, to explain the success or veridicality of various types of visual representation.

I now turn to a third point that is a natural corollary of the second and that will be critical for my argument that the theory is nonindividualistic: The information carried by representations—their intentional content—is individuated in terms of the specific distal causal antecedents in the physical world that the information is about and that the representations normally apply to. The individuation of the intentional features of numerous representations depends on a variety of physical constraints that our knowledge of the external world gives us. Thus, the individuation of intentional content of representational types presupposes the veridicality of perception. Not only the explanations but also the intentional kinds of the theory presuppose contingent facts about the subject's physical environment.

Example 3
In building up information or representational primitives in the primal sketch, Marr states six general physical assumptions that constrain the choice of primitives. I shall state some of these in order to give a sense of their character: that the visible world is composed of smooth surfaces having reflectance functions whose spatial structure may be complex, that markings generated on a surface by a single process are

often arranged in continuous spatial structures (curves, lines, etc.), and that if the direction of motion is discontinuous at more than one point (along a line, for example) then an object boundary is present. These assumptions are used to identify the physical significance of—that is, the objective information given by—certain types of patterns in the image. The computational theory states conditions under which these primitives form to carry information about items in the physical world (Marr 1982, pp. 44–71). The theory in example 1 is a case in point: Conditions are laid down under which certain patterns may be taken as representing an objective physical condition—as being edge, boundary, bar, or blob detectors. Similar points apply for more advanced primitives.

Example 4

In answering the question of what assumptions we reasonably and actually apply when we interpret silhouettes as three-dimensional shapes, Marr motivates a central representational primitive by stating physical constraints that lead to the proof of a theorem: that each line of sight from the viewer to the object grazes the object's surface at exactly one point, that nearby points on the contour in an image arise from nearby points on the contour generator on the viewed object (i.e., points that appear close together in the image actually are close together on the object's surface), and that the contour generator lies wholly in a single plane. Obviously, these are conditions of perception that may fail, but they are conditions under which humans seem to do best at solving the problem of deriving three-dimensional shape decriptions from representations of silhouettes. *Definition:* A generalized cone is a three-dimensional object generated by moving a cross section along an axis; the cross section may vary smoothly in size, but its shape remains the same (e.g., footballs, pyramids, legs, and stalagmites are, or approximate, generalized cones). *Theorem:* If the surface is smooth and if the physical constraints given just above hold for all distant viewing positions in any one plane, then the viewed surface is a generalized cone. The theorem indicates a natural connection between generalized cones and the imaging process. Marr (1982, pp. 215–225) infers from this, and from certain psycho-physical evidence, that representations of generalized cones—that is, representations with intentional content concerning generalized cones—are likely to be fundamental among our visual representations of three-dimensional objects.

Throughout the theory, representational primitives are selected and individuated by considering specific, contingent facts about the physical world that typically hold when we succeed in obtaining veridical visual information about that world. The information or content of the visual representations is always individuated by reference to the physical objects, properties, or relations that are seen. In view of the success orientation of the theory, this mode of individuation is grounded in its basic methods. If theory were confronted with a species of organism reliably and successfully interacting with a different set of objective visible properties (by perhaps a different set of optical laws), the representational types that the theory would attribute to the organism would be different, regardless of whether the individual organism's physical mechanisms were different.

I am now in a position to argue that the theory is not individualistic: (1) The theory is intentional. (2) The intentional primitives of the theory and the information they carry are individuated by reference to contingently existing physical items or conditions by which they are normally caused and to which they normally apply. (3) Thus, if these physical conditions and, possibly, attendant physical laws were regularly different, the information conveyed to the subject and the intentional content of his or her visual representations would be different. (4) It is not incoherent to conceive of relevantly different physical conditions and perhaps relevantly different (say, optical) laws regularly causing the same nonintentionally, individualistically individuated physical regularities in the subject's eyes and nervous system. It is enough if the differences are small; they need not be wholesale. (5) In such a case (by point 3), the individual's visual representations would carry different information and have different representational content, though the person's whole nonintentional physical history (at least up to a certain time) might remain the same. (6) Assuming that some perceptual states are identified in the theory in terms of their informational or intentional content, it follows that individualism is not true for the theory of vision.

I shall defend the argument stepwise. First, I take it that the claim that the theory is intentional is sufficiently evident. The top levels of the theory are explicitly formulated in intentional terms. And their method of explanation is to show how the problem of arriving at certain veridical representations is solved.

The second step of the argument was substantiated through examples 3 and 4. The intentional content of representations of edges or generalized cones is individuated in terms of specific reference to those very contingently instantiated physical properties, on the assumption that those properties normally give rise to veridical representations of them.

The third step in the argument is supported both by the way the theory individuates intentional content (see the preceding paragraph and examples 3 and 4) and by the explanatory method of the theory (see the second point illustrated above, and examples 1 and 2). The methods of individuation and explanation are governed by the assumption that the subject has adapted to his or her environment sufficiently to obtain veridical information from it under certain normal conditions. If the properties and relations that normally caused visual impressions were regularly different from what they are, the individual would obtain different information and have visual experiences with different intentional content. If the regular, lawlike relations between perception and the environment were different, the visual system would be solving different information-processing problems, it would pass through different informational or intentional states, and the explanation of vision would be different. To reject this third step of our argument would be to reject the theory's basic methods and questions. But these methods and questions have already borne fruit, and there are no good reasons for rejecting them.

I take it that the fourth step is a relatively unproblematic counterfactual. There is no metaphysically necessary relation between individualistically individuated processes in a person's body and the causal antecedents of those processes in the surrounding world.[7] (To reject this step would be self-defeating for the individualist.) If the environmental laws and conditions were different, the same proximal visual stimulations could have regularly had different distal causes. In principle, we can conceive of some regular variation in the distal causes of perceptual impressions with no variation in a person's individualistically specified physical processes, even while conceiving the person as well adapted to the relevant environment—though, of course, not uniquely adapted.

Steps three and four, together with the unproblematic claim that the theory individuates some perceptual states in terms of intentional content or representational type, entail that the theory is nonindividualistic.

Steps two and three are incompatible with certain philosophical approaches that have no basis in psychological theory. One might claim that the information content of a visual representation would remain constant even if the physical conditions that lead to the representation were regularly different. It is common to motivate this claim by pointing out that one's visual representations remain the same, whether one is perceiving a black blob on a white surface or having an eidetic hallucination of such a blob. So, runs the reasoning, why should changing the distal causes of a perceptual representation affect its content? On this view, the content of a given perceptual representation is commonly given as that of *the distal cause of this representation,* or *the property in the world that has this sort of visual appearance.* The content of these descriptions is intended to remain constant across possible situations in which the microphysical events of a person's visual processes remain the same while the distal causes of those processes are regularly and significantly different. It is thought that the representations themselves (and our experiences of them) remain constant under these circumstances. Thus, as the distal antecedents of one's perceptual representations vary, the reference of those representations will vary, but their intentional content will not.[8]

There is more wrong with this line than I have room to develop here. I will mention some of the more straightforward difficulties. The motivation from perceptual illusion falls far short. One is indeed in the same perceptual state whether one is seeing or hallucinating. However, that is because the intentional content of one's visual state (or representation) is individuated against a background in which the relevant state is normally veridical. Thus, the fact that one's percepts or perceptual states remain constant between normal perception and hallucinations does not even tend to show that the intentional visual state remains constant across circumstances in which different physical conditions are the normal antecedents of one's perceptions.

Let us consider the proposals for interpreting the content of visual representations. In the first place, both descriptions (*the distal cause of this representation* and the property in the world that uses this sort of visual appearence et al.) are insufficiently specific. There are lots of distal causes and lots of things that might be said to appear *thus* (e.g. the array of light striking the retina as well as the physical surface). We identify the relevant distal cause (and the thing that normally appears thus and so) as the thing that we actually see. To accurately pick out the "correct" object with one of these descriptions would at the very least require a more complex specification. But filling out the descriptive content runs into one or both of two difficulties: Either it includes kinds that are tied to a specific environment (*the convex, rough-textured object that is causing this representation*). In such a case, the description is still subject to our argument, for these kinds are individuated by reference to the empirical environment. Or it complicates the constraints on the causal chain to the extent that the complications cannot plausibly be attributed to the content of processes in the early visual system.

Even in their unrevised forms, the descriptions are overintellectualized philosophers' conceits. It is extremely implausible, and empirically without warrant, to think that packed into every perceptual representation is a distinction between distal cause and experiential effect, or between objective reality and perceptual appearance. These are distinctions developed by reflecting on the ups and downs of visual perception. They do not come in at the ground, animal level of early vision.

A further mistake is the view that perceptual representations never purport to specify particular physical properties *as such*, but only via some relation they bear to inner occurrences, which are directly referred to. (Even the phrase *the convex object causing this percept* invokes a specification of objective convexity as such.) The view will not serve the needs of psychological explanation as actually practiced. True descriptions of information are too inspecific to account for specific success in solving problems in retrieving information about the actual, objective world. Moreover, the view raises difficulties in epistemology.

The best empirical theory that we have individuates the intentional content of visual representations by specific reference to specific physical characteristics of visible properties and relations. The theory does not utilize complicated, self-referential, attributively used role descriptions of those properties. It does not individuate content primarily by reference to phenomenological qualities. Nor does it use the notions of cause or appearance in specifying the intentional content of early visual representations.[9]

The second and third steps of my argument are incompatible with the claim that the intentional content of visual representations is determined by their "functional role" in each person's system of dispositions, nonintentionally and individualistically specified. This claim lacks any warrant in the practice of the science. In the first place, the theory suggests no reduction of the intentional to the nonintentional. In the second, although what a person can do, nonvisually, constitutes evidence for what he or she can see, there is little ground for thinking that either science or common sense takes an individual person's nonvisual abilities fully to determine the content of his or her early visual experience. A person's dispositions and beliefs develop by adapting to what the person sees. As the person develops, the visual system (at least at its more advanced stages—those involving recognition) and the belief and language systems affect one another. But early vision seems relatively independent of these nonvisual systems. A large part of learning is accomodating one's dispositions to the information carried by visual representations. Where there are failures of adaptation, the person does not know that the visual apparatus is presenting to him or her. Yet the presentations are there to be understood.

Conclusion

There is a general argument that seems to me to show that a person's nonintentional dispositions could not fix (individuate) the intentional content of the person's visual presentations. The argument begins with a conception of objectivity. As long as the person's visual presentations are of public, objective objects, properties, or relations, it is possible for the person to have mistaken presentations. Such mistakes usually arise for a single sensory modality—so that when dispositions associated with other modalities (e.g. touch) are brought into play, the mistake is rectified. But as long as the represented object or property is objective and physical, it is in principle possible, however unlikely, that there may be a confluence of illusions such that all an individual person's sensory modalities would be fooled and all the person's nonintentional dispositions would fail to distinguish between the normal condition and the one producing the mistaken sensory representations. This is my first assumption. In the argument, I shall employ a corollary: Our concept of objectivity is such that no one objective entity that we visually represent is such that it must vary with, or be typed so as necessarily to match exactly, an individual's proximal stimuli and discriminative abilities. The point follows from a realistic, and even from a nonsubjectivistic, view of the objects of sight.[10]

I argued above that intentional representational types are not in general individuated purely in terms of an attributive role description of a causal relation, or a relation of appearance-similarity, between external objects and qualitative perceptual representatives of them. For present purposes, this is my second assumption: Some objective physical objects and properties are represented as such; they are specifically specified.

Third, in order to be empirically informative, some visual representations that represent objective entities as such must have the representational characteristics that they have partly *because* instances regularly enter into certain relations with those objective entities.[11] Their carrying information, their having objective intentional content, consists partly in their being the normal causal products of objective entities. And their specific intentional content depends partly on their being the normal products of the specific objective entities that give rise to them. That is why we individuate intentional visual representations in terms of the objective entities to which they normally apply for members of a given species. This is the core of truth in the slogan (sometimes misapplied) that mistakes presuppose a background of veridicality.

The assumptions in the three preceding paragraphs make it possible to state a general argument against individualism regarding visual states. Consider a person P who normally correctly perceives instances of a particular objective visible property O. In such cases, let the intentional type of P's perceptual representation (or perceptual state) be O'. Such perceptual representations are normally the product of interaction with instances of O. But imagine that for P perceptual representations typed O' are on some few occasions the product of instances of a different objective property, C. On such occasions, P mistakenly sees an instance of C as an O; P's perceptual state is of type O'. Assume that O' represents any instance of O as such (as an O), in the sense of the second premise, not merely in terms of some attributive role description. Since O' represents an objective property, it is possible, by the first premise, to conceive of P as lacking at his or her disposal (at every moment up to a given time) any means of discriminating instances of C from instances of O.

Now hold fixed both P's physical states (up to the given time) and his or

her discriminative abilities, nonintentionally and individualistically specified. But conceive of the world as lacking O altogether. Suppose that the
optical laws in the counterfactual environment are such that the impressions on P's eyes and the normal causal processes that lead to P's visual
representations are explained in terms of instances of C (or, at any rate, in
terms of some objective, visible entities other than instances of O). Then,
by the third premise, P's visual representation (or visual state) would not be
of intentional type O'. At the time when in the actual situation P is
misrepresenting a C as an O, P may counterfactually be perceiving something (say, a C) correctly (as a C) if the processes that lead to that visual
impression are normal and of a type that normally produces the visual
impression that P has on that occasion. Thus, P's intentional visual states
could vary while his or her physical states and nonintentionally specified
discriminative abilities remained constant.

The first premise and the methodology of intentional-content individuation articulated in the third premise entail the existence of examples. Since
examples usually involve shifts in optical laws, they are hard to fill out in
great detail. But it is easiest to imagine concrete cases taken from early but
still conscious vision. These limit the number of an individual's dispositions
that might be reasonably thought to bear on the content of his or her visual
states. Early vision is relatively independent of language or other cognitive
abilities. It appears to be thoroughly modular.

Suppose that the relevant visible entities are very small and not such as
to bear heavily on adaptive success. An O may be a shadow of a certain
small size and shape on a gently contoured surface. A C may be a shallow
crack of similar size. In the actual situation, P sees Os regularly and correctly as Os: P's visual representations are properly explained and specified
as shadow representations of the relevant sort. Assume that P's visual and
other discriminative abilities are fairly normal. P encounters the cracks of
relevant size very rarely and, on those few occasions, not only misperceives them as shadows but has no dispositions that would enable him or
her to discriminate those instances from shadows. We may assume, given
P's actual abilities and the actual laws of optics, that P would be capable, in
ideal circumstances, of visually discriminating some instances of C (relevantly similar cracks) from instances of O (the relevant sort of shadows).
But our supposition is that in the actual cases where P is confronted by
instances of the cracks, the circumstances are not ideal. All P's abilities
would not succeed in discriminating those instances of relevant cracks, in
those circumstances, from instances of relevant shadows. P may not rely on
touch in cases of such small objects, or touch may also be fooled. P's ability
to have such mistaken visual states is argued for by the objectivity premise.

In the counterfactual case, the environment is different. There are no
instances of the relevant shadows visible to P, and the laws of optics differ

in such a way that P's physical visual stimulations (and the rest of P's physical makeup) are unaffected. Suppose that the physical visual stimulations that in the actual case are derived from instances of the relevant sort of shadows are counterfactually caused by and explained in terms of cracks of relevant size. Counterfactually, the cracks take the places of the shadows. On the few occasions where, in the actual case, P misperceives shadows as cracks, P is counterfactually confronted with cracks; the optical circumstances that lead to the visual impressions on those occasions are, we may suppose, normal for the counterfactual environment.[12] On such counterfactual occasions, P would be visually representing small cracks as small cracks. P would never have visual representations of the relevant sort of shadows. One can suppose that even if there were the relevant sort of shadows in the counterfactual environment, the different laws of optics in that environment would not enable P ever to see them. But since P's visual states would be the normal products of normal processes and would provide as good an empirical basis for learning about the counterfactual environment as P has for learning about the actual environment, it would be absurd to hold that (counterfactually) P misperceives the prevalent cracks as shadows on gently contoured surfaces. Counterfactually, P correctly sees the cracks as cracks. Thus, P's intentional perceptual states differ between actual and counterfactual situations. This general argument is independent of the theory of vision that I have been discussing. It supports and is further supported by that theory.

Acknowledgments

A version of this chapter was given orally at the Sloan Conference at MIT in May 1984. I have made use of discussions with David Israel, Bernie Kobes, and Neil Stillings. Except for a few expository adjustments, this is part of a larger paper: "Individualism and Psychology," *Philosophical Review* 95 (1986): 3–45.

Notes

1. "Individualism and the Mental," *Midwest Studies* 4 (1979): 73–121; "Other Bodies," in *Thought and Object*, ed. A. Woodfield (Oxford University Press, 1982); "Two Thought Experiments Reviewed," *Notre Dame Journal of Formal Logic* 23 (1982): 284–293; "Cartesian Error and the Objectivity of Perception," in *Subject, Thought, and Context*, ed. MacDowell and Pettit (Oxford University Press, 1986); "Intellectual Norms and Foundations of Mind," *Journal of Philosophy* 83 (1986): 697–720. The aluminum argument is adapted from an argument in Hilary Putnam's "The Meaning of 'Meaning'" (*Philosophical Papers*, vol. 2 [Cambridge University Press, 1975]). What Putnam wrote in his paper was, strictly, not even compatible with this argument (see the first two papers cited in this note for discussion). However, the aluminum argument lies close to the surface of the argument he does give. The arthritis argument raises rather different issues, despite its parallel methodology.

2. *Representational type* (also *intentional type*) is a relatively theory-neutral term for intentional content, or even intentional state-kinds. See note 3. One could about as well speak of concepts, percepts, and the representational or intentional aspects of thought contents—or of the counterpart states.

3. In what follows I make use of Marr's important book *Vision* (San Francisco: Freeman, 1982). Marr writes:

   The purpose of these representations is to provide useful descriptions of aspects of the real world. The structure of the real world therefore plays an important role in determining both the nature of the representations that are used and the nature of the processes that derive and maintain them. An important part of the theoretical analysis is to make explicit the physical constraints and assumptions that have been used in the design of the representations and processes.... (p. 43)

   It is of critical importance that the tokens [representational particulars] one obtains [in the theoretical analysis] correspond to real physical changes on the viewed surface; the blobs, lines, edges, groups, and so forth that we shall use must not be artifacts of the imaging process, or else inferences made from their structure backwards to the structures of the surface will be meaningless. (p. 44)

   Marr's claim that the structure of the real world figures in determining the nature of the representations that are attributed in the theory is tantamount to the chief point about representation or reference that generates my nonindividualistic thought experiments—the first step in the schema. I shall show how these remarks constitute the central theoretical orientation of the book.

   Calling the theory Marr's is convenient but misleading. Very substantial contributions have been made by many others, and the approach has developed rapidly since Marr's death. See, for example, D. Ballard, G. Hinton, and T. Sejnowski, "Parallel Vision Computation," *Nature* 306 (November 1983): 21–26. What I say about Marr's book applies equally to more recent developments.

4. It is an interesting question when to count the visual system as having gone intentional. I take it that information is, in a broad sense, carried by the intensity values in the retinal image; but I think that this is too early to count the system as intentional or symbolic. I'm inclined to agree with Marr that where zero crossings from different-size filters are checked against one another (see example 1), it is reasonable to count visual processes as representational of an external physical reality. Doing so, however, depends on seeing this stage as part of the larger system, in which objective properties are often discriminated from subjective artifacts of the visual system.

5. Marr 1982, pp. 68–70. See also D. Marr and E. Hildreth, "Theory of Edge Detection," *Proceedings of Royal Society of London* B 207 (1980): 187–217, where the account is substantially more detailed.

6. Marr 1982, pp. 111–116, 205–212; D. Marr and T. Poggio, "A Computational Theory of Human Stereo Vision," *Proceedings of Royal Society of London* B 204 (1979): 301–328; S. Ullman, *The Interpretation of Visual Motion* (Cambridge, Mass.: MIT Press, 1979).

7. As I have intimated above, I doubt that all biological (including physiological) processes and states in the human body are individualistically individuated. The failures of individualism for these sciences involve different but related considerations.

8. Descartes went further in the same direction. He thought that the perceptual system, and indeed the intellect, could not make a mistake. Mistakes derived from the will. The underlying view is that we primarily perceive or make perceptual reference to our own perceptions. This position fails to account plausibly for various visual illusions and errors that precede any activity of the will, or even the intellect. And the idea that perceptions are in general what we make perceptual reference to has little to recom-

mend it and, nowadays, little influence. The natural and, I think, plausible view is that we have visual representations that specify external properties specifically, that these representations are pre-doxastic in the sense they are not themselves objects of belief, and that they sometimes (when they result from abnormal processes) fail to correctly represent what is before the person's eyes.

9. Of course, at least in the earliest stages of visual representation, there are analogies between qualitative features of representations in the experienced image and the features that those representations represent. Representations that represent bar segments are bar-shaped, or have some phenomenological property that strongly tempts us to call them bar-shaped. Similarly for blobs, dots, lines, and so forth. (See page 211 of Marr and Hildreth 1980 for a remark on this dual aspect of representations.) These "analogies" are hardly fortuitous. Eventually they will probably receive rigorous psychophysical explanation. But they should not tempt one into the idea that visual representations in general make reference to themselves, much less into the idea that the content of objective representation is independent of empirical relations between the representations and the objective entities that give rise to them. Perhaps these qualitative features are constant across all cases where one's bodily processes, nonintentionally specified, are held constant. But the information they carry, their intentional content, may vary with their causal antecedents and causal laws in the environment.

10. There is no need to assume that the abnormal condition is unverifiable. Another person with relevant background information might be able to infer that the abnormal condition is producing a perceptual illusion. In fact, another person with different dispositions might even be able to perceive the difference.

11. Not all perceptual representations that specify objective entities need have their representational characteristics determined in this way. The representational characters of some visual representations (or states) may depend on the subject's background theory or primarily on interaction among other representations. There are hallucinations of purple dragons. (Incidentally, few if any of the perceptual representations—even the conscious perceptual representations—discussed in Marr's theory depend in this way on the subject's conceptual background.) Here, I assume only that some visual representations acquire their representational characters through interaction. This amounts to the weak assumption that the formation of some perceptual representations is empirical.

Some of interaction that leads to the formation and the representational characters of certain innate perceptual tendencies (or perhaps even representations) may occur in the making of the species, not in the learning histories of individuals. Clearly this complication could be incorporated into a generalization of this third premise without affecting the anti-individualistic thrust of the argument.

12. What of the nonintentionally specified dispositions that in the actual environment (given the actual laws of optics) would have enabled P to discriminate Cs from Os in ideal circumstances? In the counterfactual environment, in view of the very different optical laws and different objects that confront P, one can suppose that these dispositions have almost any visual meaning that one likes. These dispositions would serve to discriminate Cs from some other sort of entity. In view of the objectivity premise, the nonintentional dispositions can always be correlated with different, normal antecedent laws and conditions—in terms of which their intentional content may be explained.

The argument of this section is developed in parallel but different ways in my "Cartesian Error and the Objectivity of Perception" (see note 1 above).

19

Modularity and Naturalism in Theories of Vision

Neil Stillings

I begin this chapter by discussing the links between modularity and naturalism in Marr's theory and in classical perceptual theories. I then discuss the challenges to modular theories that arise from work on cooperative computation, object recognition, and interactions between vision and language.

Naturalism in Marr's Theory of Vision

David Marr (1977, 1982) distinguished three levels of theoretical analysis, which he called the computational, the algorithmic, and implementational level. The implementational level is the physical level of description. The algorithmic is roughly the formal level, at which the data structures and algorithms that operate during perception are formally specified. The computational level is somewhat analogous to Chomsky's notion of a competence model. Part of the goal at this level is to give a concise characterization of the input-output relations of the system, suppressing algorithmic detail. That is, a computational analysis specifies the mapping that the algorithm has to compute. Typically, there will be an indefinite range of algorithms that satisfy a given computational characterization. For both Chomsky and Marr, this third, abstract level of analysis is methodologically prior to the other two and is to be undertaken in a way that yields the major explanatory insights of the theory. Chomsky seeks to develop a theory of language universals. A competence theory explicitly characterizes the formal properties that define the range of possible human languages. It therefore directly predicts the range of grammars that actually occur. More indirectly, it makes strong predictions about languages acquisition and the biological basis of language; even more indirectly, it makes predictions about language processing. Linguistic-competence theories are individualistic, however, in that they are strictly formal accounts of linguistic structure, excluding meaning and saying nothing about the relationship between speakers and their worlds. The thesis of strong modularity is virtually built into the theory of linguistic competence. If the modularity thesis is true for the linguistic input system, then scientific generalizations about grammatical structure are likely to be possible and interesting. If it is false, all bets are off.

The explanatory burden of Marr's computational analysis, in contrast, is explicitly semantic, and naturalistic. A computational analysis explains why a particular perceptual computation yields correct perception. A computational theory includes a formal, causal analysis of how the physical world delivers a particular kind of input to the perceiver. The theory proceeds to explain how the hypothesized computation extracts correct information about the physical world from that input. Computational analysis is also expected to come up with optimal or ideal computations, partly because the computer-vision theorist is striving for optimal solutions but partly because of the heuristic value of assuming that biological systems have evolved to embody ideal solutions to the problem of vision.

There are several assumptions underlying the notion that computational analysis is central to theorizing about vision. First, it is argued that the relationship between the world and the array of reflected light available to the perceiver is not a simple one. The relationship requires extensive analysis. Second, upon analysis it turns out that certain properties of reflected light are unambiguously related to the world only if we make certain assumptions about how the world nearly always is. For example, the recovery of three-dimensional structure from visual motion is crucially aided by the constraint that "most of the structures in the visual world are rigid, or at least nearly so" (Marr 1982, p. 209). Third, because of this ambiguity, the visual system is not a system that can respond to any kind of structure that happens to be present in dynamic, two-dimensional arrays of numbers (images). It is not a generalized perceptron or a connectionist learning network. The particular assumptions that disambiguate visual information in our physical world are hypothesized to be built into the perceptual system. Thus, Ullman (1979) proposes that the rigidity constraint just quoted is built into the perceptual system. The system is built to interpret two-dimensional motion in the image in terms of the motion of rigid bodies in three-dimensional space. Fourth, because the perceptual system is so precisely tuned to environmental constraints, any attempt to analyze its operation purely formally will probably fail and will surely miss major generalizations.

Burge's chapter in this volume neatly establishes the philosophical implications of this kind of naturalistic analysis by placing the perceptual system in a counterfactual world in which the physical constraints on the relation between objects and reflected light do not hold. An individualistic analysis can not explain the perceptual results.

Carrying out a naturalistic research program requires that the needed analysis of the world be within reach of the cognitive scientist. The immediate value of the strong-modularity thesis is that it carves out a limited domain of the world and demands only that the output of an input system be reasonably reliable and quickly delivered. What is ultimately true about the physical world is left to the central processes. Thus, the modularity thesis allows us to adopt a modular approach to the world as well. Marr not only followed this general strategy, he also adopted further hypotheses about the modularity of the world. As already mentioned, he made the basic Gibsonian cut between perceiving the three-dimensional layout of surfaces and object recognition, avoiding the problem of physically characterizing objects. Under this decomposition of the problem, large chunks of the physical description of the environment-organism relationship have proved relatively tractable. The further modular assumption that there are independent sources of information about surface layout that arise from independent physical causes was particularly valuable. Problems such as edge detection, stereopsis, color constancy, shape from shading, optical flow, and spatial structure from motion can be quite well defined, and plausible, even provably correct solutions can be found. The modularity of early vision seems to be possible because of a contingent modularity in the environment. It simply happens (under Marr's view) that reflected light makes available information about the layout of surfaces in three dimensions and in a neatly packaged way. This makes possible the evolution of organisms with modularized early vision. Environmental modularity makes possible fast, hardwired, informationally encapsulated computation.

The progress of the Marrian research program illustrates Jerry Fodor's original pressimism about being at the mercy of physics and the solution offered by strong modularity. Marr's program is driven by the development of physical descriptions of the relationship between light and the physical world. Although no cutting-edge particle physics is involved, Marr, Horn, Ullman, and others have come up with new mathematical descriptions of the two-dimensional structure imposed on light by its physical interaction with the world at the macroscopic level. However, although the proposal of algorithms and neuronal implementations follows the development of a kind of physical description, there is no sense in which visual scientists have to wait for someone else to do the physics or get interested in quarks, charm, or GUTS. They can do the physics themselves (as long as they are comfortable with convolving Laplacians with Gaussians and such). This involves specific applications of well-understood physical principles that operate at a macroscopic level and thus are largely impervious to invasion from current theoretical physics. An enormous amount of creativity is involved in working out these applications (witness the fact that Helmholtz, who applied one-dimensional spectral analysis to the auditory system, failed to develop spatial-frequency analysis), but that is no cause for a special solipsistic pessimism.

Naturalism in Classical Perceptual Theory

Perceptual theorists have always been preoccupied with the adaptive character of vision, and one way or another they have all proposed the building of contingent facts about the environment into the perceptual process. Many classical and contemporary solutions to the constancy problems and explanations of visual illusions involve the exploitation of contingent facts about the world. Burge's philosophical argument could be reconstructed within any of these theories.

To take an example of a theorist who is about as far from Marr as it is possible to be, consider Adelbert Ames (see Ittelson and Kilpatrick 1958), whose various demonstrations (such as the Ames room and chair) were designed to demonstrate the radical ambiguity of the visual stimulus. He argued that (under stationary, monocular viewing conditions) we see a wildly nonrectilinear room as rectilinear and some wildly disconnected chair parts as a coherent chair because assumptions about the way the world is are part of the perceptual process. Although Ames was a sort of ultra-radical Helmholtzian in the matter of stimulus ambiguity, his armchair argument is strikingly similar to an assumption of Marr's that physical objects are locally continuous and coherent. Both Ames and Marr leaned heavily on the fact that in our world spatially disconnected clusters of "parts" do not hang together in such a way that their ends fall precisely along viewer-centered projective geometric paths (as if suspended from invisible wires strung along those paths).

Although they are both naturalists, Ames and Marr differ on exactly how this kind of assumption is built into the perceptual process. Marr proposes that it is biologically preprogrammed. Ames leans toward explanations that involve perceptual learning, and he is quite willing to treat fundamental physical facts such as object coherence in the same manner as default assumptions, such as a simplicity principle that selects rectilinearity for the Ames room. The choice of everyday objects and scenes was also designed to illustrate the influence of higher-level knowledge of typical room and chair construction. Although the assumptions or inferences operate powerfully, unconsciously, and independent of language in Ames's theory, vision is less modular in that it is potentially adaptable to a wider range of environmental contingencies (possibly at the price of being less reliable) and is influenced by higher knowledge sources.[1]

A similar point could be made about Gregory's (1968) theory of the Muller-Lyer illusion. His theory states that the illusion results from the visual system imposing a perspective interpretation on the converging lines in the display and applying size-distance constancy scaling. The major difference between Gregory and Marr, relative to this example, is that Marr sees little reason to make perspective cues a centerpiece of perceptual theory. There are many other, more reliable, sources of information about depth. Waltz (1975) developed a computational analysis of the information available in line drawings and a cooperative algorithm that efficiently applied various constraints to arrive at a local depth map. Marr suggested that this information might be used in the computations that establish consistency in the $2\frac{1}{2}$-D sketch but that they do not play a strong role in early vision. The main reason is that we do not live in a high-contrast, straight-edged world.

The general point is that naturalistic assumptions have been adopted by all theorists who have tried to explain how the visual system gives us information about the world. Theorists differ on what assumptions about the world and its optical relation to the perceiver are part of the perceptual process, on how the assumptions come to be part of the process, and on how modifiable the assumptions are. The ultimate reason for adopting naturalistic assumptions, however, always seems to be the same: The relationship between the visible physical world and reflected light is complex, and it is ambiguous unless the perceptual apparatus has various assumptions about the relationship built into it.[2]

At first sight it might appear that the naturalistic assumptions of perceptual theories fall into two major categories. "Gibsonian" theorists (including Marr) emphasize the power and reliability of early vision and propose hardwired assumptions that operate early in the perceptual process. "Helmholtzian" theorists (including much of the computer vision community) emphasize the ambiguity of early vision and propose learned, higher-level inferences. Thus, Helmholtzian naturalism would appear not to be linked to modularity in the mind and the environment. Many of Helmholtz's unconscious inferences establish a form of weak modularity, which can be modified by further perceptual experience. Virtually, any central mental process or theory about the physical world might come to have decisive influences on perception. Naturalistic assumptions that arise only at the level of central mental processes might also deprive Burge's argument of some of its force. Burge's argument is distinctively perceptual because it assumes a Marr-type theory of early vision in which the naturalistic assumptions are encapsulated. If the naturalistic assumptions in perception are essentially the same as central thought processes, then Burge's argument would appear to be much more similar to some of his previous arguments about language. The form of the argument might also have to be reconstructed, because a Helmholtzian perceptual system might adapt to Burge's counterfactual worlds.

This proposed distinction between Gibsonian and Helmholtzian theory is incorrect, however, because Helmholtzian theorists also make naturalistic assumptions about early vision. The strongest example is that they assume that visual systems represent the light entering the system intentionally, prior to any computation. That is, the retinal image itself, given how it is treated, embodies naturalistic assumptions. The simplest example is that a point on the image is assumed by the system to originate somewhere along a ray traced from the retina out into space according to the laws of geometric optics. To quote Helmholtz (1910, p. 2):

> ... *objects are always imagined as being present in the field of vision as would have to be there in order to produce the same impression on the nervous mechanism, the eyes being used under ordinary normal conditions.* ... suppose that the eyeball is mechanically stimulated at the outer corner of the eye. Then we imagine that we see an appearance of light in front of us somewhere in the direction of the bridge of the nose. Under ordinary conditions of vision, when our eyes are stimulated by light coming from outside, if the region of the retina in the outer corner of the eye is to be stimulated, the light actually has to enter the eye from the direction of the bridge of the nose. Thus, in accordance with the above rule, in a case of this kind we substitute a luminous object at the place mentioned in the field of view, although as a matter of fact the mechanical stimulus does not act on the eye from in front of the field of view nor from the nasal side of the eye, but, on the contrary, is exerted on the outer surface of the eyeball and more from behind.[3] [emphasis in original]

Image coordinates carry information about direction in space that is intrinsic to the scene-perceiver relation before any computation is done on them.[4] This directional information depends on the contingent laws of geometrical optics. Theories of perception make use of this fact so pervasively that the assumption often passes with little comment. Although Helmholtz (in translation) says that "we substitute" an object according to the "rule" under discussion, he did not believe that we can acquire arbitrary rules mapping image coordinates onto directions in space or that we had to learn the correct rule.[5]

A similar point could be made about other information-bearing properties of the retinal image that are not so completely reliable but are still relied upon. For example, points that are nearby in the image are highly likely to be near each other in space. Marr is quite explicit about this assumption, but the assumption was certainly made by classical theorists who did not spell it out. The pervasiveness of retinotopic mapping in visual physiology, which classical theorists were aware of and impressed with, might be taken to suggest that the informational properties of image coordinates are thoroughly wired into the system. Within physiology and psychology, classical arguments for sensation vs. perception (or sense data vs. perceptual interpretation) did not assume that the retinal image was completely arbitrary. No one assumed that the system could bootstrap veridical information about the world from an image with no intrinsic, immediate representational character.

Avoidance of Naturalism in Psychophysics

The approach to the visual system that is most clearly individualistic, or methodologically solipsistic, is psychophysics. Although psychophysics, as its name suggests, attempts to find generalizations that relate psychological responses to physical input, the physics is limited to properties of light that can be defined without reference to the world of visible objects. For example, the trichromatic theory and the data on trichromatic color matching say nothing about the role of three-channel wavelength sensitivity in the perception of objects. They say nothing about the problem of color constancy (the relatively unchanging colors of objects when illuminated by varying distributions of spectral energy), which Marr takes to be central to theorizing about color vision and which leads him to explore the retinex theory, which is commonly rejected by psychophysicists. Now, a tongue-in-cheek solipsist might say that the psychophysicists do not go far enough. After all, they attempt to study the response of the visual system to light, which is a physical phenomenon outside the organism. Thus, they are probably mired in their own set of naturalistic assumptions about quanta, waves, the applicability of Fourier-transform theory to two-dimensional distributions of electromagnetic energy, and so on. A strict solipsist would study the formal processing of two-dimensional arrays of numbers, classically known as the retinal mosaic. Why don't psychophysicists do this? One possibility is that a suitable technology was not available until recently. Now that we can produce random-dot displays on a CRT, we are in a position to study the visual equivalent of Ebbinghaus's nonsense syllables. (Assumptions about physics still sneak in here, but just as a matter of instrumentation.) Why haven't psychophysicists adopted such a methodology?[6] The answer seems to be that everyone has felt that some sort of theoretical generalization about the stimulus was a necessary part of scientific investigations of the visual system.

Conservative psychophysics is methodologically solipsistic, however, in the sense that it eschews theorizing about the world of objects. One of the reasons for this is precisely that many psychophysicists, in tune with Fodor's (1981) earlier pessimism, think that they have a good shot at characterizing light and very little shot at characterizing the visible world and its causal relations with reflected light. To give a more recent example: Psychophysics-oriented investigators have attempted to characterize the visual system in terms of Fourier optics. Fourier optics is a marvelously general way of studying the response of an optical system to the input image, but it bears a less certain relation to the perception of the world.

Psychophysical and physiological evidence for spatial-frequency filtering in the visual system has been steadily accumulating for twenty years. Many psychophysicists proposed that the visual system performed a Fourier analysis of the input image and hoped that, since an image can be reconstructed from its Fourier transform, Fourier analysis would solve the problems of perception. It should be immediately clear, however, that simply recording the input image in an encoded form has nothing to do with perception. One has to go on to show that the transformed image makes information about the visible world explicitly available to the system.

Researchers in computer vision immediately recognized this burden and concluded that the Fourier transform is not very useful in encoding information about the world. As a result, although the Fourier transform is efficiently computable, it is not being used in research on computer vision. Marr (see Marr and Hildreth 1980; Marr 1982, pp. 75 ff.) develops the computational argument against the Fourier transform with particular clarity. One of the most interesting aspects of Marr's theory is that he was able to give a perceptual rather than a psychophysical interpretation of the evidence for spatial-frequency filtering in the visual system. The notion that the visual system is a Fourier analyzer has died very slowly in the psychophysical community, however, and it has died in response to psychophysical data rather than perceptual arguments. Julesz, Gilbert, and Victor (1978) showed that textures with identical Fourier spectra can be discriminated; Wilson (1983) showed that a wide variety of the psychophysical data on spatial-frequency analysis in the visual system can be fitted by a model with six broadly tuned spatial filters of the type proposed by Marr; and pervasive nonlinearities have shown up in electrophysiological recording from single cells in cat and monkey retina, lateral geniculate nucleus, and visual cortex (Shapley and Lennie 1985).

It seems increasingly clear that the (quasi-) individualistic methodology of psychophysics has to be combined with naturalistic research strategies in order to yield a convincing scientific account of the visual system.

Fundamental Challenges: Cooperative Computation And Adaptation

Many researchers believe that cooperative computation plays a considerably more important role in visual perception than Marr allowed. The empirical, theoretical, and heuristic reasons for Marr's avoidance of cooperative modeling have all been challenged.

In this volume Arbib describes a representative approach to computer vision that involves considerable top-down information flow from object and scene schemas (Hanson and Riseman 1978a). This system is particularly interesting because knowledge about objects interacts intimately with image information in edge and region finding. In his chapter Arbib gives an example in which the initial segmentation of an image by low-level processes was revised via the influence of a higher-level hypothesis that there was a typical projection of a house in the image. The high-level hypothesis included an edge that was not detected by the low-level processes on their first pass. The low-level processes then resegmented the critical region and looked for evidence of a low-contrast edge, which was present. If the low-level processes accepted this kind of evidence without higher guidance, however, they would find many spurious edges. Hanson and Riseman's reliance on top-down information flow is based partly on an empirical claim and is partly heuristic. Empirically, they are arguing that in many naturally occurring images the low-level visual information simply isn't good enough to compute a $2\frac{1}{2}$-D sketch without some hypothesis-driven help. Heuristically, their system is a demonstration that a particular scheme of top-down cooperation can be implemented and should be explored further.

Hanson and Riseman's system seems to be a clear violation of strong modularity, although it could be argued that the top-down influence is constrained by modularity. The higher-level hypothesis resets a parameter on the edge-finding process, which is still operating as a module, and the higher-level hypothesis might be regarded as a basic-level object schema (Fodor claims that such schemas are part of the visual input system). Here again, however, we see the potential loss of empirical content in the strong-modularity view. If it covers both Marr's approach and that of Hanson and Riseman, it is failing to discriminate among the theories that are being actively pursued in research on computer vision.

As mentioned above, Marr's claims about modularity rest partly on demonstrations that information sources, such as stereopsis and visual motion, can be psychophysically isolated. Psychophysical evidence can cut the other way, however. Todd (1985), for example, has synthesized displays that seem to violate some of the constraints on visual motion that have been assumed in arguments that it operats as a module. Stable perceptions of objects moving in space nevertheless occurred. Some of Todd's displays contained large amounts of visual noise, and others were based on deformations of shading, texture, or self-occluding contours, which are not part of current modular models. Todd argues that motion perception arises from cooperation among a number of bottom-up information sources, and that there may be contextual contributions as well.

Another area that has not been addressed by Marrian theory is the degree of plasticity in the visual system. Perceptual development, learning, and adaptation show that, at least to a limited extent, the contingencies of the normal world-organism relationship are not fixed in the system. The adaptation of visuomotor coordination to prismatic goggles, for example, shows that behavior can be tuned to a variety of Euclidean transformations of the normal optical situation. However, there is evidence that it is the proprioceptive system that is tuned rather than the visual system (see e.g., Harris 1968), although there is still controversy in this area. This result is an example of the general tendency for the visual system to get epistemic priority (called *visual capture* or *visual dominance*) when it is brought into conflict with another sensory modality. Regardless of the exact source of the adaptation, most experiments on adaptation concern well-behaved Euclidean transformations, and hence they do not conflict with a suitably abstract characterization of evolution's commitments, such as that of Shepard (1981). If a system makes two-dimensional projective measurements on a three-dimensional Euclidean space, there are certain mathematically natural parameters that could be open to recalibration or tuning.

We do not know what the limits of perceptual development and learning are, but research techniques in this area provide further tools for testing the commitments of the visual system. The prediction of strong, naturalistic modularity would presumably be that the remarkable plasticity of the visual system and of the total space-perception system is constrained by the modular organization and by some suitably generally stated set of assumptions about contingencies of the world-perceiver relation, which are built into the perceptual process.

Is Object Recognition Modular?

Although Marr argued that expectations and stored descriptions of objects do not influence the computation of the $2\frac{1}{2}$-D sketch, he did hypothesize top-down influences on shape description and object identification (1982, p. 321). In addition, he was pessimistic about the prospects for a computational analysis of object recognition. He essentially said that, although the problem of object representation and recognition is solvable for machine vision systems, he can't think of a way to show "what systems and schemes are actually used by humans" (1982, p. 313). It is not clear whether his tentative ideas are consistent with Fodor's sketch of an argument that object identification at Rosch's basic level is modular (1983, pp. 93 ff.), since Fodor is willing to argue that certain kinds of associative interactions among concepts or schemas are consistent with modularity (pp. 76 ff.). In view of how little we know about shape description and object recognition, Marr's reticence in this area is understandable, and Fodor's argument is necessarily sketchy and highly speculative.

Why have the problems of high-level vision not yielded readily to all the mathematics that the MIT School has been able to throw at it (generalized cones, differential geometry, and so on)? Part of the difference is that object description is firmly within the domain of three-dimensional modeling and not in the domain of describing the relationships between the world and reflected light. The physical processes involved in reflection and image formation constrain mathematical proposals in this domain tremendously. Possible proposals for the mathematical description of shape do not, so far, seem so constrained. When one is confronted with Horn's (1975) analysis of shape from shading, one has a tendency to say "Yes, that's a complete and correct analysis of the problem." When one is confronted with, say, Marr and Nishihara's (1978) proposals about shape representation, one has a tendency to say "Gee, that's interesting, but it may be an arbitrary solution."

The question here is whether the search for provably correct and optimal analyses that characterizes the computational level of analysis can be carried through for object recognition. We might imagine two directions in which further work on shape description and object recognition might play out. In the first case, Marr's pessimism about developing an ideal theory of shape for both humans and machines would be overcome. The problem would be solved in just the way that the problems in early vision were solved. In the second case, it would turn out that a much more detailed analysis of the human ecological niche would have to be undertaken, and that human shape description depends critically on our particular fit to our (primal) environment. Machines for the perception of small, machined parts on assembly lines would use a different scheme of shape description, and so on.

Let us begin with the first case. An important aspect of Marr's work on early vision is the use of an idealized design stance. There is an assumption that the early visual system can recover a description of surface layout with no loss of information. The only assumption about the organism/system is that three-dimensional surface layout is the goal of early vision. Because of the assumption that the system is an ideal detector for this information, there is no need for further assumptions about particular aspects of surface layout that humans, other primates, or particular machine systems are adapted to perceive. The limits on the system are limits of resolution that can be defined in engineering terms. The assumption of ideal design is a crucial element of the argument for unique solutions. Marr goes to great lengths to dispose of potential arguments that there might be something arbitrary about his proposals. For example, he argues (1982, p. 67) that the digitization involved in taking the zero crossings on the image causes no loss of information. Similarly, he argues (Marr 1982, pp. 54 ff.; Marr and Hildreth 1980) that the isotropic Mexican-hat operator is the best possible operator for detecting zero crossings.

Marr's work on shape and the work of those with similar views can be seen as an attempt to make the idealized design strategy work for shape. The question is what is the best way to describe the shapes of objects in general, not what aspects of the shapes of objects naturally encountered are human beings adapted to (Marr and Nishihara 1978; Hoffman and Richards 1984). Although the ideal design strategy is powerful in its minimization of assumptions, it has a pre-Darwinian flavor. Nevertheless, a successful scheme of ideal shape description would still undoubtedly be naturalistic. It would probably make contingent assumptions about local coherence and continuity of curvature, for example. And it might use computability from a $2\frac{1}{2}$-D sketch as a criterion.

The second possible strategy for a theory of shape description would undertake to constrain theories via a more detailed examination of the human ecological niche. Here, rather than assume that humans are idealized-shape detectors in some defensible abstract sense, we would undertake an empirical analysis of human visual adaptation. The history of research on frogs and toads, initiated by Lettvin et al. (1959), provides a model for this endeavor. Lettvin et al. began with very informal notions of objects in the world that were of ecological importance to the frog, such as bugs and predators. They were able to get evidence that the frog's visual system contained channels that were tuned to visual stimulation of the kind caused by the motions of these objects. At its informal beginnings, this methodology was vacuous as scientific naturalism (Fodor 1981, pp. 251–252). It was not a discovery to announce that frogs ate bugs and avoided predators. The science was on the formal side: Frogs appeared to have neural networks in the retina that were tuned to bugs and predators. However, the initially superficial ecological analysis has now been replaced by an analysis of the significant objects in physical terms (Arbib, this volume). Thus, worms happens to be (among other things) long and thin in a horizontal orientation, and the toad's visuomotor system is tuned to snap at long and thin things. The toad's success is completely dependent on contingent relationships among wormness, three-dimensional shape, and two-dimensional shape, which have been noncircularly characterized.

I do not see any principled argument against the use of this methodology to find the human scheme for shape description. I think it is probably Gibson's methodology. The impressive flexibility of human shape recognition and our lack of a firm informal grasp of our ecological niche argue against early success, but maybe clever mathematics and good experiments can save the day. On the other hand, our impressive flexibility might lead right back to Marr's ideal design approach. Somehow it came out that we are not very highly adapted to any particular three-dimensional, terrestial environment, but are well adapted in the abstract.

Regardless of whether the idealized design stance or a more ecological stance proves to be the best way to investigate strong modularity in shape description and object recognition, it seems certain that difficult questions will arise concerning the balances between strong and weak modularity and between modular processes and general problem-solving processes. There are aspects of shape description and recognition that appear to be fixed in the perceptual-cognitive architecture; two examples are the segregation of the $2\frac{1}{2}$-D sketch into objects and the interdependence of form and orientation, as demonstrated in the studies of Rock (1973) and Shepard and Cooper (1982). Another possibility is the proposal of Hoffman and Richards (1984) that objects are naturally segmented into parts at points of maximum concave curvature. The relation between orientation and form may be an example of a phenomenon that emerges from a constraint that is more specific to the ecology of terrestrial animals than those so far proposed by Marr and his associates: By and large, we and the objects we perceive have a canonical orientation relative to a ground plane that is perpendicular to gravity.

Other aspects of object identification seem likely to be weakly modular or penetrated by central cognitive processes. Shape memory, for example, might show the same kind of sensitivity to strategy and general knowledge that is found for memory in general. The impressive amount of perceptual learning displayed in the mastery of visual categories is also a problem that has not been seriously addressed. There is evidence that rather arbitrary visual categories can be learned to a degree that satisfies the criteria for modularity (Shiffrin and Schneider 1977), although the experiments involved sets of letters and digits and were not based on an explicit theory of early vision. Other similar examples seem to demonstrate a mastery of visual categories that is specifically tuned to a specific problem-solving context: Master chess players can fluently recognize thousands of strategically important visual configurations of chess pieces, although they develop no special ability to recognize random configurations of pieces (Chase and Simon 1973).

The strong-modularity theorist might argue that perceptual learning is constrained by built-in machinery for object description. One approach is to ask whether learning is strongly constrained by the kinds of general schemes for shape decomposition (Hoffman and Richards 1984) or object description (Marr and Nishihara 1978) that have been proposed. Marr and Nishihara's hierarchical approach to object description leads naturally to an account of perceptual learning (Marr 1982, p. 306). These theories allow for great flexibility in the varieties of visual categories that can be learned. In his discussion of Rosch's basic level, Fodor (1983) seems to be aiming for a higher degree of constraint that picks out particular naturally occurring visual categories rather than specifying highly general principles of description. The evidence that the basic level is a property of the visual system is extremely weak, however, since there has been no formal analysis of the visual properties that define basic objects. It is quite plausible that the special properties of basic-level identification result from regularities in the task environment and from practice rather than from strong constraints built into the neural/computational architecture. Some of the task regularities may well have genuine ecological validity (for example, categories like *bird* and *horse* may represent actual commonalities in visual shape), but it appears that human beings are well equipped to cope with vastly altered ecologies.

There is also evidence concerning various kinds of priming effects in object recognition. Kroll and Potter (1984) found evidence for visual representations of common objects in an object-decision task in which subjects judged whether line drawings were pictures of common objects or pseudo-objects. Repetition of an item facilitated the second response time. However, in a "reality decision" task, in which object-decision trials were mixed with lexical-decision trials, a lexical decision on the name of an object did not facilitate a later object decision on a picture of the object. That is, the name of an object apparently did not prime its visual representation. Other evidence, however, indicates that various kinds of semantic and contextual priming occur in tasks involving object identification (Palmer 1975; J. F. Kroll, personal communication, January 1986). Kroll has found that specific sentential contexts facilitate object decisions. The speed of the responses seems to rule out a simple model in which the facilitation occurs after the activation of a lexical or semantic representation.

The problems facing a naturalistic theory of object perception are indeed formidable. Fodor (1981) discussed a strong semantic criterion for successful perception (e.g. truly, in fact, seeing a horse) that makes the entire natural science of visible objects potentially relevant to perception (e.g. new discoveries about the genetics of horses). His proposal (Fodor 1983) that basic-level object perception is strongly modular is an attempt to overcome this difficulty by arguing that the perceptual system can deliver reasonably reliable outputs without being saddled with making generalized nondemonstrative inferences. An empirical theory focuses on aspects of objects that are potentially visibly encodable (according to the going theory of early vision) under certain boundary conditions that define normal perceptual situations. One contribution of an empirical theory to an account of semantically successful seeing is its ability to explain illusions in terms of some object accidentally leading to an image that falls under the physical description normal for some other object. (The theory can explain rigorously why an object was mistaken for a horse.) This can happen because the boundary conditions for the normal case are violated (as might be argued of the Ames demonstrations) or because under normal conditions the object's reflected array happens to meet the description.

A certain open-endedness in the variety of ways that illusions can happen makes it difficult to get a complete semantical account of correct perception going. Nevertheless, Fodor's earlier worry that the notion of a pencil, or a horse, or a worm being the discriminative stimulus for an action is vacuous as naturalistic science now seems wrong. Granted, wormness does not figure in any of the laws of physics, and it would be hard to give an exhaustive account of truly seeing a worm. However, Ewert (see Arbib, this volume) has given a nonvacuous, naturalistic account of why toads are almost always successful when they snap at worms. First, toads snap at any object that projects an image satisfying a certain physical description. Second, in the natural environment of the toad, most worms satisfy this description and very little else does.

Modularity and Interactions between Vision and Language

Interactions between vision and language provide one of the most fertile testing grounds for the strong-modularity thesis. Fodor argues that the substantial evidence for cooperative and expectation-driven computation in language processing is consistent with strong modularity. The basic argument is that the interactions occur within the language module at a restricted level. Fodor argues that an associative network among lexical items that facilitates their identification is part of the language module. According to this theory, the semantic priming of, say, *salt* by an occurrence of *pepper* is evidence for interactive computation in the lexical access system rather than for semantic associations in the central processing system. One line of support is the disputed evidence that associations like *salt-pepper* seem to be fixed and rather insensitive to the meaningful details of the situation. Thus, an occurrence of *bug* in a spying context is sometimes found to facilitate *insect*, which is not relevant to the context. The evidence in this area is growing increasingly complex, however.

To cite one line of evidence that supports strong modularity: In many cases where details of the semantic context do facilitate responses, it can be argued that the facilitation occurs after lexical access and the assignment of syntactic structure. For example, in a property-verification task Barsalou (1982) found that rather intricate properties of concepts can be facilitated by complex sentential contexts. In one stimulus, the judgment that *can be walked upon* is a property of *roof* was facilitated by the sentence *The roof creaked under the weight of the repairman* but not by the sentence *The roof had been renovated prior to the rainy season*. Property verification arguably engages central processes rather than the linguistic input system, and, as Fodor would predict, we find exactly the kind of detailed semantic effect that seems hard to elicit in on-line linguistic tasks.

The growing evidence for cross-modality semantic priming is more difficult to handle within strong-modularity theory. For example, Vanderwart (1984) found that pictures could semantically prime lexical decisions. One way to handle this kind of evidence is to argue that the lexical-decision task includes a post-lexical access component. This style of reasoning tends to diminish the theory's falsifiability, however. In general, it is not yet clear that psychological experiments have the power to discriminate between strong and weak modularity in this area. Well-developed weak-modularity theories such as Anderson's (1983) have considerable predictive power. Anderson's theory contains several mechanisms that can predict qualitative effects of the kind reviewed above. The distinction between unskilled and skilled performance in Anderson's theory makes strikingly parallel predictions to Fodor's distinction between input systems and central processes.

The issue of cross-modality effects is a particularly vexing one, in part because Fodor did not discuss it in detail. In this volume, Arbib argues that reading may violate strong modularity. Reading is a particularly interesting case, because it represents a skilled coordination of the visual and linguistic input systems that is not hardwired. It might be argued that the strongest version of strong modularity predicts that processing the alphabetic aspect of print would be impossible. Since the linguistic system evolved to retrieve lexical items and assign syntactic-logical form to acoustic inputs in a bottom-up fashion, we should not be able to phonologically encode alphabetic input or retrieve lexical items in response to alphabetic input. Even Chinese logographic orthography should be processed without access to the lexicon: A printed character should undergo shape analysis within the visual input system, resulting in the retrieval of a concept without any internal linguistic analysis. There is extremely strong evidence, however, that the processing of alphabetic orthography taps into the linguistic system at both the phonological level and the lexical-access level in normal readers.

Presumably, the strong-modularity theorist would handle reading by arguing that the cross-modality connections established in alphabetic or syllabic reading systems are restricted—perhaps even predicted—by the modular structures of the visual and linguistic input systems. For example, alphabetic writing can tap into the phonological system only because its visual shapes can be translated into that system's output vocabulary. A writing system that assigned visual shapes to arbitrary chunks of the sound stream would be difficult or impossible to learn. Similarly, the modular character of the visual system would have to be shown to influence the reading process. Carroll and Slowiaczek's chapter in this volume illustrates the kind of comparative research that has to be done to explore the implications of the modularity thesis for reading. Their work on regressive eye movements suggests lines of argument for both strong-modularity and weak-modularity theorists. On the one hand, regressive eye movements seem to be a clear case of top-down information flow. They can probably be triggered by detailed semantic and pragmatic factors that are outside the linguistic input system. On the other hand, the proponent of strong modularity could argue that the post-perceptual triggering of a reanalysis is entirely consistent with modularity if the reanalysis either reruns the perceptual system or goes off-line into a central problem-solving mode.

Connectionist models of reading potentially provide a powerful analysis of cross-modal connections and top-down influences, and they provide an interesting challenge for the modularity theorist. Many connectionist theorists seem to begin by assuming extremely weak modularity: Anything can be and probably is connected to everything else. However, there are at present no connectionist models of a complete visual process in a natural stimulus domain, going from visual input to object identification. Most detailed connectionist models concern processing within parts of the visual input system and are consistent with a version of strong modularity that allows constrained top-down information flow within an input system.

McClelland and Rumelhart's (1981; see also Rumelhart and McClelland 1982) model of context effects in letter perception is one of the few connectionist models to have been subjected to extensive empirical tests. The model has five levels of representation: visual input, visual letter features, letters, words, and higher levels. The visual-input level and the higher level of representation are not formally specified. At the letter level there is one node for each letter at each possible position in a word; for example, there are separate nodes for word-initial a, second-letter a, third-letter a, and so on. The word level is amodal and would therefore be associated with the lexical component of the linguistic input system. That is, word nodes are activated by both visual and auditory input; there are not separate visual word nodes and auditory or linguistic word nodes. There is a bottom-up flow of excitatory and inhibitory influence from the feature level to the letter level to the word level. There are inhibitory interactions among nodes at the feature, letter, and word levels. Finally, there is both excitatory and inhibitory top-down influence from the word level to the letter level. That is, if a word node has been activated by the activation of some of the letter nodes that have excitatory connections to it, then the word node feeds excitation back to letter nodes that are consistent with it and feeds inhibition back to letter nodes that are not consistent with it. This top-down flow of information is critical to the explanation of a wealth of findings on the tachistoscopic perception of letters embedded in words and nonwords.

Feedback from lexical representation (which is part of the language module) to the letter-position nodes (which are a level of visual representation) is somewhat problematic for Fodor, since it represents top-down information flow across two major input systems. However, it is constrained by modularity in two ways. First, it is not a case of top-down influence from genuinely central representations. Second, the interface between words and letters is well behaved in the sense that the activation of a word activates only its largest parts, the letters, which are the output of visual processing in this case. All the known findings can be fitted by the model without, for example, allowing a word to directly activate letter features. In fact, it turned out to be unnecessary to include top-down influences from letters to features in the simulation model. In view of this line of argument, the major criticism of strong modularity that might emerge is that its empirical content is limited. If strong modularity allows top-down computation within and across the major input systems, then it appears that its only empirical claim is that detailed central representations have small or no influences on input processing.

Although McClelland and Rumelhart have no model for semantic and pragmatic processing, they did attempt to simulate higher-level effects by preactivating word nodes before starting processing at the feature level. The simulation did not show striking effects of higher-level input on letter perception. It appears that the priming effect, which must percolate down via one or more primed word nodes, is overwhelmed by the way in which the feature input drives the massively interconnected network. This appears to be an interesting case of weak modularity mimicking strong modularity. The theory includes top-down influences from central levels of representation; however, given the structure of the task and all the other influences that are operating within and between levels, the top-down activation has extremely small effects, which are difficult to detect empirically and are of no functional importance.

Acknowledgments

The author gratefully acknowledges the help of Judith Kroll and Joseph Cohen during the preparation of this chapter.

Notes

1. Ames and his followers claimed not to be realists and were fond of remarks such as " . . . the world each of us knows is a world created in large measure from our experience in dealing with the environment" (Ittelson and Kilpatrick 1958, p. 434). Their various epistemological claims have always seemed to me to be inconsistent, however, and the most straightforward reading of their theory seems to be that the perceptual system adjusts quite rationally to the probabilistic contingencies in the environment and in the mapping from the environment to the retinal image. On this reading, their claims seem to be roughly equivalent to Brunswik's.

2. It should be clear that Gibson's theory is not an exception to this claim. Although Gibson claimed that visual stimulation is not ambiguous under normal viewing conditions, his claim rested on the assumption that organisms were precisely tuned to relationships between objects and the structure of reflected light. In fact, Gibson was the theorist most willing to build assumptions about such relations into the visual system.

3. If readers attempt this demonstration using gentle finger pressure, they may fail to perceive genuinely bright spots, or "phosphenes," in the visual field. In a lighted environment, gentle pressure tends to produce a darkish blob with perhaps a light fringe that has very little feeling of localization in space but is definitely in a nasal direction relative to the stimulated eye.

4. This remark defines direction relative to the visual axis of the eye. The computation of direction relative to the head or relative to 3-D world coordinates defined by gravity requires information about the position of the eyes relative to the head and of the head relative to the world. These complications do not change the fundamental point about the information value of retinal coordinates, however.

5. It would take some scholarly research to verify the claim that all the classical perceptual theories built this assumption into the perceptual process. Among the theories that emphasized stimulus ambiguity, did any argue that the organism has to learn the correct map from image coordinates to spatial directions from the infinite set of possible arbitrary maps? Some philosophical sense-data theories may be exceptions. Anyone who believes the strongest version of this theory should be willing to try the following perceptual learning experiment. The observer wears a goggle that presents a CRT display to his eyes as he moves about the world. The CRT display is generated in the following way: A miniature TV camera is mounted to the observer's forehead, pointed at what would be his normal field of view. The TV signal is digitized into a two-dimensional array of values and fed to a microcomputer which consistently maps each point in the array onto another randomly chosen point in the array. This entirely consistent but geometrically scrambled array is then fed to the CRT screen. The true believer in the strongest version of sense-data theory would predict that the observer would adapt to this stimulus situation. My claim is that no one has ever believed this.

6. Although random-dot displays are widely used in contemporary psychophysical and perceptual research, they are invariably used to eliminate all sources of organization in the visual stimulus except the one under study. Thus, Julesz's stereograms are random except for the presence of stereoscopic depth cues, which are hypothesized to be important by a prior ecological analysis. Posner and Keele's (1968) use of random dot patterns to study visual prototype formation is much closer to the Ebbinghausian tradition, because the random prototypes are chosen with no attention to the kinds of shapes and forms that have to be identified in the real world. The same goes for the ubiquitous N-sided random polygons.

Bibliography

Ades, A., and M. Steedman. 1982. "On the Order of Words." *Linguistics and Philosophy* 4: 517–558.

Ajdukiewicz, K. 1935. "Die syntaktische Konnexitat." *Studia Philosophica* 1: 1–27. Reprinted in English as "Syntactic Connection" in McCall 1967.

Altmann, G. T. M. 1986. Reference and the Resolution of Local Syntactic Ambiguity: The Effect of Context during Human Sentence Processing. Ph.D. Dissertation, University of Edinburgh.

Altmann, G. T. M., and M. J. Steedman. Interaction with Context during Human Sentence Processing. In preparation.

Amari, S., and M. A. Arbib. 1977. "Competition and Cooperation in Neural Nets." In Metzler 1977.

Aoun, J., and N. Hornstein. 1985. "Quantifier Types." *Linguistic Inquiry* 16: 4.

Aoun, J., and D. Sportiche. 1983. "On the Formal Theory of Government." *Linguistic Review* 3: 211–235.

Anderson, J. R. 1983. *The Architecture of Cognition*. Harvard University Press.

Anderson, S., and P. Kiparsky, eds. 1973. *A Festschrift for Morris Halle*. Holt, Rinehart & Winston.

Arbib, M. A. 1972. *The Metaphorical Brain: An Introduction to Cybernetics as Artificial Intelligence and Brain Theory*. Wiley-Interscience.

Arbib, M. A. 1981. "Visuomotor Coordination: From Neural Nets to Schema Theory." *Cognition and Brain Theory* 4: 23–39.

Arbib, M. A., and A. R. Hanson, eds. 1987. *Vision, Brain, and Cooperative Computation*. MIT Press.

Arbib, M. A., and D. H. House. 1983. "Depth and Detours: Towards Neural Models." In *Proceedings of the Second Workshop on Visuomotor Coordination in Frog and Toad: Models and Experiments*, Technical Report 83-19, Department of Computer and Information Science, University of Massachusetts, Amherst.

Arbib, M. A., and D. H. House. 1987. "Depth and Detours: An Essay on Visually Guided Behavior." In Arbib and Hanson 1987.

Arbib, M. A., C. C. Boylls, and P. Dev. 1974. "Neural Models of Spatial Perception and the Control of Movement." In Keidel et al. 1974.

Arbib, M. A., J. Conklin, and J. C. Hill. 1986. *From Schema Theory to Language*. Oxford University Press.

Bach, E. 1979. "Control in Montague Grammar." *Linguistic Inquiry* 10: 515–531.

Bach, E. 1980. "In Defense of Passive." *Linguistics and Philosophy* 3: 297–341.

Bach, E. 1983a. "Generalised Categorial Grammars and the English Auxilliary." In Heny and Richards 1983.

Bach, E. 1983b. "On the Relationship between Word Grammar and Phrase Grammar." *Natural Language and Linguistic Theory* 1: 65–80.

Bach, E., and R. T. Harms, eds. 1968. *Universals in Linguistic Theory.* Holt, Rinehart.

Bach, K. 1982. *"De Re* Belief and Methodological Solipsism." In Woodfield 1982.

Baker, C. L. 1979. "Syntactic Theory and the Projection Problem." *Linguistic Inquiry* 10, no. 4: 533–581.

Baker, C. L., and J. J. McCarthy, eds. 1981. *The Logical Problem of Language Acquisition.* MIT Press.

Bar-Hillel, Y. 1953. "A Quasi-Arithmetical Notation for Syntactic Description." *Language* 29: 47–58.

Barlow, H. 1953. "Summation and Inhibition in the Frog's Retina." *Journal of Physiology* 119: 69–88.

Barlow, M., D. Flickinger, and M. Wescoat, eds. 1983. Proceedings of the Second West Coast Conference on Formal Linguistics.

Barsalou, L. W. 1982. "Context-Independent and Context-Dependent Information in Concepts." *Memory and Cognition* 10: 82–93.

Barss, A., E. Hale, M. Perkins, and M. Speas. 1985. Untitled manuscript, Massachusetts Institute of Technology.

Bates, E., and B. MacWhinney. 1982. "Functionalist Approaches to Language Acquisition." In Wanner and Gleitman 1982.

Bayer, J. The Processing of German Particles: Research for Aphasia and Cognitive Disorders. Unpublished.

Beardsley, D. C., and M. Wertheimer, eds. 1958. *Readings in Perception.* Van Nostrand.

Belletti, A., L. Brandi, and L. Rizzi, eds. 1979. *Theory of Markedness in Generative Grammar.* Scuola Normale Superiore di Pisa.

Berwick, R. C. 1985. *Computational Linguistics.* MIT Press.

Berwick, R. C., and A. S. Weinberg. 1982. "Parsing Efficiency, Computational Complexity, and the Evaluation of Grammatical Theories." *Linguistic Inquiry* 13: 165–192.

Berwick, R. C., and A. S. Weinberg. 1983. "The Role of Grammars in Models of Language Use." *Cognition* 13: 1–62.

Berwick, R. C., and A. Weinberg. 1984. *The Grammatical Basis of Linguistic Performance.* MIT Press.

Berwick, R. C., and A. Weinberg. 1986. "Deterministic Parsing and Linguistic Explanation." *Language and Cognitive Processes* 1: 465–490.

Bever, T. 1970. "The Cognitive Basis for Linguistic Structures." In Hayes 1970.

Bever, T. G., M. F. Garrett, and R. Hurtig. 1973. "Ambiguity Increases Complexity of Perceptually Incomplete Clauses." *Memory and Cognition* 1: 279–286.

Bever, T. G., J. M. Carroll, and L. A. Miller, eds. 1984. *Talking Minds: The Study of Language in the Cognitive Sciences.* MIT Press.

Bischof, N. 1980. "Remarks on Lorenz and Piaget: How Can 'Working Hypotheses' Be 'Necessary'?" In Piattelli-Palmerini 1980.

Bouchard, D. 1984. *On the Content of Empty Categories.* Foris.

Bouma, H., and D. G. Bouwhuis, eds. 1984. *Attention and Performance X: Control of Language Processes.* Erlbaum.

Braddick, O. J., and A. C. Sleigh, eds. 1983. *Physical and Biological Processing of Images.* Springer-Verlag.

Braunstein, M. 1976. *Depth Perception through Motion.* Academic.

Bresnan, J. W., ed. 1982. *The Mental Representation of Grammatical Relations.* MIT Press.

Bresnan, J. W., R. M. Kaplan, S. Peters, and A. Zaenen. 1982. "Cross-Serial Dependencies in Dutch." *Linguistic Inquiry* 13: 613–636.

Bruce, V., and P. R. Green. 1985. *Visual Perception: Physiology, Psychology, and Ecology.* Erlbaum.

Burge, T. 1979. "Individualism and the Mental." *Midwest Studies in Philosophy* 4: 73–121.

Burge, T. 1986. "Individualism and Psychology." *Philosophical Review* 95: 3—45.

Cairns, H. S. 1983. "Current Issues in Language Comprehension." In Naremore 1983.

Cauman, L., et al., eds. 1983. *How Many Questions? Essays in Honor of Sidney Morgenbesser.* Hackett.

Cervantes-Perez, F., R. Lara, and M. A. Arbib. 1985. "A Neural Model of Interactions Subserving Prey-Predator Discrimination and Size Preference in Anurans." *Journal of Theoretical Biology* 113: 117—152.

Chambers, S. M., and K. I. Forster. 1975. "Evidence for Lexical Access in a Simultaneous Matching Task." *Memory and Cognition* 3: 549—559.

Chase, W. G., ed. 1973. *Visual Information Processing.* Academic.

Chase, W. G., and H. A. Simon. 1973. "The Mind's Eye in Chess." In Chase 1973.

Chierchia, G. 1984. Topics in the Syntax and Semantics of Infinitives and Gerunds. Doctoral dissertation, University of Massachusetts, Amherst.

Chierchia, G. 1985. "Formal Semantics and the Grammar of Predication." *Linguistic Inquiry* 16: 417—443.

Chomsky, N. 1965. *Aspects of the Theory of Syntax.* MIT Press.

Chomsky, N. 1973. "Conditions on Transformations." In Anderson and Kiparsky 1973.

Chomsky, N. 1975a. "Questions of Form and Interpretation." *Linguistic Analysis* 1: 1. Reprinted in Chomsky 1977.

Chomsky, N. 1975b. *Reflections on Language.* Pantheon.

Chomsky, N. 1976. "Conditions on Rules of Grammar." *Linguistic Analysis* 2: 4. Reprinted in Chomsky 1977.

Chomsky, N. 1977. *Essays in Form and Interpretation.* North-Holland.

Chomsky, N. 1980a. "Remarks on Nominalisation." In Jacobs and Rosenbaum 1980.

Chomsky, N. 1980b. *Rules and Representations.* Columbia University Press.

Chomsky, N. 1981. *Lectures on Government and Binding.* Foris.

Chomsky, N. 1982. *Some Concepts and Consequences of the Theory of Government and Binding.* MIT Press.

Chomsky, N. 1986. *Knowledge of Language: Its Nature, Origin, and Use.* Praeger.

Churchland, P. S. 1986. *Neurophilosophy: Toward a Unified Science of the Mind-Brain.* MIT Press.

Clark, H. H. 1973. "The Language-as-Fixed-Effect Fallacy: A Critique of Language Statistics in Psychological Research." *Journal of Verbal Learning and Verbal Behavior.* 12: 335—359.

Clark, H. H., and S. E. Haviland. 1977. "Comprehension and the Given-New Contract." In Freedle 1977.

Collett, T. S., and L. I. K. Harkness. 1982. "Depth Vision in Animals." In Ingle et al. 1982.

Coltheart, M., R. Job, and G. Sartori, eds. 1986. *The Cognitive Neuropsychology of Language.* Erlbaum.

Connine, L. M., and C. Clifton. 1984. Interactive Use of Lexical Information in Speech Perception. Unpublished.

Cooper, R. 1979. "Variable Binding and Relative Clauses." In Guenthner and Schmidt 1979.

Cooper, R. 1983. *Quantification and Syntactic Theory.* Reidel.

Cooper, W. E., and E. C. T. Walker, eds. 1979. *Sentence Processing: Psycholinguistic Studies Presented to Merrill Garrett.* Erlbaum.

Cottrell, G. W. 1985a. A Connectionist Approach to Word Sense Disambiguation. Ph.D. thesis, University of Rochester.

Cottrell, G. W. 1985b. "Connectionist Parsing." In Proceedings of the Seventh Annual Conference of the Cognitive Science Society.

Cottrell, G. W., and S. L. Small. 1983. "A Connectionist Scheme for Modelling Word-Sense Disambiguation." *Cognition and Brain Theory* 6: 89—120.

Cowart, W. 1983. Reference Relations and Syntactic Processing: Evidence of Pronoun's Influence on a Syntactic Decision that Affects Naming. Indiana University Linguistics Club.

Crain, S. 1980. Contextual Constraints on Sentence Comprehension. Ph.D. dissertation, University of Connecticut.

Crain, S., and J. Fodor. 1985. "How Can Grammars Help Parsers?" In Dowty et al. 1985.

Crain, S., and M. Steedman. 1985. "On Not Being Led Up the Garden Path." In Dowty et al. 1985 (presented in 1982).

Curry, H. B. 1963. "Some Logical Aspects of Grammatical Structure." In *Structure of Language and Its Mathematical Aspects: Proceedings of the Twelfth Symposium in Applied Linguistics*, ed. R. Jakobson (American Mathematical Society).

Curry, H. B., and R. Feys. 1958. *Combinatory Logic*, volume 1. North-Holland.

Cutler, A., and J. D. Fodor. 1979. "Semantic Focus and Sentence Comprehension." *Cognition* 7: 49–60.

Cutler, A., and D. J. Foss. 1977. "On the Role of Sentence Stress in Sentence Processing." *Language and Speech* 20: 1–10.

Cutting, J. E., and B. S. Rosner. 1974. "Categories and Boundaries in Speech and Music." *Perception and Psychophysics* 16: 564–570.

Davidson, D., and G. Harman, eds. 1972. *Semantics of Natural Language*. Reidel.

Dell, G. S. 1986. "A Spreading Activation Theory of Retrieval in Sentence Production." *Psychological Review* 93: 283–321.

Dev, P. 1975. "Perception of Depth Surfaces in Random-Dot Stereograms: A Neural Model." *International Journal of Man-Machine Studies* 7: 511–528.

Dornic, S., ed. 1977. *Attention and Performance VI*. Erlbaum.

Dowty, D. 1982. "Grammatical Relations and Montague Grammar." In Jacobson and Pullum 1982.

Dowty, D., L. Kartunnen, and A. M. Zwickey, eds. 1985. *Natural Language Parsing: Psycholinguistic, Computational, and Theoretical Perspectives*. Cambridge University Press.

Dresher, B. E., and N. Hornstein. Restructuring and Interpretation in the T-Model. Unpublished.

Ehrlich, K., and K. Rayner. 1983. "Pronoun Assignment and Semantic Integration during Reading: Eye Movements and Immediacy of Processing." *Journal of Verbal Learning and Verbal Behavior* 22: 75–87.

Eimas, P. D., and J. D. Miller, eds. 1981. *Perspectives on the Study of Speech*. Erlbaum.

Ellis, A., ed. 1985. *Progress in the Psychology of Language*. Erlbaum.

Elman, J. L., and J. L. McClelland. 1984. "The Interactive Activation Model of Speech Perception." In Lass 1984.

Engdahl, E. 1981. "Multiple Gaps in English and Swedish." In *Proceedings of the Sixth Scandinavian Conference of Linguistics*, ed. T. Fretheim and L. Hellan (Tapir).

Engdahl, E. 1983. "Parisitic Gaps." *Linguistics and Philosophy* 6: 5–34.

Ewert, J.-P. 1976. "The Visual System of the Toad: Behavior and Physiological Studies on a Pattern Recognition System." In Fite 1976.

Ewert, J.-P., and W. von Seelen. 1974. "Neurobiologie und System-theorie: Eines visuellen Master-Erkennungmechanismus bei Kröte." *Kybernetik* 14: 167–183.

Feldman, J. A. 1985. "Four Frames Suffice: A Provisional Model of Vision and Space." *Behavioral and Brain Sciences* 8: 265–289.

Feldman, J. A. 1986. Neural Representation of Conceptual Knowledge. Cognitive Science Technical Report 33, University of Rochester.

Feldman, J. A., and L. Ballard. 1982. "Connectionist Models and Their Properties." *Cognitive Science* 6: 205–254.

Ferreira, F. 1985. The Role of Context in Resolving Syntactic Ambiguity. M. S. thesis, University of Massachusetts.

Ferreira, F., and C. Clifton. 1984. Role of Context in Resolving Syntactic Ambiguity. Presented at annual meeting of Psychonomic Society.

Ferreira, F., and C. Clifton. 1985. "The Independence of Syntactic Processing." *Journal of Memory and Language* 25: 348–368.

Fiengo, R., and J. Higginbotham. 1981. "Opacity in NP." *Linguistic Analysis* 7: 395–422.

Fillmore, C. 1968. "The Case for Case." In Bach and Harms 1968.

Fischer, D. F., R. A. Monty, and J. W. Senders. 1981. *Eye Movements: Cognition and Visual Perception.* Erlbaum.

Fite, K., ed. 1977. *The Amphibian Visual System: A Multidisciplinary Approach.* Academic.

Flores d'Arcais, G. B. 1982. "Automatic Syntactic Computation in Sentence Comprehension." *Psychological Research* 44: 231–242.

Flynn, M. 1983. "A Categorial Theory of Structure Building." In Gazdar et al. 1983.

Fodor, J. A. 1975. *The Language of Thought.* Crowell.

Fodor, J. A. 1979. "Superstrategy." In Cooper and Walker 1979.

Fodor, J. A. 1981. "Methodological Solipsism Considered as a Research Strategy in Psychology." In *Representations: Philosophical Essays on the Foundations of Cognitive Science,* ed. J. A. Fodor (MIT Press).

Fodor, J. A. 1983. *The Modularity of Mind.* MIT Press.

Fodor, J. A., and T. G. Bever. 1965. "The Psychological Reality of Linguistic Segments." *Journal of Verbal Learning and Verbal Behavior* 4: 414–420.

Fodor, J. A., and I. Sag. 1982. "Referential and Qualificational Indefinites." *Linguistics and Philosophy* 5: 344–398.

Fodor, J. A., T. G. Bever, and M. F. Garrett. 1974. *The Psychology of Language: An Introduction to Psycholinguistics and Generative Grammar.* McGraw-Hill.

Ford, M., J. Bresnan, and R. M. Kaplan. 1982. "A Competence-Based Theory of Syntactic Closure." In Bresnan 1982.

Forster, K. I. 1979. "Levels of Processing and the Structure of the Language Processor." In Cooper and Walker 1979.

Forster, K. I. 1980. "Absence of Lexical and Orthographic Effects in a Same-Different Task." *Memory and Cognition* 8: 210–215.

Forster, K. I. 1981. "Priming and the Effects of Sentence and Lexical Contexts on Naming Time: Evidence for Autonomous Lexical Processing." *Quarterly Journal of Experimental Psychology* 33: 465–495.

Frauenfelder, U., and S. M. Marcus. 1984. Phonetic Decisions and Lexical Constraints in the Real-Time Process of Speech Perception. Manuscript 488, Institute for Perception Research, Eindhoven.

Frazier, L. 1978. On Comprehending Sentences: Syntactic Parsing Strategies. Indiana University Linguistics Club.

Frazier, L. 1985a. "Modularity in the Representation of Hypotheses." *Proceedings of the Northeastern Linguistics Society* 131–144.

Frazier, L. 1985b. Syntactic Processing: Evidence from Dutch. Max-Planck-Institut, Nijmegen.

Frazier, L., and J. Fodor. 1978. "The Sausage Machine: A New Two-Stage Parsing Model." *Cognition* 13: 187–222.

Frazier, L., and K. Rayner. 1982. "Making and Correcting Errors during Sentence Comprehension: Eye Movements in the Analysis of Structurally Ambiguous Sentences." *Cognitive Psychology* 14: 178–210.

Frazier, L., C. Clifton, and J. Randall. 1983. "Filling Gaps: Decision Principles and Structure in Sentence Comprehension." *Cognition* 13: 187–222.

Freedle, R. O., ed. 1977. *Discourse Production and Comprehension*. Ablex.

Freedman, S. A. 1982. Behavioral Reflexes of Constraints on Transformations. Doctoral thesis, Monash University.

Freedman, S. A., and K. I. Forster. 1985. "The Psychological Status of Overgenerated Sentences." *Cognition* 19: 101–131.

Ganong, W. F. 1980. "Phonetic Categorisation in Auditory Word Perception." *Journal of Experimental Psychology: Human Perception and Performance* 6: 210–217.

Garnes, S., and Z. Bond. 1976. "The Relationship between Semantic Expectation and Acoustic Information." *Phonologica* 285–293.

Garrett, M. F. 1978. "Word and Sentence Perception. In Held et al. 1978.

Garrett, M., T. Bever, and J. Fodor. 1966. "The Active Use of Grammar in Speech Perception." *Perception and Psychophysics* 1: 30–32.

Gazdar, G. 1981. "Unbounded Dependencies and Coordinate Structure." *Linguistic Inquiry* 12: 155–184.

Gazdar, G., and G. K. Pullum. 1981. "Subcategorization, Constituent Order, and the Notion 'Head.'" In Moortgat et al. 1981.

Gazdar, G., E. Klein, and G. K. Pullum, eds. 1983. *The Nature of Syntactic Representation*. Reidel.

Gazdar, G., E. Klein, I. A. Sag, and G. K. Pullum. 1985. *Generalised Phrase Structure Grammar*. Blackwell.

Geach, P. T. 1972. "A Program for Syntax." In Davidson and Harman 1972.

Gibson, J. J. 1966. The Senses Considered as Perceptual Systems. Houghton Mifflin.

Goodman, G. O., J. L. McClelland, and R. W. Gibbs. 1981. "The Role of Syntactic Context in Word Recognition." *Memory and Cognition* 9: 580–596.

Gough, P. B., J. A. Alford, Jr., and P. Holley-Wilcox. 1981. "Words and Contexts." In Tzeng and Singer 1981.

Green, K. P. 1984. The Availability and Use of Visual Prosodic Information during Spoken Language Processing. Ph.D. thesis, Northeastern University.

Green, K. P., and J. L. Miller. 1985. "On the Role of Visual Rate Information in Phonetic Perception." *Perception and Psychophysics* 38: 269–276.

Gregory, R. 1968. "Visual Illusions." *Scientific American* 219: 66–76.

Grimshaw, J. 1981. "Form, Function, and the Language Acquisition Device." In Baker and McCarthy 1981.

Grimshaw, J., and A. Prince. The Prosodic Constraint on Dative Verbs. In preparation.

Grimson, W. E. L. 1981. *From Images to Surfaces*. MIT Press.

Guenthner, F., and S. J. Schmidt, eds. 1979. *Formal Semantics and Pragmatics for Natural Languages*. Reidel.

Haber, R. N., ed. 1968. *Contemporary Theory and Research in Visual Perception*. Holt, Rinehart & Winston.

Haddock, N. J. 1985. Computing Noun Phrase Reference. DAI Working Paper 182, University of Edinburgh.

Halle, M. 1959. *The Sound Pattern of Russian*. Mouton.

Halle, M., J. Bresnan, and G. Miller, eds. 1978. *Linguistic Theory and Psychological Reality*. MIT Press.

Hanson, A., and E. Riseman 1978a. "VISIONS: A Computer System for Interpreting Scenes." In *Computer Vision Systems*, ed. A. Hanson and E. Riseman (Academic).

Hanson, A., and E. Riseman. 1978b. "Segmentation of Natural Scenes." In *Computer Vision Systems*, ed. A. Hanson and E. Riseman (Academic).

Harris, C. S. 1968. "Perceptual Adaptation to Inverted, Reversed, and Displaced Vision." In Haber 1968.

Hart, J., R. S. Berndt, and A. Caramazza. 1985. "Category-Specific Naming Deficit Following Cerebral Infarction." *Nature* 316: 439–440.

Haviland, S., and H. H. Clark. 1974. "'What's New?' Acquiring New Information as a Process in Comprehension." *Journal of Vebal Learning and Verbal Behavior* 13: 512–521.

Hayes, J. R., ed. 1970. *Cognition and the Development of Language*. Wiley.

Hécaen, H., and M. L. Albert. 1978. *Human Neurophysiology*. Wiley.

Held, R., H. L. Teuber, and H. Leibowitz, eds. 1978. *Handbook of Sensory Physiology*, volume 8: *Perception*. Academic.

Helmholtz, H. von. 1910. *Helmholtz's Treatise on Physiological Optics*, volume III, tr. J. P. C. Southall. McGraw-Hill, 1962.

Heny, F., and B. Richards, eds. 1983. *Linguistic Categories, Auxiliaries, and Related Puzzles*. Reidel.

Higginbotham, J. 1980. Review of *Montague Grammar* (ed. B. Partee). *Journal of Philosophy* 77: 278–312.

Higginbotham, J. 1985. "On Semantics." *Linguistic Inquiry* 16: 547–593.

Hintikka, J. 1974. "Quantifiers vs. Quantification Theory." *Linguistic Inquiry* 5: 153–177.

Hinton, G. E., and T. J. Sejnowski. 1983. "Optimal Perceptual Inference." In Proceedings of the IEEE Computer Society Conference on Computer Vision and Pattern Recognition, Washington, D.C.

Hirschbühler, P. 1982. "VP-Deletion and Across the Board Quantifier Scope." In Proceedings of NELS, University of Masaschusetts, Amherst.

Hoffman, D. D., and W. A. Richards. 1984. "Parts of Recognition." *Cognition* 18: 65–96.

Holmes, V. M. 1979. "Some Hypotheses about Syntactic Processing in Sentence Comprehension." In Cooper and Walker 1979.

Hook, S., ed. 1969. *Language and Philosophy*. NYU Press.

Horn, B. K. P. 1975. "Obtaining Shape from Shading Information." In Winston 1975.

Hornby, P. A. 1971. "The Role of Topic-Comment in the Recall of Cleft and Pseudocleft Sentences." In Papers from the Seventh Regional Meeting of the Chicago Linguistics Society.

Hornby, P. A. 1974. "Surface Structure and Presupposition." *Journal of Verbal Learning and Verbal Behavior* 13: 530–538.

Hornstein, N. 1977. "S and the X' Convention." *Linguistic Analysis* 3: 2.

Hornstein, N. 1984. *Logic as Grammar*. MIT Press.

Hornstein, N. 1986. Restructuring and Interpretation in the T-Model. Unpublished.

Hornstein, N., and D. Lightfoot. 1986. "Predication and PRO." *Language* 64.

Hornstein, N., and D. Lightfoot. Rethinking Predication. Unpublished.

House, D. H. 1982. "The Frog/Toad Depth Perception System—A Cooperative/Competitive Model." In Proceedings of the Workshop on Visuomotor Coordination in Frog and Toad: Models and Experiments, Technical Report 82-16, Department of Computer and Information Science, University of Massachusetts, Amherst.

House, D. H. 1984. Neural Models of Depth Perception in Frogs and Toads. Ph.D. dissertation (Technical Report 84-16), Department of Computer and Information Science, University of Massachusetts, Amherst.

Huang, J. 1982. Logical Relations in Chinese and the Theory of Grammar. Ph.D. thesis, Massachusetts Institute of Technology.

Hubel, D. H., and T. N. Wiesel. 1974. "Sequence Regularity and Geometry of Orientation Columns in the Monkey Striate Cortex." *Journal of Comparative Neurology* 158: 267–294.

Ingle, D. J., M. A. Goodale, and R. J. W. Mansfield, eds. 1982. *Analysis of Visual Behavior*. MIT Press.

Ittelson, W. H., and F. P. Kilpatrick. 1958. "Experiments in Perception." In Beardsley and Wertheimer 1958.

Jackendoff, R. 1972. *Semantic Interpretation in Generative Grammar*. MIT Press.

Jackendoff, R. 1975. "On Belief Contexts." *Linguistic Inquiry* 6: 53–93.

Jackendoff, R. 1977. *X̄ Syntax: A Study of Phrase Structure*. MIT Press.

Jackendoff, R. 1980. "Belief Contexts Revisited." *Linguistic Inquiry* 11: 391–414.

Jacobs, R., and P. Rosenbaum, eds. 1980. *Readings in Transformational Grammar*. Ginn.

Jacobson, P., and G. Pullum, eds. 1982. *The Nature of Syntactic Representation*. Reidel.

Jarvella, R. J. and W. Klein, eds. 1982. *Speech Place and Action*. Wiley.

Jasper, H. H., et al., eds. 1958. *Reticular Formation of the Brain*. Little, Brown.

Johnson-Laird, P. N. 1983. *Mental Models*. Cambridge University Press.

Joshi, A., B. Webber, and I. Sag, eds. 1981. *Elements of Discourse Understanding*. Cambridge University Press.

Julesz, B. 1971. *Foundations of Cyclopean Perception*. University of Chicago Press.

Julesz, B., E. Gilbert, and J. Victor. 1978. "Visual Discrimination of Textures with Identical Third-Order Statistics." *Biological Cybernetics* 31: 137–140.

Juscyk, P. W., and A. Cohen. 1985. "What Constitutes a Module?" *Behavioral and Brain Sciences* 8: 20–21.

Just, M., and P. Carpenter. 1980. "A Theory of Reading: From Eye Fixations to Comprehension." *Psychological Review* 87: 329–354.

Karmiloff-Smith, A. 1980. "Psychological Processes Underlying Pronominalization and Non-Pronominalization in Children's Connected Discourse." In Papers from the Parasession on Pronouns and Anaphora, ed. J. Kreiman and A. E. Ojeda (Chicago Linguistic Society).

Karmiloff-Smith, A. 1985. "Language and Cognitive Processes from a Developmental Viewpoint." *Language and Cognitive Processes* 1: 61–85.

Keidel, W. D., W. Handler, and M. Spreng, eds. 1974. *Cybernetics and Bionics*. Munich.

Kilmer, W. L., W. S. McCulloch, and J. Blum. 1969. "A Model of the Vertebrate Central Command System." *International Journal of Man-Machine Studies* 1: 267–294.

Kimball, J. 1973. "Seven Principles of Surface Structure Parsing." *Cognition* 2: 15–47.

Kimball, J. 1975. "Predictive Analysis and Over-the-Top Parsing." In *Syntax and Semantics*, volume 4, ed. J. Kimball (Academic).

Klein, E., and I. A. Sag. 1985. "Type Driven Translation." *Linguistics and Philosophy* 8: 163–201.

Knuth, D. 1965. "On the Translation of Languages from Left to Right." *Information and Control* 8: 607–639.

Koopman, H. 1984. "On Deriving Deep and Surface Order." In Proceedings of NELS 14, University of Massachusetts, Amherst.

Koster, J. 1978. *Locality Principles in Syntax*. Foris.

Kreiman, J., and A. Ojeda, eds. 1983. Papers from the Parasession on Pronouns and Anaphora. Chicago Linguistics Society.

Kroll, J. F., and M. C. Potter. 1984. "Recognizing Words, Pictures, and Concepts: A Comparison of Lexical, Object, and Reality Decisions." *Journal of Verbal Learning and Verbal Behavior* 23: 39–66.

Kubovy, M., and J. R. Pomerantz, eds. 1981. *Perceptual Organization*. Erlbaum.

Kuhl, P. K., and J. D. Miller. 1975. "Speech Perception by the Chinchilla: Voiced-Voiceless Distinction in Alveolar-Plosive Consonants." *Science* 190: 69–72.

Kuhn, T. 1962. *The Structure of Scientific Revolutions*. University of Chicago Press.

Küng, G. 1966. *Ontology and the Logistic Analysis of Language*. Reidel.

Lackner, J. R., and M. F. Garrett. 1972. "Resolving Ambiguity: Effects of Biasing Contexts in the Unattended Ear." *Cognition* 1: 359–372.

Lambek, J. 1958. "The Mathematics of Sentence Structure." *American Mathematical Monthly* 65: 154–170.

Lara, R., M. A. Arbib, and A. S. Cromarty. 1982. "The Role of the Tectal Column in Facilitation of Amphibian Prey-Catching Behavior: A Neural Model." *Journal of Neuroscience* 2: 521–530.

Lasnik, H. 1976. "Remarks on Coreference." *Linguistic Analysis* 2: 1.

Lasnik, H. 1983. "On Certain Substitutes for Negative Data." In Proceedings of the Workshop on Learnability and Linguistic Theory, University of Western Ontario.

Lass, N. 1984. *Language and Speech.* Academic.

Lehnert, W. G. 1981. "Human Question Answering." In Joshi et al. 1981.

Lettvin, J. Y., H. Maturana, W. S. McCulloch, and W. H. Pitts. 1959. "What the Frog's Eye Tells the Frog's Brain." *Proceedings of the IRE* 47: 1940–1951.

Levelt, W. J. M., G. B. Flores d'Arcais, eds. 1978. *Studies in the Perception of Language.* Wiley.

Lewis, D. 1970. "General Semantics." *Synthese* 22: 18–67. Reprinted in Partee 1976.

Liberman, A. M., and A. G. Mattingly. 1985. "The Motor Theory of Speech Perception Revisited." *Cognition* 21: 1–36.

Lisker, L., and A. S. Abramson. 1964. "A Cross-Language Study of Voicing of Initial Stops: Acoustical Measurements." *Word* 20: 384–422.

Lisker, L., and A. S. Abramson. 1970. "The Voicing Dimension: Some Experiments in Comparative Phonetics." In *Proceedings of the Sixth International Congress of Phonetic Sciences* (Prague: Academia).

Llinas, R., and W. Precht, eds. 1976. *Frog Neurobiology.* Springer-Verlag.

Lukatela, G., A. Kostic, L. B. Feldman, and M. T. Turvey. 1983. "Grammatical Priming of Inflected Nouns." *Memory and Cognition* 11: 59–63.

Lyons, J. 1968. *Introduction to Theoretical Linguistics.* Cambridge University Press.

MacKay, D. B. 1966. "To End Ambiguous Sentences." *Perception and Psychophysics* 1: 426–436.

McCall, S., ed. 1967. *Polish Logic 1920–1939.* Clarendon.

McCawley, J. 1968. "Concerning the Base Component of a Transformational Grammar." *Foundations of Language* 4: 243–269.

McClelland, J. L., and A. H. Kawamoto. 1986. "Mechanisms of Sentence Processing: Assigning Roles to Constituents." In McClelland and Rumelhart 1986.

McClelland, J. L., and D. E. Rumelhart. 1981. "An Interactive Activation Model of Context Effects in Letter Perception. I. An Account of Basic Findings." *Psychological Review* 88: 375–407.

McClelland, J. L., and D. E. Rumelhart, eds. 1986. *Parallel Distributed Processing: Explorations in the Structure of Microcognition.* MIT Press.

McConnell-Ginet, S. 1982. "Adverbs and Logical Form." *Language* 58: 144–184.

McDermott, D. 1986. "We've Been Framed: Or, Why AI is Innocent of the Frame Problem." In Pylyshyn 1986.

McGurk, H., and J. MacDonald. 1976. "Hearing Lips and Seeing Voices." *Nature* 264: 746–748.

Manzini, M. R. 1983a. "On Control and Control Theory." *Linguistic Inquiry* 14: 421–446.

Manzini, M. R. 1983b. Restructuring and Reanalysis. Ph.D. thesis, Massachusetts Institute of Technology.

Marcus, M. P. 1980. *A Theory of Syntactic Recognition for Natural Language.* MIT Press.

Marcus, M. P. 1984. "Some Inadequate Theories of Sentence Processing." In Bever et al. 1984.

Marcus, S. M., and U. Frauenfelder. 1985. Word Recognition—Uniqueness or Derivation? Unpublished.

Marr, D. 1977. "Artificial Intelligence—A Personal View." *Artificial Intelligence* 9: 37–48.

Marr, D. 1982. *Vision: A Computational Investigation into the Human Representation and Processing of Visual Information.* Freeman.

Marr, D., and E. Hildreth. 1980. "Theory of Edge Detection." *Proceedings of the Royal Society of London* B 207: 187–218.

Marr, D., and H. K. Nishihara. 1978. "Representation and Recognition of the Spatial Organization of Three-Dimensional Shapes." *Proceedings of the Royal Society of London* B 200: 269–294.

Marr, D., and T. Poggio. 1976. "Cooperative Computation of Stereo Disparity." *Science* 194: 283–287.

Marr, D., and T. Poggio. 1979. "A Computational Theory of Human Stereo Vision." *Proceedings of the Royal Society of London* B 204: 301–328.

Marslen-Wilson, W. D. 1975. "The Limited Compatibility of Linguistics and Perceptual Explanations." In CLS Papers from the Parasession on Functionalism.

Marslen-Wilson, W. D. 1980. "Sentence Perception as an Interactive Parallel Process." *Science* 189: 226–228.

Marslen-Wilson, W. D. 1984. "Function and Process in Spoken Word Recognition: A Tutorial Review." In Bouma and Bouwhuis 1984.

Marslen-Wilson, W. D. 1985. "Speech Shadowing and Speech Communication." *Speech Communication* 4: 55–73.

Marslen-Wilson, W. D., and L. K. Tyler. 1975. "Processing Structure of Sentence Perception." *Nature* 257: 784–786.

Marslen-Wilson, W. D., and L. K. Tyler. 1980a. "The Temporal Structure of Spoken Language Understanding." *Cognition* 8: 1–71.

Marslen-Wilson, W. D., and L. K. Tyler. 1980b. "Towards a Psychological Basis for a Theory of Anaphora." In Kreiman and Ojeda 1983.

Marslen-Wilson, W. D., and L. K. Tyler. 1981. "Central Processes in Speech Understanding." *Philosophical Transactions of the Royal Society* B 295: 317–322.

Marslen-Wilson, W. D., and A. Welsh. "Processing Interactions and Lexical Access during Word Recognition in Continuous Speech." *Cognitive Psychology* 10: 29–63.

Marslen-Wilson, W. D., E. Levy, and L. K. Tyler. 1982. "Producing Interpretable Discourse: The Establishment and Maintenance of Reference." In Jarvella and Klein 1982.

May, R. 1977. The Grammar of Quantification. Doctoral dissertation, Massachusetts Institute of Technology.

May, R. 1985. *Logical Form.* MIT Press.

Mayhew, J., and J. Frisby. 1984. "Computer Vision." In O'Shea and Eisenstadt 1984.

Mazurkewich, I., and L. White. "The Acquisition of the Dative Alternation: Unlearning Overgeneralization." *Cognition* 16: 261–283.

Metzler, J., ed. 1977. *Systems Neuroscience.* Academic.

Miller, J. L. 1981. "Effects of Speaking Rate on Segmental Distinctions." In Eimas and Miller 1981.

Miller, J. L. 1985. "Rate Dependent Processing in Speech Perception." In Ellis 1985.

Miller, J. L., E. R. Dexter, and K. A. Pickard. 1984. "Influence of Speaking Rate and Lexical Status on Word Identification." *Journal of the Acoustical Society of America* 76: 589.

Miller, J. L., K. P. Green, and A. Reeves. 1986. "Speaking Rates and Segments: A Look at the Relation between Speech Production and Speech Perception for the Voicing Contrast." *Phonetica* 43: 106–115.

Miller, J. L., K. Green, and T. M. Schermer. 1984. "A Distinction between the Effects of Sentential Speaking Rate and Semantic Congruity on Word Identification." *Perception and Psychophysics* 36: 329–337.

Miller, J. L., F. Grosjean, and C. Lomanto. 1984. "Articulation Rate and Its Variability in Spontaneous Speech: A Reanalysis and Some Implications." *Phonetica* 41: 215–225.

Mitchell, D. C. 1982. *The Process of Reading.* Wiley.

Montague, R. 1973. "The Proper Treatment of Quantification in Ordinary English." In Thomason 1974.

Moortgat, M., H. V. D. Hulst, and T. Hoekstra, eds. 1981. *The Scope of Lexical Rules.* Foris.

Morris, D. 1958. "The Reproductive Behavior of the Ten-Spined Stickleback (*Pygosteus pungitius* L.)." *Behavior* Suppl. 6: 1–154.

Motley, M. T., B. J. Baars, and C. T. Camden. 1981. "Syntactic Criteria in Prearticulatory Editing: Evidence from Laboratory-Induced Slips of the Tongue." *Journal of Psycholinguistic Research* 5: 503–522.

Mountcastle, V. B. 1978. "An Organizing Principle for Cerebral Function: The Unit Module and the Distributed System." In *The Mindful Brain,* ed. G. M. Edelman and V. B. Mountcastle (MIT Press).

Murray, W. S. 1982. Sentence Matching: The Influence of Meaning and Structure. Doctoral thesis, Monash University.

Nagel, T. 1969. "Linguistics and Epistemology." In Hook 1969.

Naremore, R., ed. 1983. *Recent Advances in Language Sciences.* College Hill.

Neely, J. H. 1977. "Semantic Priming and Retrieval from Lexical Memory: Role of Inhibitionless Spreading Activation and Limited Capacity Attention." *Journal of Experimental Psychology (General)* 106: 226–254.

Newmeyer, F. J. 1980. *Linguistic Theory in America.* Academic.

Nooteboom, S. G., J. P. Brokx, and J. J. deRooij. 1978. "Contributions of Prosody to Speech Perception." In Levelt and Flores d'Arcais 1978.

Oehrle, R. T., E. Bach, and D. Wheeler, eds. 1987. *Categorial Grammars and Natural Language Structures.* Reidel.

O'Regan, K. 1981. "The 'Convenient Viewing Position' Hypothesis." In Fischer et al. 1981.

O'Shea, T., and M. Eisenstadt, eds. 1984. *Artificial Intelligence: Tools, Techniques, and Applications.* Harper & Row.

Palmer, S. E. 1975. "The Effects of Contextual Scenes on the Identification of Objects." *Memory and Cognition* 3: 519–526.

Papert, S. 1980. "The Role of Artificial Intelligence in Psychology." In Piattelli-Palmarini 1980.

Pareschi, R. 1985. Combinatorial Categorial Grammar, Logic Programming, and the Parsing of Natural Language. DAI working paper, University of Edinburgh.

Partee, B. H., ed. 1976. *Montague Grammar.* Academic.

Pastore, R. E. 1981. "Possible Psychoacoustic Factors in Speech Perception." In Eimas and Miller 1981.

Pesetsky, D. 1983. Paths and Categories. Doctoral dissertation, Massachusetts Institute of Technology.

Piattelli-Palmarini, M., ed. 1980. *Language and Learning: The Debate between Jean Piaget and Noam Chomsky.* Harvard University Press.

Pinker, S. 1984. *Language Learnability and Language Development.* Harvard University Press.

Pisoni, D. B. 1981. "In Defense of Segmental Representations in Speech Processing." In Research in Speech Perception, Progress Report 7, Indiana University, Bloomington.

Pisoni, D. B., T. D. Carrel, and S. J. Gans. 1983. "Perception of the Duration of Rapid Spectrum Changes in Speech and Nonspeech Signals." *Perception and Psychophysics* 34: 313–332.

Pitts, W. H., and W. S. McCulloch. 1947. "How We Know Universals: The Perception of Auditory and Visual Forms." *Bulletin of Mathematical Biophysics* 9: 127–147.

Pollard, C. 1985. Lectures on HPSG. Unpublished.

Pollard, C., and I. A. Sag. 1983. "Reflexives and Reciprocals in English: An Alternative to the Binding Theory." In Barlow et al. 1983.

Port, R. F., and J. Dalby. 1982. "Consonant/Vowel Ratio as a Cue for Voicing in English." *Perception and Psychophysics* 32: 141–152.

Posner, M., and S. Keele. 1968. "On the Genesis of Abstract Ideas." *Journal of Experimental Psychology* 77: 353–363.

Posner, M., and C. Snyder. 1975. "Attention and Cognitive Control." In Solso 1975.

Powell, T. P. S., and V. B. Mountcastle. 1959. "Some Aspects of the Functional Organization of the Cortex of the Post-Central Gyrus of the Monkey: A Correlation of Findings Obtained in a Single Unit Analysis with Cytoarchitecture." *Bulletin of the Johns Hopkins Hospital* 105: 133–162.

Putnam, H. 1980. "What is Innate and Why: Comments on the Debate." In Piattelli-Palmarini 1980.

Pylyshyn, Z. 1980. "Computation and Cognition: Issues in the Foundations of Cognitive Science." *Behavioral and Brain Sciences* 1: 93–127.

Pylyshyn, Z. 1986. *The Robot's Dilemma: The Frame Problem in Artificial Intelligence.* Ablex.

Quine, W. V. 1951a. "Two Dogmas of Empiricism." *Philosophical Review* 60: 20–43. Reprinted in Quine 1960.

Quine, W. V. 1951b. "The Problem of Meaning in Linguistics." Reprinted in Quine 1960.

Quine, W. V. 1960. *From a Logical Point of View.* Harvard University Press.

Ratcliff, J. 1983. Inference Processes in the Early Stages of Sentence Comprehension: A Study of the Plausibility Effect. Doctoral dissertation, Monash University.

Rayner, K. 1978. "Eye Movements in Reading and Information Processing." *Psychological Bulletin* 85: 618–660.

Rayner, K., M. Carlson, and L. Frazier. 1983. "The Interaction of Syntax and Semantics during Sentence Processing: Eye Movements in the Analysis of Semantically Based Sentences." *Journal of Verbal Learning and Verbal Behavior* 22: 358–374.

Reinhart, T. 1983a. *Anaphora and Semantic Intepretation.* Croom Helm.

Reinhart, T. 1983b. "Coreference and Bound Anaphora: A Restatement of the Anaphora Questions." *Linguistics and Philosophy* 6: 1.

Reisbeck, C., and R. Schank. 1978. "Comprehension by Computer: Expectation-Based Analysis of Sentences in Context." In Levelt and Flores d'Arcais 1978.

Richards, W. 1971. "Anomalous Stereoscopic Depth Perception." *Journal of the Optical Society of America* 61: 410–414.

Rock, I. 1973. *Orientation and Form.* Academic.

Rodman, R. 1976. "Scope Phenomena, 'Movement Transformations,' and Relative Clauses." In Partee 1976.

Rosch, E. 1973. "Natural Categories." *Cognitive Psychology* 4: 328–350.

Rucker, J. 1986. A or The Proper Retreatment of Quantification in Ordinary English. Thesis, Hampshire College.

Rumelhart, D. 1977. "Toward an Interactive Model of Reading." In Dornic 1977.

Rumelhart, D. E., and J. L. McClelland. 1982. "An Interactive Activation Model of Context Effects in Letter Perception: Part 2. The Contextual Enhancement Effect and Some Tests and Extensions of the Model." *Psychological Review* 89: 60–94.

Rumelhart, D., and J. L. McClelland. 1986. *Parallel Distributed Processing: Explorations in the Microstructure of Cognition,* volume 1: *Foundations.* MIT Press.

Rumelhart, D. E., and D. A. Norman. 1982. "Simulating a Skilled Typist: A Study of Skilled Cognitive-Motor Performance." *Cognitive Science* 6: 1–36.

Rumelhart, D., G. E. Hinton, and R. J. Williams. 1986. "Learning Internal Representations by Error Propagation." In Rumelhart and McClelland 1986.

Sag, I., and J. Hankamer. 1982. Toward a Theory of Anaphoric Processing. Unpublished.

Sag, I., and S. Weisler. 1979. "Temporal Connectives and Logical Form." In Proceedings of the Berkeley Linguistics Society.

Samuel, A. 1981. "Phoneme Restoration: Insights from a New Methodology." *Journal of Experimental Psychology: General* 110: 474–494.

Sanford, A. J., and S. C. Garrod. 1981. *Understanding Written Language*. Wiley.

Schank, R. 1975. *Conceptual Information Processing*. North-Holland.

Scheibel, M. E., and A. B. Scheibel. 1958. "Structural Substrates for Integrative Patterns in the Brain Stem Reticular Core." In Jasper et al. 1958.

Schönfinkel, M. 1924. "Über die Bausteine der mathematischen Logik." *Mathematische Annalen* 92: 305–316.

Seidenberg, M. S., M. K. Tanenhaus, J. M. Leiman, and M. A. Bienkowski. 1982. "Automatic Access of the Meanings of Ambiguous Words in Context: Some Limitations of Knowledge-Based Processing." *Cognitive Psychology* 14: 489–537.

Seidenberg, M. S., G. S. Waters. M. Sanders, and P. Langer. 1984. "Pre- and Post-Lexical Loci of Context Effects on Word Recognition." *Memory and Cognition* 12: 315–328.

Seligman, M. E. P., and J. Hager, eds. 1972. *Biological Boundaries of Behavior*. Appleton-Century-Crofts.

Selman, B., and G. Hirst. 1985. "A Rule-Based Connectionist Parsing System." In Proceedings of the Seventh Annual Conference of the Cognitive Science Society.

Shaply, R., and P. Lennie. 1985. "Spatial Frequency Analysis in the Visual System." *Annual Review of Neuroscience* 8: 547–583.

Shastri, L. 1985. Evidential Reasoning in Semantic Networks: A Formal Theory and Its Parallel Implementation. Ph.D. thesis, University of Rochester.

Shaumyan, S. K. 1977. *Applicational Grammar as a Semantic Theory of Natural Language*. Edinburgh University Press.

Shepard, R. N. 1981. "Psychophysical Complementarity." In Kubovy and Pomerantz 1981.

Shepard, R. N., and L. A. Cooper. 1982. *Mental Images and Their Transformations*. MIT Press.

Shiffrin, R., and W. Schneider. 1977. "Controlled and Automatic Human Information Processing: 2. Perceptual Learning, Automatic Attending, and a General Theory." *Psychological Review* 84: 127–190.

Simpson, G. 1984. "Lexical Ambiguity and Its Role in Models of Word Recognition." *Psychological Bulletin* 96: 316–340.

Slowiaczek, M. L. 1981. Prosodic Units as Language Processing Units. Doctoral dissertation, University of Massachusetts, Amherst.

Solso, R. L., ed. 1975. *Information Processing and Cognition*. Erlbaum.

Sproat, R. Dissertation in progress.

Stanovich, K. E., and R. F. West. 1983. "On Priming by a Sentence Context." *Journal of Experimental Psychology: General* 112: 1–36.

Steedman, M. J. 1985a. "Dependency and Coordination in the Grammar of Dutch and English." *Language* 61, no. 3: 523–568.

Steedman, M. J. 1985b. Combinatory Grammars and Parasitic Gaps. Unpublished.

Steedman, M. J. 1985c. "Combinators and Grammars." Paper given to Conference on Categorial Grammar, Tucson. In Oehrle et al. 1987.

Stemberger, J. P. 1985. "An Interactive Activation Model of Language Production." In Ellis 1985.

Sternberg, R. J. 1985. "Controlled versus Automatic Processing." *Behavioral and Brain Sciences* 8: 32–33.

Sternberg, S. 1969. "Memory-Scanning: Mental Processes Revealed by Reaction-Time Experiments." *American Scientist* 57: 421–457.

Stevenson, B. 1984. An Investigation of Constraint Violations in the Context of the Same-Different Matching Task. Honors thesis, Monash University.

Stowell, T. 1981. Origins of Phrase Structure. Doctoral dissertation, Massachusetts Institute of Technology.

Stroud, B. 1977. *Hume*. Routledge & Kegan Paul.

Summerfield, A. Q. 1975. "Aerodynamics vs. Mechanics in the Control of Voicing Onset in Consonant-Vowel Syllables." *Speech Perception* 4: 61–72.

Summerfield, Q. 1981. "On Articulatory Rate and Perceptual Constancy in Phonetic Perception." *Journal of Experimental Psychology: Human Perception and Performance* 7: 1074–1095.

Suszko, R. 1958. "Syntactical Structure and Semantical Reference." *Studia Logica* 8: 213–244.

Szabolcsi, A. 1983. ECP in Categorial Grammar. Unpublished.

Szekely, G., and G. Lazar. "Cellular and Synaptic Architecture of the Optic Tectum." In Llinas and Precht 1976.

Szentagothai, J., and M. A. Arbib. 1974. "Conceptual Models of Neural Organization." *Neurosciences Research Program Bulletin* 12: 310–479.

Tanenhaus, M. K., and S. Donnenwerth-Nolan. 1984. "Syntactic Context and Lexical Access." *Quarterly Journal of Experimental Psychology* 36A: 649–661.

Tanenhaus, M. K., and M. M. Lucas. 1986. "Context Effects in Lexical Processing." *Cognition* 23.

Tanenhaus, M. K., J. M. Leiman, and M. S. Seidenberg. 1979. "Evidence for Multiple Stages in the Processing of Ambiguous Words in Syntactic Contexts." *Journal of Verbal Learning and Verbal Behavior* 18: 427–440.

Tanenhaus, M. K., G. N. Carlson, and M. S. Seidenberg. 1985. "Do Listeners Compute Linguistic Representations?" In Dowty et al. 1985.

Taraldsen, T. 1979. "The Theoretical Interpretation of a Class of Marked Extractions." In Belletti et al. 1979.

Thomason, R., ed. 1974. *Formal Philosophy: Selected Papers of Richard Montague*. Yale University Press.

Tinker, M. A. 1958. "Recent Studies of Eye Movements in Reading." *Psychological Bulletin* 55: 215–231.

Todd, J. T. 1985. "Perception of Structure from Motion: Is Projective Correspondence of Moving elements a Necessary Condition?" *Journal of Experimental Psychology: Human Perception and Performance* 11: 689–710.

Townsend, D. J., and T. G. Bever. 1982. "Natural Units Interact during Language Comprehension." *Journal of Verbal Learning and Verbal Behavior* 28: 681–703.

Travis, L. 1984. Parameters and Effects of Word Order Variation. Doctoral dissertation, Massachusetts Institute of Technology.

Triesman, A. M., and G. Gelade. 1980. "A Feature-Integration Theory of Attention." *Cognitive Psychology* 12: 97–136.

Turner, D. A. 1979a. "A New Implementation Technique for Applicative Languages." *Software Practice and Experience* 9: 31–49.

Turner, D. A, 1979b. "Another Algorithm for Bracket Abstraction." *Journal of Symbolic Logic* 44: 267–270.

Tyler, L. K. 1985. "Real-Time Comprehension Processes in Agrammatism: A Case Study." *Brain and Language* 26: 259–275.

Tyler, L. K. 1986. "Spoken Language Comprehension in Aphasia: A Real-Time Processing Perspective." In Coltheart et al. 1986.

Tyler, L. K., and W. D. Marslen-Wilson. 1977. "The On-Line Effects of Semantic Context on Syntactic Processing." *Journal of Verbal Learning and Verbal Behavior* 16: 683–692.

Tyler, L. K., and W. D. Marslen-Wilson. 1982. "The Resolution of Discourse Anaphors: Some On-Line Studies." *Text* 2: 263–291.

Tyler, L. K., and J. Wessels. 1983. "Quantifying Contextual Contributions to Word-Recognition Processes." *Perception and Psychophysics* 34: 409–420.

Tzeng, O. J. L., and H. Singer, eds. 1981. *Perception of Print: Reading Research in Experimental Psychology.*

Ueda, M. 1984. Notes on Parsing in Japanese. Unpublished.

Ullman, S. 1979. "The Interpretation of Structure from Motion." *Proceedings of the Royal Society of London* B 23: 67–83.

Vanderwart, M. 1984. "Priming by Pictures in Lexical Decision." *Journal of Verbal Learning and Verbal Behavior* 23: 67–83.

van Dijk, T. A., and W. Kintsch. 1983. *Strategies of Discourse Comprehension.* Academic.

Waltz, D. 1975. "Understanding Line Drawings of Scenes with Shadows." In Winston 1975.

Waltz, D., and J. Pollack. 1985. "Massively Parallel Parsing: A Strongly Interactive Model of Natural Language Interpretation." *Cognitive Science* 9: 51–74.

Wanner, E. 1980. "The ATN and the Sausage Machine: Which One is Baloney?" *Cognition* 8: 209–225.

Wanner, E., and L. Gleitman, eds. 1982. *Language Acquisition: The State of the Art.* Cambridge University Press.

Wanner, E., and M. Maratsos. 1978. "An Augmented Transition Model of Relative Clause Comprehension." In Halle et al. 1978.

Wanner, E., R. Kaplan, and S. Shiner. 1974. Garden Paths in Relative Clauses. Unpublished.

Weinberg, A. 1987. "Mathematical Properties of Grammars." In *Cambridge Survey of Linguistics*, ed. F. Newmeyer (Cambridge University Press).

Weinberg, A., J. Aoun, N. Hornstein, and D. Lightfoot. 1987. "Two Notions of Locality." *Linguistic Inquiry* (in press).

Weisler, S. 1979. Daughter Dependency Grammar, VP-Deletion, and Logical Form. Presented at winter meeting of LSA, Los Angeles.

West, R. F., and K. E. Stanovich. 1982. "Source of Inhibition in Experiments on the Role of Sentence Context in Word Recognition." *Journal of Experimental Psychology: Learning, Memory, and Cognition* 8: 385–399.

West, R. F., and K. E. Stanovich, 1986. "Robust Effects of Syntactic Context on Naming." *Memory and Cognition* 14: 104–112.

Wexler, K. 1985. Modularity and Language Acquisition. Presented at Conference on Modularity in Knowledge Representation and Natural Language Understanding, Hampshire College.

Wexler, K., and P. Culicover. 1980. *Formal Principles of Language Acquisition.* MIT Press.

Williams, E. 1977. "Discourse and Logical Form." *Linguistic Inquiry* 8: 1.

Williams, E. 1980. "Predication." *Linguistic Inquiry* 11: 3.

Williams, E. 1984. "Semantic vs. Syntactic Categories." *Linguistics and Philosophy* 6: 423–446.

Wilson, H. R. 1983. "Psychophysical Evidence for Spatial Channels." In Braddick and Sleigh 1983.

Winograd, T. 1972. "Understanding Natural Language." *Cognitive Psychology* 3: 1.

Winston, P. H., ed. 1975. *The Psychology of Computer Vision.* McGraw-Hill.

Wittgenstein, L. 1922. *Tractatus Logico-Philosophicus.* Routledge & Kegan Paul.

Woodfield, A. 1982. *Thought and Object.* Oxford University Press.

Wright, B., and M. F. Garrett. 1984. "Lexical Decision in Sentences." *Memory and Cognition* 12: 31–45.

Authors

Gerry Altmann   University of Edinburgh
Michael A. Arbib   University of Southern California
Tyler Burge   University of California, Los Angeles
Greg Carlson   University of Iowa
Patrick J. Carroll   University of Texas, Austin
Charles Clifton, Jr.   University of Massachusetts, Amherst
Gary S. Dell   University of Rochester
Mark Feinstein   Hampshire College
Fernanda Ferreira   University of Massachusetts, Amherst
Michael Flynn   Carleton College
Jerry A. Fodor   City University of New York
Kenneth I. Forster   Monash University
Lyn Frazier   University of Massachusetts, Amherst
Jay L. Garfield   Hampshire College
Jane Grimshaw   Brandeis University
James Higginbotham   Massachusetts Institute of Technology
Norbert Hornstein   University of Maryland
William Marslen-Wilson   Max Planck Institute for Psycholinguistics, Nijmegen; Cambridge University
Joanne L. Miller   Northeastern University
Maria L. Slowiaczek   University of Texas, Austin
Mark Steedman   University of Edinburgh
Neil Stillings   Hampshire College
Michael K. Tanenhaus   University of Rochester
Lorraine Komisarjevsky Tyler   Max Planck Institute for Psycholinguistics, Nijmegen; Cambridge University
Amy Weinberg   University of Maryland
Steven Weisler   Hampshire College

Index

Vision
  ambiguity of stimulus in, 386
  color, 389
  computational analysis of, 383–384
  computer, 331, 351–359, 390–392
  cooperative computation in, 330–331,
    359, 390–392
  and distal stimuli, 368, 371–372, 374–376
  of frog, 339, 394
  high-level, 349–350, 359, 392–397
  as information-processing problem, 367
  low-level, 326, 328–331, 349–352, 366,
    368–373, 385–386, 393
  motion constraints and, 391
  naturalistic theories of, 368–373, 376–
    379, 383–389
  and psychological theory, 366
  and reliability, 368, 377–379
  as skill, 327
  top-down effects in, 326, 356–359, 386,
    390–392
  as weakly modular, 327–328, 395
Visual cortex, 334, 340
Visuomotor coordination, 344–349
Voluntary control, 3
VP-ellipsis, 114, 158–168

Waltz, D., 387
Weinberg, A., 187
Well-formedness conditions, 121
West, R., 104–105
Wexler, K., 208–209
Wh-raising, 134
Williams, E., 151–152, 158–164
Wittgenstein, L., 182
Word frequency, and fixation, 235
Word length, and processing, 235
Word monitoring, 44–48
Word order, 192
Word recognition, 235–239
Wrapping rules, 115
Writing, perception of, 217

Zero-crossings, 369–370, 393